WHAT DID THE BIBLICAL WRITERS KNOW
AND WHEN DID THEY KNOW IT?

WHAT DID THE BIBLICAL WRITERS KNOW AND WHEN DID THEY KNOW IT?

*What Archaeology Can Tell Us
about the Reality of Ancient Israel*

William G. Dever

WILLIAM B. EERDMANS PUBLISHING COMPANY
GRAND RAPIDS, MICHIGAN / CAMBRIDGE, U.K.

© 2001 Wm. B. Eerdmans Publishing Co.
255 Jefferson Ave. S.E., Grand Rapids, Michigan 49503 /
P.O. Box 163, Cambridge CB3 9PU U.K.
All rights reserved

Paperback edition 2002

Printed in the United States of America

10 09 08 07 06   8 7 6 5 4 3

Library of Congress Cataloging-in-Publication Data

Dever, William G.
What did the biblical writers know and when did they know it?:
what archaeology can tell us about the reality of ancient Israel / William G. Dever.
p.   cm.
Includes bibliographical references.
ISBN-10: 0-8028-2126-X / ISBN-13: 978-0-8028-2126-3 (pbk.: alk. paper)
1. Bible. O.T. — History of Biblical events.   2. Bible. O.T. — Antiquities.
3. Bible. O.T. — Historiography.   4. Jews — History — 1200-953 B.C.
5. Jews — History — 953-586 B.C.   I. Title.

BS1180.D66   2001
200.9′5 — dc21

00-067678

www.eerdmans.com

For G. Ernest Wright (1909-1974)
my teacher

Contents

CONTENTS

Foreword

This book has been 35 years in the making, and readers may be interested to know what has gone into it. In any case, the "ideology" of writers is in the air today, so I shall be up-front about how my own was shaped.

I was reared on the Bible, in a series of small towns in the South and Midwest, as well as in Jamaica, where my father was a preacher in various churches (he would never have said "clergyman"). Although I see in retrospect that he was no doubt a rather old-fashioned fundamentalist, I remember him not for his orthodoxy, but as a warm and compassionate man whose life was centered upon what he believed to be the Bible's eternal truths and values. I can still hear the cadence of his booming voice as he read Scripture from the pulpit; and I suspect that some of my own homiletical style in the classroom and in popular lectures comes from him.

I went from a small Christian liberal arts college in Tennessee to a liberal Protestant theological seminary, where for the first time I was exposed to the critical study of the Bible. I resisted mightily, knowing that my faith was at risk. But in the end I was won over to the love, and the risks, of learning, so in 1960 I went on to Harvard to do a doctorate in biblical theology. That was how I met Professor George Ernest Wright, who knew me better than I knew myself and set me on the path to a career in archaeology, starting with fieldwork under him at Shechem in 1962. I abandoned theology, but I continued to read in the field. However, I served as a Congregational minister in a liberal parish throughout my years at Harvard, and found it a positive experience. I began to see something of the wider world.

Upon graduation I went to Israel for a year at the Hebrew Union College — Jewish Institute of Religion; fell under the spell of Rabbi-archaeologist Nelson Glueck; and stayed on for 11 years. I became director of that school, and later director of the W. F. Albright Institute of Archaeological Research in Jerusalem, as well as directing excavations at Gezer, Shechem, West Bank sites, and elsewhere. I soon took up an interest in trends in biblical and Syro-Palestinian archaeology (and helped to set a few). But above all, I began to see how the *realia* of archaeology could illuminate ancient Israel. And I caught a vision of a dialogue between archaeology and biblical studies.

In 1975 I returned somewhat reluctantly to the United States to take up an academic career at a university renowned for the "new," anthropologically-oriented archaeology. In addition to teaching and writing, I did a great deal of traveling and lecturing to popular audiences and experienced the satisfaction of communicating the results of archaeology and biblical studies to a wider public. At the same time, I began to turn my attention from fieldwork to larger syntheses, especially to the possibilities of a *new* style of "biblical archaeology." I also converted to Judaism during this period, at least nominally — although I am not a theist, and indeed remain a secular humanist. But the Jewish *tradition* suits me in many ways.

In 1992 I read Philip R. Davies' *In Search of "Ancient Israel"* (Sheffield: JSOT) and saw immediately a new, irresistible challenge. By 1995 I was writing to oppose the "revisionists," as some called them. Gradually I began to immerse myself in "revisionist" and "postmodern" literature, intuitively sensing that this was leading me to a larger work — the present volume, as it turned out.

Why did I write this book? Because I had to, not only to counter the "revisionists'" abuse of archaeology, but to show how modern archaeology brilliantly illuminates a *real* "Israel" in the Iron Age, and also to help foster the dialogue between archaeology and biblical studies that I had always envisioned.

A word of warning to the reader. This is meant to be a "popular" book, designed to be accessible to the nonspecialist, so it may be at times overly simplistic, and it is certainly polemical. Yet for those who wish to pursue some scholarly matters further, there are detailed footnotes and references.

For further information on the dozens of archaeological sites and topics discussed here, I recommend several handbooks, especially *The New Encyclopedia of Archaeological Excavations in the Holy Land,* ed. Ephraim Stern (Jerusalem: Israel Exploration Society and Carta, 1993); and Amihai Mazar, *Archaeology of the Land of the Bible, 10,000-586 B.C.E.* (New York: Doubleday, 1990).

I want to acknowledge many who contributed to this book in many ways that they probably never imagined. My parents inculcated in me not only a love of the Bible, but a devotion to duty and a certain moral earnestness that has (I hope) informed everything that I have ever done. To Professor George Ernest Wright, my teacher and mentor, I owe more than I can say. My Israeli archaeological colleagues over the past 35 years have shared with me the thrill of discovery and have challenged me in many ways. From my "public," I have learned that archaeology really matters, and is always exciting. I must also thank my many graduate students, who probably taught me more than I taught them, and who remain my most satisfying achievement. The future is theirs.

I with to thank my colleague, Prof. J. Edward Wright, whose reading of the manuscript in a draft version saved me from several errors in the field of biblical studies, but who is not to be blamed for the remaining idiosyncrasies.

Finally, I express my appreciation to my family — wives and children — who have kept me part-time in the real world, while I was mostly off tilting at various windmills.

WILLIAM G. DEVER
Tucson, Arizona
Turn-of-the-millennium

Abbreviations

AASOR	Annual of the American Schools of Oriental Research
ABD	*Anchor Bible Dictionary*
ANET	*Ancient Near Eastern Texts*, ed. J. B. Pritchard
AOAT	Alter Orient und Altes Testament
AUSS	*Andrews University Seminary Studies*
BA	*Biblical Archaeologist*
BAR	*Biblical Archaeology Review*
BASOR	*Bulletin of the American Schools of Oriental Research*
BETL	Bibliotheca ephemeridum theologicarum lovaniensium
BR	*Bible Review*
BZAW	Beihefte zur Zeitschrift für die alttestamentliche Wissenschaft
EAEHL	*Encyclopedia of Archaeological Excavations in the Holy Land*, ed. M. Avi-Yonah
ErIsr	*Eretz Israel*
ExpTim	*Expository Times*
HSM	Harvard Semitic Monographs
HSS	Harvard Semitic Studies
HUCA	*Hebrew Union College Annual*
IDB	*Interpreter's Dictionary of the Bible*, ed. G. A. Buttrick (Nashville: Abingdon, 1962)
IEJ	*Israel Exploration Journal*
JAOS	*Journal of the American Oriental Society*
JBL	*Journal of Biblical Literature*
JR	*Journal of Religion*
JSOT	*Journal for the Study of the Old Testament*
NEA	*Near Eastern Archaeology*

ABBREVIATIONS

NEAEHL	*The New Encyclopedia of Archaeological Excavations in the Holy Land,* ed. E. Stern
OBO	Orbis biblicus et orientalis
SBLMS	Society of Biblical Literature Monograph Series
SBLSBS	Society of Biblical Literature Sources for Biblical Study
SBT	Studies in Biblical Theology
SHANE	Studies in the History of the Ancient Near East
SJOT	*Scandinavian Journal of the Old Testament*
Sup	Supplement
TA	*Tel Aviv*
TynBul	*Tyndale Bulletin*
VT	*Vetus Testamentum*
VTSup	Supplements to *Vetus Testamentum*

CHAPTER 1

The Bible as History, Literature, and Theology

The Mysterious Bible

The Bible, including the Old Testament, or as we prefer here, the Hebrew Bible, is so familiar to those of us still steeped in the Western cultural tradition that it would seem to need little explanation, much less defense. For centuries the Bible has been *the* Classic — although that really means (1) that we take it for granted; and (2) that we revere it, but don't bother to read it any more.

Yet for all the lip service still paid to the Bible in our society, it remains largely a mystery to lay people. A recent, long-running television series in which I became involved was entitled "Mysteries of the Bible." Obviously it capitalized (so to speak) on the public's continuing fascination with the unresolved riddles of the Bible: Where was the Garden of Eden? Did Jericho's walls really come tumbling down? Why did the biblical writers think Jezebel such a wicked woman? Such examples could go on and on.

Even though I was somewhat surprised, and indeed gratified, to see the public's enthusiasm for the series (I now am recognized when I go to the local barber shop), I became skeptical in the end. The commercial and somewhat cynical exploitation of biblical topics is clearly designed to titillate more than to educate the public. Any gratuitous educational benefits aside, the Bible remains a mysterious book to most people.

The Nature of the Hebrew Bible

The above is true partly because we forget that the Bible is not a book at all, but a whole shelf of books. That means that you cannot simply pick up the Bible and read it from beginning to end, as a connected story with a structured plot and believable characters. One of my friends was required to do that for a "book report" in a college class on "The Bible as Literature" (he confessed later that he could never bring himself to pick up the Bible again). What *is* the Bible's "story" really about? Who wrote it, and why? And can we moderns really believe any of it?[1]

The many "books" that make up our Hebrew Bible (39 in English versions, but 24 in Hebrew) have many stories to tell, written almost entirely by anonymous authors. These stories were set down over a period of a thousand years, the whole finally woven into a composite, highly complex literary fabric sometime in the Hellenistic era (ca. 2nd century B.C.). This vast "library" — for that is what the Bible really is — contains such diverse and indeed contradictory literary forms as myths, legends and folktales, sagas, heroic epics, oral traditions, annals, biographies, narrative histories, novellae, *belles lettres,* proverbs and wisdom-sayings, poetry (including erotic poems — read the Song of Songs without your spiritual blinders on), prophecy, apocalyptic, and much more.

All of this vast compilation of literature comes down to us from a long-lost Oriental world almost entirely foreign to our modern consciousness and worldview. Furthermore, the Bible is written in a dead language. (Hebrew has been revived as a spoken language only recently, as in Israel, but in any case it differs considerably from Biblical Hebrew.) Finally, the librarians in charge of the biblical corpus seem to be mostly clerics of one sort or another, intent upon forcing their "orthodox" interpretations upon the rest of us, although no two of them agree. Or else they are academics, who seem to delight in making the Bible even more mysterious and therefore accessible only through them, although I suspect that many professional biblical scholars are closet agnostics.

The Biblical Tradition under Attack

Where does all this leave the intelligent layperson, whether formally religious or not, who wishes simply to understand the Bible better? And is the effort worth

---

1. The relevant literature is vast; but for the nonspecialist a number of recent "handbooks" are most helpful, among them Howard Clark Kee, Eric M. Meyers, John Rogerson, and Anthony J. Saldarini, eds., *The Cambridge Companion to the Bible* (Cambridge: Cambridge University Press, 1997); and Michael D. Coogan, ed., *The Oxford History of the Biblical World* (New York: Oxford University Press, 1998). Also recommended is Richard E. Friedman, *Who Wrote the Bible?* (Englewood Cliffs: Prentice Hall, 1987).

it any longer, at a time when the biblical literature — indeed the entire biblical tradition — is being dismissed by so many as "irrelevant," even by those in Synagogue, Church, and Seminary? My colleagues tell me that many priests and clergy no longer know Hebrew and Greek and thus cannot read the Bible in the original. The study of the history of ancient Israel, long fundamental to our understanding of biblical Israel and her faith, is scarcely taught in many Protestant seminaries. History and historical exegesis have been replaced by more stylish courses in liberation theology; feminist approaches to the Bible; new literary criticism, including structuralism, semiotics, rhetorical criticism, and even more esoteric "schools" that we shall discuss in more detail later.

The *Atlantic Monthly* ran an article in December 1996 entitled "The Search for a No-frills Jesus," by Charlotte Allen. Here Burton L. Mack, longtime Professor of New Testament at the School of Theology of Claremont in California, is quoted as saying of the latest studies in the "quest for the historical Jesus" that the forthcoming publication of *Documenta Q* by the International Q Project "should bring to an end the myth, the history, the mentality, of the Gospels." Says Mack, who spent his entire professional life training Christian ministers: "It's over. We've had enough apocalypses. We've had enough martyrs. Christianity has had a two-thousand-year run, and it's over." I see here a hypocrisy whereby one so long "professes" a history that he thinks did not exist. As I shall note in Chapter 6, the malaise in the scholarly pursuit of "the historical Jesus" parallels almost exactly the current crisis in the search for "the historical Israel." The same methodological issues are involved.

The irony is that the most deadly attack on the Bible and its veracity, in either the historical or the theological meaning, has come recently not from its traditional enemies — atheists, skeptics, or even those "Godless Communists" feared by Bible-believing people until recently — but from the Bible's well-meaning friends.

If its professional custodians no longer take the Bible seriously, at least as the foundation of our Western cultural tradition, much less a basis for private and public morality, where does that leave us? If we simply jettison the Bible as so much excess baggage in the brave new postmodern world, what shall we put in its place?

Is the Bible "Historical" at All?

For the purposes of the present discussion, I would argue that the most serious challenge to the Hebrew Bible in its long history of interpretation and controversy comes from a small but vocal group of scholars, mostly European, who have recently undertaken what they sometimes allude to as "revisionist" histories of ancient Israel. Of course, every generation in the history of Judaism and Christianity has assayed to write its own, "new" histories of ancient Israel — and rightly so, because the spirit of the biblical tradition is dynamic, ever-changing. Even within the biblical period itself, as Michael Fishbane, Jeffrey Tigay, and other rather conservative scholars have shown, the biblical writers are constantly in a kind of "inner dialogue" with themselves.[2] These writers dare to rework the literary tradition, even though it was regarded from early on as Scripture, "sacred writings." And now, after centuries of such "recycling the Bible," the effort has been made even more necessary — and rewarding. That is because of the gradual development of basic tools of modern scholarship since the Enlightenment that no scholars, even Fundamentalists, can ignore: literary criticism, historical exegesis, comparative religion, and especially, as we shall see, archaeology in its broadest sense.

Given these considerations, what is menacing about the revisionists and their program? Simply this: if we look carefully at their agenda, the revisionists do not intend merely to rewrite the history of ancient or biblical Israel; they propose rather to abolish it altogether. As Philip R. Davies puts it in his little book that started much of the fuss, *In Search of "Ancient Israel"* (1992), there was no "ancient" or "biblical" Israel. These are all late "intellectual constructs," forced back upon an imagined past by centuries of Jewish and Christian believers. The notion of "ancient Israel" stems ultimately from the Bible itself; but the Bible is "pious fiction," not historical fact. The Bible, too, is a late literary construct, written in and reflecting the realities of the Persian-Hellenistic era (ca. 5th-1st centuries), not the Iron Age of Palestine (ca. 12th-6th centuries) that purports to be its setting.

In Chapter 2 I shall expose the dangers of the revisionist challenge in much more detail. Here I wish only to acknowledge the thrust of their major questions. Is there any real "history," at least in the modern sense, in the Hebrew

---

2. On the "meaning" of the Bible, an older but still useful work is that of James Barr, *The Bible in the Modern World* (1973, repr. Philadelphia: Trinity, 1990); from a much more conservative (if not evangelical) perspective, see Roy A. Harrisville and Walter Sundberg, *The Bible in Modern Culture: Theology and Historical-Critical Method from Spinoza to Käsemann* (Grand Rapids: Wm. B. Eerdmans, 1995). See further William G. Dever, "Philology, Theology, and Archaeology: What Kind of History Do We Want, and What Is Possible?" in *The Archaeology of Israel: Constructing the Past/Interpreting the Present,* ed. Neil A. Silberman and David Small. JSOTSup 237 (Sheffield: Sheffield Academic, 1997), 290-310; and references in Chapter 4, n. 16. See also Michael Fishbane, *Biblical Interpretation in Ancient Israel* (New York: Oxford University Press, 1985); Jeffrey H. Tigay, ed., *Empirical Models for Biblical Criticism* (Philadelphia: University of Pennsylvania Press, 1985).

Bible? And if not, how can we any longer write a history of ancient Israel or its religion(s) at all? These questions deserve to be taken seriously, even though the revisionists are hardly the first to have posed them. (As happens so often, self-styled revisionists are not nearly as radical as they suppose.)

The urgency here is simply that (1) not even the most extreme "modern-ists" in critical biblical scholarship of the late 19th-20th century ever went so far as to deny any historicity to the Hebrew Bible; (2) the current visibility of the revisionists in the professional journals, at national and international sympo-sia, and increasingly on the Internet has scarcely come to the attention of lay people and may seem frivolous to scholars, but it reveals a disturbing trend to-ward what I would call nihilism. In adopting the term "nihilism" (Lat. *nihil,* "nothing"), I have in mind its common and current usage in philosophy to mean "the denial of the existence of any basis for knowledge or truth." The revi-sionists will reject this term; but their own declared methodology and results betray them, as we shall see presently. "No history" means no history. Here, however, I wish only to sound a preliminary alarm, while at the same time tak-ing the revisionist challenge seriously.

What Kind of "History"?

When we are challenged as to whether there is any "history" in the Hebrew Bible, we ought to reply first by asking: "What kind of history?" It should be obvious that everything in the quest for history depends upon qualifications that must be demanded at this point. The fundamental point is that there are many kinds of history, and thus many differing but appropriate methods, aims, and materials for history-writing. English has only one basic word, "history." But German, for instance, has (1) *Geschichte,* or the academic discipline of history-writing; (2) *Historie,* or less formal narrative history; and (3) *Storie,* which may contain many mythical and folkloric elements, but nevertheless aims at a connected ac-count of the past. To put matters another way, we may distinguish: (1) political history, the history of great public figures and institutions; (2) intellectual history, the history of formative ideas; (3) socio-economic history, the history of social and economic structures; (4) technological history, the history of things and their use; (5) art history, the history of aesthetics; (6) ideological history, the history of how certain concepts, specifically ethnic and religious, have shaped culture; (7) natural history, the history of the environment and the natural world (such as Pliny's *Historia naturalis*); and (8) perhaps a culture history, or total history.[3]

3. See further Dever, "Philology, Theology, and Archaeology."

Yet even most professional biblical scholars (and, I fear, nearly all archae-ologists) have scarcely given serious, critical thought to historiography — the aims and methods of history-writing — even though they must presume them-selves to be historians. This may seem like a harsh criticism of my colleagues, but consider the scholarly literature. As late as 1988, Giovanni Garbini com-plained in his *History and Ideology in Ancient Israel* that "all those who have been occupied with and have written about the story of the ancient Hebrew Bi-ble are not historians by profession, though for the sake of brevity I have called them 'historians'; almost without exception they are all professors of theol-ogy."[4]

The first full-scale critical study of historiographic issues in dealing with ancient Israel in English-speaking biblical studies was John Van Seters' 1983 work, *In Search of History: History and Historiography in the Ancient World and the Origins of Biblical History*,[5] followed in 1988 by Baruch Halpern's provoca-tive *The First Historians: The Hebrew Bible and History*.[6] The first publications, by a biblical or Syro-Palestinian archaeologist (for the terms, see below), that dealt extensively with historiography and ancient Israel, were by myself, begin-ning in 1987.[7] The literature since these early publications should have bur-geoned, but it has not. Why? Is it because we historians have lost confidence in our ability to deal with a seemingly intractable past? Surely the current skepti-cism about history-writing cannot be due to inadequate data, since both textual and archaeological sources have mushroomed in the past century, and new ar-chaeological discoveries are now coming at a dizzying pace.

The Bankruptcy of "Mere Philology"

If one examines the malaise further, it soon becomes apparent that a "historiographical crisis" is perceived only among those scholars who deal spe-cifically with the texts of the Hebrew Bible. I would argue that these scholars — some trained originally as philologians, others secondarily as theologians,

4. (New York: Crossroads, 1988), 2.
5. (1983; repr. Winona Lake: Eisenbrauns, 1997).
6. (San Francisco: Harper & Row, 1988).
7. See, e.g., "Unresolved Issues in the Early History of Israel: Toward a Synthesis of Archaeological and Textual Reconstructions," in *The Bible and the Politics of Exegesis: Es-says in Honor of Norman K. Gottwald on His Sixty-Fifth Birthday*, ed. David Jobling, Peggy Lynne Day, and Gerald T. Sheppard (Cleveland: Pilgrim, 1991), 195-208; and "'Will the Real Israel Please Stand Up?' Archaeology and Israelite Historiography: Part I," *BASOR* 297 (1995): 61-80 and literature cited there.

many now attempting to recycle themselves as "new literary critics" — are undergoing an identity crisis that they are projecting upon the rest of us. We archaeologists have no such hesitation about writing histories, however provisional, of Israel and the ancient Near East; we have been doing this for more than a century now, with ever more promising results.

Here it may be instructive to compare two recent books, announced in the same issue of the catalogue of the trendy Sheffield Academic Press. One is a collection of essays from the 1994 Dublin meetings of the European Seminar on Methodology in Israel's History, entitled *Can a "History of Israel" Be Written?*[8] The other volume results from an international seminar held by archaeologists in America the same year; it carries the upbeat title, *The Archaeology of Israel: Constructing the Past/Interpreting the Present*. My own chapter in the latter volume is entitled "Philology, Theology, and Archaeology: What Kind of History Do We Want, and What Is Possible?"[9] My Israeli archaeological colleagues, who now dominate the field and who were at the symposium in force, were incredulous; I was attacking a straw man. They all said: "Of course we can write histories of ancient Israel; let's get on with it!"

I wish I could be as sanguine as they. But the fact is that mainstream European biblical scholarship, which for two centuries has led the international field in new directions, has virtually given up on writing a satisfactory history of ancient Israel. In America, the revisionist discourse has not yet created much stir, certainly not among the public. But at national professional meetings, European scholars attend and make sweeping, doctrinaire pronouncements that would have been regarded as arrant nonsense only a decade ago, but are now applauded by audiences of hundreds. At the 1996 national meetings of the Society of Biblical Literature, Thomas L. Thompson of Copenhagen triumphantly announced to a standing-room-only crowd that not only was there no "ancient Israel," but there was "no Judaism until the 2nd century A.D." His remarks were greeted with applause. Mine was the only voice raised in protest; but I was drowned out, and the chairman closed the session. Afterward, I found many of my colleagues dismayed, but only a few of us had seen the handwriting on the wall (a biblical allusion — Belshazzar's feast — for those who still respond to such images). What is going on here? Should we be alarmed?

The sad state of our art is perhaps best seen in several recent developments. One is an international seminar convened by European scholars in Jeru-

8. Lester L. Grabbe, ed., *Can a "History of Israel" Be Written?* JSOTSup 245 (Sheffield: Sheffield Academic, 1997).

9. See n. 2 above.

salem in 1995, published in 1996 as *The Origins of the Ancient Israelite States.*[10] The opening address was a scathing, personal attack on me by Thompson, who asserted among many other things that I had deliberately dismantled stones of the "Solomonic" city gate at Gezer and had thrown out all the pottery that might disagree with my preconceived notions of a 10th-century B.C. date. Although I was unable to attend, having just returned from Jerusalem, "our" side was ably defended by one of America's most brilliant young biblical scholars, Baruch Halpern.[11]

The latest "exchange" of views was at the 1996 Dublin methodology seminar, to which apparently we dissidents were not invited. The papers have now been published, and again Thompson's contribution, "Defining History and Ethnicity in the South Levant," is largely a mean-spirited caricature of my views and those of my North American and Israeli colleagues. As Thompson had already put it, we are guilty of "an interpretation of Palestine's archaeology [i.e., all of it] in the context of an anachronistically projected biblical Israel." I, in particular, have been throughout my long career "dependent on (a) commitment to find a harmony between archaeologically derived socio-cultural scenarios and (a) reading of the bible *(sic)*." As for Thompson's own conclusion, he declares: "I cannot imagine what a biblical text would look like that was judged to be 'historically wholly reliable.'"[12] In much of what follows, I shall supply many such materials, to be "read historically," both textual and archaeological.

Another deplorable development, one hailed by Thompson, was the 1996 publication by Keith W. Whitelam of *The Invention of Ancient Israel: The Silencing of Palestinian History.*[13] Whitelam claims that biblical scholars, and especially archaeologists like the Israelis and myself, have "usurped" the history of the Palestinians, the real occupants of the land from the Bronze Age onward. In the name of a fraudulently conceived "biblical Israel," we have conspired to deprive the Palestinians of their cultural heritage and dispossess them of their rightful homeland. In Whitelam's reading of history, the charge

10. Ed. Volkmar Fritz and Philip R. Davies. JSOTSup 228 (Sheffield: Sheffield Academic, 1996).

11. Cf. Thomas L. Thompson, "Historiography of Ancient Palestine and Early Jewish Historiography: W. G. Dever and the Not So New Biblical Archaeology," in Fritz and Davies, 26-43, esp. 27-29, 37; and Baruch Halpern, "The Construction of the Davidic State: An Exercise in Historiography," 44-75.

12. The first two quotations here are from Thompson's original manuscript, which he sent to me, and differ somewhat from the published version. The latter quotation is from Grabbe, *Can a "History of Israel" Be Written?* 180.

13. (New York: Routledge, 1996).

of "inventing ancient Israel" comes perilously close to anti-Semitism, as some reviewers have pointed out.

Before moving on, we need to be aware of the "shorthand" that is developing to categorize the protagonists in the growing debate, much of the terminology in the "electronic gossip" on the Internet. Apparently the terms "maximalists" and "minimalists" stem from my own writings a decade ago. Now, however, we encounter "positivists" vs. "nihilists," "crypto-Fundamentalists" vs. "scientific historians," "triumphalists" vs. "supercessionists." Next, I suppose, we will see "Zionists" vs. "Anti-Semites."[14] Such name-calling is perhaps inevitable in the heat of the battle; but it certainly seems silly to lay people, and by oversimplifying, it serves only to obscure the substantial and serious differences between two emergent "schools" of biblical interpretation that are likely to dominate biblical scholarship for some time. In any case, the increasing rancor of the discussion is the clearest indication of the desperation among exclusively text-based historians that Halpern, quoting Jacob Burckhardt, has characterized as the "spiritual bankruptcy of philology" in itself.[15] The revisionists are right about one thing: the impasse is such that neither they nor we can write a history of ancient Israel based entirely on the biblical texts. That is their despair, however, not ours.

In the remainder of this book, I hope to clarify these issues and to focus upon what I consider to be the crux of the matter: How and whether we can write a history of ancient Israel, and how biblical texts and archaeological evidence can interact as legitimate sources for history-writing. Before proceeding, however, we need to set the stage by noting what the revisionists substitute for the now-rejected notion of "the Bible as history": "the Bible as literature."

---

14. The epithet of "Zionist" has now indeed been applied to me, at least implicitly, by Niels Peter Lemche. See "Response to William G. Dever, 'Revisionist Israel Revisited,'" *Currents in Research: Biblical Studies* 5 (1997): 9-14, esp. 12: "Dever is defending a political agenda found within a certain strand of modern Zionism, which considers biblical history to legitimate the politics of the present state of Israel. . . ." Thompson's rhetoric in "Historiography of Ancient Palestine" is no less inflammatory. For a perceptive review of Whitelam's *The Invention of Ancient Israel,* see Benjamin D. Sommer, *Middle East Quarterly* (March 1998), 85, 86. See further Chapter 2, n. 43; Chapter 6, n. 15.

15. Halpern, *The First Historians,* 23, citing Jacob Burckhardt, letter to Gottfried Kinkel, 7 Feb 1845, in *Briefe,* ed. Fritz Kaphahn (Leipzig: Kröner, 1935).

History, Literature, and Faith

It has always been apparent that the Hebrew Bible is, among other things, literature — and immortal literature at that. Thus the modern, critical study of the Bible began properly in the mid-19th century as "literary criticism" (sometimes called "Higher Criticism"). This approach was, and still is, despite many detractors today, a fundamental starting-point. From the beginning, however, literary criticism — the detailed analysis of the historical setting of texts; their sources, authorship, and date; and the complex history of their transmission — had as its ultimate goals (1) the recovery from the texts of a real *history of events;* and (2) the exegesis of these texts so as to reevaluate the *theological interpretations* to be derived from or attached to these events, both ancient and modern. In short, the classical literary approach to the Hebrew Bible incorporated a tacit recognition of the Bible's fundamentally "historical" character. To be sure, over time literary-critical study has seemed to many to undermine that very history, perhaps irretrievably. Again, the revisionists have a point: it is no longer possible simply to read the Hebrew Bible at face value as "history." The Bible is, rather, a series of theological reflections by later Israel on its past experience, not a "history of Israel." Yet that fact does not mean that there is no history to be gleaned from the literature, as I shall show presently.

For the "revisionists," however, one must make a choice: we are constrained to regard the Bible either as "history" or as "literature." Given their historiographical nihilism, the choice is a foregone conclusion: the Hebrew Bible is only literature. As Niels Peter Lemche and Thompson put it recently: "the Bible is not history, and only very recently has anyone ever wanted it to be."[16] Never mind that the statement is patently false (the Bible's millions of readers over two millennia have almost always thought it to be "history"). What is at work here? What is the ideological motivation behind the revisionists' determination to view the Hebrew Bible merely as literature? And what do they mean by "literature"?

The "Bible as Literature" Movement

Once again, the revisionists are scarcely innovators, for the beginnings of the so-called "new literary critical" approach to the Hebrew Bible can be traced

---

16. See Niels Peter Lemche and Thomas L. Thompson, "Did Biran Kill David? The Bible in the Light of Archaeology," *JSOT* 64 (1994): 18.

back nearly 30 years. What distinguishes the "new" literary approach from the traditional? According to J. Cheryl Exum and D. J. A. Clines (of the "Sheffield school" of Davies and others) in their edited collection of essays, *The New Literary Criticism and the Hebrew Bible*, the "new" literary approach "is not a historical discipline, but a strictly literary one, foregrounding the *textuality* (italics mine) of the biblical literature."[17] According to these leading proponents of the method, who are among the first to set it forth explicitly, it is rather eclectic, embracing for instance newer (i.e., nonhistorical) literary-critical approaches, poststructuralist methods, feminist criticism, political and materialist (but not classically Marxist) criticism, psychoanalytic criticism, and above all deconstruction.[18]

If one pursues the essays in this provocative volume, along with other recent literature on new literary criticism, the following composite portrait emerges. It should be no surprise that the resulting portrait resembles quite closely the movement of the past decade or so known in wider literary circles as "deconstruction," which in my judgment is the parent of this particular radical school of biblical criticism. My categorization here may be somewhat cryptic in the interest of brevity, but browsing a bit in recent literature will show that it is valid.

What Are "Texts"?

1. A text is an individual "work of art in its own right," not something to be pursued as a means to an end.
2. There is no single, authoritative "meaning" for a text.
3. *How* a text "signifies" is as important as *what* it "signifies."
4. "Structure" is more important than content.
5. There are multiple, almost limitless, approaches to a text that may be legitimate and productive.
6. All texts, because of the "unbounded" nature of language, are incomplete, often contradictory; most even lack any "conscious intentionality" on the writer's part.
7. Texts have no intrinsic "meaning"; any meaning must be supplied, and it depends largely on the reader's response, as well as the "social context of knowledge," the author's and ours.
8. "Meaning" is best "produced" by reading the text imaginatively and sym-

17. (Sheffield: Sheffield Academic, 1993), 11.
18. Exum and Clines, 12-20.

bolically, on many levels at once, as well as in conjunction with other texts ("intertextuality").

9. Readings far beyond the text's original boundaries are not only possible but desirable.

10. The only "test" of a reading's "authenticity" (if any) is acceptance by the reader's particular community.

Such new literary critical manifestations may not necessarily be subscribed to by all practitioners of the method, but they are typical. The theory, however, is best understood in practice, particularly if we look at how texts are treated specifically. Again, my point of departure is standard, recent literature in mainstream biblical studies.

How to "Read" a Text: Deconstruction in Practice

First, we should look at the essays in Exum and Clines' basic handbook. Here we learn that we must:

1. Read the text "against its demand, its coercion"; "identify its Achilles' heel."

2. Look for "cognitive dissonance," rather than integrity.

3. Regard the text as a "coherent intelligible whole, independent of its author."

4. Read the "biblical" text in Spanish, or whatever our own language is, so as to appropriate it to our own situation.

5. Read the text "politically," as a "representation of power," "interrogate it for what it fails to say."

6. Rid ourselves resolutely of the old-fashioned notion that "literature is a reflection of reality."

Perhaps the most instructive example of how texts should be treated by the new literary critic is the chapter by Clines himself, a reinterpretation of Psalm 24 from an admittedly deconstructionist position. Here we learn that the appropriate strategy for reading this text is an "ideologically slanted reader-response criticism." This intent is "a goal-oriented hermeneutic, which I shall call a 'bespoke' or 'customized' interpretation." Clines explains later on that his is an "end-user theory of interpretation, a market philosophy of interpretation." The text thus means anything Clines can "sell"; he says that sometimes he is lucky to find six "buyers." Is that any wonder?

Lest it seem that I am caricaturing Clines' position, here is his own summary:

> If there are no "right" interpretations, and no validity beyond the assent of various interest groups, biblical interpreters have to give up the goal of determinate and universally acceptable interpretations, and devote themselves to producing interpretation they can sell — in whatever mode is called for by the communities they choose to serve.

Clines ends his essay by musing: "I have often wondered what one should do after deconstructing a text. A true deconstructionist would say, Start deconstructing the deconstruction." Somehow, Clines is reluctant to do that. He concludes simply that "We float on a raft of signifiers under which we signifieds slide playfully like porpoises; but we have to live *as if* the foundations were solid all the way down to bedrock."[19]

All of this would seem a counsel of despair. Clines is a belated borrower of the notions of Stanley Fish, professor in the English Department of Duke University (whom Clines does not cite), one of the founders of the deconstructionist movement, who seems now to be going out of favor. It was Fish, in his *Is There a Text in This Class? The Authority of Interpretive Communities,* who argued that "it is the reader who 'makes' literature."[20]

Behind Fish, really a rather banal exponent of deconstruction, there stand pivotal founding figures like the poststructuralists Michel Foucault and Jacques Derrida. The latter, for instance, has declared that "reading" a text is all about "catching at a word," i.e., being brought up short by its "unresolvable contradictions."

> If a metaphor seems to suppress its (the word's) implications, we shall catch at that metaphor. We shall follow its adventures through the text coming under a structure of concealment, revealing its self-transgression, its undecidability.[21]

Deconstruction's basic approach to texts — which I would call "hostile," rather than, as formerly presumed necessary, "sympathetic" — is illustrated in other recent works of biblical New Literary Criticism. Let us look, for instance,

---

19. Quotations from D. J. A. Clines, "A World Established on Water (Psalm 24): Reader-Response, Deconstruction and Bespoke Interpretation," in Exum and Clines, 87, 90.

20. (Cambridge: Harvard University Press, 1980), esp. 167-73.

21. Jacques Derrida, *Of Grammatology* (Baltimore: Johns Hopkins University Press, 1976), lxxv.

at a volume of essays stemming from a 1994 conference of mostly "liberation theologians" in Pretoria, South Africa, entitled *Rhetoric, Scripture, and Theology*.[22] Here we learn that we must:

1. Approach texts with the "politics and the hermeneutics of suspicion."
2. "Protect" ourselves from the text, and the text from us.
3. "Forget" the distance between the two.
4. "Celebrate diversity and plurality."
5. Remember that texts are "rhetorically invented."
6. Acknowledge that all ancient texts are "kyriocentric" (i.e., male chauvinist).
7. Grasp that "readings" are "autobiographical," "circular."

Even a recent mainstream handbook on methods in biblical scholarship — *To Each Its Own Meaning: An Introduction to Biblical Criticisms and Their Application* — reveals the inroads that new literary criticism, deconstruction, and related literary approaches have made.[23] Various authors assert of texts that:

1. A text is an "interpretable entity independent of its author."
2. The "author's intention" is an "illusion created by readers." What matters is only the author's "semantic universe."
3. Language is "infinitely unstable and meaning is always deferable."
4. All texts are to be "resisted."
5. An author's "convictions" are not to be confused with "theological, ethical, or narrative expressions."
6. Others' "legitimate readings" are as good as ours.

The above notions of how texts, here particularly biblical texts, are to be read would seem to require little comment, since readers with much common sense will regard them as too absurd to be taken seriously. But such notions now prevail among the many biblical scholars who have abandoned the Bible as history for a new "literary Bible." Thus I think that some more formal rebuttal is re-

22. Stanley E. Porter and Thomas H. Olbricht, eds. JSOTSup 131 (Sheffield: Sheffield Academic, 1996). The quotations here are typical of most of the essays, but they are perhaps most explicit in the piece by Harvard Divinity School's Elizabeth Schüssler-Fiorenza, "Challenging the Rhetorical Half-Turn: Feminist and Rhetorical Biblical Criticism," 28-53.

23. Steven L. McKenzie and Stephen R. Haynes, eds. (Louisville: Westminster John Knox, 1993). See esp. the essays of Daniel Patte, "Structural Criticism," 153-70; and William A. Beardslee, "Poststructuralist Criticism," 221-35.

quired. After all, the biblical texts have until recently been regarded as the basic data — indeed the only data we have — for writing a history of ancient Israel. That this is being questioned by the revisionists is seen in the not-entirely rhetorical question now frequently raised in the literature: "Is it possible to write a history of ancient Israel *without* the Bible?" We shall answer that presently. But whatever the case, if the biblical texts are to be "salvaged" for the historian in any sense, we shall have to address questions about the nature of these texts and the best ways to read them. We would have to do that — which is what the revisionists have conspicuously failed to do — even to dismiss texts in the end.

A Brief Critique of New Literary Criticism

My own misgivings about the new literary critical approach to texts concern primarily the following:

1. Its determined "anti-historical" stance, for which I find no justification.
2. Its promise of superior results; but does this approach truly edify us, or merely entertain us?
3. Its lack of sophistication, despite its claims, particularly in its inchoate theories of "literary production." These are usually borrowed from other disciplines long after they have become obsolete.
4. Its largely reactionary character, self-consciously situated on the "margins" of society and preoccupied with questions of ideology and power and political discourse that may be totally foreign to the text.
5. Its stress on the "social context" of all knowledge, but its ignoring the original context of the text itself.
6. Its minimalization of the importance of philological, historical, and comparative-analytical competence; its "know-nothing" attitude toward, or denial of, any original context.
7. Its contradiction in insisting upon the "isolation" of an individual text, but at the same time arguing that "intertextuality" is essential in reading texts.
8. Its positing that a text must be "tested," but producing no criteria by which that might be accomplished.
9. Its denial of "authorial intent," which defies common sense.
10. Its ultimate cultural relativism, which makes the text mean anything the reader wants. This is no different from the distortion and exploitation of texts of which they accuse both Fundamentalists and the liberal religious establishment in the past.

11. Its fondness for "posing questions" of the text, but its lack of any answers.
12. Its elevation of the reader's subjective concerns to the status of final arbiter of "meaning," which I find arrogant and self-indulgent.
13. The oppressively ideological and polemical character of the entire movement, which substitutes slogans for sustained rational argument.
14. The superiority of this approach is often asserted, usually dogmatically; but its actual reading of texts often borders on the fantastic.
15. A typical postmodern stance is assumed as essential, but it is rarely defended. Is the latest fad (for that is what it will in time be seen to have been) really the best?

In Defense of Ancient Texts

As an archaeologist, I admit to being "premodern" in outlook, an unreconstructed traditionalist by temperament and training. Consider, by contrast, traditional assumptions in approaching ancient texts, which I find infinitely preferable and more rewarding.

1. A text is a product of a particular time, place, culture, language, and it must be placed back in that context to be understood at all.
2. A text is written by an author with a specific intent, usually for a specific audience.
3. An original "meaning" is inherent and is expressed in language that is both deliberate and potentially intelligible.
4. The reader's first task in approaching a text is to place himself and his situation in the background, attempting to be as "objective" as possible so as to be open to the text's original (i.e., "true") meaning in its own terms as far as possible.
5. Methodically, there is no substitute for mastery of the text's original language, geographical and cultural setting, and the light that other contemporary texts may shed.
6. Since there are, at best, always personal, subjective factors at work in interpreting an ancient text, these must be acknowledged, but they may then be usefully exploited. These factors include intuition; an educated imagination; and, above all, empathy, or "positioning oneself within understanding distance."
7. Above all, the question of the modern appropriation of the perceived meaning of a text must be kept strictly separate during the initial interpretation in fulfillment of the requirement of "disinterestedness." Even

thereafter, the applied meaning is tentative and is not possessed of the same "authority" that the text may have had in its original context. In short, theological concerns must be rigidly distinguished from historical exegesis. As Krister Stendahl, distinguished theologian, New Testament scholar, and former Dean of Harvard Divinity School, once observed, there are two separate questions to be asked in all historical inquiry, especially in biblical studies: (1) What *did* the text mean? and (2) What *does* it mean?[24]

If all this makes me a positivist, so be it. At least I have not unwittingly put myself out of business as a historian by denying the existence of my fundamental data, which I think the revisionists have done. In any case, I may not be so old-fashioned after all. A number of astute trend-spotters have already observed that the fascination with deconstruction may have peaked in many university English and comparative literature departments, where the trend first arose. In its place they predict a new approach, one that would seem to be the obvious antidote to deconstruction's bleak outlook: "Neo-pragmatism." With that, it seems to me that, after a generation of floundering around in literary criticism, we have come full circle. Some of us, however, did not take that journey; we have always been "pragmatist" — not "idealistic," much less "positivist" — in trying to read ancient texts (and, as we shall see, artifacts as well). Sometimes, as Freud might have put it, "a text is only a text." But it is that.

I am hardly the only embattled traditionalist around. We may be in the minority in the face of trendy academic fashions these days, but the battle is not lost. Fads, being extremist by definition, usually trigger reactions that bring about their demise and a return to the center.

What Is "Literature," and How Is It Produced?

Having examined the nature of texts as the fundamental issue in our conversation with the "revisionists," we must now briefly move the discussion to the next higher level of analysis, namely the question of literature, or the larger construct of which texts are simply the fundamental building-blocks. The essential notion of "literature" would seem to be self-evident, particularly in the work of those scholars who are preoccupied with literary criticism. Yet definitions are rare. The revisionists, for instance, simply assume that the Bible is "literature." Why so? And what do they mean by that assertion?

24. Krister Stendahl, "Biblical Theology, Contemporary," *IDB* 1:418-32.

Rarer still is a straightforward, reasoned exposition of any theory of "literary production." Thus Robert Carroll, who has published widely on the book of Jeremiah, seems forced to admit that "our knowledge of the processes that gave rise to the book of Jeremiah in the first place is absolutely nil."[25] That is simply untrue. We know a great deal about the political crisis provoked in Judah by the Neo-Babylonian advance in the late 7th–early 6th centuries, both from biblical and nonbiblical sources. Surely that was the formative situation in which Jeremiah (or his "schools") lived and worked. Such statements simply illustrate how absurdly wrong scholars can be when they are willfully blind to historical context. I would attribute the failure to produce a coherent body of literary theory among new literary critics to the fact that most biblical scholars have no formal training in literary theory and comparative literature, as Exum and Clines candidly acknowledge.[26] It is significant that those scholars who do have such training, like Robert Alter, a distinguished Hebraist and pioneer in newer literary critical approaches to the Hebrew Bible, have never gone to the extremes of many of the new literary critics. Alter's literary analyses in such works as *The Art of Biblical Narrative*[27] are more persuasive, precisely because they do not necessarily exclude other readings, even historical ones, nor do they eschew more traditional exegesis of the texts. Not incidentally, Alter is also a Hebraist far superior to most biblical scholars. Compare this with the much-quoted works of the Dutch "narratologist" Mieke Bal, who does not read Hebrew.[28] Somehow all this does not inspire much confidence.

Literature may be thought of as simply a "form of discourse" (a favorite term of new literary critics) that is written, rather than verbal — although many ancient texts may well have originated in long-standing oral traditions. I would distinguish several salient points to be considered in any definition of literature.

1. Literature is the product of the creative, intellectual imagination of a very few, especially in the largely-illiterate ancient world. Literature is written by elites, for elites.
2. Literature is largely fiction, even if it is sometimes "historicized," as in much of the biblical narratives. It does not and cannot reveal "how it

25. Robert P. Carroll, "Intertextuality and the Book of Jeremiah: Animadversions on Text and Theory," in Exum and Clines, 62.

26. Exum and Clines, 13.

27. (New York: Basic Books, 1981).

28. Mieke Bal, *Death and Dissymmetry: The Politics of Coherence in the Book of Judges* (Chicago: University of Chicago Press, 1988).

actually was in the past" (in the 19th-century positivist historian Leopold von Ranke's famous phrase, *Wie es eigentlich gewesen war*), at least for the vast majority of people.

3. Despite the fact that literature is not a direct reflection of reality, it is deliberately "intentional." It is (a) written for a specific audience, however limited; and (b) intended to communicate a certain vision of reality, primarily the "inner reality" of the author's experience, but inevitably reflecting at least something of the external (or "real") world. It both reflects and refracts a vision of reality, perhaps transcending history, but not thereby obliterating it.

An apt metaphor for understanding literature may be to regard it as a form of "symbolically encoded thought and behavior," words being the specific symbols chosen and language the code. To the extent that we can "break the code" — difficult at best with ancient texts — we may be able to read the symbols and thus penetrate behind them to the reality that the author sought to express. To be sure, symbols (including verbal ones) are only "signs" pointing beyond themselves, and therefore will always remain somewhat enigmatic. Yet "reading" symbols is possible; and it is not mere guesswork unless it is ignorant of the language, vocabulary, grammar, or syntax of the symbols, in this case the texts. Texts, however encoded, are not "mute"; but historians are sometimes deaf. Shortly we shall see how artifacts are "symbols," precisely like texts, and are to be read with similar principles of interpretation (hermeneutics).

The Bible as Theology

Thus far I have argued in a preliminary way that the Bible is history in the sense that it at least contains some history; and that the Bible is without doubt literature, although not "mere literature." Does the fundamental nature of the Bible, however, as we are examining it here, include theology? This may seem to many a non-question; of course the Bible is theology, primarily theology. What else? Yet we must remember what theology is: it is a systematic, unified body of propositions about the nature of God, his revelation of himself, and his requirements of the human family. In the light of this definition of theology, there is no such thing as a "biblical theology," if only because the diversity of materials in the biblical literature noted above militates against the very notion of unity, much less a rational, systematic presentation of ideas such as theology would require.

"Theology," in the sense of an academic *or* confessional discipline, is a

19

comparatively modern notion, i.e., at least post-Classical. It is worth noting that there is no Hebrew term equivalent to "theology" in the Bible — indeed, no word for "religion" (that phenomenon is simply taken for granted, needing no definition). To be sure, there are many theological concepts in the Hebrew Bible, because it is a profoundly religious document throughout; but there is no single "biblical theology" that characterizes the biblical literature as a whole.

Having made this necessary qualification, I must nevertheless hasten to say that we cannot simply secularize the Hebrew Bible, or "sanitize" it, by excising those religious notions that we moderns find objectionable. Such radical surgery may be tempting in works like Robert Oden's *The Bible Without Theology*[29] or Davies' *Whose Bible Is It Anyway?*[30] To eliminate, however, the very element that is the irreducible core of the Hebrew Bible — its deeply religious sensibilities — is to violate its integrity as literature. Not even the revisionists would go to that extreme. They would merely "liberate theology from history," as Lemche has phrased it.[31] Yet it is questionable whether we can in fact do that, as we shall see when we examine "biblical theology" further below.

The question here is whether the radical depreciation of the Hebrew Bible as history and the subsequent attempt to re-evaluate it as literature, sketched above, compromises the Bible's authority as Scripture. Certainly the interpretation and use of the Bible in Synagogue and Church over many centuries had assumed that the Bible was "true" in every sense, including the historical, simply because it was the Word of God. The Enlightenment and the rise of modern biblical criticism, however, began the process of undermining that confidence, a process that would now seem to have reached its logical conclusion in the revisionist dehistoricization of the Bible.

Among the many attempts in the past century or so to resist the supposedly destructive impact of biblical criticism was the notorious Fundamentalist-Modernist controversy that shook the very foundations of American religious life early in the 20th century. Nearly every Protestant denomination split into warring camps that remain at odds even to this day, precisely over the question: "Is the Bible historically true?"

As we shall see, archaeology was drawn into this controversy almost from the beginning, in the guise of the peculiarly American phenomenon known as "biblical archaeology." The hope of many was that archaeology would prove the

---

29. Robert A. Oden, Jr., *The Bible Without Theology: The Theological Tradition and Alternatives to It.* New Voices in Biblical Studies (San Francisco: Harper & Row, 1987).

30. JSOTSup 204 (Sheffield: Sheffield Academic, 1995).

31. Niels Peter Lemche, "Early Israel Revisited," *Currents in Research: Biblical Studies* 4 (1996): 9.

Bible to be true. My own mentor at Harvard, George Ernest Wright, was a prominent biblical archaeologist in the 1940s-1970s, and at the same time a leading Old Testament theologian. Heavily influenced in the 1950s by the post-war "Neo-orthodox" theological movement that grew out of Europe's devastation and despair in those years, Wright published in 1952 a highly influential little book entitled *God Who Acts: Biblical Theology as Recital.* Wright the archaeologist and theologian (a combination unimaginable today) summed up the matter by declaring that history was the "primary datum" of faith. Said Wright: "In Biblical faith, everything depends upon whether the central events actually occurred."[32] By central events of Israel's faith Wright meant events such as the call of Abraham, the exodus, the promise of the gift of the land of Canaan, and the conquest. In these *historical* events, God intervenes in human experience to reveal himself and his will uniquely — thus Wright's title, *God Who Acts.* All of this was resounding theology, and reassuring to many devout believers (and even many not-so-devout biblical scholars of conservative persuasion).

But suppose that the "central events" did not happen at all? Worse still, what if it was archaeology, not simply liberal biblical criticism, that provided the actual proof? Significantly, it was Wright's own students in archaeology who were in the forefront of resolving the historiographical crisis that he foresaw. The "archaeological revolution" in biblical studies confidently predicted by Wright and his teacher, the legendary William Foxwell Albright, had come about by the 1980s, but not entirely in the positive way that they had expected. Many of the "central events" as narrated in the Hebrew Bible turn out not to be historically verifiable (i.e., not "true") at all. But is there any history left? And how might it form the basis for modern religious life, or even for a secular morality? To these questions we shall turn in subsequent chapters, and especially in Chapter 6.

---

32. SBT 8 (Chicago: Regency, 1952), 126, 127. For a critique, see William G. Dever, "Syro-Palestinian and Biblical Archaeology," in *The Hebrew Bible and Its Modern Interpreters,* ed. Douglas Knight and Gene M. Tucker (Chico: Scholars, 1985), 54-59.

CHAPTER 2

The Current School of Revisionists
and Their Nonhistories of Ancient Israel

In Chapter 1 we explored the nature of the biblical narratives as "history," noting briefly the skepticism of a newer generation of biblical scholars who sometimes style themselves "revisionists," but whom others now regard as "minimalists" or even the "new nihilists."[1] There we faced resolutely the question that they have now raised with some urgency: "Is it any longer possible to write a history of ancient or biblical events at all?" Their answer, by and large, is: No.

In proceeding now to analyze the revisionist agenda in more detail, we should note several things. (1) The revisionists have pointed to a real crisis. (2) They did not themselves bring about this crisis, however, since the fundamental philosophical issues of reason and historical knowledge arose in the En-

---

1. For the term "new nihilist," which I coined, see my first foray into the "revisionist" controversy, "'Will the Real Israel Please Stand Up?' Archaeology and Israelite Historiography: Part I," *BASOR* 297 (1995): 61-80; and for more recent treatments, with full references to recent literature, cf. "Archaeology, Ideology, and the Quest for an 'Ancient' or 'Biblical' Israel," *NEA* 61 (1998): 39-52; "Histories and Nonhistories of 'Ancient Israel,'" *BASOR* 316 (1999): 89-105. For a sharp reaction, see Robert P. Carroll, "Madonna of Silences: Clio and the Bible," in *Can a "History of Israel" Be Written?* ed. Lester L. Grabbe, 89. On ideology, see further Chapter 1, n. 11; Chapter 2, nn. 6, 24; Chapter 6, nn. 1-20, 23, 37-39; and discussions below on the ideology of the revisionists. The scant more recent revisionist literature would include Niels P. Lemche, *The Israelites in History and Tradition* (Louisville: Westminster John Knox, 1998); *Prelude to Israel's Past: Background and Beginnings of Israelite History and Identity* (Peabody: Hendrickson, 1998); and Thomas L. Thompson, *The Mythic Past: Biblical Archaeology and the Myth of Israel* (London: Basic Books, 1999).

lightenment in the 18th century. (3) It is the entire history of modern critical biblical scholarship since the mid-19th century that created the momentum that has led text-based studies of ancient Israel to this denouement. (4) Many more recent and contemporary trends in biblical studies have contributed to a devaluation of texts as history, including especially the new literary-critical schools outlined above, and this has hastened the crisis. (5) The revisionists, while still a very small minority of biblical scholars, have provoked the present historiographical crisis only by being the most extreme, the most vocal, the best coordinated strategists, and easily the most effective propagandists. In less than 10 years the revisionists have created a storm of controversy in the scholarly literature and in national professional meetings, on the Internet, and now even in the media and in popular magazines. This controversy is so recent, however, that mainstream biblical scholarship has been slow to respond, and archaeologists, with a few exceptions like myself, have not gotten directly involved at all.

The Postmodern Agenda

It is my contention here that behind the revisionists' program lurks a hidden agenda. This agenda, in turn, can be understood best in the context of the postmodern milieu in which they are steeped. But what is the intellectual and social construct that goes under the general name of postmodernism?[2]

2. For an introduction to postmodernism, see the incisive critique of David Gress, *From Plato to NATO: The Idea of the West and Its Opponents* (New York: Free Press, 1998); and cf. Richard Tarnas, *The Passion of the Western Mind: Understanding the Ideas That Have Shaped Our World View* (New York: Harmony, 1991). See also the devastating case-studies in postmodern historiography in Keith Windschuttle, *The Killing of History: How Literary Critics and Social Theorists Are Murdering Our Past* (New York: Free Press, 1997); Terry Eagleton, *The Illusions of Postmodernism* (Oxford: Blackwell, 1997). For a more sympathetic view, see Charles C. Lemert, *Post-modernism Is Not What You Think* (Oxford: Blackwell, 1997). See in much more detail Chapter 6. For documentation of the revisionists' postmodern stance, see Dever, *NEA* 61 (1998): 39-52; cf. also Iain W. Provan's independent and somewhat different exposé in "Ideologies, Literary and Critical: Reflections on Recent Writing on the History of Israel," *JBL* 114 (1995): 585-606. Thompson's tortured reply to Provan is, I think, the best clue to his own ideology; see Thomas L. Thompson, "A Neo-Albrightian School in History and Biblical Scholarship?," *JBL* 114 (1995): 683-98. Note that the editor of a collection of essays by the largely revisionist European Seminar on Methodology in Israel's History candidly admits that there is "strong agreement that the implications of postmodernism for the historical question need to be accepted"; see Lester L. Grabbe, "Reflections on the Discussion" in *Can a "History of Israel" Be Written?* 189.

First, we must understand what this reactionary movement was reacting against — in this case, late 19th- and early 20th-century modernism, or positivism. Among the main propositions of positivism were the following. (1) There are immutable and universal "laws" governing the universe and the relationships of all its parts, including human society. (2) These "laws" are objective facts and thus can be discovered by science, based on observation of the empirical evidence. (3) This modern, rational, and positivist way of thinking supersedes all earlier stages of thinking, such as (a) "theological/fictive," (b) "metaphysical abstract," or (c) both "materialism" and "spiritualism."

Postmodernism must be understood as a reaction against positivism. Thus its main features were and are: (1) rebellion against all authority; (2) distrust of all universal, "totalizing" discourse; (3) the assumption that "social constructs" determine all knowledge; (4) it is only "discourse" and "realms of discourse" that matter; (5) all "truth" is relative; (5) there is no intrinsic "meaning," only that which we supply; (6) there is no operative "consensus" view, so that everything becomes ideology, ultimately politics; (7) one ideology is as appropriate as another (sometimes the more "radical" the better); (8) ideological discourse need not be rational or systematic, but may be intuitive or even eccentric, representing the neglected "peripheries" of society rather than the "center."

Such postmodern thinking has affected nearly all disciplines in the social sciences since ca. the 1970s, to such an extent that it is now taken for granted as the reigning paradigm. Yet its very name is negative; can any movement define itself largely by what it follows and still maintain our confidence? And what marvelous new paradigm will come after this penultimate postmodernism? "Pre-apocalyptic"? If all this amounts to modernism and its aftermath, will someone please show me the way back to the Enlightenment?

Deconstructionism

One particular expression of postmodernism is a movement or a method called deconstructionism. Recently it has been prominent in literary criticism, especially in some university English and comparative literature departments, but it has also spread to other areas of the humanities, even biblical studies, as we saw in Chapter 1. Deconstruction's major premise, derived from its overall postmodern stance, is that texts have no intrinsic "meaning," at least none that is recoverable in the case of ancient texts; the modern interpreter gives to the text whatever "meaning" seems appropriate in the social context of his or her own "realm of discourse," whatever the "realm" of the original author may have been. The more extreme deconstructionists even argue that the original author may not have had any specific intention (a curious conceit). Instead, the critical and sensitive reader must inquire what the author's subjective inner world was about, who the audience may have been, and what the reason for the particular style of discourse was. Ultimately, one must ask not *what* a text "signifies," but *how*. We can go no further; seeking a "historical context," an original meaning, or an agreed-upon interpretation is methodologically suspect.

In the past decade or so, the deconstructionist mode of textual analysis — especially in the form of new literary criticism sketched above — has made such inroads in biblical studies that the traditional historical exegesis and criticism that have ruled for more than a century are often dismissed today as *passé*. If the search for "history" and for historical exegesis of texts is obsolete, the archaeology of the "biblical world" is irrelevant. That may explain why archaeology is neglected or at best misunderstood almost everywhere in biblical studies and theology today.[3]

Postmodern Ideology and the Revisionist Agenda

It is at this point that I think we can comprehend the revisionist agenda in biblical studies. It is, I suggest, thinly-disguised postmodernism, in this case specifically deconstruction. If the reader thinks this proposal too far-fetched, or too severe an indictment, consider the following, which are the main points that the revisionists themselves have set forth — what I would call the manifesto of a movement that self-consciously portrays itself as revolutionary.

(1) All the texts of the Hebrew Bible in its present form date to the Hellenistic era (as late as the 2nd-1st century). They are therefore "unhistorical," of little or no value for reconstructing a "biblical" or an "ancient Israel," both of which are simply modern Jewish and Christian literary constructs.

(2) Interpretation of the biblical texts should be "liberated from historical

---

3. Virtually all Syro-Palestinian archaeologists — American, European, and Israeli — instinctively feel the isolation of their discipline from biblical and theological studies; and a few even rejoice in that fact, such as Israel Finkelstein, "Bible Archaeology or Archaeology of Palestine in the Iron Age? A Rejoinder," *Levant* 30 (1998): 167-74. For a tacit admission of the lack of dialogue from a biblicist, see Baruch Halpern, "Text and Artifact: Two Monologues?" in *The Archaeology of Israel*, ed. Neil A. Silberman and David B. Small, 311-40. Note that a recent collection of basic essays, *Israel's Past in Present Research: Essays on Ancient Israelite Historiography*, ed. V. Phillips Long (Winona Lake: Eisenbrauns, 1999), contains 33 chapters, but not one by an archaeologist, although several of us have written extensively on the subject.

consideration." It should proceed strictly on the basis of literary analysis of the Bible's "stories," which reveal mainly the "self-perception" of the narrators.

(3) This radically "anti-historic movement" in the study of ancient Israelite "history" has at last brought us such "new knowledge" that it makes all other approaches obsolete, indeed illegitimate. Those who persist in traditional approaches may be dismissed as either servants of the religious Establishment, or simply crypto-Fundamentalists.

(4) Attempts to write any more histories of "Israel" should be abandoned. Instead, we should be writing "Palestinian history," which American and Israeli biblicists and archaeologists have conspired to "suppress" because of their biblical and nationalistic biases.

The quotes above are all taken directly from the current literature; and I can supply numerous other quotations from the principal spokesmen of revisionism, including Philip R. Davies, Thomas L. Thompson, Niels Peter Lemche, and Keith W. Whitelam.[4] That my paraphrase above fairly represents the revisionist position in general is easy to document (although this "school," like others, is not necessarily monolithic). I suggest simply that the reader reflect on the obviously ideological pronouncements above, then compare them with the postmodern/deconstructionist agenda that I have outlined. Can there be any other background against which to portray the revisionists and their stated objectives?[5]

A "Revolution"?

It is true that most of the revisionists have either carefully avoided the terms "deconstruction" and "new literary criticism," or else have denied that the terms describe them. Nevertheless, I think that it is always instructive to pay more attention to what people actually do, than to what they say or think they are doing. And in my judgment the revisionists are carrying out a classic, deliberate, single-minded deconstructionist agenda. It is also evident that their program is complete with all those elements that typically characterize "revolutionary" movements: pretense to authoritative credentials; ideological manifestos; po-

4. The above agenda is perhaps seen most succinctly in Lemche, *Currents in Research* 4 (1996): 9-34; see my reply in the same issue, "Revisionist Israel Revisited: A Rejoinder to Niels Peter Lemche" (35-50). The agenda is also quite clear in Lemche and Thompson, "Did Biran Kill David? The Bible in the Light of Archaeology," *JSOT* 64 (1994): 3-22; and Thompson, *JBL* 114 (1995): 683-98. For the other revisionist literature — all of it rather explicitly programmatic — see nn. 1 and 2 above.

5. See further below in this chapter.

larization of viewpoints; extremist rhetoric; personal polemics; evangelical (!) fervor; apparatus for disseminating their own views; prevailing dogmatism; and Utopian ideals. Readers can readily confirm these programmatic objectives by browsing through the flood of recent revisionist publications. If I perceive their intentions wrongly, I would welcome other readings (that is, if texts really have any "meaning").

On Ideology, Bias, and "Realms of Discourse": Some Case-studies

Even if my attempt here to identify the revisionists as "ideologues" is persuasive to some, others may protest. They could say, for instance, that all scholars are in a sense ideologues, i.e., they have a position to defend; and that the revisionists' ideology is not necessarily wrong-headed or particularly menacing. If the latter qualifications are valid, then the whole controversy is a "tempest in a teacup." But I think that there is more to it than that.

Before proceeding, let me define "ideology" and "ideologue." The former term is often taken only in the negative sense, i.e., as the obvious bias of the "other." I use "ideology" here, however, in its proper and neutral meaning, since we all have "ideologies," or a "system of ideas," a way of thinking. It should be content that determines whether a given ideology is good or bad (I do not espouse to be a relativist). By "ideologue," on the other hand, I refer to those who espouse a particular ideology, often uncritically examined, to the exclusion of others, and who then become obsessed with visionary ideas.[6] Space prohibits more than a few specific examples of how ideology typically shapes revisionist discourse.

Philip R. Davies

Much of the present controversy began with Philip R. Davies, of the University of Sheffield, in his provocative little book *In Search of "Ancient Israel"* (1992).[7] Here Davies sets forth the basic revisionist premises noted above, which be-

---

6. See further Provan, *JBL* 114 (1995): 585-606; and Tina Pippin, "Ideology, Ideational Criticism, and the Bible," *Currents in Research: Biblical Studies* 4 (1996): 51-78 and full literature cited there. See also V. Phillips Long, "The Future of Israel's Past: Personal Reflections," in Long, *Israel's Past in Present Research*, 580-92.

7. JSOTSup 148 (Sheffield: JSOT, 1992).

came the foundation for most subsequent discussions. The casual, off-hand, sometimes outrageous style of Davies' book tempts one to dismiss it as either an example of British eccentricity, or perhaps intended only as a tongue-in-cheek piece for our amusement. But I suspect that Davies, with all his disarming flair, is in deadly earnest: there *was* no "ancient" or "biblical" Israel; and the "historical Israel" that archaeology might recover in theory is beyond our reach due to archaeology's deficiencies. Yet I would point out that nowhere that I can see does Davies document the basic premise on which his basic statement rests — that all the literature of the Hebrew Bible in its present form was composed long after the fact, and thus yields no real "history." In 1992 Davies simply asserted this, not informing his readers that his is a decidedly minority view, one that goes against a long tradition of mainstream biblical historical-critical scholarship, as well as many studies in oral transmissions and literary production.

As for archaeology's potential for writing a history of "ancient Israel," Davies rejects this as anything more than a remote possibility. Only once does he cite any of the basic archaeological handbooks we noted above — Amihai Mazar's *Archaeology of the Land of the Bible, 10,000-586 B.C.E.*[8] — merely to dismiss it as irrelevant, since Mazar ends with the Iron Age in Palestine and does not cover Davies' "biblical world" in the Persian-Hellenistic period. He does not even cite Helga Weippert's *Palästina in vorhellenistischer Zeit,*[9] which although only a handbook is the single work cited by Thompson and most other revisionists. Together these two fundamental sources contain some 700 pages of detailed presentation of archaeological data on the Iron Age. If this complex, or archaeological assemblage, is not "Israelite," what is it?

An even more egregious example of Davies' tailoring the evidence to fit his presuppositions is his notorious attempt (along with others) to discredit the recently discovered 9th-century inscription from Tel Dan in northern Israel, mentioning the "house of David" and a "king of Israel," a king we can now identify as Jehoram, ca. 840.[10] Davies simply refuses to take the Dan inscription seriously as a historical datum for the United Monarchy, in this case one that would effectively contradict his assertion that there were no early Iron Age Israelite and Judean "states." But Lemche and Thompson (below) have gone so far

---

8. *In Search of "Ancient Israel,"* 24 n. 4.

9. (Munich: C. H. Beck, 1988).

10. See Avraham Biran and Joseph Naveh, "An Aramaic Stele Fragment from Tel Dan," *IEJ* 43 (1993): 81-98; "The Tel Dan Inscription: A New Fragment," *IEJ* 45 (1995): 1-18; and cf. the devastating rebuttal by Anson Rainey, "The 'House of David' and the House of the Deconstructionists," *BAR* 20/6 (1994): 47. See also n. 11 below.

as to imply that the inscription is a forgery, a hoax "planted" on the unsuspecting dig director, the venerable Avraham Biran. Several of the other revisionists have turned amusing intellectual somersaults to avoid the obvious meaning of the Dan inscription.[11] The irony is that biblical scholars have long demanded that an archaeologist supplement our "mute" artifacts with texts. But when we do find a spectacular text, they discard it! More recently, Davies has alleged that our most secure ancient Hebrew monumental inscription — the Hezekiah tunnel inscription, dated to the siege of Sennacherib in 701 (2 Chr. 32:1-5) — is a Hasmonean/Hellenistic work of the 2nd century, in effect "fraudulent" as used by epigraphers and paleographers.[12]

As for "Biblical" Hebrew, Davies regards this as a *Bildungssprache,* an artificial "literary" language that was invented by the late scribes who wrote the Bible. He ignores the fact that we have hundreds, probably thousands, of ostraca,inscriptions on stone, inscribed pots, seals, and seal-impressions from well-dated 10th-6th century contexts, in precisely this "nonexistent" Iron Age Hebrew. What is one to make of all this, unless we suppose that we are dealing here with ideological pronouncements, rather than with honest, competent, fully documented *scholarship?*

At least Davies' bias is obvious, and he has recently defended it: he is resolutely anti-theological.[13] Here I might agree with Davies, since one can easily show, as I shall do below, that theology constitutes a separate quest and must be clearly distinguished from historical and archaeological inquiries, which have a different motivation. But it appears to me that Davies is largely reacting against what may be his own Fundamentalist background.

Thomas L. Thompson

Another of the current revisionists, Thomas L. Thompson, actually set out on this path, although apparently not deliberately, many years ago with his icono-

11. Cf. Lemche and Thompson, *JSOT* 64 (1994): 3-22; Frederick H. Cryer, "Of Epistemology, Northwest-Semitic Epigraphy and Irony: The '*BYTDWD*/House of David' Inscription Revisited," *JSOT* 69 (1996): 3-17; Keith W. Whitelam, *The Invention of 'Ancient Israel,* 166-69. On the genuineness of the inscription and its significance, see most recently André Lemaire, "The Tel Dan Stela as a Piece of Royal Historiography," *JSOT* 81 (1998): 3-14.

12. See references in Chapter 5, n. 49.

13. See his *Whose Bible Is It Anyway?* (Sheffield: Sheffield Academic, 1995); cf. "Method and Madness: Some Remarks on Doing History with the Bible," *JBL* 114 (1995): 669-705.

clastic work, *The Historicity of the Patriarchal Narratives* (1974),[14] a radical attack on Albright and his school. An "outsider" for many years, never accepted by the religious establishment, Thompson has finally ended up in Copenhagen with Niels Peter Lemche (below). In a very defensive piece in the *Journal of Biblical Literature,* Thompson describes himself as "a Joycean Catholic Irish-American emigré" and as a "neo-Albrightian."[15] However, the first characterization helps us to account only for Thompson's oblique writing style; and the latter is simply absurd.

Thompson's real point of departure is revealed in comments elsewhere in this article. He is "strongly influenced by the political, ideological, and religious turmoil of the late 1960s"; 1968 was the year that meant "denying authority to old opinions and institutions which are no longer able to present a decent argument in favor of their continued existence." Thompson and the other revisionists are committed rather to *Wissenschaft* (or "scientific knowledge"), in this case partly a real theology of some sort. As Thompson says, we "never gave up the hope that we could do something positive for this world."[16] Commendable; but hardly a sturdy theology.

Somehow, all this does little to reassure me on the issue of ideology. Social constructionism and political activism, combined with an appeal to "New Age" theo-babble, hardly provide the most fruitful orientation to the "objective and critical" study of the biblical texts that Thompson claims to be doing. On the other hand, such an orientation — complete with the Utopian ideal — does characterize postmodernism generally, and the biblical deconstructionists in particular. Can one be forgiven for suggesting that there may be a connection here?

The issue, however, is whether or not Thompson's ideological agenda, or ours, has adversely affected scholarship. I think that in Thompson's case it has, both in method and in results. Positing in Thompson's work a "revolutionary" ideology explains many things, such as his exaggerations. Among them are the following statements. (1) There were no real "cities" in the Bronze Age heartland. (2) Archaeology "cannot distinguish" Israelite from Canaanite culture. (3) Albright's "Canaanites" existed only "in his head." (4) In the Iron I period (12th-11th centuries) the notion of an "indigenous Israel . . . is historically meaningless." (5) "The Bible's stories about Saul and David are no more factual than the tales of King Arthur." (6) There was no Judean "state" until the 7th century,

---

14. *The Historicity of the Patriarchal Narratives: The Quest for the Historical Abraham.* BZAW 133 (New York: de Gruyter, 1974).

15. Thompson, *JBL* 114 (1995): 696.

16. See Thompson, *JBL* 114 (1995): 694, n. 32.

because "only a few dozen villagers lived as farmers in all the Judaean highlands." (7) Jerusalem finally became a political and religious center or capital only in the 2nd century B.C. (8) "The very existence of an 'exilic' period . . . is open to serious challenge." (9) The concept of "Israel" was a literary and theological creation of the Persian, if not the Hellenistic, period. (10) Our "new knowledge" proves that the Hebrew Bible is a late "Jewish construct." (11) There was no "Judaism" until the 2nd century A.D., and claims to the contrary are "literary fiction."[17]

Such exaggerations — which I can easily multiply — will no doubt be defended by countering that they are quotations taken out of context or simply part of Thompson's deliberately provocative style of debate. Nonetheless, this is irresponsible scholarship — simply ideological rhetoric, with no attempt at documentation or a well-balanced presentation that might enlighten the reader. If Davies is a propagandist, Thompson appears to be a pamphleteer.

Thompson's latest book, *The Mythic Past: Biblical Archaeology and the Myth of Israel* (1999), only confirms my suspicions. Here the statements are even more outrageous. A few typical quotations will give the flavor of the book: (1) "It is only a Hellenistic Bible that we know: namely the one that we first begin to read in the texts found among the Dead Sea scrolls near Qumran." (2) "The Bible's 'Israel' [is] a literary fiction. . . . The Bible is not a history of anyone's past." (3) "There never was a United Monarchy in history, and it is meaningless to speak of preexilic prophets and their writings." (4) "The literary nature of the Mesha stele [a 9th-century B.C. monumental inscription from Moab, in Transjordan, mentioning Omri, king of Israel] needs to be taken seriously. It is quite doubtful that it refers to an historical person when it refers to Israel's king." (5) "The central core of biblical tradition, this *torah* of instruction, was centered on the belief in a universal and transcendent God. This belief is more philosophical than religious." (6) "The concept of [Israelite] ethnicity, however, is a fiction, created by writers. It is a product of literature, of history-writing." (7) "Gods are created, but the true God is unknown. This important maxim lies at the centre of the Bible's theology." (8) "The [biblical] text doesn't speak to us, nor was it addressed to us. To pretend that it does and was, is among theology's least critical and most self-serving lies."[18]

---

17. See Thomas L. Thompson, *Early History of the Israelite People from the Written and Archaeological Sources* (Leiden: Brill, 1992); *JBL* 114 (1995): 683-98; "Historiography of Ancient and Early Jewish Historiography: W. G. Dever and the Not So New Biblical Archaeology," in *The Origins of the Ancient Israelite States,* ed. Volkmar Fritz and Philip R. Davies, 26-43; "Defining History and Ethnicity in the South Levant," in Grabbe, *Can a "History of Israel" Be Written?,* 166-87; *The Mythic Past.*

18. Thompson, *The Mythic Past,* xiv, xv, 13, 32, 234, 305, 387. Thompson's book contains no footnotes or documentation.

Is it any wonder that I have suggested elsewhere[19] that Thompson and his fellow revisionists have become the new nihilists?

Another aspect of Thompson's ideology is his misrepresentation or suppression of the views of those who would oppose him. Typical are Thompson's charges against me. From the beginning, he says, I have really been an old-fashioned, Albrightian "biblical archeologist" (despite my much-publicized opposition to this kind of archaeology for 25 years). I have distorted archaeological data by using them to prove the "historicity of the biblical Patriarchs" (although in fact I wrote to oppose this 20 years ago). Others have argued for the methodological separation of Bible, archaeology, and the history of ancient Palestine, but I have uncritically combined them; my "project has always been the relationship asserted by biblical and Christian fundamentalism" (i.e., between Bible and archaeology). I have "never recognized the methodological and historical issues that were involved." I and other archaeologists "only visit ideas." Proof of my "biblical bias" is that I went to Gezer in 1967 deliberately to find a "Solomonic" city gate, where we pulled out large *in situ* stones and rolled them down the hill, suppressing this evidence in our report. And "when it came to questions of chronology and the gate itself, all pottery discrepancies were consciously discarded prior to recording." Thompson says that I refuse to address the issue that the revisionists raise, that my "ancient Israel (is) a scholarly figment, rather than the goal of current research," a "harmonistic scenario" with which to wed our "own hardly independently derived phantasms." "Dever's methods . . . have little to do with archaeology." Mine is "history by committee," "not history at all," "wholly bereft of method." By contrast, the revisionists' separation of archaeological and historical pursuits is "a hard-won gain that has been accepted by all but fundamentalists." Even my pioneering work on Early Bronze IV, begun in 1966, derives from Thompson's "archaeological" publications.[20]

My few recent attempts to counter Thompson's charges are now dismissed as seeking "credit for initiating the now dominant historiographical development in our *(sic)* field which understands archaeology and the history of the southern Levant as independent disciplines," or at worst simply "acrimonious" debate and *ad hominem* attacks. I and others who are finally compelled to expose the blatant ideology here are introducing irrelevant issues such as ques-

19. See William G. Dever, review of Thompson, *The Mythic Past, BAR* 25 (1999): 64-66. See Chapter 3, n. 60.

20. See Thompson, "Historiography of Ancient Palestine," *passim.* Such undocumented charges are all too typical of revisionist discourse. Its frequent substitution of rhetoric for fair and balanced judgment is a telling fault.

tions of competence and integrity, and even of faith and morality. We are simply obstructionists who stand in the way of acceptance of the New Truth that will soon triumph and will resolve the "historiographical crisis" that many have acknowledged. The "newer archaeology" that will support this historiographical breakthrough is not that which I and others have developed, but is rather the work of biblical scholars whom I do not even cite ("a form of Harvard censorship"), such as Gösta Ahlström, Ernst Axel Knauf, Niels Peter Lemche, J. Maxwell Miller, John Van Seters, and Thompson himself. (Never mind that I have cited and discussed all in detail.) These scholars are not "ideologues" or "radicals"; their critics are. They are not "skeptics" about the history of ancient Israel, but their opponents are "maximalists" or "credulists." They are embattled protagonists for *Wissenschaft*, "scientific historical knowledge," the New Truth.[21]

What is the fair-minded reader to make of all this fulmination? Let me suggest that here, as in the other voluminous literature being spewed forth by this vocal minority, are all the classic hallmarks of the "ideologue": the claim to be "voices from the margin"; unmasking others' ideology, while denying their own; "liberation" rhetoric; the deliberate intent to overthrow the Establishment and to repudiate its "power to sanction"; dogmatic assertions with little documentation; caricatures of the views of opponents; claims to have discovered a New Truth, but without telling how and why they have repudiated their own *former* "truth"; and revolutionary slogans and even claims to have won the victory already (see further below).

Keith W. Whitelam

A more recent convert to revisionism is Keith W. Whitelam of the University of Stirling, who had earlier collaborated with Robert B. Coote in an innovative settlement-history of ancient Palestine entitled *The Emergence of Early Israel in Historical Perspective*.[22] This foray into archaeology was followed by Whitelam on his own in several programmatic statements on "early Israel." Then in late 1996 there appeared a full-scale work, *The Invention of Ancient Israel: The Si-*

---

21. Most of the quotations here come from Thompson's most programmatic (and revealing) work, *JBL* 114 (1995): 683-98.

22. Social World of Biblical Antiquity 5 (Sheffield: Sheffield Academic, 1987); Whitelam, "The Identity of Early Israel: The Realignment and Transformation of Late Bronze-Iron Age Palestine," *JSOT* 63 (1994): 57-87; see William G. Dever, "The Identity of Early Israel: A Rejoinder to Keith W. Whitelam," *JSOT* 72 (1996): 3-24.

lencing of Palestinian History. Whitelam's basic thesis is similar to that of Davies and Thompson, except for one twist. Not only have scholars been preoccupied with reconstructing an imaginary "ancient Israel," but American and Israeli biblicists and archaeologists have meanwhile conspired to deprive the modern Palestinians of *their* history.

Whitelam's main arguments[23] are that both archaeology and biblical studies have conspired to "usurp Palestinian history" and that the conspiracy results from the biases of European and American scholarship regarding an "ancient Israel," as well as the program of Zionism coupled with modern Israeli archaeology. According to Whitelam (with Davies, Lemche, and Thompson), "the 'ancient Israel' of biblical studies is a scholarly construct based upon a misreading of the biblical tradition and divorced from historical reality." The result of the preoccupation with an "Israel" has been that "in effect, Palestinian history, particularly for the thirteenth century BCE to the second century CE, has not existed except as the backdrop to the histories of Israel and Judah or of Second Temple Judaism."

As proof of this bias, Whitelam asserts that recent Israeli archaeological surveys of the West Bank have been "heavily influenced by biblical scholarship and the all-consuming search for 'ancient Israel.'" These are research strategies that have "invented and located Israel in the Late Bronze-Iron Age transition and early Iron Age." The surveys "are also an expression of a claim to the land by the mapping and conceptualization of that land." Biblical studies and Israeli archaeological scholarship have "dispossessed Palestinians of a land and a past." The "new paradigm" in both disciplines must be to rediscover the "Palestinians" in the Iron Age and even in the Bronze Age; all who oppose that agenda are "distracting" us from the proper objectives of scholarship.

Here the sensitive reader will see red flags all over the place; but let me suggest only my chief misgivings about Whitelam, quite apart from his belated conversion to the revisionist movement. (1) He does not document any of his charges against Israeli (and other) archaeologists. That archaeologists, Israelis or others, are not "objective," that they too are conditioned by their social context, is a truism. But Whitelam would need to give some specific "case-histories" to show how a connection with the Bible or the Land of the Bible has adversely influenced scholarly conclusions. For instance, Whitelam castigates Israel Finkelstein in particular as one of the leading Israeli archaeologists who carried out the West Bank surveys, charging him with using this research to create an "early Israel" and to validate modern Israeli claims to these territories.

23. See Whitelam, *The Invention of Ancient Israel*, esp. chs. 2-6, from which the following quotations are taken.

Whitelam does not inform his readers that (a) since 1991 (even earlier, in Hebrew), Finkelstein has repudiated the use of the label "Israelite" or even my "Proto-Israelite" for the 12th-11th century hill-country archaeological assemblage that he himself did so much to place on our settlement map. (b) Finkelstein does not belong to the political right in Israel, which defends the modern settlements, but is strongly affiliated with the opposition on the left. (c) Finkelstein — like all Israeli archaeologists — is a secularist whose work is entirely separated from programs of biblical and religious studies at every level, and who is adamantly opposed to the religious establishment in Israel.[24]

Finkelstein's current negative views on "Israelite ethnicity" do indeed pose some serious problems, which is why he and I are constantly engaged in controversy in print. But these are strictly archaeological disputes — not ideological, nationalistic, religious, or personal, much less biblical. They have to do with legitimate professional differences in interpretation. And here, Whitelam, not being an archaeologist, really lacks credentials that would entitle him to enter the debate.

(2) The latter point leads me to the second problem that I have with Whitelam's ideology: his appeal to archaeology is bogus. The fraud here lies in the fact that Whitelam has no experience in fieldwork, no first-hand acquaintance with the material culture of ancient Palestine (or *his* "Palestine") and its interpretation, and only superficial and secondary knowledge of the critical literature. Furthermore, if Whitelam wishes to complain of scholarly "usurpation," let him confront his own *hubris* in claiming that he and other biblicists must now take up the burden of the "neglected history of ancient Palestine." We archaeologists have been doing precisely that history for nearly 150 years! Are he and the other revisionist biblical historians better equipped for this task? Are they better equipped than the *real* "Palestinians," who now have their own Department of Archaeology in the Palestinian Authority, and have no need for outsiders to patronize them or to write their history? These Palestinians are already collaborating with American, Israeli, and Jordanian archaeologists to write a history of ancient Palestine in all periods, not just that of the Israelite monarchy.

24. For Finkelstein's early about-face on "Israelite ethnicity," see "The Emergence of Israel in Canaan: Consensus, Mainstream and Dispute," *SJOT* 5 (1991): 47-59. See further the discussion on early Israel in Chapter 4. On Whitelam's caricature of the surveys carried out principally by Finkelstein, the final report has now appeared in Israel Finkelstein, Zvi Lederman, and Shlomo Bunimovitz, *Highlands of Many Cultures. The Southern Samaria Survey: The Sites* (Tel Aviv: Institute of Archaeology, 1997); see my review, completely vindicating Finkelstein and others from the charge of "pro-Israel" bias, in *BASOR* 313 (1999): 87, 88. For my critique of Whitelam generally, see *BASOR* 316 (1999): 89-105. For other about-faces, see references in Chapter 6, n.34.

(3) Finally, several of Whitelam's statements border dangerously on anti-Semitism; they are certainly anti-Jewish and anti-Israel. There is a clear bias here, as early critics have pointed out.[25] Where does it come from, in a scholar who is otherwise modest, quiet, and personally charming, and who in the past has written perceptively and sensitively about a real "ancient Israel"? What has happened to convert Whitelam to revisionism? In any case, other critics on the horizon will be less charitable. These critics will charge (and perhaps document) "anti-Semitism"; others will be outraged and will come to the defense of the revisionists. Thus our several disciplines are likely to be further polarized and isolated by the acrimonious discussions of what are essentially nonissues. I choose to believe that Whitelam is sincere, although naïve, and that he did not consciously intend to precipitate such a furor. But that is what he has done; and it is not just his scholarship that is at fault, but also and principally his ideological agenda.

Niels Peter Lemche

Niels Peter Lemche, of the University of Copenhagen, came to international prominence in 1985 with what at the time seemed a revolutionary new socio-anthropological history, *Early Israel: Anthropological and Historical Studies on the Israelite Society Before the Monarchy* (popularized in 1988 as *Ancient Israel: A New History of Israelite Society*). By 1994, however, his mind had changed sufficiently that he could write a programmatic article entitled "Is It Still Possible to Write a History of Ancient Israel?" Practically speaking, his answer was No. His full-scale work in German in 1996 appeared in English in 1998, *Prelude to Israel's Past: Background and Beginnings of Israelite History and Identity*. This was followed in 1999 by *The Israelites in History and Tradition*. While less radical than Thompson's *Early History of the Israelite People* (and later, nonhistories), Lemche's most recent works leave no doubts that his "history" is so minimal that it scarcely merits the term. For instance, David, Solomon, and

---

25. See, e.g., the review of Benjamin D. Sommer, *Middle East Quarterly* (1998): 85, 86, who speaks of "the political agenda that dominates his book" (85). See also Baruch A. Levine and Abraham Malamat, *IEJ* 46 (1996): 284-88, who conclude that "ideological scholarship is flawed scholarship, no matter who engages in it." According to Levine and Malamat, Whitelam's book "comes close to being a political manifesto" (288). For my own review, see *BASOR* 316 (1999): 89-106; and for Lemche's almost embarrassingly laudatory review, see "Clio Is Also Among the Muses! Keith W. Whitelam and the History of Palestine: A Review and a Commentary," in Grabbe, *Can a "History of Israel" Be Written?*, 123-55.

the United Kingdom are all "invented." And "without a Davidic empire there was no Israel in the biblical sense. The only thing that remains is the tradition of two tiny states of Palestine in the Iron Age, which were long after their disappearance chosen as the basis of a history of a new nation to be established on the soil of Palestine in the postexilic period."[26] Earlier Lemche had written an article entitled "Early Israel Revisited," in which he argued that no traditional history of Israel is possible, even works such as his own previously radical but rather well received histories.[27] Lemche now repudiates these, because they were too close to a "paraphrase of the Bible," relying "far too much on the biblical narratives."

Here I can give only something of the flavor of an exchange of views (an attempt at dialogue — one of the few thus far in the scholarly literature) which appeared in Sheffields's *Journal for the Study of the Old Testament.* (Archaeologists rarely write, and are still more rarely invited to write, for biblical journals; in this case, I invited myself, and the editor accepted.) Lemche begins his overview by suggesting one dimension of the historiographical crisis we face: the decline in university positions in biblical history and archaeology, and even in theological seminaries, where these subjects "are increasingly deemed unnecessary luxuries." He is absolutely right, as I also pointed out in a somewhat alarmist article in the *Biblical Archaeology Review* entitled "Death of a Discipline?"[28] Lemche predicts that "Should Whitelam's plea (1996) for the replacement of Israelite history with a proper history of Palestine find an audience, the anti-historic movement among theologians will probably gain momentum." Lemche thinks that it should, that despite certain risks — the possibility of "bad exegesis" and "a kind of ethical morass" — theology should be "liberated from historical considerations." Indeed, Lemche thinks that this has already happened by and large, and that "the debate in this area is almost at an end." The reason for this triumph of a new "secular theology" (as I would call it) is, according to Lemche, the fact that "the old-fashioned endeavor to extract historical information from the Old Testament narratives is considered a thing of the past."[29]

Lemche's view is that the biblical texts reveal only "the self-perception of the people who wrote this narrative," and they lived in the Persian period in the Exile (ca. 6th-5th centuries). Thus genuine "historical recollections of Israel's

---

26. For the article, see *JSOT* 8 (1994): 163-88. For the more recent books, see n. 1 above; the quotation here is from *The Israelites in History and Tradition*, 155.

27. *Currents in Research: Biblical Studies* 4 (1996): 9-34. I replied to Lemche, a friend of long standing, in the same issue, 35-50.

28. *BAR* 21 (1995): 50-55, 70.

29. For the quotations from Lemche, see *Currents in Research* 4 (1996): 9, 10.

early history are not to be found in the Old Testament historical narrative." Therefore "we cannot save the biblical history of early Israel." In his conclusion, Lemche observes:

> Coming back to the field of studies on the history of early Israel is like visiting an old house, formerly resplendent in all its glory, full of life and merry conversation, but now forsaken by its inhabitants. It is hardly a place to stay for long. In the corners a few ghosts of the past may still be lurking, maintaining the basic historical truth of the historical biblical narrative.[30]

Lemche is speaking here of the Premonarchical period, the 12th-11th centuries, but he notes that his basic historiographical skepticism could be extended to cover the whole of the Monarchy, and even the exilic and postexilic periods. In short, the Hebrew Bible should be "studied as what it is — a narrative." For Lemche, as for the other revisionists, the Hebrew Bible for the most part is *only* literature, not history. Is there, however, *any* "history" left? When I pressed this point in a closed session at national meetings, Lemche could only respond that "we (may) have a number of historical recollections" in the Bible," that "we love these stories, but we don't believe them to be true." Thompson chimed in: "We don't deny that there's early material in the Bible. But we do think it's small, only fragmentary material." When P. Kyle McCarter (the other "maximalist" invited to this private debate) and I pressed both Lemche and Thompson, citing among other historical data the Tel Dan inscription and a brand new Aramaic inscription found at biblical Ekron and mentioning "Ekron," they both argued that the latter might be a forgery — just as they had said of the Tel Dan inscription in a joint article in 1994.[31] What can one do with scholars who refuse to regard as legitimate any data that confound their theories? Don't bother them with facts; their minds are made up.

Here is the crux of the matter: What is left of Israelite history after the devastating attack of the revisionists on the biblical texts? I have yet to discover in all their writings any real awareness of the "historical core" of the biblical narrative, a core that I argue here can now be reconstructed by means of a sophisticated reading of archaeological and textual evidence, taken together.

Further details of my critique of Lemche's position (and others) will be given below in Chapters 3-6, but as I pointed out, such a negative approach

---

30. *Currents in Research* 4 (1996): 27, 28.

31. See Lemche and Thompson, *JSOT* 64 (1994): 3-22. For the symposium, at a joint meeting of the American Schools of Oriental Research and the Society of Biblical Literature, see Hershel Shanks, "Face to Face: Biblical Minimalists Meet Their Challengers," *BAR* 23/4 (1997): 26-42, 66.

does indeed come dangerously close to nihilism. All the revisionists, in my judgment, are rapidly becoming:

philologians — with no pertinent texts

historians — with no history

theologians — with no empathy with religion

ethnographers — with no recognizable "ethnic groups," no training, and no field experience

anthropologists — with no theory of culture and cultural change

literary critics — with little coherent concept of literary production

archaeologists — with no independent knowledge or appreciation of material culture remains

If this is an unfair characterization, I would welcome their defense; but it must be documented. Meanwhile, I regard theirs as "nonhistories" of ancient Israel. What results when historians like the revisionists leap from narrative to archaeology and back again — says one whom they claim as their own, Ernst Axel Knauf — is "a pseudohistory of nonevents."[32]

Israel Finkelstein

The only Syro-Palestinian archaeologist who has become involved with the revisionist camp, except for a few critics like myself, is Israel Finkelstein of Tel Aviv University. This in itself is significant, since all of the revisionists have appealed to archaeology in one way or another, as we have seen. To be sure, Thompson has claimed in print and on the Internet that several other archaeologists support his approach, such as Peter Parr, J. Maxwell Miller, John Woodhead, Henk Franken, James Strange, David Ussishkin, Ze'ev Herzog, a certain "Tuft," and the vast majority of archaeologists working in Jordan. The reader should be warned that none of these archaeologists has either written anything expressly on the subjects at hand or espoused a basic method that is any different from what Thompson calls our "harmonizing" approach. Finkelstein alone might be said to remain in Thompson's camp, but he has not acknowledged any such affiliation; nor does he share the revisionists' negative historiographic or so-called archaeological views.[33]

32. Ernst Axel Knauf, "From History to Interpretation," in *The Fabric of History: Text, Artifact and Israel's Past*, ed. Diana V. Edelman (Sheffield: JSOT, 1991), 49.

33. See, most recently, *Levant* 30 (1998): 167-73.

Thompson's reasons for attempting to co-opt Finkelstein are simply that Finkelstein has written in what seem to be supportive ways on two topics that are critical to the revisionist agenda: (1) "ethnicity" and (2) the date of the rise of the Israelite state.

(1) It was Finkelstein's own pioneering work in *The Archaeology of the Israelite Settlement* that triggered much of the discussion of "Israelite origins" in the past decade.[34] Here Finkelstein published the first English version of his extensive surface surveys north of Jerusalem, i.e., in the biblical "tribal territory" of Manasseh. He also summarized the results of several other Israeli archaeological survey projects in all parts of the country. The data revealed nearly 300 small settlements of the late 13th-12th/11th centuries. Most were not founded above "destruction layers" of Canaanite Late Bronze Age urban sites, as a former generation of "biblical archaeologists" had argued, but were early Iron Age foundations *de novo*. Located mostly in the hill country, this network of agricultural villages represents not a large-scale military invasion of "newcomers," as the Joshua story has it, but rather a largely indigenous socio-economic movement. This is marked by a shift of population with the collapse of the Late Bronze Age society to the rural frontiers and hinterland, accompanied by a new agrarian economy and lifestyle, characterized by certain "reformist" notions and a new religious sensibility (later to develop as Yahwism). While the rural-style farmhouses and some aspects of agricultural technology (terraces, cisterns, silos, and iron tools) are new on the Late Bronze/Iron I horizon ca. 1250-1150, other diagnostic traits of the emergent hill-country culture show strong continuity with the Late Bronze Age Canaanite culture. This is especially true of the pottery of the highland villages — always our most sensitive medium for perceiving cultural contact and change — which is a direct outgrowth of the 13th-century Late Bronze Age repertoire. Today, on the basis of the evidence that Finkelstein and his colleagues have presented in many subsequent publications, all archaeologists and virtually all biblical scholars have abandoned the older conquest model, or even "peaceful infiltration" and peasants' revolt models, for "indigenous origins" and/or "symbiosis" models in attempting to explain the emergence of early Israel in Canaan.

In an early review of Finkelstein's seminal work I criticized him for adopting somewhat uncritically the *ethnic* term "Israelite" for his highland ar-

---

34. (Jerusalem: Israel Exploration Society, 1988). This was a preliminary report of the field surveys; for the final report and its significance, see Finkelstein, et al., *Highlands of Many Cultures.* For my own characterization of the settlement complex revealed by the Israeli (and other) surveys, see Chapter 4.

chaeological assemblage.[35] To be sure, we have an undisputed contemporary, extrabiblical reference to "Israel" in the well-known Victory stele of Pharaoh Merneptah, ca. 1210. I suggested, however, caution in connecting the 13th-12th century *archaeological* "Israel" directly either with Merneptah's "Israel" or the later, fully-developed state of "Israel" of the Monarchy and the biblical narratives. Nevertheless, because of the direct continuity between the 12th-11th century material culture complex and that of the 10th-8th century in the Iron II period, I suggest calling Finkelstein's material "Proto-Israelite." Other scholars, among them several of the revisionists, also criticized Finkelstein's original "ethnic" designations, charging that this derived improperly from *biblical* considerations.[36]

By 1991 Finkelstein had begun to soften his position on "Israelite ethnicity." Then in several publications in 1994-97, he reversed himself completely, arguing that it was impossible to identify an "Israel" in the Iron I material culture.[37] Why this dramatic about-face? The reader will search Finkelstein's numerous recent publications in vain for any new archaeological data; there are none since the late 1980s, so we are all basing ourselves on the same, original data that Finkelstein had. It is clear that Finkelstein has done much more reading in the socio-anthropological literature on ethnicity since 1988, so his theoretical arguments are now more sophisticated, but also more cautious. Such intellectual growth is commendable, but I fear that in this case Finkelstein has changed his mind not on the basis of any empirical data, but simply out of an inherent iconoclasm, evident in much of his writing, as well as a sense of "political correctness." When a scholar does such a radical about-face, without offering any evidential basis, or even acknowledging the change in views, it seems to me that we are entitled to be skeptical, to raise certain questions. Was he wrong then, but right now? Or right then, and wrong now? Or, perhaps, wrong both times? (As we shall see, the revisionists have all proven to have similar chameleonlike qualities).

Elsewhere Finkelstein and I have debated the issue of "Israelite ethnicity"

---

35. William G. Dever, "Archaeological Data on the Israelite Settlement: A Review of Two Recent Works," *BASOR* 284 (1991): 77-90.

36. Cf. Whitelam, *The Invention of Ancient Israel*, 156-60; Philip R. Davies, "Whose History? Whose Israel? Whose Bible? Biblical Histories, Ancient and Modern," in Grabbe, *Can a "History of Israel" Be Written?*, 108, 109; Lemche, "Clio," 145-47; Thompson, "Defining History and Ethnicity," 167-70.

37. See n. 24 above. For a critique of Finkelstein's more recent ideological stance, see William G. Dever, "Why the Biblical and Archaeological 'Revisionists' Are Wrong — And Why We Should Be Concerned" (forthcoming in the proceedings of a University Museum, University of Pennsylvania symposium, November 1998, ed. B. Routledge).

extensively in the literature, so we need not dwell on details here.[38] But it is significant that ours is a strictly *anthropological* and *archaeological* difference, one that has nothing whatsoever to do with *biblical* maximalists and minimalists, much less the revisionists' insistence that there was no "early Israel." Unfortunately, Finkelstein may have unwittingly played into the hands of deconstructionists with whom he otherwise would have nothing in common.

(2) The second area in which Finkelstein's work seems to lend credence to revisionist claims is the chronology of the early Israelite Monarchy. Finkelstein has long questioned the proposed 10th-century date of the nearly identical Hazor, Megiddo, and Gezer monumental city gates and walls, which for many point to a degree of centralized planning that reflects the rise of a centralized government, i.e., a state (below), and in this case that of the biblical Solomon. Finkelstein first argued for a 9th-century date for these defenses, and recently has attempted to lower the entire 12th-9th century chronology by as much as 50 years.[39]

Lemche and Thompson have hailed Finkelstein's new chronology as a triumph, arguing that it proves their contention that there was no Israelite (or northern) kingdom before the 9th century and thus that the biblical accounts of a "King Solomon" are simply myths. What they do not tell the reader is that Finkelstein does not deny an Israelite state, but only down-dates its origins somewhat; and that his idiosyncratic "low chronology" is scarcely accepted by any other archaeologist. Leading Israeli archaeologists such as Amnon Ben-Tor, now excavating Hazor, and Amihai Mazar, digging contemporary levels at nearby Beth-shan and Tel Reḥov, argue strongly that Hazor, Megiddo, Beth-shan, Gezer, and other sites all belong to a mid- to late-10th century state, and were all simultaneously destroyed by the raid of Shishak ca. 930 (as we shall note below in discussing Gezer).[40]

38. Cf. Israel Finkelstein, "On Archaeological Methods and Historical Considerations: Iron Age II Gezer and Samaria," *BASOR* 277/278 (1990): 109-19 (but cf. my rebuttal, "Of Myths and Methods," 121-30); "The Archaeology of the United Monarchy: An Alternative View," *Levant* 28 (1996): 177-87; *Levant* 30 (1998): 167-73; "State Formation in Israel and Judah: A Contrast in Context, A Contrast in Trajectory," *NEA* 62 (1999): 35-52, with full bibliography. See also n. 40 below and Chapter 4, nn. 30-32.

39. Lemche, *The Israelites in History and Tradition*, 54; Thompson, cited in Shanks, *BAR* 23/4 (1997): 34, 35. On Finkelstein's continued insistence on a 10th-century "state" of some sort, with its capital in Jerusalem, see most recently *Levant* 30 (1998): 172, 173. This is a position that Finkelstein has consistently maintained; yet I have not found a single revisionist citing him for this "inconvenient" opinion.

40. On the controversy over "10th or 9th century," Finkelstein still stands alone in the current literature, although his Tel Aviv colleague David Ussishkin generally supports

Once again, the arguments of Thompson and other revisionists treat the archaeological data selectively and cavalierly. Their obvious bias makes one suspect that we are dealing here with a tendentious ideology, not honest, competent scholarship. There are legitimate disagreements among archaeologists, but they are *archaeological* disagreements, and nonspecialists must not be allowed to make hocus-pocus of them. Ironically, the revisionists are guilty of the very same flawed methods for which they castigate "biblical archaeologists" — using selected archaeological data as proof-texts with reference to the Bible, in this case *their* view of the Bible and its history (or nonhistory). "Anti-biblical" archaeology is no improvement over "biblical" archaeology.

A Brief Critique of the Methodology
and Agenda of the Revisionists

The positive constructive aspects of our rejection of the revisionists' deconstructionist agenda will be presented in Chapters 4 and 5 below, i.e., our own suggested reconstruction of ancient Israel's history. In anticipation of that, however, we need to do a bit of "deconstruction" of our own, showing how flimsy most of the revisionists' arguments are methodologically. The following are, I believe, consistent fallacies.

(1) All the revisionists follow in one way or another Davies' original 1992 attempt to distinguish three "Israels": "biblical" and "ancient" Israel, both of which are antiquarian and modern "social constructs," that is, fictitious; and a "historical" Israel, which admittedly did exist, although little can be said about it.[41] Yet it is obvious even to the uninitiated that Davies, like so many

---

him in public remarks. For strong rebuttals to the "low chronology," see Amihai Mazar, "Iron Age Chronology: A Reply to I. Finkelstein," *Levant* 29 (1997): 157-67; "The 1997-1998 Excavations at Tel Rehov: Preliminary Report," *IEJ* 49 (1999): 1-42; Amnon Ben-Tor and Doron Ben-Ami, "Hazor and the Archaeology of the Tenth Century B.C.E.," *IEJ* 48 (1998): 1-38; Anabel Zarzeki-Poleg, "Hazor, Jokneam and Megiddo in the Tenth Century B.C.E.," *TA* 24 (1997): 258-88. For my detailed defense of a 10th-century Israelite state, see William G. Dever, "Archaeology and the 'Age of Solomon': A Case-Study in Archaeology and Historiography," in *The Age of Solomon: Scholarship at the Turn of the Millennium*, ed. Lowell K. Handy (Leiden: Brill, 1997), 217-51, with full bibliography, including my own views going back to 1990. For full discussion of the early Israelite monarchy, see further Chapter 4.

41. See Davies, *In Search of "Ancient Israel,"* 21-74. Elsewhere, Davies protests that critics who have charged that he has no real "historical" Israel are wrong; cf. "Whose History?," 107. Yet nowhere in his writing will one find anything more than the rather grudg-

postmodernists, is partly playing word-games here. The terms "ancient" and "historical" Israel clearly must refer to a single entity, however inadequately known one claims it to be, that is, the tangible Israel of the past.

There is merit in recognizing that the ideal *theological* "Israel" of the Hebrew Bible, as well as that of many Jewish and Christian commentators and believers, is not to be automatically equated with the *real* Israel of the Iron Age of ancient Palestine. Furthermore, the revisionists are right in asserting that our relatively recent rediscovery of data on the latter Israel has resulted in a theoretical historical "reconstruction," rather than an absolutely certain and fully accurate portrait. No responsible historian or archaeologist would claim otherwise. In that sense, all "histories of ancient Israel" are indeed "social constructs." But it is obvious that so is all our knowledge of the human past, the external world, or any other purported "reality." Religion is a "social construct"; is it thereby irrelevant?[42] The question is not whether claims to knowledge are "social constructs" — intellectual formulations within a social context that gives them particularity, relevance, and meaning — but a question of whether the constructions are based on facts or merely on fancies. In short, the fundamental historiographical and epistemological presuppositions of the revisionists with regard to writing a history of Israel are either naïve, or, even when unobjectionable, banal. There is nothing sophisticated or new here.[43]

(2) The revisionists, having isolated a "biblical" Israel as the principal focus of their attack, miss their target for several reasons. They fail to identify specifically what they mean by "biblical" Israel. Do they mean the "Israel" of the

---

ing admission that we do have the biblical king-lists, plus a few nonbiblical textual correlations. Davies' "history" would run to about 10 pages at most; note that his section on the Israelite and Judean states in *In Search of "Ancient Israel"* runs to about three pages (66-70). See further below and n. 48.

42. The revisionists' fundamental dependence on the notion of "social construct," like that of all postmodernists, rests on a specious epistemology. For an exposé of the folly of "social constructivism," see the discussion in Chapter 6 below.

43. More than a century ago Julius Wellhausen — whom Thompson is fond of quoting — said most of what Thompson and the other revisionists have trumpeted. Note his oft-quoted statement:

> We attain to no historical knowledge of the patriarchs, but only of the time when the stories about them arose in the Israelite people: this latter age is here unconsciously projected, in its inner and outward features, into hoar antiquity, and is reflected there like a glorified mirage. (*Prolegomena to the History of Israel* [Berlin: Georg Reimer, 1985], 318)

See further Robert Oden, "Historical Understanding and Understanding the Religion of Israel," in *Community, Identity, and Ideology: Social Science Approaches to the Hebrew Bible,* ed. Charles E. Carter and Carol L. Meyers (Winona Lake: Eisenbrauns, 1996), 201-29.

Pentateuch? The "Deuteronomistic" or historical school? The prophets? The Wisdom, poetic, or apocalyptic literature? "Israel" in the earliest, or the latest writings? There is no systematic, comprehensive, uniform portrait of Israel among the many writers of the Hebrew Bible, as is well known. Clearly some "Israels" are more idealistic retrojections than others, some more genuinely historical than others. Lumping them all together to discredit them does not do justice to the richness and variety of the biblical literature, nor does it constitute sound critical and historical method.

What the revisionists seem to mean by "biblical" Israel is the Israel of "*mythic* proportions." This is the Israel reflected in numerous "stories" that are embellished with exaggerations and fanciful features such as miracles, compiled partly from sagas, legends, folk-tales, and outright inventions. Above all, it is the story of an Israel that is set in an over-arching theocratic framework whose intent is always didactic. It aims not at historical narrative *per se,* but at elucidating the hidden theological meaning of events and their moral significance.[44] Of course this "Israel" is not historical, except for revealing something of the historical context of its writers and final editors. But then few modern readers except Fundamentalists ever thought that it was. Here we see again one of the favorite devices of the revisionists: caricature. Furthermore, their everrecurring theme that the "biblical" Israel does not correspond with the "real" Israel — knowable for them only through a few extrabiblical texts and scant archaeological data — is true, but in the end irrelevant in the quest for ancient Israel. Fortunately, the Hebrew Bible is not our only source.

Throughout their publications, the revisionists jump from the conclusion that because the Hebrew Bible's "Israel" is really couched in idealistic terms, there was no *real* "Israel" of the biblical period, that is (as we shall show), the Iron Age of ancient Palestine. Such a conclusion is either naïve, the result of semantic confusion, or simply disingenuous. Were the revisionists better historians, seriously engaged in a search for ancient/historical Israel, they would have built upon their own pertinent observations on the limitations of the biblical texts as sources for history-writing. They would then have turned to the now primary source of new data, archaeology, in order to write *truly* revisionist histories of ancient Israel. That they have consistently failed to do so (below) suggests to me that they do not want to see the reconstruction of the history of *any* Israel: it does not suit their ideological purposes.[45]

---

44. The revisionists grant these points, indeed insist upon them. But they fail to see that even "myth" may contain some genuine history. See Alan R. Millard, "The Old Testament and History: Some Considerations," *Faith and Theology* 110 (1983): 41.

45. On the failure to utilize archaeological data, at least properly, see further below.

Finally, the "revisionists," for all their insistence on the Bible as literature, have a curiously simplistic sense of literary theory, particularly in their notions of literary production. For them, the Hebrew Bible must be either reliable history (which it is clearly not), or blatant propaganda. They see no middle ground. They do not appreciate the fact that all literature in effect is fundamentally "propaganda," that is, self-conscious expression of a worldview, usually in the advocacy of a cause. That the Hebrew Bible is in that sense "propaganda" is not in dispute among responsible scholars; the only question is whether or not such propaganda reflects anything of the *real* world of the time. And it inevitably does, otherwise it would not have been credible for those to whom it was originally addressed. Propaganda characteristically and deliberately exaggerates and distorts; but it does not freely invent. Even a caricature is an accurate, recognizable portrait in some respects, or otherwise it would have no impact. The task of the *real* historian is to get at the "history behind the history" in the Hebrew Bible, as we shall attempt in the following. The inability of the revisionists to separate fact from fiction in the ancient texts at their disposal, biblical or other, as discriminating commentators must do, is one of their more conspicuous failures.[46]

(3) Even when the revisionists do occasionally acknowledge the existence of a hypothetical Israel in the Iron Age (Davies' "historical Israel"), their approach is consistently "minimalist," to use one of the common terms in the current discussion.[47] Given their skepticism about the trustworthiness of one po-

---

46. Curiously, they seem able to make this discrimination easily enough when dealing with the nonbiblical texts from the ancient Near East. Is there some animus here against the Hebrew Bible?

47. The most common epithets nowadays seem to be: traditionalist vs. revisionist, maximalist vs. minimalist, positivist vs. nihilist, credulist/theist vs. skeptic, neo-conservative vs. scientific. I agree with several of the revisionists who have objected that these epithets are not helpful; but note that it is they who have engaged in the most egregious name-calling, especially Davies and Thompson. Cf. Davies, *In Search of "Ancient Israel,"* 47; *JBL* 114 (1995): 669-705; "Whose History?," esp. 108, 109; Thompson, *JBL* 114 (1995): 683-98; "Historiography of Ancient Palestine." More recently Lemche has labeled me a "Zionist," despite the fact that there is scarcely a word on Middle Eastern politics in anything I have written in the past 30 years; cf. *Currents in Research* 5 (1997): 12; cf. Norman K. Gottwald's generally helpful attempt at mediation in the same issue, "Triumphalist versus Anti-Triumphalist Versions of Early Israel," 15-42 (although I am certainly not a "triumphalist"). Thompson has implicitly labeled me a "crypto-Fundamentalist"; I think that he may be a "neo-supercessionist." Surely all this is a reflection that the current debate is not only about historical methodology, but about ideology and belief as well. See further Lemche, "Clio," 142-48; Dever, *NEA* 61 (1998): 39-52; and further below. My term here, "revisionist," is taken from Lemche and Thompson themselves and is not used in a neces-

tential source, the texts of the Hebrew Bible, it is not surprising that they can salvage little useful information there. But what of archaeology, which most acknowledge in one way or another?

The fact is that one of the revisionists' major faults is that they ignore, cite selectively and cavalierly, misinterpret, distort, or otherwise abuse modern archaeology and the rich data that it produces. Davies pointedly ignores actual, specific archaeological data altogether, even in his chapter on "historical Israel," except to comment here and there on its "silence." And of course he does not even attempt a history.[48]

Lemche's 1998 work, *The Israelites in History and Tradition,* has a chapter on "Archaeology and Israelite Ethnicity," which does mention favorably several recent developments in the archaeology of Israel, including my own contributions; but again he cites only minimal data, largely negative in Lemche's view. As he states: "The Israel of the Iron Age proved to be most elusive, in historical documents as well as in material remains, where hardly anything carries an ethnic tag that helps the modern investigator to decide what is Israelite and what is not. . . . The only thing that remains is the tradition of two tiny states of Palestine in the Iron Age, which were long after their dissolution chosen as the basis of a new nation to be established on the soil of Palestine in the postexilic period." Lemche concludes: "At the end we have a situation where Israel is not Israel, Jerusalem not Jerusalem, and David not David. No matter how we twist the factual remains from ancient Palestine, we cannot have a biblical Israel that is at the same time the Israel of the Iron Age."[49] Elsewhere, he repudiates his own quite successful pioneering work, *Early Israel: Anthropological and Historical Studies on the Israelite Society Before the Monarchy,*[50] as not radical enough, in effect not sufficiently deconstructionist.[51]

Thompson's *The Mythic Past* is subtitled *Biblical Archaeology and the Myth of Israel,* but throughout it mentions archaeology only to caricature it as the oldfashioned "prove-the-Bible" kind, never once citing and documenting any actual archaeological data. Thompson is even more of a minimalist than Lemche. In a 397-page book, supposedly devoted to a search for *some* Israel, he devotes only three pages to early Israel, mentioning without documentation some of the recent archaeological evidence, but never alluding to the 12th-11th century high-

---

sarily pejorative sense; see Lemche, *The Israelites in History and Tradition,* 157; Lemche and Thompson, *JSOT* 64 (1994): 17. See further Chapter 1, n. 11.

48. Davies, *In Search of "Ancient Israel,"* 24, 60-74. Cf. n. 41 above.

49. Lemche, *The Israelites in History and Tradition,* 166.

50. VTSup 37 (Leiden: Brill, 1985); popularized as *Ancient Israel: A New History of Israelite Society* (Sheffield: JSOT, 1988).

51. Cf. "Clio," 146-48.

land settlers in Canaan as "Israelites."[52] (Elsewhere Thompson deigns to refer to these folk only as the Iron Age population of "Syria's southern fringe."[53]) To the entire development of the states of Israel and Judah in the 10th-7th centuries, Thompson allots barely seven pages. The rest of his ponderous disputation is given over to arguing, again without documentation, that the "effort to integrate the results of Palestinian archaeology, biblical research and ancient Near Eastern studies in a comprehensive synthesis has been refuted in both principle and detail." Thompson concludes that "The Bible's 'Israel' [is] a literary fiction. . . . The Bible is not the history of anyone's past."[54] One might aspire to write a "history of *Palestine*," which in 1992 Thompson actually attempted to do (*Early History of the Israelite People*). But he now rejects even this (really no more than prolegomenon, in my opinion), confessing that this "was after all hardly history, critically speaking, but rather just another rationalistic paraphrase for biblical Israel."[55]

Whitelam had collaborated in 1987 with Coote to produce *The Emergence of Early Israel in Historical Perspective,* which was provocative and generally well-received. By 1996, however, not only did he castigate virtually every biblical scholar and archaeologist who had ever even attempted to document an "early Israel," but he declared that there never had been any such Israel. Thus the title of his 1996 book, *The Invention of Ancient Israel.* The goal itself being inadmissible, the only proper procedure was for scholars to repudiate the whole tradition of writing a history of "Israel" and concentrate instead on a history of Palestine. His own earlier, confident treatment he now dismissed as "not radical enough," "misleading," simply another aspect of the "invention" of ancient Israel.[56] A telling clue to all the revisionists' basic antipathy toward any real "Israel" in the Iron Age is their consistent emphasis on how "small and insignificant" Israel was (as though that had anything to do with the issues at hand); how it was really only a part of "Syria's southern fringe" throughout its history; how almost no contemporary nonbiblical documents ever refer specifically to either Israel or Judah. In particular, they are hesitant even to use the name "Israel" for the northern kingdom (if any), instead following, for instance, the Neo-Assyrian references to "the house (i.e., dynasty) of Omri" or the province of Samaria/"Samarina." Even when the name Israel is admitted to have existed, it is argued that it refers only to a "religious community," not to an ethnic group, much less a real state. Such blatant misrepresentation of the textual evidence — including the Neo-Assyrian

52. Thompson, *The Mythic Past,* 158-68; cf. 9, 252.
53. "Defining History and Ethnicity," 176-78.
54. Thompson, *The Mythic Past,* 7.
55. Thompson, "Defining History and Ethnicity," 178-79.
56. Whitelam, *The Invention of Israel,* 35.

texts, the 9th-century Mesha stele from Moab, and the 9th-century Dan inscription — is perhaps the best evidence of the revisionists' anti-biblical bias.[57]

In view of their rejection of traditional historical and literary-critical methodologies in the effort to reconstruct Israel's past, as well as their deliberate search for newer methods, one might think that the revisionists would seize upon what is probably the most promising recent trends, "social-scientific" approaches to the Hebrew Bible and the history of ancient Israel. Yet only Lemche's *The Israelites in History and Tradition* comes even close. Despite the popularity of these approaches for the past 25 years or so, and the fact that the revisionists have taken note of their promise, they themselves have produced nothing like a "sociology of the history and religions of ancient Israel."[58] Surely if no history of Israel is possible, a "sociology" might be. But that, too, would be out of the question if the texts of the Hebrew Bible are indeed late and historically untrustworthy — unless one would assay to use them to produce a "sociology of *Hellenistic-Roman* Judaism."[59] By contrast, Paula M. McNutt, without any vaunted claims to "revolutionary methods," has produced a superb social-scientific work, *Recon-*

57. Cf. Davies, *In Search of "Ancient Israel,"* 17, 55, 63, 66-69, 73; Lemche, "Clio," 128, 140, 141, 153; *The Israelites in History and Tradition,* 51-55, 62-64, 81-85, 155, 166; Thompson, "Defining History and Ethnicity," 176-78; *The Mythic Past,* xv, 9, 11-15, 158-60; Whitelam, *The Invention of Ancient Israel,* 160-74. Lemche accepts the reading "Israel" on the 9th-century Mesha and Dan inscriptions, and even the clear reference to "Ahab of Israel" on the inscription of Shalmaneser III following the Battle of Qarqar in 853. Nevertheless, he argues that "it is simply Samaria that is used as the name of the country" (*The Israelites in History and Tradition,* 52, 53). Cf. also Thompson's astounding assertion that the reference on the Moabite stele of King Mesha to "Omri, King of Israel" "belongs to the world of stories"; "it is quite doubtful that it refers to an historical person" (*The Mythic Past,* 13). This is either ignorance or dishonest scholarship. For a convenient correlation of Israelite and Judean kings with Neo-Assyrian and Neo-Babylonian texts and kings, see Baruch Halpern, "Erasing History: The Minimalist Assault on Ancient Israel," *BR* 11/6 (1995): 26-35, 47; esp. 32. See also generally, Nadav Na'aman, "The Contribution of Royal Inscriptions for a Re-Evaluation of the Book of Kings as a Historical Source," *JSOT* 82 (1999): 3-17. See further Chapter 5, n. 1.

58. For an excellent introduction to these methods, including reference to some of the revisionists like Lemche, see Carter and Meyers, *Community, Identity, and Ideology,* and the many essays there, esp. Carter, "A Discipline in Transition: The Contributions of the Social Sciences to the Study of the Hebrew Bible," 3-36.

59. If the revisionists are correct that the composition of the Hebrew Bible belongs early in this era, and that they are leading biblical scholars, then *they* ought to be producing such a study. It is obvious, however, that they do not have even an elementary knowledge of the required disciplines: the early Classical period in the Levant, early Rabbinic Judaism, intertestamental studies, and the archaeology of late antiquity. See further Chapter 6 below.

structing the Society of Ancient Israel.[60] Not only does she take the texts of the Hebrew Bible seriously as both literature and history, but she also makes extensive
and discriminating use of the archaeological data. The result is, to put it simply,
the history of ancient Israelite society that the revisionists are unable or unwill-
ing to write. It is instructive to compare McNutt's book with Lemche's *The Israelites in History and Tradition,* both published a year apart in the same Library of
Ancient Israel series. The former is a fresh, balanced, positive work, fully documented; the latter is little more than a tendentious prolegomenon.

With this in view — and much more revisionist literature that I could
easily cite — is it any wonder that most mainstream scholars regard them as
"minimalists" or that I have dubbed them the "new nihilists"? A close reading
of their voluminous output in the past decade suggests to me that here we confront not properly speaking a coherent scholarly "school," but rather an ideological movement with revolutionary aspirations, one that as with most such
movements is characterized by a distinct, recognizable methodology and
agenda. In the following summary, I may be engaging in a bit of tongue-in-
cheek caricature of my own. But having steeped myself in revisionist literature
("discourse," I suppose we must say) for several years, I assure the reader that
the principal revisionists are all easily recognizable here.[61]

---

60. (Louisville: Westminster John Knox, 1999).

61. For devastating critiques of the revisionists' methodology and agenda, from
leading biblical scholars, see Halpern, *BR* 11/6 (1995): 26-35, 47. According to Halpern,
none of them is trained as a "real historian"; "their exposure to history as it is practiced
with respect to other times and other places is almost always marginal." Halpern states further: "The most extreme forms of this new historiography do not even engage the archaeology in an intellectually honest fashion. They appeal to archaeology, instead, to subvert
the validity of the textual (biblical) presentation" (28-31). Furthermore, "at the extremes,
the reaction against tradition is emotional, not intellectual"; "at the base of the extremism
of contemporary 'minimalism' lies a hysteria" (23, 26). See also Sara Japhet, "In Search of
Ancient Israel: Revisionism at All Costs," in *The Jewish Past Revisited: Reflections on Modern Jewish Historians,* ed. David N. Meyers and David B. Ruderman (New Haven: Yale University Press, 1998), 213-33, which is less polemical than my remarks here, but deftly exposes the superficiality and biases of the revisionists. See also R. N. Whybray, "What Do
We Know About Ancient Israel?," *ExpTim* 108 (1996): 71-74; Peter B. Machinist, "The Crisis of History in the Study of the Hebrew Bible," forthcoming in the proceedings of a symposium at the University of Hartford in September 1998; Marc Brettler, "The Copenhagen
School: The Historiographical Issues," forthcoming in the proceedings of a Northwestern
University symposium in October 1999 on "The Origins of the Jewish People in Contemporary Scholarship," ed. J. Lassner. My own paper, also forthcoming in the volume, is entitled "Archaeology and the Emergence of Israel in History: Why the Revisionists Are
Wrong." See further Chapter 6, nn. 1-2, 28-30, 39, 42.

1. Always attack the Establishment on principle, and in the name of "revolutionary progress." Set in motion a counter-culture, even if it means repudiating your own earlier works, but pretending that you have not done so.
2. Pose a set of convenient false issues; create an imagined dichotomy between positions; polarize the discussion.
3. Reject consensus scholarship; deplore the middle ground; carry the argument to its most extreme; celebrate the bizarre, since it gets attention.
4. Caricature the history of traditional scholarship; demonize any remaining opponents.
5. Deny that there are objective facts; insist that everything is relative, and that all interpretations (except your own) are under suspicion.
6. Pretend to be scientific, but discard evidence that doesn't fit; falsify the rest.
7. Be "politically correct" at all times; pretend to identify with the oppressed minorities, while still maintaining your elitist privileges.
8. Substitute clever epigrams for sustained rational argument; use catchy slogans to conceal the real agenda.
9. Declare yourself innovative and "revolutionary"; inflate banalities into presumptuous social pronouncements.
10. Reject empiricism and positivism as outdated and perverse; but promote your own Utopian visions.
11. Elevate skepticism into a scholarly method; cherish cynicism; pride yourself on how little real knowledge you possess, since that suggests modesty and honesty.
12. Remember that the real issue is always ideology: race, gender, class, power, and above all politics. Expose others' ideology, but deny that you have any.
13. Escalate the level of rhetoric, so that the issues are obscured.
14. Announce the "New Truth" triumphantly.
15. When exposed, decamp; accept martyrdom gracefully.

If all this sounds familiar, it is. It is precisely the method and agenda of the extreme forms of postmodernism that I have posited above as the intellectual and social matrix of revisionism. This is not sound, careful, balanced, honest scholarship: it is demagoguery. If that charge sounds extreme, let us turn in the remaining chapters to the case-studies that will prove it correct.

CHAPTER 3

What Archaeology Is and What It Can Contribute to Biblical Studies

The Nature of Archaeology, Old and New

The public seems to be perennially fascinated by archaeology. This is evident by frequent headline stories of discoveries in all the media, the fact that hundreds will turn out for popular lectures on any archaeological topic, and an apparently endless flood of publications, from semi-scholarly books for laypeople, to lavishly illustrated coffee-table volumes, to sensational stories in periodicals from the *Wall Street Journal* to *Biblical Archaeology Review* and the *National Enquirer.* Whenever I tell people that I am an archaeologist, they invariably exclaim "Oh, how exciting!" Perhaps they have seen too many "Raiders of the Lost Ark" movies. Archaeology isn't really like that: the elusive but available field director isn't as dashing as Harrison Ford, even in the right fedora; his female companion isn't necessarily young and beautiful, ripe for adventure (she may be the over-burdened director of the project); the chase rarely leads to anything spectacular, just bits and pieces of other peoples' garbage; the funds never magically materialize, if at all; and the daily routine is long, hard, hot, dirty, and mostly dull — hardly "glamorous"!

Modern, real-life archaeology is not treasure-hunting; it is simply another kind of historical research. In this case, the research focuses not on texts (although some may be found), but rather on what we call "material culture." This basic body of data consists largely of artifacts of various kinds, together with the immediate physical setting and larger environmental context in which they are found. It may be said that an archaeologist writes "history from things," as a distinguished colleague, David Kingery, has recently titled his book on the history of early technologies.[1] Another way of putting it is to say that an archaeologist is an anthropologist who deals with "the ethnography of the dead." The archaeologist attempts to "reconstruct" extinct social systems from traces of the scattered physical remains that may happen to have been left behind. Archaeology may thus best be thought of simply as a way of making inferences about "how it was in the past" by examining material culture remains.

Modern archaeology might be said to have begun as early as the 17th-18th century, with accidental discoveries of exciting relics in Europe and elsewhere. The large-scale exploration and mapping of sites and the first attempts at systematic excavation began, however, only in the late 19th century. Even so, much of the early archaeological work was little better than "treasure-hunting." One thinks of the British, French, Germans, and others who plundered the treasures of Egypt and what is now Iraq and Iran to fill their national museums in the 1840s-1890s. (We Americans would undoubtedly have been just as rapacious, but we weren't yet a colonial power.) Or picture Heinrich Schliemann at Troy in the 1860s, bedecking his young Greek wife with the jewels of "Priam's Treasure" (now partly lost).[2]

Roots in the 19th Century: The Exploratory Era

The archaeology of the "Holy Land," in the broad sense of the exploration of biblical topography and antiquities, goes back centuries to hundreds of pilgrim's accounts since the Byzantine period. The modern discipline of Palestinian archaeology, however, can be said to have begun with the pioneering visits of the American biblical scholar Edward Robinson in 1838 and 1852, published as *Biblical Researches in Palestine and the Adjacent Regions* (1852). Robinson and his traveling companion Eli Smith correctly identified dozens of long-lost ancient sites. The first modern maps, however, after those of Napoleon's cartographers in 1798-99, were those drawn up by C. R. Conder and H. H. (later Lord) Kitchener for the great Survey of Western Palestine (1878; published in six volumes in 1884), sponsored by the British Palestine Exploration Society (1865–), which also undertook the first actual fieldwork, C. W. Wilson and Charles Warren's soundings around the Temple Mount in Jerusalem (1867-1870).

1. Steven Lubar and W. David Kingery, eds., *History from Things: Essays on Material Culture* (Washington: Smithsonian Institution, 1993).
2. See now the critical re-analysis of Schliemann in D. A. Traill and I. Bogdanov, "Heinrich Schliemann: Improbable Archaeologist," *Archaeology Odyssey* 2/3 (1999): 30-39.

In Egypt and Mesopotamia, dramatic archaeological discoveries beginning in the 1840s — partly by chance and partly the results of the first deliberate excavations — soon drew attention to Palestine, largely because of its biblical connections. Several foreign societies soon joined the British Palestine Exploration Fund: the German Deutsches Palästina-Vereins (1878-); the French École Biblique et archéologique in Jerusalem (1892-); and finally the American School of Oriental Research (1900-).[3]

Despite mounting interest, however, true excavations did not begin in Palestine until the brief campaign of the legendary Sir William Flinders Petrie at Tell el-Ḥesī in the Gaza area (possibly biblical Eglon) in 1890, followed by American work there under F. J. Bliss in 1893. It was Petrie who laid the foundations of all subsequent fieldwork and research by demonstrating, however briefly and intuitively, the importance of detailed stratigraphy of Palestine's complex, multi-layered tells or mounds; and the potential of comparative ceramic typology and chronology.

This first, formative era of archaeological exploration and discovery in Palestine in the 19th century was characterized by adventurism, nationalism and competition among the colonial powers, and growing expectations that archaeology would shed unique light upon the biblical world. Yet ancient Syria has scarcely been touched, although some archaeological exploration had begun as early as the 1860s under French scholars such as Ernest Renan.

From the Turn of the Century Until World War I:
The Formative Period

The first two decades of the 20th century constituted a sort of "golden age" in Syro-Palestinian archaeology, one that saw the first large-scale, reasonably well-

---

3. On early explorations in Mesopotamia, see Seton Lloyd, *Foundations in the Dust: The Story of Mesopotamian Exploration*, rev. ed. (London: Thames & Hudson, 1980); and on Egypt, see John A. Wilson, *Signs and Wonders upon Pharaoh: A History of American Egyptology* (Chicago: University of Chicago Press, 1964). For accounts of the early history of the British, French, and German schools in Jerusalem, see several of the essays in *Benchmarks in Time and Culture: An Introduction to Palestinian Archaeology*, ed. Joel F. Drinkard, Gerald L. Mattingly, and J. Maxwell Miller (Atlanta: Scholars, 1988). For the American school, now the W. F. Albright Institute of Archaeological Research, see Philip J. King, *American Archaeology in the Mideast: A History of the American Schools of Oriental Research* (Philadelphia: American Schools of Oriental Research, 1983). On the general history of "biblical archaeology" in the Middle East, see P. R. S. Moorey, *A Century of Biblical Archaeology* (Louisville: Westminster John Knox, 1991).

staffed and funded field projects.[4] These included the work of the Americans at Samaria (1908-10); of the British at Tell Gezer (1902-9); and of the Germans at Ta'anach (1902-4), Megiddo (1903-5), Jericho (1907-9), and Galilean synagogues (1905). In Syria, Howard Crosby Butler's splendid surveys of Byzantine Christian sites for Princeton University (1904-9) deserve mention; but by and large Syria was ignored as peripheral to the Holy Land. None of these excavations, however, with the exception of George A. Reisner's work at Samaria (not published until 1924), demonstrated more than the rudiments of stratigraphy. Pottery chronology was off by centuries; and the publication volumes, although sometimes lavishly illustrated, are largely useless today. An almost exclusively architectural orientation or biblical biases marred most work.

All these and other projects were brought to a halt by the onset of World War I, but the foundations of both Syro-Palestinian and "biblical" archaeology had been laid. Nevertheless, neither an academic discipline nor a profession had yet emerged in this second, formative period.

Between the Great Wars: The Classificatory Period

Following the corrupt bureaucracy of Ottoman Turkish rule, Palestine was turned over to a British mandate in 1918 at the close of World War I. The British government opened a Department of Antiquities, promulgated modern antiquities laws, and undertook the first systematic, comprehensive program of archaeological investigation of the entire area, including Transjordan. During the ensuing period the foreign schools in Jerusalem noted above flourished. This was particularly true of the American School of Oriental Research (founded in 1900), which now dominated the field under the direction of William F. Albright (1920-29; 1933-36). Albright, one of the most eminent Orientalists of the 20th century, was then followed (1932-33; 1936-1940; 1942-47) by his protégé Nelson Glueck, a rabbi famed for his explorations in Transjordan. It was Albright who became known as the "Father of Biblical Archaeology," through his unparalleled mastery of the pottery of Palestine, of the broad ancient Near Eastern context in which the results of Palestinian archaeology needed to be placed to illuminate them properly, and of the vast scope of biblical history with which individual discoveries often seemed to correlate. Al-

---

4. For the following, in addition to Moorey, see my more detailed critique of early work in Palestine in William G. Dever, "Syro-Palestinian and Biblical Archaeology," in *The Hebrew Bible and Its Modern Interpreters*, ed. Douglas A. Knight and Gene M. Tucker (Chico: Scholars, 1985), 31-74.

though Albright himself used the term "Syro-Palestinian archaeology" alternately, his overriding concern was with the biblical world. Through his genius,
his towering status, and his own excavations at Tell el-Fûl (1922), Bethel (1934),
and especially at Tell Beit Mirsim (1926-1932) and his innumerable disciples,
Albright dominated "biblical archaeology" from the early 1920s through the
1960s. One of his protégés, G. Ernest Wright of McCormick Seminary and Harvard, carried on the tradition by coupling "biblical archaeology" more specifically with the "biblical theology" movement current in the 1950s-1970s. A tran-
sitional figure, Wright trained most of the older American generation still
working in the field today.

Many of the American excavations in Palestine between the two wars, under Albright's influence, were at biblical sites, staffed by Protestant seminarians
and clergy, and supported by funds from church circles. These included
Albright's own excavations (above), those at Tell en-Naṣbeh (1926-1935), at
Beth-shemesh (1928-1933), and many smaller sites. Nevertheless, there existed
a parallel, secular American tradition, especially in the large projects of the
University of Pennsylvania at Beth-shan (1926-1933); of the Oriental Institute
of the University of Chicago at Megiddo (1926-1939), well funded by the
Rockefellers; and of Yale University at Jerash in Transjordan (1928-1934).
These, too, were biblical sites; but the secular stream of American Palestinian
archaeology never captured the imagination of the public or succeeded in per-
petuating itself as the Albright school did. In retrospect, it seems that, in the
United States at least, archaeology in "poor Palestine" was not thought able to
justify itself without the biblical connection.

The Heyday and Decline of "Biblical Archaeology": 1950-1970

American-style "biblical archaeology" reached its zenith soon after the postwar
resumption of fieldwork in Palestine in the early 1950s. The principal excavations were in Jordan now, those of Wright at Shechem (1957-1968); James B.
Pritchard at Gibeon (1956-1962); Joseph A. Callaway at ʿAi (1964-69); Paul W.
Lapp at Tell er-Rumeith, Tell el-Fûl, and Taʿanach (1964-68); and Pritchard at
Tell es-Saʿaidiyeh (1964-67). All these excavations, affiliated with the American
School in Jerusalem, were at biblical sites; the directors in every case were clergy
and professors of theology or religion; the agenda was often drawn from issues
in biblical studies; and funds came largely from religious circles. In addition,
the generation of younger American archaeologists who would come to the
fore in the 1970s was trained here. Finally, a series of publications by Albright,
Wright, and others attracted international attention to American biblical ar-

chaeology and provoked heated controversy in Europe. At issue were both fundamental questions of method in general (biblically biased or not) and certain specific historical questions in biblical studies (e.g., the historicity of the patriarchs and the Israelite conquest; Moses and monotheism; Israelite religion and cult). Neither Albright nor Wright was a Fundamentalist (although certainly conservative by more recent standards), yet outside of America suspicions prevailed. Indeed, the misgivings were prescient; by the early 1970s biblical archaeology (along with the biblical theology movement, an outgrowth of postwar neo-orthodoxy) was moribund, if not dead.

In retrospect, the demise of biblical archaeology was probably inevitable.[5] The reasons are many. First, what may be called internal weaknesses of the movement were numerous: its reputation for amateurish fieldwork, naïve or biased scholarship, and poor publications; its parochial character, related as it was largely to the conservative (if not Fundamentalist) character of so much of American religious life; its reactionary nature, locked into dated theological issues, which left it unable to respond creatively to new developments in or outside the field; its resistance to growing trends toward specialization and professionalism, which made it extremely vulnerable; and, above all, the fact that it failed to achieve its own major objective, i.e., the demonstration of the "historicity" of the Bible (at least as it was seen at the time).

There were also significant, indeed critical, factors that may be regarded as external to biblical archaeology *per se*, although very much a part of archaeology in general in modern Israel-Jordan and elsewhere. These included: the stratigraphic revolution of the 1950s-1960s led by the British archaeologist Kathleen Kenyon and others, which promised "total retrieval," automatically generating much more and more varied data that required analysis by interdisciplinary specialists; the growing complexity and costs of excavation, especially in Israel, which pushed the field inevitably toward professionalization and secular sources of support; field schools and student volunteerism, which not only constituted an intellectual challenge but broke the monopoly of biblical scholars on dig staffs and thus contributed to the secularization of the discipline; the increasing sense that biblical archaeology was indeed parochial and had failed to achieve even its own limited agenda of historical-theological issues; increasing competition among the "national schools" — especially those now rising in the Middle East (below) — which highlighted fundamental and legitimate differences in approach and thus called into question any exclusively biblicist view

5. See "Syro-Palestinian and Biblical Archaeology" and references there; also "Impact of the 'New Archaeology,'" in Drinkard, Mattingly, and Miller, 337-52; "Archaeology, Syro-Palestinian and Biblical," *ABD* 1:354-67.

of ancient Syria-Palestine; and finally the advent of the "new archaeology," which began in American New World archaeology in the early 1960s and by the end of that decade was beginning to have an impact on archaeological theory and method generally.

The principal aspects of the new archaeology[6] were: an orientation more anthropological than historical, i.e., away from particularization and more toward the study of culture and culture change generally; a "nomothetic" approach that sought to formulate and test law-like propositions that were thought to govern the cultural process (thus the common designation "processualist" archaeology), in order to develop a body of theory that would qualify archaeology as not only a discipline but a true science; an ecological thrust, which emphasized techno-environmental factors (rather than simply evolutionary trajectories) in the role of adaptation in culture change; a multidisciplinary strategy that involved many of the physical sciences and their statistical and analytical procedures in attempting to reconstruct the ancient landscape, climate, population, economy, socio-political structure, and other sub-systems (often using the model of General Systems Theory); and an insistence on an overall, up-front "research design" for projects that would integrate all the above and thus would advance archaeology as a culturally relevant enterprise.

The "New Archaeology"

By the 1970s, the initial efforts to excavate mounds in the Middle East with proper stratigraphic (or "three-dimensional") methods were being supplemented by newer field and analytical methods.

Perhaps the most typical aspect of the new archaeology in practice was its interdisciplinary character. This approach, now commonplace on almost all modern excavations, includes such disciplines as geomorphology and geology, paleo-botany and paleo-zoology, climatology and paleo-ecology, hydrology, physical and cultural anthropology, the history of technology, and any number of other specialized branches of the natural and social sciences.

Newer techniques for analyzing excavated materials include: radiocarbon and other chronometric means of dating; neutron activation analysis to "fingerprint" the sources of clays for pottery making and thus to trace trade pat-

---

6. On the following, see William G. Dever, "The Impact of the 'New Archaeology' on Syro-Palestinian Archaeology," *BASOR* 242 (1981): 15-29, and extensive literature cited there.

terns; gas chromatography analysis to determine residues present; "use-wear" analysis of objects using high-powered electron microscopes to define manufacturing techniques, function, and reuse; and, more recently, DNA analysis to identify the relationships between ancient populations and possibly even their long-distance migrations.

Technical devices that aid immensely in field excavation and in the workup of materials for publication now include: aerial photography and mapping; geographical information systems, which can model ancient landscapes in detail; electrical-resistivity surveying and ground-penetrating radar; laser transits, which greatly simplify surveying; a whole range of photographic techniques, including digital systems; and a vast array of computer-based systems of recording, data-retrieval, manipulating models, preparing graphics, and even final publication.

The development of the so-called "new archaeology" since the early 1970s has radically transformed all branches of archaeology today. However, the rapid progress of archaeology — once called "the handmaiden of history" — toward independent professional and academic status, a full-fledged discipline of its own, has not been greeted by enthusiasm in all quarters. It had been assumed all along that archaeology had been an ancillary discipline (Latin *ancillaris*, from *ancilla*, "maidservant"), or a sub-branch of history. Today, however, many archaeologists regard themselves primarily as anthropologists (the discipline from which they derive most of their theory), or even as full-fledged scientists whose methods, aims, theory-testing, and generation of knowledge scarcely differ from the "laws of behavior" of natural scientists. Where does all this leave our branch of archaeology and its relation to the Bible as "history" in any sense?

"Biblical Archaeology" — or "The Archaeology of Syria-Palestine"?

Against this background of the "coming of age" of archaeology in general, we now need to look more closely at one branch, namely ours. It has been called "biblical archaeology" until recently, but now it is more commonly styled "the archaeology of Syria-Palestine," or increasingly "the archaeology of the Southern Levant." What's in a name? And, beyond mere semantics, what underlying shifts in intellectual orientation and methodology are implied in the change? Until we can characterize this peculiar (!) subdivision of Near Eastern archaeology more accurately, we cannot assess any potential contributions that it might make to biblical studies. In particular, we must ask whether the impact of the new archaeology on our branch of archaeology renders it more "historical" or less so.

Elsewhere I have written extensively on the history of the "biblical archaeology" movement.[7] I have argued that it was more an aspect of theological studies than a deliberate "school of archaeology" properly speaking, and that it was largely an American phenomenon. A brief look at the actual development of excavations in general in Palestine in the era 1900-1950 will confirm the first point. The majority of American digs (and many others) were at sites identified with biblical places, staffed almost exclusively by seminary professors and clerics, funded largely by religious institutions, and having as their primary aim the elucidation of problems in biblical history, not least of all the perennial "faith-and-history" issue. The exceptions, such as the Chicago excavations at Megiddo and the Pennsylvania work at Beth-shan, only proved the rule. American archaeology in Palestine was "biblical archaeology," whether of the more respectable type epitomized by Albright or the Fundamentalist, "prove-the-Bible" type all too common among his less enlightened (or conscientious) imitators.

The scandalous stories of archaeological misadventures in the Holy Land during the heyday of biblical archaeology in the 1920s-1950s may make for entertaining reading, but they have left our field with a bad reputation for amateur, substandard, biased archaeological work that remains an embarrassment to this day — and this despite the fact that most of my generation repudiated old-fashioned biblical archaeology 30 years ago. The current generation, our students, regard it merely as a curiosity, a Stone Age relic. Due to my own outspoken opposition, I have often been accused of "killing biblical archaeology." I am flattered that anyone supposes that I might have that much influence. But the truth is simply that I happened to be one of the first to observe biblical archaeology's passing and to write its obituary, back in the early 1970s.

Archaeology as an Independent Discipline?

For at least the past 20 years, the branch of Near Eastern archaeology that deals with ancient Palestine has been known chiefly as "Syro-Palestinian" or sometimes simply "Palestinian," rather than "biblical," archaeology (the other branches being Anatolian, Mesopotamian, Iranian, Egyptian, and occasionally Cypriot archaeology). I did indeed insist upon and popularize the term "Syro-Palestinian." But that was Albright's original, alternate term for "biblical archaeology" in the 1930s-1940s. I simply revived it, and it caught on because

7. See references in nn. 4-6 above.

others agreed with the rationale. Even Israeli archaeologists, who obviously find "Palestine" problematic, use the term when speaking or writing in English.[8]

It is not, however, the label that matters, but what it says about the transformations brought about by the new archaeology in our field. That field is now a full-fledged, autonomous *archaeological* discipline, no longer an ancillary branch of biblical or theological studies. Its geographical purview is not "Bible Lands" as such, but ancient southern-central Syria and Palestine, both west and east of the Jordan (i.e., modern Israel, Jordan, Lebanon, and parts of Syria), or more properly ancient "Greater Canaan." Its time-frame extends far beyond the "biblical period," embracing everything from the Lower Paleolithic to the Ottoman period. Its aims and methods are exactly the same as those of other branches of archaeology (and anthropology). Where questions pertinent to the "biblical world," as envisioned by the biblical writers, arise from the archaeological data, they will be addressed; but the agenda is not drawn from the Bible, much less from theological questions.

Syro-Palestinian archaeology today is characterized, in my view, by three "watchwords": specialized, professional, and secular. By the latter term I mean simply to say that in the past generation Syro-Palestinian archaeology has at last come "out of the cloister," into the academy, and now even into the marketplace. That marks the full evolution of our discipline toward independent status. That is not to say that it will not develop even further — and dramatically so in the next decade, I think — but that there is now no turning back. There can be none of what I have called "nostalgia for a biblical past that never existed."

A Crucial Issue: Can Archaeology Write History?

It was generally assumed that the older-style biblical archaeology could and should be employed in writing a history of ancient Israel, even though the histories that it produced are now generally discredited — even works such as Albright's magisterial *From the Stone Age to Christianity* (1940) — and ironically by the very same archaeology in its later incarnation as "Syro-Palestinian archaeology." Thus a "patriarchal era," an "exodus from Egypt," and a pan-military "conquest of Palestine," as portrayed in the biblical narratives, have all

---

8. This can be seen simply by browsing through the principal Israeli journal, the *Israel Exploration Journal.* See also the introductory remarks of Amihai Mazar, in the standard Israeli handbook, *Archaeology of the Land of the Bible, 10,000-586 B.C.E.* (New York: Doubleday, 1990), 33, n. 1.

now been shown to be essentially nonhistorical, "historicized fiction" at best. And the proof has come largely *not* from radical biblical scholars, attempting to undermine the historicity of the biblical texts. It has come from "secular" archaeologists, Israeli and American, who have no theological axes to grind. So apparently archaeology, even of the "new" variety, *can* write histories of ancient Israel, if not conventional ones.

Yet archaeology has not always been conceived as a basically historical discipline, nor was it assumed that it can contribute productively to history-writing. Following the early history of biblical archaeology sketched above, with its strong historical (some would say "historicist") thrust, the new archaeology of the 1960s-1980s brought about a radical change in orientation. One fundamental tenet of the new archaeology was that "archaeology is anthropology, or it is nothing." The older "culture-history" approach, so typical of both Americanist and Near Eastern archaeology in the formative phases in the 1900-1960 era, was now rejected as unproductive. "Historical particularism," the attempt to classify and describe successive individual cultural and historical phases, was now passé. That was because, it was argued, archaeology of that sort could only *describe* cultural stages. It could not "explain" them, particularly in terms of testing the "universal laws of the cultural process" that the new, scientific archaeology thought was the only legitimate goal of archaeology. A turning point in North America was marked by the appearance of Patty Jo Watson, Steven A. LeBlanc, and Charles L. Redman's *Explanation in Archeology: An Explicitly Scientific Approach.*[9] The "modernization" of the spelling of "archeology" was intended apparently to signal how *avant garde* the new approach was to be. Despite spirited resistance from the Old Guard in American archaeology, by the late 1970s the anti-historical crusade of the new archaeology had triumphed. No respectable archaeologist would any longer style himself or herself a "historian." We were now scientists.

Nearly two decades ago I analyzed the impact of the new archaeology on Near Eastern and Syro-Palestinian archaeology.[10] It was slow to be felt, largely because nearly all of us in the general field of Near Eastern archaeology considered ourselves basically historians, not anthropologists, much less scientists. I pointed out early on that most of the Americans who led the new movement were essentially prehistorians, and that led to a bias. They worked with New World cultures that, even though comparatively recent (from our point of view), were still preliterate. But those of us who dealt with the ancient Near East *had* a history — a long, complex history of various peoples and cultures, copi-

9. (New York: Columbia University Press, 1969).
10. See n. 6 above.

ously illustrated from the late 4th millennium on by a wealth of written re-mains of every kind. There was good reason for our resisting the new archaeol-ogy's prejudice against history and its rejection of history-writing as a legitimate goal of archaeology (one among many, to be sure).

Toward a Rapprochement

Today, it seems, a proper balance is emerging in all branches of Near Eastern ar-chaeology. It seeks a *modus vivendi* that allows us to borrow appropriate socio-economic and cultural theories from many other disciplines, especially anthro-pology. It provides us with a framework for integrating and interpreting our data in a broader and much more sophisticated framework of knowledge, but nevertheless does not imprison us in rigid or mechanistic evolutionary schemes (what one distinguished new archaeologist himself called the search for "Mickey Mouse" laws[11]). The new *rapprochement* also enables us to borrow freely from any and all of the natural sciences their more precise analytical pro-cedures, which help us understand the artifacts that we dig up, how they were made and used, and how they were a part of a larger functioning ecology and technology.

Thus the basic inter-disciplinary approach pioneered by the new archae-ology is here to stay — not so much because the theory was persuasive, but be-cause of the essentially pragmatic nature of Near Eastern archaeology from the beginning. The "newer archaeology" is better for us because it works; it pro-duces superior data, data that can be understood and accepted by scholars in fields far beyond our own. Thus the course of civilization in ancient Palestine, so thoroughly investigated, finally becomes an instructive "case-study" in what is widely called "the rise of complex society."[12] What is lost of the "uniqueness" once attributed to ancient Israel is more than compensated for in the new ap-preciation that archaeology brings us of "Israel among the nations" — not

11. The phrase is that of Kent V. Flannery, in "The Golden Marshalltown: A Parable for the Archeology of the 1980s," *American Anthropologist* 84 (1982): 265-78.

12. The phrase is still used mostly of the prehistorical periods; for an excellent case-study of Palestine in the Early Bronze Age (late 4th-3rd millennium B.C.), see Alexander H. Joffe, *Settlement and Society in the Early Bronze I-II Southern Levant* (Sheffield: Sheffield Academic, 1993). For the 2nd millennium, see William G. Dever, "The Rise of Complexity in Palestine in the Early Second Millennium B.C.E.," in *Biblical Archaeology Today, 1990: The Proceedings of the Second International Congress on Biblical Archaeology, Pre-Congress Symposium: Population, Production and Power,* ed. Avraham Biran and Joseph Aviram (Je-rusalem: Israel Exploration Society, 1993), 98-109.

unique, but distinct. Presently we shall see in detail how modern archaeology can make the Bible and its story *more* "real" because it becomes more "tangible" — a real story, about a real people, in a real time and place, like us.

"Post-Processual" Archaeology

The potential of archaeology for illuminating the past in unique ways — for history-writing on a broad scale — has always seemed clear to some of us. But our traditional instincts have been confirmed by one of the most recent trends in archaeology. Reacting against the new archaeology's fascination with positivist philosophies of science and its extreme anti-historicism, a group of younger archaeologists began a decade ago to explore "post-processualist" approaches to archaeology.[13] Most had been raised up on "explicit science," structuralism, Neo-Marxism, and other new critical archaeologies. But ultimately they became disillusioned with the search for universal laws of cultural process and change — the "processualism" that they saw as the essential thrust of the new archaeology. They pointed out that the elegant theories had scarcely been confirmed in actual fieldwork. What if there *were* no "universal laws of the cultural process"? If not, why not go back to the task of trying to delineate individual societies and cultures, doing it better than traditional archaeology had done, with the new tools now at hand? Thus there emerged among the post-processualists a renewed interest in history, but accompanied now by a determination to write more satisfying histories.

One of the most prominent and engaging spokesmen for postprocessualism is Ian Hodder. Once a structuralist himself, Hodder became dissatisfied with all forms of the "newer archaeology," largely because of the same failure to "explain" cultural process that was charged against historical archaeologists. In his 1986 work, *Reading the Past: Current Approaches to Interpretation in Archaeology,*[14] Hodder lays out a program for postprocessual approach. Moving substantially beyond the new archaeology, with its largely functionalist notion of culture as ecological/technological adaptation, as well as his own previous structuralist models, Hodder advocates a more idealist and historical approach

---

13. An excellent introduction is the series of essays in *Reader in Archaeological Theory: Post-Processual and Cognitive Approaches,* ed. David S. Whitley (New York: Routledge, 1998). For an earlier orientation, see the essays in *Processual and Postprocessual Archaeologies: Multiple Ways of Knowing the Past,* ed. Robert W. Preucel (Carbondale: Center for Archaeological Investigations, Southern Illinois University, 1991). See also n. 15 below.

14. (Cambridge: Cambridge University Press, 1986).

that he calls "contextual" — literally, artifacts "with texts." But he goes even further in defining the archaeological record itself as a "text," and conversely written texts as "artifacts." Thus both can and must be "read" — indeed in similar ways, if a common "generative grammar" can be developed. Hodder says that such a notion "has long been tacitly assumed in archaeology." But he gives few examples; and he does not expand much on this fecund idea, beyond saying that artifacts are not necessarily "mute," if we can work out suitable principles of interpretation. Yet, as Hodder observes, somewhat ruefully, "there are no grammars and dictionaries of material culture language."

Postprocessualism is still being resisted by die-hard new archaeologists — now ironically the "old archaeologists," having become the Establishment they once fought so hard. In Syro-Palestinian and Near Eastern archaeology to date, usually a trend or two behind, little notice has been taken of postprocessualism, although I argued some years ago (1993) that this trend augured well for us since it made history-writing respectable once again.[15] Meanwhile, the revisionists, who must perforce turn to archaeology for data since they have jettisoned the biblical texts as history, are oblivious to postprocessualism and its potential (see above, Ch. 2). Astonishingly, they are still beating the dead horse of "biblical archaeology," as the current revisionist literature shows. These would-be biblical historians have no comprehension of modern archaeology, its aims and methods, its recent accomplishments, its enormous momentum, or its potential for truly revolutionizing our understanding of a *real* "ancient Israel."

Texts as Data

If the postprocessualists have set us back again upon the right track in studying the past — assaying to write history based on archaeological data — we must confront once again questions raised earlier. What *kind* of history do we want? *How* do artifacts constitute data, and are such data primary or secondary? Here we may take a clue from the postprocessualists themselves. One of their persistent themes is "reading" the artifacts, not unlike reading texts. In fact, artifacts *are* "texts," and similarly informative when skillfully and sympathetically interpreted. (Won't *that* be news to the revisionists?)

We might begin to move beyond this impasse by developing a tentative outline of a "grammar" of texts, based on what I would argue are parallels be-

15. See William G. Dever, "Biblical Archaeology: Death and Rebirth," in Biran and Aviram, *Biblical Archaeology Today, 1990,* 706-22. See also n. 13 above.

tween artifacts and texts. Here, in chart form, is what we must know in order to "read" or interpret texts and artifacts, both as "objects" in themselves and as "signs."

Texts	Artifact
Writing system	"Language" of material culture
Vocabulary	Artifacts of all types
Grammar	Formation processes
Syntax	Ecological, socio-cultural context
Author, composition, date	Date, technology
Cultural context *(Sitz im Leben)*	Overall historical setting
Intent	"Mental template" of makers
Later transmission, interpretation	Natural-cultural transformation
What the text "symbolizes"	What the artifact "symbolizes"
How its "meaning" is relevant today	How its "meaning" is relevant today

Once again, the parallels in reading the two types of "texts" are striking. Although I am sanguine about the possibilities for eventually reading the archaeological record as effectively as the textual record in the Hebrew Bible has been read in the past century of critical scholarship, examples of such readings — what have been called "formalist-structuralist" interpretations — are still relatively rare. One thinks, however, of New World examples such as James Deetz' analysis of early New England houses and their furnishings; Henry H. Glassie's similar study of folk-housing in Georgia; J. Muller's study of the American Southwest; Kenneth Washburn's of ceramic design; J. Hill's interpretation of Indian peace-pipes; and even of the revealing studies of modern discard patterns by my colleague William Rathje and his fellow "garbologists." All these are studies in "reading" material culture texts.[16]

In Old World prehistory, Andre H. Leroi-Gourhan has elucidated what appear to be underlying structural principles that can be useful in understanding Paleolithic cave art. This is a sort of "vocabulary, grammar, and syntax" for reading the "statements" made by the various representations and arrangements of animal drawings — what Leroi-Gourhan considers a "cave-as-text," or "mythogram." Here is a striking example of the potential of poststructural "ar-

---

16. For the analysis here, as well as references to this and other literature, see William G. Dever, "On Listening to the Text — and the Artifacts," in *The Echoes of Many Texts: Reflections on Jewish and Christian Traditions,* ed. Dever and J. Edward Wright (Atlanta: Scholars, 1997), 23.

chaeology of mind" for doing prehistory, if not history itself. It is from such challenges to "realism" and "naturalism" that the reader of cultural texts — such as literary myths, visual images, and archaeological artifacts — can profit. As Terence Hawkes points out, however, the textual-artifactual record is not simply a static, one-to-one representation of an underlying "reality" in the natural world, but is dynamic in nature, subject interacting with object. Thus, he says, all art (and, we would add, texts and artifacts) "acts as a mediating, molding force in society rather than an agency which merely reflects or records." The conclusion might be that in the structuralist and new literary-critical view, as opposed to the empiricist/rationalist view, "reality" is not expressed by culture (or language) but *produced* by it. Yet I think we need not go that far. There is a real, tangible world "out there"; but intervening between us and our perceptions of it are always ideas, beliefs, and meanings, both individual and cultural. Nevertheless, as George Cowgill, a leading anthropologist and formalist, puts it: "I believe it is possible to construct models of the world that increasingly approximate how it really is, even if we never get beyond approximations."[17] On this "positivist" note, I cannot help remarking how ironic I find it that at the very time when biblical historians, basing themselves on texts, are rejecting von Rankian notions of *wie es eigentlich gewesen war* ("how it actually *was* in the past") — despairing of writing a genuinely historical picture of ancient Israel — some archaeologists are about to take up the challenge. How is that possible? And how can the unique artifactual data that we possess lead us to any certain knowledge of the past? *Are* there archaeological "facts," and if so how are we to interpret them? Here we must turn to *epistemology,* theories of knowledge.

Toward an Epistemology

By the general term epistemology, sometimes called hermeneutics in textual studies, I mean simply the study of theories of knowledge, as in philosophy, of the question of how and whether we can know *anything* with certainty. Is our preserved knowledge verifiable in any way, related to a real world out there, or is the reality only our perceptions, which after all may be illusory?[18]

17. For references to Leroi-Gourhan and Hawkes, as well as further discussion, see Margaret Wright Conkey, "The Structural Analysis of Paleolithic Art," in *Archaeological Thought in America,* ed. C. C. Lamberg-Kazlousky (Cambridge: Cambridge University Press, 1989), 135-54. For Cowgill, see Lamberg-Kazlousky, 74. See also references in n. 13 above.

18. The following section is adapted from my "Archaeology, Texts, and History-Writing: Toward an Epistemology," in *Uncovering Ancient Stones: Essays in Memory of*

In one fundamental dimension, the new archaeology has so far proven as deficient as the old, namely its failure to address the fundamental issue of epistemology. It has built a much more adequate foundation in some aspects of general theory, but it has not probed deeply enough to reach the philosophical and methodological level at which all archaeological and historical inquiry must begin: how is it possible to know anything with certitude about the human past? Until this question has been addressed, both disciplines will remain superficial, arcane, and too speculative to have anything of substance to say to each other. I begin with some definitions.

To make archaeology and biblical history truly intellectual rather than antiquarian enterprises, we need to think much more profoundly about what we are doing. By this I do not mean simply more attention to "method" — which in our field has usually meant asking how to dig better, how to collect and record more information. Improvements in archaeology at this level are indeed important, and the past two decades have seen remarkable progress. However, archaeological advances and the proliferation of new material have now brought archaeologists to a critical stage where they must ask: What is the point? What are we trying to learn?

It might have been better to have asked these theoretical questions at the outset of the new archaeology. But as Thomas S. Kuhn has stated in *The Structures of Scientific Revolutions,* theory often follows rather than precedes the practical "shift in paradigm" that he regards as constituting a revolution in most research disciplines.[19] Thus it is indeed "better late than never" to raise these questions. In the discussion that follows I begin by reflecting on terms that all use but seldom bother to define, wrongly assuming that their meaning is self-evident.

On Archaeological "Facts"

Archaeology's original fascination for Albright, and I suspect for many of his followers, was that it could serve as an antidote. Archaeology promised new *facts* to offer the speculation of various schools of critical biblical scholarship,

---

H. Neil Richardson, ed. Lewis M. Hopfe (Winona Lake: Eisenbrauns, 1994), 105-17. Epistemology is one of the most urgent issues in general archaeology today, yet there is virtually no literature in our field. Israeli archaeologists, in particular, seem uninterested; but see, provisionally, Shlomo Bunimovitz, "How Mute Stones Speak: Interpreting What We Dig Up," *BAR* 21/2 (1995): 58-67, 96.

    19. 3rd ed. (Chicago: University of Chicago Press, 1996).

which seemed to have reached the limits of useful inquiry. This was what Albright meant when he spoke so confidently of *realia*. But archaeologists must delimit for themselves the facts that are recoverable through archaeology or, for that matter, define the so-called "facts of history."

By "fact" (derived from Latin *factum*, past participle of the verb *facere*, "to do") we usually mean those discrete, irreducible, empirically observable things or events whose existence cannot be doubted by reasonable persons. That is, facts are theoretically provable and correspond to reality. In practice, however, facts are merely inferences that each person draws, based not only on observations, but also on our own social conditioning and the intent of our investigation. Even in the natural sciences, this is true and is increasingly recognized; and in all the social sciences, such as archaeology and history, the factor of individual bias is even more operative. Thus, while in theory archaeology does recover objective "facts" from the past — for example, a pot, a stone tool, a figurine, the foundations of a building, perhaps the entire plan of a village, or even a written text — the apprehension of the reality of any of these is always dependent on present, subjective human interpretation. Facts do not speak directly. They may in principle have a concrete existence of their own; but they come to life, empowered to speak to me of the past, only as I am able to incorporate them into my consciousness. This process is obviously an extraordinarily complex matter.

A useful analogy is still the old philosophical puzzle: if a tree falls in the woods and there is no human or animal in hearing range, is there any sound? One may say "No," because sound, like meaning, is dependent on response, in this case the impact of airwaves set in motion by the crash upon human eardrums or other biological hearing mechanisms. Similarly, facts may be assumed to "speak," but until meaning — a uniquely human quality — is supplied, there is no message (see below). These inherent limitations of the facts brought to light by archaeology must always be kept in mind.

Are there, then, *no* facts in archaeology? There are, but they are relatively few and generally of minimal significance in themselves. Even these facts, however, must be carefully established as such before becoming admissible evidence. For example, using the list of items above, one might make an assertion that a particular pot is a "wheelmade cooking pot"; but laboratory analysis may show that it was handmade or that it was made for cooking but used for something else. In another instance, the plan of a building may be used as evidence that it was a "domestic house," not a temple. But it is important to keep in mind that no one can be absolutely sure of this analysis.

The element of subjectivity increases in the case of archaeological stratigraphy, or the science of untangling layers in a mound. It is possible to conclude, using the geological "law of superimposition," that the material in the upper-most of a sectioned series of earth layers is the latest; but further exposure may reveal that the entire series is an inverted fill, and the earliest material is on top. Again, a floor may be said to abut a wall rather than being cut by it, and so is contemporary. But a careful scholar will bear in mind the fact that foundation trenches can be surfaced-over so skillfully by later floors that the earlier purpose of the wall remains undetected.

For all these and other reasons, I suggest that archaeologists ought rarely to use the word "proof," because the kind of verification that is possible in sciences that investigate the physical world is simply not obtainable for material-culture remains, even though they are also physical objects. New archaeologists today do formulate and test hypotheses, do seek regularities in the cultural process, and in that sense they may aspire to "scientific" status of a sort. Ultimately, however, they are dealing with human behavior, and behavior cannot be replicated in the laboratory, nor is it predictable.

Thus archaeologists are better off speaking not of "laws" or "proofs" or even of "facts," but rather of various "probabilities," some of which are better (i.e., more useful) than others. They may also speak of "levels of inference," of which the lower are more certain than the higher. For example, to infer that the structure above is a "house" may be relatively safe; but to conclude that "the family is nuclear" is riskier, that "the social structure is segmentary" is still more risky. What is essential in the necessary process of interpretation is not to deny or minimize the difficulties, but rather to make presuppositions absolutely clear and above all not to claim more than is actually known. This — *knowledge of what is true* — is what the epistemological dilemma is all about.

Before leaving the topic of facts, it is worthwhile distinguishing four *kinds* of facts with which the archaeologist (and biblical historian) works: artifacts, textual facts, ideofacts, and ecofacts. Artifacts have already been mentioned, and all who work in the fields of historical archaeology are well acquainted with the necessity for using biblical and extrabiblical texts wherever possible for the illumination of the past. These two classes of facts are much more similar than usually thought. Both texts and artifacts symbolically represent a particular perception of reality; both are "encoded messages" that must be decoded, using rational, critical methods as well as empathy; both remain somewhat enigmatic, however skillful and persistent the attempts to penetrate their full meaning. Finally, I would argue simply that both objects and texts *are* artifacts, that is, thought and action frozen in the form of matter, the "material correlates of human behavior." Even the Bible is an artifact, in this case what I have called a "curated artifact," or an item that originally functioned in one social context but has subsequently been reused in other ways and settings. Thus the Bible is what it once was, in addition to what it has become over the centuries of interpretation as Scripture by Synagogue and Church. This fact must always be kept in mind when biblical texts are used as evidence in archaeological reconstructions.[20]

What Are "Data"?

Both archaeologists and historians refer constantly to the basic *data* on which their arguments rest. That is why an archaeological epistemology must begin with a definition of the word *datum*. Etymology suggests that *data* (plural past participle of Latin *dare*, "to give") are those facts that are "given" to us, the bedrock evidence upon which conclusions are based. What is "given" and how it is given, or by whom, are fundamental epistemological questions.

Ordinarily the terms "fact" and "data" are used interchangeably, but I contend that they represent two successive stages of the interpretive process. Archaeological facts in themselves, as has been seen, may possess intrinsic value, but this is not true for meaning, which must be supplied by human beings. In that sense, facts *become* data — that is, useful information — only as interpreted within an intellectual framework that is capable of giving them significance. Or put another way, it is possible to learn about the past, not simply by amassing more and more bits and pieces of disjointed "evidence," but rather by coordinating the pieces of evidence and situating them within a context, relating knowledge to a deliberate quest.

In all disciplines, but particularly in archaeology, the advance of real and lasting knowledge comes not so much from chance discovery (as the popular misunderstanding assumes), but rather from the systematic investigation of specific questions. Thus what is learned depends largely on what is already known, the goals and orientation of the investigation, and the method of inquiry. Simply put, the best answers — true "data" — result from framing appropriate questions. The use of the word "appropriate" does not imply any value judgment about what the "right" questions are, but a notion of what may be possible, given the nature of the material at one's disposal and the intellectual stage of the discipline at the moment.

20. See further William G. Dever, "The Silence of the Text: An Archaeological Commentary on 2 Kings 23," in *Scripture and Other Artifacts: Essays on the Bible and Archaeology in Honor of Philip J. King*, ed. Michael D. Coogan, J. Cheryl Exum, and Lawrence E. Stager (Louisville: Westminster John Knox, 1994), 143-68. The title of the volume is taken from the metaphor used in my chapter.

All of the foregoing is what should be intended by the use of the current phrase "research design" in archaeology, but the typical design entails more practical field strategy than it does an adequate theoretical base for the expansion of knowledge.

As Lewis R. Binford and other new archaeologists remind us, limitations of knowledge are more the results of inadequate research design than poor data. The archaeological record can be *much* more efficiently exploited, if only we better understand what cultural formation processes are and how superior data can be generated from broader and more sophisticated research strategies. Again, it all depends on asking appropriate questions. David Noel Freedman, one of Albright's protégés and a leading biblical scholar, sums up the wrong approach:

> Albright's great plan and expectation to set the Bible firmly on the foundation of archaeology buttressed by verifiable data seems to have foundered or at least floundered. After all the digging, done and being done and yet to be done, how much has been accomplished? The fierce debates and arguments about the relevance of archaeology to the Bible and vice versa indicate that many issues remain unresolved. Can anyone say anything with confidence about the patriarchs or the patriarchal age? The fact that skeptical voices now dominate the scene indicates that the Albrightian synthesis has become unglued and we are further from a solution than we ever were. Archaeology has not proved decisive or even greatly helpful in answering the questions most often asked and has failed to prove the historicity of biblical persons and events, especially in the early periods.[21]

I contend, however, that it was not archaeology that went wrong, but a generation of biblical historians who were asking the wrong questions — not wrong in a moral sense, but certainly wrong heuristically. Much of classical biblical archaeology was an exercise in futility in that the questions posed were either parochial and so received trivial answers at best, or were basically theological in nature and so received no answers at all. Only as scholars learn to structure questions more appropriate to the archaeological record itself and to socioeconomic history, rather than religious and political history, will archaeology become the powerful interpretive tool that Albright envisioned for reconstructing biblical life and times.

21. David Noel Freedman, quoted in "The Relationship of Archaeology to the Bible," *BAR* 11/1 (1985): 6.

What Is "Context"?

"Context" is another term that is used loosely in biblical archaeology. While recognizing the theoretical importance of context, archaeologists often mean by it little more than the immediate provenience of an object — its locus or stratum, or at most its associated materials. Rarely do they grasp that it is the *total* systemic context that is essential, that is, an ascending hierarchy of find-spot, stratigraphic phase, site-wide chronological horizon, multi-site evolutionary stage, ecological setting, and indeed long-term settlement-history. Lying behind this holistic approach is often General Systems Theory, which assumes that any given archaeological item functions within a larger environmental and sociocultural system, without which it cannot be understood.[22] It is this larger setting that provides significance, for without it an artifact is torn out of its original context, isolated as a curio, fit for little more than viewing in a museum. It can tell us little of the culture that produced it and was in turn partly shaped by it.

Biblical historians are often just as myopic in using biblical texts, fragmenting sources into verses and verses into still smaller units. Ultimately the critic becomes bogged down in the minutiae of literary analysis and loses sight of the larger picture of Israel's whole life and history. This narrowness of vision is all too prevalent, despite the broadening horizons of such newer approaches as rhetorical and canonical criticism. It is true that from the beginning form criticism stressed the importance of the *Sitz im Leben* ("life-setting"), but in practice this tended to mean simply *situating* a text within the *literary* tradition, not within the larger social and historical context of "real life." There were many times when the broader context could be recovered only through archaeology, but the dialogue between archaeology and biblical studies proved once again to be deficient. However, refreshing exceptions can be found: Robert B. Coote and Keith W. Whitelam's *The Emergence of Israel in Historical Perspective*, for example, takes a settlement-history approach over very long time-spans.[23]

---

22. On General Systems Theory and its possibilities for application to our branch of archaeology, see William G. Dever, "The Collapse of the Urban Early Bronze Age in Palestine: Toward a Systemic Analysis," in *L'urbanisation de la Palestine à l'âge Bronze ancien,* ed. Pierre de Miroschedji (Oxford: BAR, 1989), 225-46. General Systems Theory has recently been criticized by postprocessualists for its supposedly functionalist and deterministic biases, but I find a moderate and sensible application still useful.

23. This adopts the approach of Fernand Braudel and other *annales* historians who emphasize the importance of *la longue durée*. Cf. Dever, "Impact of the 'New Archaeology.'"

Archaeology and History: Epistemological Principles

It is fashionable once again to speak of history-writing as a primary goal of archaeology, and for this reason I turn now to the matter of defining the term "history." Unfortunately, both biblical scholars and archaeologists have neglected historiography until very recently, except for a few scholars such as John Van Seters, Baruch Halpern, and Giovanni Garbini.[24] Syro-Palestinian archaeologists, historians of a sort, usually manifest a naïveté regarding the nature of history and the task of history-writing. Albright, on the other hand, was familiar with and responded to works of such philosophers of history as Arnold Toynbee, Benedetto Croce, R. G. Collingwood, and Eric Voegelin, but his followers have shown little such inclination. The current result is highly technical archaeological studies of isolated problems and periods, but nothing approaching the full-scale synthetic history of ancient Palestine that today's proficient archaeology is capable of producing. This criticism is true even of the best recent works, such as Helga Weippert's *Palästina in vorhellenistischer Zeit* or Amihai Mazar's *Archaeology of the Land of the Bible, 10,000-586 B.C.E.*[25]

This lamentable deficiency is the direct result of an attenuated notion of history-writing among both archaeologists and biblical scholars. Scholars have produced a bare-bones "political history" based exclusively on select biblical texts and highly visible, monumental archaeological remains such as temples, palaces, and destruction-layers. This "history" has emphasized public events and the deeds of great men, but largely ignores socioeconomic history, much less the kind of long-term history of the masses that Fernand Braudel and the *annales* school undertake.[26] Such an elitist history is unsatisfactory on many accounts, not least of which is the modern biblical historian's apparently unconscious (and certainly uncritical) appropriation of the ideological bias of the ancient writers. It is history written "from within," rather than from the perspective of the external evidence now available from the ancient Near East, both in abundant texts and artifacts. Here again, even the most critical current works, such as J. Maxwell Miller

---

24. John Van Seters, *In Search of History;* Baruch Halpern, *The First Historians;* Giovanni Garbini, *History and Ideology in Ancient Israel.* For a review of the literature on historiography and its relevance to our branch of archaeology, see William G. Dever, "'Will the Real Israel Please Stand Up?'" *BASOR* 297 (1995): 61-80. I omit the biblical revisionists here because I do not think that they have sufficiently addressed the issue of historiography, and by-and-large their works are nonhistories.

25. Both are standard, up-to-date handbooks. More sophisticated and comprehensive is the collection of essays in *The Archaeology of Society in the Holy Land,* ed. Thomas E. Levy, 2nd ed. (London: Leicester University Press, 1998).

26. See n. 23 above.

and John H. Hayes' *A History of Ancient Israel and Judah,* are a disappointment.[27] Yet progress in this matter is unlikely without a more adequate concept of history and of the historian's task. At this point I wish to present a methodology for what I foresee to be a more adequate written history of ancient Israel in the future. Since, as I have argued, epistemology is basic, I begin with an appeal for theory.

Archaeological Theory-Building

In his 1977 work *For Theory Building in Archaeology,* Binford elaborates on one of the original motifs of the new archaeology of 25 years ago, stressing that archaeology is unlikely to advance further unless this earlier revolution in basic theory is carried forward.[28] Unfortunately, the new archaeology has come and gone, and most Syro-Palestinian archaeologists have missed the signal for change. To judge from the scant discussions in the literature, the notion of "theory" meets with apathy at best and often with open hostility. American archaeologists, striving to reeducate themselves in newer approaches, have shown some interest in what is usually called "theory and method"; but they have construed *method* to mean simply improved digging and recording techniques, rather than an inquiry that concerns the very intellectual foundations of the discipline. Israelis view the few attempts at theory-building by Americans or archaeologists in other fields with a skepticism revealing only their innocence.

Both Middle Eastern and American archaeologists fail to understand that "theory" does not mean idle speculation (which our field has indeed seen too much of) but simply a body of principles that guide research. The purposes of theory-building are: to make explicit and examine the presuppositions that are brought to research, whether consciously or not; to define a discipline with respect to methods and objectives; to establish a common ground for discussion within a discipline and for dialogue with other disciplines; and to promote the health and advancement of a particular discipline and the branch of knowledge that it represents. I seriously doubt that archaeologists who resist theory really believe these goals are undesirable. And surely it is obvious that such goals will not be achieved automatically.[29]

27. (Philadelphia: Westminster, 1991).

28. Lewis R. Binford, *For Theory Building in Archaeology: Essays on Faunal Remains, Aquatic Resources, Spatial Analyses, and Systemic Modeling* (New York: Academic, 1977), 1-10.

29. William G. Dever, "The Importance of Research Design," in *Archaeology's Publication Problem,* ed. Hershel Shanks (Washington: Biblical Archaeology Society, 1996), 37-48.

I contend that the unprofessional standards in biblical and Syro-Palestinian archaeology, the failure to keep pace with other branches of archaeology, the endless controversies, the isolation, and the failure to engage in productive dialogue with biblical and historical studies are *all* largely the result of a reluctance to confront basic questions of theory. Syro-Palestinian archaeology will "come of age" only when it addresses the issue of theory, the first consideration in developing an epistemology.

Archaeological Reasoning

A second step in developing an epistemology is reflecting on the nature of the reasoning process of archaeology, as well as the reasoning process of history. It is evident that both disciplines employ critical methods to sift the evidence, whether artifactual or textual, in order to select data that can be judged useful in reconstructing the past. Whatever the principles employed in this initial sifting task, they should be made explicit.

Biblical scholars over the past century have indeed developed explicit methodologies, but archaeologists are far behind. Often the assessment of excavated evidence is based on little more than intuition or on the competence of the excavator. Data of varying quality are categorized indiscriminately. Wide-ranging historical and cultural conclusions are drawn from the flimsiest of evidence or based on the cavalier citation of various "authorities." It is true, unfortunately, that archaeology today is so specialized and so esoteric that the non-specialist (historian or biblical scholar, for instance) is at a loss to know whom or what to trust. For this reason, among others, Syro-Palestinian archaeologists need desperately to develop a hermeneutic, preferably one that takes into account a number of parallel methods of interpreting artifacts and texts, as pointed out by Hodder in *Reading the Past*.[30]

One aspect shared by both biblical scholarship and archaeology is a dependence on *analogy* as a fundamental method of argument. It is possible to know the past only by making inferences from artifacts preserved from that past. Inferences, by definition, are observations (one might say "guesses") made by individuals who experience the present world. Only by using analogies — parallels thrown alongside — can one hope to illuminate these enigmatic relics. Without some point of contact, it is impossible to determine the use of objects from the past. This is true of ancient texts as well as ancient objects, since translation is analogy, an attempt to render the images of the text into images familiar to the reader.

30. See above and n. 14.

The challenge is to find *appropriate* analogues, those offering the most promise yet capable of being tested in some way. Ethnoarchaeology is useful in this regard, particularly in places where unsophisticated modern cultures are still found superimposed, as it were, upon the remains of the ancient world, as in parts of the Middle East. Analogies drawn from life in modern Arab villages or Bedouin society can, with proper controls, be used to illuminate both artifacts and texts, as many studies have shown. What is more, postulates made in this way can be partially tested: those regarding social structure, by modern usage; those regarding individual objects, by replication (a device all too infrequently employed).[31]

Nevertheless the limitations of inquiry into the meaning of both artifacts and texts must always be borne in mind by archaeologists, regardless of their method of interpretation. It is no coincidence that Wright and Roland de Vaux, leading scholars in Bible and archaeology, wrote articles near the end of their lives on both the capabilities and the limitations of archaeology.[32] All historians deal with possibilities, at best with probabilities, never with certainties. The degree of subjectivity can and should be reduced, but it can never be eliminated. It is possible to hone the tools of textual analysis and archaeology fieldwork to an ever-sharper edge, thus increasing the true data in quantity and quality, but the past will always remain partly elusive. As Hodder says, of his new postprocessual or "contextual" archaeology:

> It is characterized by debate and uncertainty about fundamental issues that may have been rarely questioned before in archaeology. It is more an asking of questions than a provision of answers.[33]

The Dialogue between Texts and Artifacts in History-Writing

If, as we have argued thus far, texts and artifacts are both data to be "read" and both may constitute sources for writing history, then they must be considered

---

31. One can count on the fingers of one hand the efforts at replication of structures, assemblages, or even individual artifacts in archaeology in Israel. A notable exception is the full-scale reconstruction of an Iron Age Israelite house and its furnishings in the Municipal Museum in Tel Aviv (formerly the Ha-Aretz Museum).

32. Cf. Roland de Vaux, "On Right and Wrong Uses of Archaeology," in *Near Eastern Archaeology in the Twentieth Century*, ed. James A. Sanders (Garden City: Doubleday, 1970), 64-80; G. Ernest Wright, "What Archaeology Can and Cannot Do," *BA* 34 (1971): 70-76.

33. *Reading the Past*, 170.

together. Or, more precisely, they must be interpreted separately and similarly, and then compared. In arguing for the necessity of a *dialogue between* these two fundamental sources for the historian, I meant just that.

The possibility for a serious dialogue seems scarcely to have occurred to either biblical scholars or Syro-Palestinian archaeologists. The former have continued until recently to produce various "histories" of ancient Israel that upon examination turn out to be little more than histories of the *literature* of the Hebrew Bible, or as Garbini has scathingly put it, mere "paraphrases of the Bible itself."[34] Given the apparent futility of that approach, a few more radical biblical scholars have recently sought to write "histories of ancient Palestine" as an alternate. These would include works such as Gosta W. Ahlström's *The History of Ancient Palestine from the Paleolithic to Alexander's Conquest*[35] and Thomas L. Thompson's *Early History of the Israelite People: From the Written and Archaeological Sources.*[36] Yet, as we have shown, these are far from satisfactory as histories of either ancient Israel *or* Palestine — precisely because, despite their paying lip-service to archaeology, out of desperation, they remain monologues, not the dialogue between specialists that I envision as necessary. Ahlström and Thompson are biblical scholars talking to other biblical scholars. The point is simple: neither Ahlström nor Thompson is an archaeologist, so their use of archaeological data is arbitrary, often amateurish, and ultimately misleading. Their works, despite a laudable attempt to break the impasse we have seen in writing text-based histories of ancient Israel, are essentially nonhistories. They constitute what one of the revisionists himself, Ernst Axel Knauf, said of a more traditional work, Miller and Hayes' *History of Ancient Israel and Judah,* "a pseudo-history of non-events."[37] Certainly no Syro-Palestinian *archaeologist* would recognize Ahlström's and Thompson's "portraits" (and none but myself has even bothered to review them).

Meanwhile, what have the archaeologists been doing? It is significant that until recently no full-scale, comprehensive diachronic treatments of the archaeology of Palestine had been published since Albright's standard *Archaeology of Palestine*[38] and Kathleen M. Kenyon's *Archaeology in the Holy Land.*[39] That was due mostly to the rapid pace of discovery, which made the task of synthesis

34. *History and Ideology,* 7.

35. (Sheffield: JSOT, 1993).

36. (Leiden: Brill, 1992). See my brief reviews in "Will the Real Israel Please Stand Up?"

37. Ernst Axel Knauf, "From History to Interpretation," in *The Fabric of History,* ed. Diana V. Edelman, 49.

38. (Harmondsworth: Penguin, 1949).

39. 4th ed. (1979, repr. Nashville: Nelson, 1985).

daunting. Then in short order there were what are now the standard hand-books: Weippert's *Palästina in vorhellenistischer Zeit;* and the works of leading Israeli archaeologists, Mazar's *Archaeology of the Land of the Bible;* and *Archaeology of Ancient Israel,* edited by Amnon Ben-Tor.[40] Yet Weippert's book, while valuable as a "handbook" (a typical German *Handbuch*), is derivative, being written by an art historian, and simply contains a mass of information. Despite Thompson's enthusiastic (and usually exclusive) citation of Weippert, hers is by no means a "history of ancient Palestine." Mazar's work is less detailed, but it has much more authority because it is written by one of Israel's leading archaeologists, whose broad knowledge and balanced judgment are widely admired. Ben-Tor's edited work is more uneven, but many chapters are superb critical summaries of what is now known archaeologically. Once again, however, the Israeli works are far from being "histories of ancient Palestine"; they are reference works, compilations of raw data plus some interpretation. There is little or no attempt at overall integration of ecological, artifactual, textual, socio-economic, cultural, and much other data; at connected narrative of events; or, much less, at the discussion of cause (or "explanation" in current archaeology) that would be essential for true history-writing.

All the above works, while extremely useful, are highly technical mono-logues among specialists, in this case specialists in material culture studies. Indeed, most Israeli (and other) Syro-Palestinian archaeologists are almost entirely aloof from biblical and historiographical discussions like the present, for reasons that we shall explore elsewhere but which have to do mostly with the highly specialized and avowedly "secular" character of Israeli archaeology. In any case, archaeologists and biblical scholars continue to labor away in their little black boxes, largely oblivious of each other. In no case do we see real collaboration. Despite Albright's original vision of a dialogue between archaeology and biblical studies, not to mention my own call for it for more than 25 years, sadly enough there is none. Beyond the occasional "joint session" at annual professional meetings in America, such as the Society of Biblical Literature/ American Academy of Religion and the American Schools of Oriental Research, there is not even much conversation, just scholars typically "talking past each other."

This situation is appalling, especially since, as we shall now see, the possibilities for dialogue have never been more promising or the rationale more compelling. That is true especially because texts and artifacts can both now be characterized as "data to be read," as I have suggested above. What I shall attempt to show in the following is that the textual and artifactual data now avail-

---

40. (New Haven: Yale University Press, 1992).

able concerning ancient Israel are remarkably similar in character; that the history of scholarly interpretation of both classes of data runs surprisingly parallel; and that these convergences point to an inter-disciplinary dialogue that holds the best hope yet for writing an adequate history of ancient Israel.

How the Textual Record and the
Archaeological Record Compare

We may begin by noting that the corpus of individual texts and artifacts constitutes in each case what we may call a "record" of the past. That the texts of the Hebrew Bible are a record of sorts is obvious, although the nature of that record is disputed. On the other hand, archaeologists have also been seeking to define a phenomenon known as "the archaeological record" since the dawn of the new archaeology some three decades ago. By consensus today, the archaeological record may be said to consist of all those physical remains that survive from past human actions, i.e., not only artifacts or objects strictly speaking; any observable traces of human impact upon the external world and the natural environment, or "cultural deposits" of many kinds (including the burials of the humans themselves); the above remains situated in their larger spatial and temporal context; and the whole of the evidence seen in the light of the intellectual and social matrix that we moderns inevitably bring to the task of interpretation. Need it be stressed that biblical texts must be seen as constituting a parallel and very similar kind of "record of the past" — indeed, with the same scope, complexity, and limitations?

Before proceeding, we may attempt in the interests of brevity to list some of the essential characteristics of both texts and artifacts — in a simplified chart form (see p. 82), noting similarities and differences.[41] Of these 12 diagnostic characteristics, fully half are the same for both texts and artifacts, and a number of others are similar or overlap. And, as I shall argue, even those characteristics that differ share something, in the fact that the same *interpretive methods* are required of the historian who works with these two types of data. Specifically, both texts and artifacts are "objective," yet require "subjective" interpretation if the record is to be read correctly. Both contain valid information about the past, but only in the form of inferences we must make that must be tested against some external criteria. These "facts," when established as such, then constitute true data when placed within an intellectual framework that gives them meaning in relation to specific questions that are appropriate to history-

---

41. See further Dever, "On Listening to the Text," 1-23.

Biblical Texts (as preserved)	Archaeological Artifacts (as preserved)
Concretize thought and behavior	Concretize thought and behavior
Symbolic, "encoded" messages of past	Symbolic, "encoded" messages of past
Express deliberate intent, imagination	Express deliberate intent, imagination
Selective, elitist by nature	Broadly representative, "populist"
Heavily edited in transmission	Constitute random sample
Reflect principal ideology	Reflect common practice
Closed corpus	Dynamic, expanding source of data
Continuous tradition	"Broken" tradition
Only a residue of past	Only a residue of past
"Curated artifact"	"Curated artifacts"
Refract the past	Refract the past
Literature	"Real" life

writing. Furthermore, the use of both classes of data requires an interpretive methodology that is fundamentally genetic, evolutionary, and comparative. Finally, if "reading" both the textual and archaeological record is the appropriate metaphor, then it is obvious that the interpreter must master the peculiar vocabulary, grammar, and syntax of each class of data, as we have seen. Otherwise, the text of the Hebrew Bible will remain as "mute" as some misguided biblical scholars maintain that the artifacts are.

Parallel Interpretive Methods

In a recent publication[42] I have shown in detail how all the 19th-20th century "schools" of interpretation in biblical studies can parallel almost exactly the history of archaeological scholarship (although the "schools" were not necessarily contemporary). That would seem to confirm the suggestion here that the two classes of data — textual and artifactual — are naturally complementary when understood properly. Space precludes detail, but for instance (1) the 19th-century philological approach, or "learning the language" of the Bible, was paralleled by the initial mapping of the landscape in early archaeology. (2) The later literary- or higher-critical approach, untangling the strands in the literary tradition, was paralleled in archaeology by the stratigraphic revolution, "untangling" the layers in a mound. (3) Form criticism, the attempt to

42. See Dever, "On Listening to the Text."

Biblical Theology	Biblical Archaeology
The Bible text taken as starting-point	The Bible text taken as starting-point
"Historical" agenda actually drawn from theological issues	"Historical" agenda actually drawn from theological issues
Conservative, tendentious throughout in basic method	Conservative, tendentious throughout in basic method
Drew heavily on popular religious mentality in America	Drew heavily on popular religious mentality in America
Operated with positivist presuppositions	Operated with positivist presuppositions
Actually begged the broader historical questions	Actually begged the broader historical questions
Resisted newer inter-disciplinary methods	Resisted newer inter-disciplinary methods
Could not accommodate "secular" approaches	Could not accommodate "secular" approaches
Gradually became parochial or obsolete	Gradually became parochial or obsolete

isolate and categorize various genres in the literary tradition, was paralleled in archaeology by the typological analysis of artifacts, especially pottery. (4) Redaction or tradition criticism, or the study of how the overall literary tradition was formed and transmitted, has been paralleled in archaeology by the recent study of "formulation processes of the archaeological record." (5) The "history of religions" approach in biblical studies has now been paralleled in archaeology by the burgeoning study of religion and cult in ancient Israel. (6) The ethnographic approach, or seeking in cross-cultural comparisons a background for life in biblical times, is paralleled by the strongly anthropological orientation of current archaeology, as well as its penchant for cross-cultural studies. (7) The socio-anthropological, or new "socio-critical," school is paralleled closely by the socio-anthropological thrust of all recent archaeology. (8) Even the much-maligned "Old Testament theology" school has its archaeological parallels, in the "biblical archaeology" movement of the early-mid 20th century.

In the latter, especially, the *convergences,* as we shall call them, are remarkable, as the chart above shows. Even though there were factors other than these that were operative in the demise of biblical archaeology in the 1970s — such as competition from foreign "national schools" and a crisis in funding — two facts remain clear. As Albright and Wright, with their peculiar combination of biblical studies and archaeological research, passed from the scene in the early 1970s, so did biblical archaeology, which had in many ways always been uniquely Protestant and American. At the very same time, Brevard S. Childs could write an obituary of the biblical theology movement, *Biblical Theology in Crisis*.[43] Both movements had construed the history of ancient Palestine and of Israel as a sort of "religio-political history" that was thought to yield a universal, self-evident cultural meaning. The effort was perhaps noble, but doomed to failure.

Toward a New Hermeneutic?

The foregoing sketch of parallel schools of interpretation in biblical and archaeological studies up until some 20 years ago is suggestive. I would argue, however, that more recent trends in both disciplines pave the way for the first dialogue between texts and artifacts, with unique possibilities for illuminating the past in general, and the phenomenon of ancient Israel in particular.

Structuralism as a putative method, much less a "school," is nearly impossible to define. But the approach as applied sporadically in recent biblical studies has sought to penetrate behind the texts to comprehend the underlying mental construct as a whole, as a closed system, yet one capable of transformation (the "deep structure"). Often the analysis focuses on bipolar opposites that constitute universal themes in the myths, and often function as symbols or "signs": e.g., male/female, life/death, good/bad, nature/culture, immanence/transcendence. Structuralism originated not in biblical studies, but in cultural anthropology, and especially in linguistics. Because of its interest in the structure of society, structuralism is sometimes allied with Marxist notions of the social relations of production, and the relation of these to ideology, as they shape society (Marx was not simply a "vulgar materialist"). Structuralism has had little if any impact on Syro-Palestinian archaeology, although it has had its advocates in the general field of archaeology. Yet if there *is* a discernible "deep structure" in texts, then it is reasonable to suppose that some such structure exists in artifactual remains as well; and, furthermore, it is evident that artifacts, like texts, are "signs" and have symbolic meaning.[44]

Similar in many ways to structuralism is semiotics — a "science of how language works as a set of symbols" — and several related approaches that sometimes go under the banner of New Literary Criticism. The effort of the lat-

43. (Philadelphia: Westminster, 1970).
44. See Dever, "On Listening to the Text," and references there.

ter is directed toward a formal description of the fundamental structure of a text as "discourse." Obviously this discourse is associated with some meaning; but the question is not primarily what texts "mean," but rather "what makes meaning possible?" In short, how is the text *able* to say what it says; how does it "signify," and to whom? The basic tool of the newer literary approaches is often "metalanguage," a special language of description that focuses on the play among "signifying elements" in the text — mostly opposites/contrasts that are said to make "meaning" possible. At the heart of these varied approaches is the notion of *symbol,* understood as a primary language that emerges directly and simultaneously out of experience. In a secondary stage, this symbolic language comes to be arranged in narrative form as "myth," but this is not, however, yet at the stage of reflective thought. These symbolized myths, in turn, must be analyzed by the interpreter in terms of a double structure, as conveying obvious, literal meaning, and as analogies. Texts, then — biblical or other — do refer to a "reality," but in different and special ways. They do say something to somebody; they offer at least the possibility of re-creating the world that was real to their authors and/or editors, if not an "objective" reality.

New Literary Criticism, as we saw above, with its emphasis on "narrative history" and the "intent" (if any) of the text, is clearly related to older approaches, as well as more recent schools like rhetorical and canonical criticism, and therefore it seems accessible to many biblical scholars (at least in its less extreme forms). Unfortunately, New Literary Criticism falls easily into a deconstructionist mode: the text itself means nothing, and *we* must supply whatever meaning we choose, largely in terms of our own contemporary needs. There are no "truths" about the past to be learned; our supposed knowledge of the past is conditioned entirely by the modern context of the quest, mostly political.

Complementary Histories?

If the parallel character of texts and artifacts as data for history-writing seems well established, can they enable us to write "parallel histories"? And could those differing but complementary histories ever converge? Again, the question: "What kinds of history?"[45]

That the two histories are indeed different seems clear. (1) A text-based history, in this case dependent upon the texts of the Hebrew Bible, while lim-

---

45. See further William G. Dever, "Philology, Theology, and Archaeology," in Silberman and Small, *The Archaeology of Israel,* 290-310.

ited could be expected to yield what I have termed "political history," a more or less connected narrative of great men and public institutions, or a "theocratic history," history as His story (what biblical scholars call *Heilsgeschichte,* or "the history of salvation"). Such an account, *if* it could be shown to be factual, might contribute to another traditional "history of the religion of Israel," or at its best an "intellectual history of ancient Palestine." But that is a very large "if," as we have noted above.

(2) Archaeology, in the broad, inter-disciplinary sense in which the discipline is conceived today, might be expected to yield several histories, as we noted above, at least in outline: a history of technology, a socio-economic history, a cultural history, something of a history of religion (at least of cult, if not of theology), and a larger portrait that might be called a "secular history of ancient Palestine."

The latter term deserves further comment. It seems to have been introduced in my 1987 paper at national meetings, which was not published however until 1991.[46] Meanwhile, it was learned that Ahlström's 1992 and Thompson's 1991 "histories of *Palestine*" were in process, with an intent similar to mine to go beyond traditional "confessional" histories of ancient or biblical history. Ahlström did not use the term "secular" history, although he did make Palestine in all periods his focus, not simply "biblical Israel."

Thompson had already outlined his program in 1987 (which I had not seen when I first wrote) for a "long range goal of reconstructing a sound and critical history of Israel and of its origins within the context of the historical geography of *Palestine*."[47] This is rather similar to Knauf's call at about the same time (1991) for "an extension of natural history into the specific realm of *homo sapiens*," suggesting that we combine Braudel's long-term history ("structures") and his medium-term history ("conjunctures") into a "processual history," an approach that Knauf says "cannot do without archaeology."[48] That is similar to my "history of cultural context" in the broadest (i.e., ecological) sense, and not unlike the "natural history" of Pliny's *Historia naturalis.*

These tentative but independent attempts to transcend "theocratic histories" of ancient Israel in the last decade, coming as they have from both biblicists and archaeologists, would seem to bode well for the dialogue that I envision. Yet ironically, it is precisely the protagonists noted here — Dever,

---

46. See William G. Dever, "Unresolved Issues in the Early History of Israel," in Jobling, Day, and Sheppard, *The Bible and the Politics of Exegesis,* 195-208.

47. Thomas L. Thompson, *The Origin Tradition of Early Israel,* 1: *The Literary Formation of Genesis and Exodus 1–23.* JSOT Sup 55 (Sheffield: JSOT, 1987), 39.

48. Knauf, "From History to Interpretation," 44.

Knauf, and Thompson — who now differ vociferously on how to proceed. That may be due in large part to the fact that we do not agree on *whose* data should be "primary," whose "secondary": texts, or artifacts?

"Primary" and "Secondary" Sources

Biblical scholars, until recently trained primarily as philologians, have always tended to overvalue texts as the more "objective" evidence, even when they acknowledge as they must the inherent differences in interpretation. In my judgment, this reflects a certain naïveté about how texts serve as "symbols," and an abysmal ignorance of how artifacts can serve in the same way (as we have seen above). It was Martin Noth, one of the giants of German biblical scholarship and long-term director of the German school in Jerusalem, who first declared in *The History of Israel* that "as far as the Israelite age is concerned, Syrian-Palestinian archaeology is almost wholly silent."[49] The German original is *dumm*, "mute, silent," which provides an extra, if unintended, irony. Noth probably only meant to point out that artifacts are usually anonymous; they usually don't come labeled with the names of historical actors. In his *History*, Noth went on to give a more positive account of archaeology's ability to contribute to biblical history, concluding that "an account of the history of Israel which does not refer constantly to the results of Syrian-Palestinian archaeology is indefensible now that this source of information has become accessible." That assessment must be balanced against Noth's other statement. And I know from personal conversations not long before his death in 1969 that, had he lived to revise his *History*, Noth would have been much more enthusiastic about archaeology's contribution to biblical studies.

Noth's new optimism was clearly attributable to the contact he had in later life with Paul W. Lapp, then director of the American School of Oriental Research in Jerusalem, and to actual contact with good field archaeology. But a later generation of biblical scholars seized upon Noth's somewhat cryptical remark, which has been repeated mindlessly by leading historians such as Siegfried Herrmann, Hartmut Rösel, Ahlström, Miller, and many others. Yet as Knauf — something of a radical himself — points out, this is a slander: "the archaeological evidence is no more silent than the Torah is to somebody who cannot read Hebrew." Even though Knauf still regarded archaeological sources as "secondary," he acknowledged their importance as "external evidence" and even conceded that a certain *kind* of history of ancient Israel/Palestine could be

49. 2nd ed. (New York: Harper & Row, 1958), 46-47.

written without using the Hebrew Bible. He thought the latter task not entirely desirable but "probably possible — and worth a try."[50]

At about the same time (indeed, in the same volume of essays) the well-known American biblical historian J. Maxwell Miller sharpened the issue by asking: "Is It Possible to Write a History of Israel Without Relying on the Hebrew Bible?" This was evidently meant as a rhetorical question, since Miller went on to maintain once again that "artifacts are silent and remain 'anonymous unless interpreted in the light of written records.'"[51] But certainly this would be news to prehistorians, who proceed confidently to do culture-history without a written word from the past. It is at this point that I have observed of Miller and others that "archaeology is not mute, but historians are often deaf." Certainly this attitude does not foster the dialogue I envision between two independent but complementary disciplines, each with its own appropriate aims, methods, and body of data. Simple honesty and integrity, not to mention scholarly competence, demand that scholars in our several fields respect the limitations of their individual knowledge and commit themselves to *teamwork*. Here texts and artifacts both must be considered "primary data," read similarly.

The position of another protagonist in this debate, Thompson, is now nuanced. His 1987 work on the origin traditions of Genesis and Exodus actually laid the foundations for his 1992 *Early History of the Israelite People*. Already disillusioned with text-based histories, Thompson declared:

> It is . . . the independence of Syro-Palestinian archaeology that now makes it possible for the first time to begin to write a history of Israel's origins. Rather than the Bible, it is in the field of Syro-Palestinian archaeology, and the adjunct field of ancient Near Eastern studies, that we find our primary source for Israel's earliest history.[52]

I couldn't have said it better myself. In fact, I *had* been saying almost precisely these things for a decade or more — using the very terms "Syro-Palestinian archaeology" and "independent discipline" (as far back as 1973). Thompson's failure is that he does not carry through his important insights into "primary sources" in writing his own subsequent full-scale *Early History*, nor can he. He is not an archaeologist himself and does not consult those who are. He makes frequent reference to Weippert's 1988 handbook (his usual preference for German works); but he does not even allude to the standard reference work, Mazar's *Archaeology of the Land of the Bible*, published in 1990 and easily available to him.

---

50. Knauf, "From History to Interpretation," 46.
51. J. Maxwell Miller, in Edelman, *The Fabric of History*, 93-102, quotation on 96.
52. *The Origin Tradition of Early Israel*, 27.

Consequently, as I have shown in reviews, Thompson's scant, arbitrary, and uncritical citation of some of the archaeological literature and evidence renders his portrait a *caricature* of ancient Palestine, one that no archaeologist would even recognize.[53] Furthermore, Thompson's later writings and nearly all of the revisionists' current outpourings in print and elsewhere feature self-confident declarations about archaeology and even about individual archaeologists that reflect ignorance, clear ideological bias, and malice (as detailed in Chapter 2 above). I cannot understand rationally how the revisionists can fall back upon archaeology in their disillusionment with the biblical texts, and then refuse to educate themselves about its results. They become "historians" with no history. Perhaps we are dealing not with reason at all, but with ideology. Yet I continue to hope for a dialogue, because it is our only hope for writing a history of ancient Israel.

Before we turn directly to that dialogue, however, let me summarize why I think archaeological data can be "primary" sources for history-writing — indeed, sometimes superior to biblical and other ancient Near Eastern texts.

1. Archaeological data in the broadest sense are by definition "external" to the texts and therefore constitute an *independent* witness. In the case of the biblical texts, this is the only such witness that we shall ever have, since the Bible is a closed corpus.

2. Archaeological data, unlike texts, have not been deliberately edited and altered in meaning over time by continuous commentary, so they allow us to leap across the centuries and encounter a past reality directly. It is true that the forces of mankind and nature may have shaped the objects in the ground since their original deposition, what we call "formation processes of the archaeological record." But we can control these factors with objects found *in situ* better than we can account for the biases of the long interpretive process in the transmission of ancient texts.

3. Archaeological artifacts constitute *realia,* as much as do texts. Far from being enigmatic, artifacts may surpass texts in being more immediate, concrete, and tangible, and therefore more "objective."

4. While surviving ancient texts will always be relatively scant, and largely the result of accidental finds, archaeological evidence is potentially almost unlimited. Archaeology provides a deliberate and productive research program, producing data that are a dynamic, ever-expanding source of genuinely new information about the past. While biblical studies everywhere seems to be exhausted, lacking in either new data or compelling paradigms, archaeology is a discipline barely beyond its infancy and full of youthful vigor and confidence.

53. Dever, "Will the Real Israel Please Stand Up?" 62-65.

5. The analysis of ancient texts will and should proceed, although I think with diminishing results. (When was the last time that we heard about "the assured results of biblical criticism"?) But it is *only* archaeology, in the broad inter-disciplinary sense in which we conceive it today, that can truly "revolutionize" biblical studies.

Rules for a Dialogue

Suppose the dialogue between texts and artifacts should begin to materialize. What ought the ground rules be? This is not in fact a difficult question, since we are merely talking about the interdisciplinary research that goes on all the time among many other disciplines today, particularly the social sciences, where such inquiries are taken for granted. Indeed our rules will sound rather banal.

1. The intellectual and professional integrity of each discipline (and archaeology today is a separate discipline) must be respected, acknowledging the "autonomous" aims and methods of each, even though that may seem at first a contradiction in terms.

2. There is no substitute for absolute competence in one's own discipline. Breadth of interests, open-mindedness, courage in crossing disciplinary lines, the willingness to test new models, and imagination and skill in synthesis are all necessary. But they cannot compensate for inferior work in one's own "home discipline." Too much of what passes for "inter-disciplinary" research is dilettantish and faddish; it is shabby, lacking a real disciplinary foundation. (I think that is particularly true of much of New Literary Criticism generally, and of the revisionists in particular.) As Knauf says wisely of the historian (and he is speaking here specifically about biblical and archaeological sources), "you either undergo training in which you are provided with a theoretical background that allows you to make sense out of your source — disputable sense, of course — or you are at the mercy of those who did."[54]

3. However impossible absolute "objectivity" may be (and all acknowledge that today), it is still a worthwhile and essential goal for the philologian and exegete, specialist in material culture, or historian. Either there are empirical data or there are not; and the historian who opts for the second alternative puts himself out of business, at least as a serious scholar and not a demagogue. Again, one of Knauf's observations is trenchant:

---

54. Knauf, "From History to Interpretation," 41.

For all its inherent fallacies, its obvious subjectivism, its biased, sometimes myopic selection of the material that is processed, we cannot totally abandon the history of events for the scientific and objective history of processes if we intend to study history as human history and if we maintain that there is some basic difference between humans and wolves.[55]

4. Simplistic as it may sound, the chief requirements for dialogue may be courage and honesty. By "courage," I mean the individual scholar's willingness to put his or her ego up for stakes; to abandon long-cherished positions when necessary; and to acknowledge how and why one's mind has changed. By "honesty," I mean simply citing other scholars accurately, in context, and crediting one's sources fully; not pretending to an expertise one does not possess; resisting the temptation to indulge in personal polemics that stem from a sense of inadequacy, either in oneself or in the evidence at hand; and refusing on principle to distort the evidence or another scholar's view.

The fact that these virtues are demanding and therefore rare (i.e., "scholars are only human") may account for the fact that almost everyone in the academic world hails "inter-disciplinary research," but few undertake it seriously. Can we provide a "case-study," an example of how it *might* work in this instance?

What Can We Know from the
Integrated Study of Texts and Artifacts

I will present many specific case-studies of what I call "convergences" between textual and artifactual evidence in Chapters 4 and 5. Here, however, I will try to show what we can obtain by way of *sure knowledge* from looking at a specific set of data from the two sources. I shall do this, not by artificially "harmonizing" the sources as Thompson charges, but simply by allowing them to speak for themselves insofar as possible.

First, let me take an isolated artifact, a pot not unlike the one of which Knauf says "almost never is it possible to identify the nationality of a cooking pot."[56] In fact, by "reading the artifact as text" in the way outlined above, we can identify much *more* than nationality. Let us exercise our reading skills on a typical mid-8th-century large storejar from southern Palestine, illustrated here. It will speak clearly to us (to be politically correct, "signify") and will answer the

---

55. Knauf, "From History to Interpretation," 47.
56. Knauf, "From History to Interpretation," 39.

Iron II C storage jar
from Tell Beit Mirsim
(Ruth Amiran, *Ancient Pottery
of the Holy Land*)

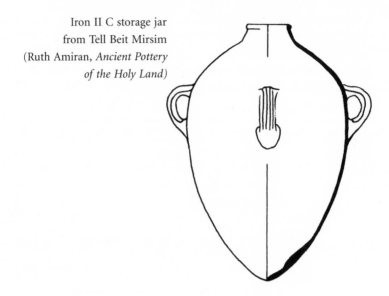

following questions — more, I suspect, if we could frame them properly: What? Where? When? Who? How? and perhaps even Why? These are not mere speculations, but "facts."

(1) In size and shape ("morphological" typology) we can confidently classify this as a "storejar," used for solid or liquid foodstuffs.

(2) It is not only from Lachish, where it was excavated under close control, but from a destruction layer in the inner chambers of the main city gate, its exact context being determined by the fact that it was "sealed" under the debris and thus cannot be considered intrusive here. No site could be more Judean than Lachish, so the storejar's "nationality" is clear, even if it was manufactured elsewhere in Judah and shipped here for use.

(3) The storejar's date ("temporal" typology) can be fixed precisely in the few years just before 701, since the destruction of Level III is correlated beyond reasonable doubt with the well-known campaign of the Neo-Assyrian king Sennacherib. This synchronism is attested by the Assyrian annals, dated by astronomical observations and synchronisms; the Assyrian stone-carved reliefs found at Nineveh, now in the British Museum, showing graphic details of the city of Lachish and its gate; extensive British and Israeli excavations at the site, which have yielded a picture that corresponds to the Assyrian texts and reliefs almost exactly; and, not least, the biblical descriptions in 2 Kgs. 18–20 and 2 Chr. 32, whatever historical value may be assigned to them.

92

(4) The question of who made the jar can be answered, even if only somewhat impersonally, through neutron activation analysis. This can "fingerprint" the source of the clay and thus pinpoint the place of manufacture within reasonable limits, in this case certainly Judah. If this storejar, like hundreds of others nearly identical, happens to bear one of the "royal stamped storejar inscriptions" in Hebrew, we can even narrow the place of manufacture to one of four pottery production centers: Socoh (in Judah), Ziph, Hebron, or *mmšlt* (identification unknown, but plausibly *memšelet,* or Jerusalem).[57]

(5) How the storejar was made ("technological" typology) need not be a mystery, since modern laboratory analysis can reconstruct the clay and temper sources, the wheel and hand techniques used, and even the firing temperature of the kiln. How the storejar was used ("functional" typology) is also easy to ascertain, since its standardized size, large shape, and features such as handles can have been intended only for storing dry or liquid commodities. Indeed, several nearly identical storejars have been found bearing such Hebrew inscriptions as *bat* (a well-known biblical measure, ca. 5 gallons); *yayin,* "wine"; or *šemen,* "oil."[58]

(6) The reason for the manufacture and use of storejars of this unique type throughout Judah is perhaps the most difficult question and had long perplexed archaeologists. As they knew, all too well, "cognitive" typology — the "Why" of things, or what Binford called "paleo-psychology" — is the most elusive category of typological analysis. Yet recently we have undertaken both neutron activation analysis of the clays, and microscopic examination of the marks of the "royal inscriptions" left by what are only a handful of signet rings. Taking the evidence of tightly controlled production, together with the occurrence of only four place-names in Judah in the inscriptions, the fact that the top line of all the inscriptions reads in Hebrew "belonging to the king," i.e., under crown aegis, and finally the well-stratified date of these jars to the very late 8th century, there can be only one reasonable conclusion. These storejars were manufactured under royal supervision (in this case, Hezekiah); certified by official inspectors of size and quality with their signet-rings; and filled with provisions and sent to principal store-cities throughout Judah such as Lachish, intended for the anticipated siege of Sennacherib in 701. If further proof were needed, it comes from the fact that *none* of the "royal stamped jars" have been found outside Judah, for instance in northern Israel, which had already been devastated by the Neo-Assyrian conquests in 735-721. And as proof of royal use of such storejars, similar ones have been found on the ancient Iron Age citadel in Jeru-

57. On the royal stamped jar handles, see H. Darrell Lance, "Stamp, Royal Jar Handle," *ABD* (1992), 6:184-86.

58. See references in Chapter 5, n. 82.

salem, dating to the 8th-7th century and inscribed in Hebrew "belonging to the governor."[59]

Surely 2 Chr. 32:1-8 is pertinent here. This text, although later, details Hezekiah's preparations for the Assyrian siege against "the fortified cities" of Judah, including not only his securing of Jerusalem's water supply (witnessed by the well-known "Hezekiah's water tunnel" and its monumental Hebrew inscription) and his restoration of the city walls and towers (undoubtedly Nahman Avigad's 8th-century "broad wall" in the Old City), but also his appointing "commanders over all the people" and placing them under royal edict.

How would the revisionists react to the remarkable "convergences" in the Lachish archaeological evidence and the textual data? Ahlström has argued that Lachish is not "Lachish," i.e., that the large mound Tell ed-Duweir (the only one anywhere in the vicinity) cannot be positively identified with ancient Lachish. Philip R. Davies has recently entered the fray by claiming that the long, beautifully executed "tunnel inscription" — our best-dated Hebrew inscription, and the fulcrum for paleographic study of all the scripts — really belongs to the period of the Hasmoneans in the early 2nd century B.C. In effect, the inscription is a "forgery" when used as a datum by epigraphers and paleographers. This is so outrageous that in recent publications, and even in popular magazines like the *Biblical Archaeology Review, all* the world's leading specialists in ancient Hebrew scripts have ridiculed Davies.[60]

As for the "eloquent storejar" discussed above, what would the revisionists say of it? Given their own presuppositions (I will not dignify them by the term "methods"), they would be obliged to say, as of texts: the storejar does not

---

59. See Eilat Mazar and Benjamin Mazar, *Excavations in the South of the Temple Mount: The Ophel of Biblical Jerusalem* (Jerusalem: Institute of Archaeology, 1989), 29-48 (the "Royal Building").

60. See references in Chapter 5, n. 12. If it should be argued that the storejar's "nationality" is unknown, the Egyptian Merneptah inscription mentioning "Israel" in central Canaan is sufficient rebuttal. Niels Peter Lemche (*The Israelites in History and Tradition,* 57, 76) mentions the existence of the Merneptah inscription twice, but acknowledges only that it may refer to "unsettled or discontented demographic elements in the central highlands of Palestine." Thompson (*The Mythic Past,* 78-81) makes the incredible claim that the mention of an "Israel" in the inscription "is hardly the same as evidence for the historical existence of the Israel of the Bible" (79). He argues that the term "Israel" refers to a "metaphorical parent" of a town in Canaan destroyed by the Egyptians (81). The leading Egyptologists I have consulted say that this is ludicrous. For a devastating critique of *The Mythic Past* by a fellow member of the European Seminar on Methodology in Israel's History, a generally revisionist group, see Lester L. Grabbe, "Hat die Bibel doch Recht? A Review of T. L. Thompson's *The Bible in History* [British title of Thompson's book]," *SJOT* 14 (2000): 117-39. Thompson's rejoinder (140-61) gives the best insight yet into his tortured reasoning.

have any concrete "existence," except as part of an extinct system; we do not know who "produced" it; there is no objective, discernible "intent" or "meaning" here; it could have had any number of meanings, since symbols (like this) are "indefinite" and "unbounded"; the storejar is, if anything, a "statement about power and social constructs"; in any case, it "communicates" nothing except whatever the viewer/reader perceives; it can and should be manipulated for our own modern purposes. The revisionists' approach, applied to nearly identical "material culture texts," or artifacts, is so absurd that the archaeologist scarcely needs to refute it.

CHAPTER 4

Getting at the "History behind the History": What Convergences between Texts and Artifacts Tell Us about Israelite Origins and the Rise of the State

The central proposition of this book is very simple. While the Hebrew Bible in its present, heavily edited form cannot be taken at face value as history in the modern sense, it nevertheless *contains* much history. Obviously most such "facts of history" lie embedded in many kinds of quasi-historical narratives, where the overriding theological framework of the writers and editors of the Hebrew Bible will tend to obscure them to all but the most critical and discerning eye. The historian must patiently dig out these nuggets of truth, a task that should never be underestimated but in my judgment is possible. That is the exact opposite of the approach of the "revisionists," who as we have seen declare that "the Hebrew Bible is not about history at all," i.e., it is mere propaganda. For them, if *some* of the Bible's stories are unhistorical, they *all* are — a rather simplistic notion.

It is not fashionable in these "postmodern" times to be a "positivist," to assert that history can be understood and can have meaning. Thus in what follows I must defend my modest but nevertheless optimistic proposal to use some portions of the Hebrew Bible as a possible source for history-writing.

Prolegomenon: Which Books?

Let me begin by clarifying which books of the Hebrew Bible I think can be utilized by the would-be historian, whether textual scholar or archaeologist. With most scholars, I would exclude much of the Pentateuch, specifically the books of Genesis, Exodus, Leviticus, and Numbers. These materials obviously constitute a sort of "pre-history" that has been attached to the main epic of ancient Israel by late editors. All this may be distilled from long oral traditions, and I suspect that some of the stories — such as parts of the Patriarchal narratives — may once have had a real historical setting. These traditions, however, are overlaid with legendary and even fantastic materials that the modern reader may enjoy as "story," but which can scarcely be taken seriously as history. For instance, no archaeologist would go looking for the Garden of Eden (even though it might make a good movie thriller). The story is really about Mankind (Heb. *'ādām*, "man") and the Mother of all living things (*ḥawwâ*, "life-giver") in an earthly Paradise (*gān 'ēden*) — in short, an idyllic and profoundly *true* story about the fact that when any man and any woman find each other, in love as it should be, there is Paradise. Eden is not a place on any map, but a state of mind.[1]

Or take the Patriarchal narratives. After a century of exhaustive investigation, all respectable archaeologists have given up hope of recovering any context that would make Abraham, Isaac, or Jacob credible "historical figures." Virtually the last archaeological word was written by me more than 20 years ago for a basic handbook of biblical studies, *Israelite and Judean History*.[2] And, as we have

---

1. No scholar, revisionist or otherwise, thinks these materials anything other than "myth." But even myths can have *meanings* that are in some sense historical, i.e., reveal an actual setting of the authors in time, place, and mentality. For a perceptive re-reading of the creation story, see Carol Meyers, *Discovering Eve: Ancient Israelite Women in Context* (New York: Oxford University Press, 1988). For the Pentateuchal literature as a whole, see Douglas A. Knight, "The Pentateuch," in Douglas A. Knight and Gene Tucker, *The Hebrew Bible and Its Modern Interpreters*, 263-296. See also several essays in *The Pentateuch: A Sheffield Reader*, ed. John W. Rogerson (Sheffield: Sheffield Academic, 1996).

2. "The Patriarchal Traditions" in *Israelite and Judean History*, ed. John H. Hayes and J. Maxwell Miller (Philadelphia: Westminster, 1977), 70-120. For one of the few updates, by a biblical scholar, see Ronald S. Hendel, "The Patriarchal Age: Abraham, Isaac and Jacob," in *Ancient Israel: A Short History from Abraham to the Roman Destruction of the Temple*, ed. Hershel Shanks, rev. ed. (Washington: Biblical Archaeology Society, 1999), 1-29. There are a few sporadic attempts of more conservative scholars to "save" the Patriarchal narratives as history, such as Kenneth A. Kitchen, "The Patriarchal Age: Myth or History?" *BAR* 21/2 (1995): 48-57, 88-95. By and large, however, the minimalist view of Thompson's pioneering work, *The Historicity of the Patriarchal Narratives*, prevails. Thompson claims that I had earlier advocated the historicity of the patriarchs, placing them in the Early Bronze IV period, ca. 2300-2000, but that it was he who overturned this notorious use of "biblical archaeology"; cf., among other references, Thomas L. Thompson, "Historiography of Ancient Palestine," in Volkmar Fritz and Philip R. Davies, *The Origins of the Israelite States*, 26-30. The fact is that I have never situated the biblical patriarchs in any archaeological period, quoting and essentially agreeing with Thompson from the beginning; cf. my "Patriarchal Traditions."

seen, archaeological investigation of Moses and the Exodus has similarly been discarded as a fruitless pursuit. Indeed, the overwhelming archaeological evidence today of largely indigenous origins for early Israel leaves no room for an exodus from Egypt or a 40-year pilgrimage through the Sinai wilderness. A Moses-like figure may have existed somewhere in southern Transjordan in the mid-late 13th century B.C., where many scholars think the biblical traditions concerning the god Yahweh arose. But archaeology can do nothing to confirm such a figure as a historical personage, much less prove that he was the founder of later Israelite religion.[3] As for Leviticus and Numbers, these are clearly additions to the "pre-history" by very late Priestly editorial hands, preoccupied with notions of ritual purity, themes of the "promised land," and other literary motifs that most modern readers will scarcely find edifying, much less historical.

Much of what is called in the English Bible "poetry," "wisdom," and "devotional literature" must also be eliminated from historical consideration. That would include books such as Psalms, an anthology of prayers and hymns for liturgical use, which come from many periods; Proverbs and Ecclesiastes, collections of wisdom-sayings, some quite late and others reflecting much non-Israelite influence; Ruth, Esther, Job, and Daniel, historical novellae with contrived "real-life settings," the latter dating as late as the 2nd century B.C. and reflecting the crisis of the Hasmonean Wars; the Song of Songs (or Solomon), a cycle of erotic Oriental love-songs that finally made it into the Bible only because both Jewish and Christian commentators "spiritualized" it; and a number of the late, "Minor Prophets," which the literary tradition itself places last and does not regard as very influential. The outline thus far omits 1-2 Chronicles, which are clearly dependent on 1-2 Kings but may have, despite many scholars, some independent traditions of occasional historical value. Of the Prophetic books we shall speak directly.[4]

---

3. Cf. William G. Dever, "Is There Any Archaeological Evidence for the Exodus?" in *Exodus: The Egyptian Evidence,* ed. Ernest S. Frerichs and Leonard H. Lesko (Winona Lake: Eisenbrauns, 1997), 67-86. On Moses as the putative "founder of Israelite religion," see, e.g., Susan Niditch, *Ancient Israelite Religion* (New York: Oxford University Press, 1997), which barely mentions the possibility of a historical Moses (cf. 7, 8, 28, 37, 38, etc.). See further P. Kyle McCarter, "The Origins of Israelite Religion," in *The Rise of Ancient Israel,* ed. Hershel Shanks (Washington: Biblical Archaeology Society, 1992), 119-36. The "indigenous origins" theory advanced below renders the question of a Moses (and Israel) in Egypt largely irrelevant. On the other hand, see the more positive view of Baruch Halpern, "The Exodus from Egypt: Myth or Reality?" in Shanks, *The Rise of Ancient Israel,* 87-113.

4. For orientation to the prophetic literature, see *The Place Is Too Small for Us: The Israelite Prophets in Recent Scholarship,* ed. Robert P. Gordon (Winona Lake: Eisenbrauns, 1995).

Most scholars regard the "epic history" of monarchical Israel and the preceding formative period ("Judges") as contained primarily in what is called the "Deuteronomistic history" (Dtr). This is a composite work, stretching from Deuteronomy through Samuel and Kings. It incorporates older sources, but is woven together with great literary sophistication into a sweeping national epic that purports to chart Israel's history from its earliest emergence in Canaan (i.e., in the 12th century as we now know) to the fall of Jerusalem and the beginning of the Exile (the early 6th century).

This literary corpus, the Deuteronomistic history, can be distinguished in its present form by unifying themes that characterize the first portion, the book of Deuteronomy (or the "Second Law," of Moses). Indeed according to both an inner biblical tradition and much of the opinion of modern scholarship, the core of the entire Deuteronomistic history is a literary work that stems from a circle of religious reformers in the days of Josiah, in the late 7th century. This "long-lost lawbook" is reported in 2 Kgs. 22:8-20 to have been found by accident by the high priest Hilkiah in the Jerusalem temple, then read to the king, after which it became the basis for a sweeping national reform. One suspects, of course, that radical members of what became the Deuteronomistic "school" compiled the core of Deuteronomy themselves, put it in the mouth of the legendary Moses for obvious reasons, then hid it in the temple where it would be dramatically discovered. Thus it would appear to be a miraculous "new" Word from Yahweh, a "second chance" for Israel to repent and save itself on the eve of the Neo-Babylonian advance. In short, the Deuteronomistic history as a composite literary work is largely "propaganda," designed to give theological legitimacy to a party of nationalist ultra-orthodox reformers, what has been called (along with the prophetic reform movements of the time) a "Yahweh alone" party.[5]

This brief sketch of the Deuteronomistic history represents the consensus of mainstream biblical scholarship since about the 1930s. There remain, however, several problems. (1) First is the date of Dtr's composition. It cannot be earlier than the time of Josiah (ca. 640-609), but biblical scholars remain divided beyond that. Some think Dtr is a unified work of the preexilic period; others see a preexilic core (Dtr1), much edited and supplemented by postexilic

---

5. The literature on the Deuteronomistic history is vast; but for orientation, see Gary Knoppers and J. Gordon McConville, eds., *Reconsidering Israel and Judah: Recent Studies on the Deuteronomistic History* (Winona Lake: Eisenbrauns, 2000); and on Deuteronomistic theology, cf. Andrew D. H. Mayes, "Deuteronomistic Ideology and the Theology of the Old Testament," *JSOT* 82 (1999): 57-82. See also Bernhard Lang, *Monotheism and the Prophetic Minority: An Essay in Biblical History and Sociology* (Sheffield: Almond, 1983).

writers in the Persian period (Dtr2); and more radical scholars, like the revisionists, date the entire work, unified or not, well down into the Hellenistic period (Philip R. Davies) or even the Roman period (Thomas L. Thompson).

(2) The answer to a second question obviously depends upon the answer to the first: How reliable is the Deuteronomistic "history," given its overarching theological agenda, complex literary composition, and uncertain date? Here we must underline how crucial the second question is, for the Deuteronomistic corpus contains not just the "core themes" attributed to Moses. The work as a whole comprises the *entire* "epic history" of Israel mentioned above, that is, it contains not only whatever basic document the Deuteronomists produced, but also presumably a radically edited and reworked version of earlier literary works, most of them lost to us. Dtr claims to be a story not only of late "Mosaic" reforms, but of Israel's entire history; it is "theocratic history" on a grand scale.[6]

At the heart of the Deuteronomistic history lies the connected narrative in 1-2 Kings, beginning with David's death and continuing the story until the fall of Jerusalem some 350 years later. It is 1-2 Kings, therefore, that will provide the best test-case for our attempt to mine "historical nuggets" from biblical texts. For that reason, Kings continues to fascinate scholars, as shown, for example, by an excellent recent attempt to grapple with the work by Steven L. McKenzie, *The Trouble with Kings: The Composition of the Book of Kings in the Deuteronomistic History.*[7]

McKenzie brings up another matter related to the date and composition of Kings, namely the question of whether there may have been later *prophetic* additions to the work, such as the Elisha-Elijah cycle (which McKenzie takes to be largely unhistorical). We shall look at some of the prophetic materials for ourselves, because I am convinced that however much they may have been edited or even composed largely by later (postexilic) "schools" bearing the prophets' names, they reflect a real historical setting, in some cases much earlier and certainly going back to the Iron Age. To be more specific, much of the material in the great prophetic books reflects Israelite "daily life," even if unintentionally and incidental to the theological message. Furthermore, I shall show that many aspects of this picture of daily life do not fit at all in the Persian period, much less the Hellenistic-Roman era. They fit in, and *only* in, the Iron II period (ca.

---

6. Among other "lost works" specifically mentioned are the Book of Jasher, the Age of Solomon, and the Chronicles of the Kings of Israel and Judah. Cf. n. 47 below.

7. VTSup 42 (Leiden: Brill, 1991). See also Iain W. Provan, *1 and 2 Kings*. Old Testament Guides 11 (Sheffield: Sheffield Academic, 1997); Knoppers and McConville, *Reconsidering Israel and Judah*.

1000-600) and therefore must have originated in a *real* history of a real, not fictional, "Israel." Such a proposition goes completely counter to that of the revisionists, who assume that the biblical writers knew very little if any real history. This allowed their imaginations a free reign in literary composition, or even resulted in complete fabrications; the Hebrew Bible overall is for them "pious fiction," in effect a literary hoax. It is precisely that assertion that I intend to challenge and refute, using archaeological data.

Sitze im Leben: The Search for a "Real-life Setting"

Modern literary-critical study of the Hebrew Bible beginning in the late 19th century isolated not only the "D school" (Dtr here), but also other blocks of literary material or "sources" that were thought to trace back to other anonymous groups of composers. These included the "J school," so-called because of its preference for the name Yahweh (*Jahve* in German) for God, thought to have originated in the 10th-9th century B.C., perhaps in the south. The "E school," by contrast, used the Hebrew name Elohim for God; it was dated to the 9th-8th century and seen as reflecting northern concerns. The J and E strands of the literary tradition constituted the bulk of the Pentateuch, or Genesis through Deuteronomy (now, as we have seen, better ended with Numbers). It was theorized that the J and E materials, perhaps containing much older traditions, were at some point combined and intricately interwoven. This would explain the doublets, contradictions, anachronisms, etc., which scholars had long since noted in the Pentateuch. This process of amalgamation and editing that produced the Pentateuch in its present form was attributed to a "P" or "Priestly school" that flourished principally in the postexilic period, when most would agree that the work we know as the Hebrew Bible was actually compiled (although, as I shall argue, not entirely composed or written). The isolation of these four "sources" — J, E, D, and P — was the lasting contribution of "higher criticism," or the "documentary hypothesis" of biblical scholarship. Although the basic theory of such separate "sources" has been attacked again and again, and has been much revised, it remains in broad outline the basis of all modern literary critical and historical study of the Hebrew Bible.[8]

---

8. Again, the literature is extensive. For general orientation, see several of the essays in Knight and Tucker, *The Hebrew Bible and Its Modern Interpreters;* and update by reference to the excellent essays in Steven L. McKenzie and Stephen R. Haynes, *To Each Its Own Meaning* (Louisville: Westminister John Knox, 1993). What was sometimes called "literary criticism" is now usually called "source criticism"; for the more recent (since ca. 1970)

The latter, the *historical* concern, must be kept in mind in this era of purely "literary" approaches. It must be recalled that "higher criticism," in contrast to "lower criticism" or the attempt to establish a correct Hebrew *text,* had as its ultimate goal *historical exegesis,* that is, an accurate reading in an original context that if correct would produce "truth," if not in the theological then at least in the historical sense. The goal of modern criticism became, and still is in most circles, the establishment of a reliable Hebrew text, corrected of errors as far as possible by philological and literary analysis; the recovery of the date, authorship, and historical circumstances of individual books and units within them; detailed exegesis or interpretation of the whole text, so as to render its historical meaning and significance; and, in the case of much Protestant scholarship, the systematic formulation of the overall religious ideas of the texts when finally understood, or a historical "biblical theology," valid precisely because it could be *shown* to be "historical" despite, or because of, modern "critical" scholarship. The whole modern literary-critical approach was thus "positivist" indeed, and many "postmodern" scholars have come to question it or even to reject it precisely because of its over-confidence, as well as its authoritarian stance. Yet the current attack on "historicism" too easily loses sight of what I as an archaeologist regard as an essential, critical dimension of all ancient textual studies: history.

One particular aspect of the modern critical study of the Hebrew Bible was "form criticism," pioneered by the great German scholar Hermann Gunkel, developed in books like *The Folktale in the Old Testament* (German original 1917) and first in his Genesis commentary (1901). Both form criticism and later "redaction criticism" (the analysis of the way the literary tradition was finally edited) sought to comprehend biblical texts and to explain how they were collected, transmitted, and finally edited into larger literary compositions by first isolating *individual* units. These could then be characterized — whether as myth, legend, saga, folktale, or the like — by tracing them back to a specific *Sitz im Leben* (lit., "life-setting") that might explain their origin and durability, first in oral and then finally in written traditions. Form criticism developed its attractions at the very time when Semitic philology, ethnography, the study of comparative religion, and especially archaeology were beginning to broaden our knowledge of the long-lost ancient Oriental setting of the Bible in exotic and often dramatic ways.[9]

The basic notion of recovering a *Sitz im Leben,* or *context,* for the biblical

---

school of "literary criticism," see the essays in Paul R. House, ed., *Beyond Form Criticism: Essays in Old Testament Literary Criticism* (Winona Lake: Eisenbrauns, 1992). For the still newer "social sciences" approach, see Charles E. Carter and Carol Meyers, *Community, Identity, and Ideology.*

9. See references in nn. 1, 5, 7 above, and n. 10 below.

texts is particularly congenial to archaeologists, because that is precisely what we had thought we were doing all along. The more recent "contextual archaeology" of Ian Hodder and others (Chapter 3) simply reinforces the basic understanding of archaeology's potential contribution to history and to history-writing that underlies all of my argument here. Yet even archaeologists of the older "biblical" persuasion have seldom juxtaposed *archaeological* context and the *Sitz im Leben* of textual scholars in just this way — probably because of the characteristic isolation of our two disciplines that we noted above.

For all the importance of context as sought by biblical scholars, in practice the search produced little more than a *Sitz in Literatur* — a "setting" that reflected much more the history of the *literature* and its transmission than of "real life" or history in the usual sense. To be sure, a few biblical scholars have sensed this deficiency. Rolf Knierim's incisive critique of recent literary criticism of the Hebrew Bible points out:

> For form criticism, the societal settings behind the texts are assumed to be the decisive generative forces for the emergence of generic texts. This assumption, however, has always meant that a comprehensive sociological picture of Israel's history is indispensable for form-critical work. The only problem is that we have never had such a comprehensive picture.[10]

Knierim goes on to decry "dubious reconstruction of settings via dubiously identified text patterns" — which I would characterize simply as a classic circular argument. He concludes:

> A new direction would evolve, however, if the sociological study of Israel's history and the study of the genres of the OT literature, each in its own right, would be programmatically correlated. Of such a programmatic correlation we have at best embryonic indications but neither a program nor an execution.[11]

Exactly; but how about including in that program *archaeology* — the only source of information on society independent of the Hebrew Bible. Indeed, I would argue, archaeology is our best source for a *real* "sociology of biblical Israel."

Thompson has also addressed this point, although obliquely, in observing that the postexilic "setting" usually delineated for the final redaction and com-

---

10. Rolf Knierim, "Criticism of Literary Features, Form, Tradition, and Redaction," in Knight and Tucker, *The Hebrew Bible and Its Modern Interpreters*, 144.

11. Knierim, 144. For attempts at a "sociology of ancient Israel," see Carter and Meyers, *Community, Identity, and Ideology;* and add the pioneering work of Paula McNutt, *Reconstructing the Society of Ancient Israel*, discussed in Chapter 2.

position of the Hebrew Bible as a whole is the work of what he terms only "a handful of tradents." "One ought not to assume, however, that such *Sitze im Leben* lie in *Leben des Volkes* ['life of the people']. Rather we are dealing with scholarly bibliophiles."[12] I would say simply that we are dealing with *literature* — a literary rather than a "real-life" setting. The essential point that many philologians (and theologians) seem to overlook is that literature does not necessarily mirror real life, at least not the life of the masses, but only of the *literati*. As noted above, the biblical texts reflect the creative, literary imagination of a very few of the elite classes. In ancient Israel, pre- and postexilic, these classes constituted a mere handful of priests, intellectuals sometimes attached to the court, writing prophets, and probably scribes. *These* were the people who wrote the Bible, for others like themselves.[13] And while they could write "disinterested" history or include details on ordinary day-to-day activities when they chose to do so, the fact is that they were simply not interested in what the vast majority of people in ancient Israel thought or did. Only archaeology, as Fernand Braudel and some *annales* historians argue, "can give history back to the people."[14] Or, to use biblical language, archaeology gives back to those anonymous folk "who sleep in the dust" (Dan. 12:2) their authentic, long-lost voice.

Perhaps the point is simply: Who *makes* history? And who *writes* it? Which count more, the principal actors, countless individuals over the slow-moving millennia, as with Braudel; or those few who rationalize events, who are often makers of myth more than of history? If "history is written by the winners," what constitutes "winning"? While I have argued here that there is much more genuine historical information in the biblical texts than supposed by many nowadays (especially if we read skillfully "between the lines"), the fact is that we are nevertheless almost totally dependent upon *archaeological* data for most of what we shall ever know, about most of the people of ancient Israel, most of the time.

"Life-setting" and Historical Method

Thus far I have been optimistic about the potential of archaeology for reconstructing a "life-setting" for some biblical texts, thereby offering independent

12. Thomas L. Thompson, *Early History of the Israelite People*, 392.

13. See Richard E. Friedman, *Who Wrote the Bible?*

14. Cf. John Bintliff, *The Annales School and Archaeology* (Leicester: Leicester University Press, 1991). For an anthropological perspective, see George E. Marcus and Michael M. J. Fischer, *Anthropology as Cultural Critique: An Experimental Moment in the Human Sciences* (Chicago: University of Chicago Press, 1986), 95-108.

corroboration of the likelihood that they preserve genuinely historical memory and information. Not only will there thus be a promising "convergence" of textual and artifactual evidence, but we will be able to offer in place of the revisionists' presupposition that texts "just mysteriously happen" a *coherent theory of literary production.* Obvious as this proposal of using archaeology as a tool in textual criticism may be, it is a novelty. Such a method has never been suggested before, much less carried through in practice, either by biblical scholars or by Syro-Palestinian archaeologists. Of course one may object at this point that seeking such "convergences" was just what the now-discredited older "biblical archaeology" sought to do.[15] The critical difference between that and what I propose here has to do with the independent but parallel investigation of the two sources of data for history-writing, and the subsequent critical dialogue between them that scholars must undertake. But we must address the methodological issues further before proceeding with our case-studies; in short, we must set forth a historiographical prolegomenon.

I offer the following as a *résumé* of common-sense, widely accepted rules for establishing the "facts" upon the basis of which history-writing can proceed fruitfully, whether these are textual facts or artifacts. (I would welcome similar methodological clarification from the revisionists before they proceed with more nonhistories of ancient Israel.) If the language sounds a bit like that of the courtroom, that may be an appropriate metaphor.[16]

---

15. Indeed, Thompson and others of the revisionists have reacted to my earlier suggestions along these lines by dismissing all this as "harmonization of the Bible and archaeology," as "credulism," or even "thinly disguised Fundamentalism" — in short, an "improper method"; Thompson, *JBL* 114 (1995): 695-96; "Historiography of Ancient Palestine," *passim.*

16. The literature on historiography and the Hebrew Bible/ancient Israel is vast. But among the works I have found most useful are Baruch Halpern, *The First Historians;* Ernest Axel Knauf, "From History to Interpretation," in Diana V. Edelman, *The Fabric of History,* 26-64; J. Maxwell Miller, "Reading the Bible Historically: The Historian's Approach," in Steven L. McKenzie and Stephen R. Haynes, *To Each Its Own Meaning,* 11-28; Marc Z. Brettler, *The Creation of History in Ancient Israel* (London: Routledge, 1995); Hans M. Barstad, "History and the Hebrew Bible," in Lester L. Grabbe, *Can a "History of Israel" Be Written?,* 37-64; Lester L. Grabbe, "Are Historians of Ancient Palestine Fellow Creatures — or Different Animals?" in *Can a "History of Israel" Be Written?,* 19-36. None of these scholars, however, uses my "courtroom" metaphor. On the perhaps related issue of "faith and history," see Barstad and Grabbe. By contrast, Thompson's theological naïveté is embarrassing; in *The Mythic Past* he cavalierly dismisses the entire issue, remarking that "the Old Testament is no longer believable and offers really no difficulty to theology" (386). His 100-page treatment of the Bible's "theological and intellectual world" is a tortured excursus in New Age theology (293-397). For essays on the "faith and history" theme from a

(1) A text or an archaeological artifact requires an external referent, an *independent witness,* to corroborate it before it can become valid testimony.

(2) In the case of the Hebrew Bible, the only possible external witness will have to come from archaeology, either in the form of artifacts and ecofacts that it recovers or in extrabiblical textual evidence.

(3) The essential, indeed the only, correct method is to "interrogate" each witness separately; to use the same or closely similar interpretive methods in "reading" the evidence, agreed upon by both textual and material culture specialists; to establish the pertinent "facts" as such, critically and selectively; and to compare the various sources of information and the facts derived from them so as to arrive at a synthesis that summarizes what is known or claimed to be known. If such a synthesis is undertaken before the independent comparison, it constitutes a presupposition, not a conclusion; and the argument will be unpersuasive because it is circular.

(4) While "objectivity" in historical investigation is clearly impossible, as all responsible scholars have long acknowledged (the revisionists hardly invented that observation), objectivity must be earnestly attempted, if only to keep the inquiry as honest and open as possible, or "disinterested" in the proper sense. Otherwise the investigation becomes a farce (as, for instance, Fundamentalist "scholarship" often is).

(5) Whenever the two sources or "witnesses" happen to converge in their testimony, a historical "datum" (or given) may be said to have been established beyond reasonable doubt. To ignore or to deny the implications of such convergent testimony is irresponsible scholarship, since it impeaches the testimony of one witness without reasonable cause by suppressing other vital evidence. Cases based on suborning the key witness should be thrown out of court.

(6) The historian is the final arbiter, or judge, of what is to be taken as "historically true," even if some cases remain circumstantial for lack of sufficient direct evidence.

(7) Historical "proof" in the scientific sense is rarely available in historical reconstruction, because the objects themselves are "subjective"; human nature and behavior are not "lawlike" except in trivial ways, and thus they are not predictable, as for instance the behavior of particles might be in physics; there are too many unknown variables in trying to determine historical "causation"; even if there were "laws of the historical process," the experiments needed to

---

conservative, often evangelical viewpoint, see *Faith, Tradition, and History: Old Testament Historiography in Its Near Eastern Context,* ed. Alan R. Millard, James K. Hoffmeier, and David W. Baker (Winona Lake: Eisenbrauns, 1994), especially the essays by Millard and Edwin Yamauchi. See also Chapter 2, n. 44.

demonstrate them are impossible or unrepeatable; thus neither confirmation nor falsification is possible.

(8) Finally, the historian must work often with "the balance of probability." This may not offer ultimate proof of what happened in history; but to overturn that would require a more *likely* scenario, replete with new and superior independent witnesses. In the absence of that, skepticism is not warranted, and indeed is suspect. The skeptic may remain a "hostile witness," but such a witness is overruled, and the case may be considered sufficiently established by all reasonable historical requirements.

(9) The final jury and court of appeal are the broader community of peers, where consensus may prevail. In the case of textual and archaeological evidence bearing on Israel's ancient history, this community will be made up of mainstream scholars as well as the educated public. This is not "doing history by vote," as Thompson charges, much less "marketing" idiosyncratic interpretations of texts, as some New Literary critics maintain as the test of truth.[17] It is, rather, a matter of seeking broad consensus — which would be a refreshing antidote to the rabble-rousing tactics of the revisionists. If mine be dismissed as "middle-of-the-road" scholarship, so be it: that is where most often the truth is likely to be found.

Some "Case-studies": Israelite Ethnicity

In refuting some of the basic assumptions of the revisionists above, I have already anticipated one test-case, namely the question of whether we can recognize in the archaeological record an "early Israel," in the sense of an ethnic group that was different from its contemporaries. The revisionists uniformly say "no," so there is no "early Israel." Building on the summary of the extensive archaeological data presented there, as well as the introduction of ethnographic and anthropological understandings of "ethnicity," let us now compare or contrast these data with the biblical/textual data, first looking at the two sources independently.[18]

17. Thomas L. Thompson, "Defining History and Ethnicity"; "Historiography of Ancient Palestine," 32: my "history by committee." Perhaps what really bothers Thompson is that he is not on the committee, since elsewhere he complains that this is "a form of Harvard censorship." On New Literary Criticism, see Chapter 1, esp. nn. 17-19.

18. This approach is hardly that ascribed to me by Thompson, who writes of my "search for harmonistic scenarios with which to wed [one's] own hardly independently derived phantasms" ("Historiography of Ancient Palestine," 37); "archaeology and history (i.e., Biblical) were for him a single discipline" (28).

Principal Iron Age sites in Israel and Transjordan

Plan of 12th-century Israelite village at Ai
(Aharon Kempinski and Ronny Reich, *The
Architecture of Ancient Israel*)

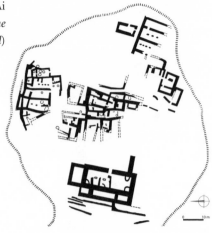

Since the early 1980s, Israeli and American archaeologists have been developing what might be called a "symbiosis" model of Israelite origins. Extensive surface surveys of the Israeli-occupied West Bank carried out by several teams of Israeli archaeologists, together with excavation in depth at a few sites, have revealed that in the heartland of ancient Israel about 300 small agricultural villages were founded *de novo* in the late 13th-12th centuries. They are quite small, a few acres at most, often situated on hilltops adjacent to arable land and good springs, almost always unwalled and without defenses of any kind. These villages are located principally in the central hill country, stretching all the way from the hills of lower Galilee as far south as the northern Negev around Beersheba. None are founded on the ruins of a destroyed Late Bronze Age site; indeed, the sites chosen for occupation in early Iron I are nearly all in areas conspicuously devoid of Canaanite urban centers. They are situated on the marginal hill-country frontier that had previously been only sparsely occupied. The dispersed pattern of settlement and the overwhelming predominance of small villages point to a distinctive nonurban society and economy, undoubtedly agrarian. Population estimates, based on well-developed ethnographic parallels and site size, indicate a central hill-country population of only about 12 thousand at the end of the Late Bronze Age (13th century), which then grew rapidly to about 55 thousand by the 12th century, then to about 75 thousand by the 11th century. Such a dramatic "population explosion" simply cannot be accounted for by natural increase alone, much less by positing small groups of pastoral nomads settling down. Large numbers of people migrated here from somewhere else, strongly motivated to colonize an underpopulated fringe area of urban Canaan, now in decline at the end of the Late Bronze Age.

Pillared courtyard house at Khirbet Raddana, 12th century
(Photo by William G. Dever)

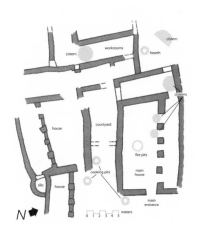

Plan of the major house complex at
Khirbet Raddana (Joint Expedition to Ai)

The villages that have been excavated are characterized by U-shaped courtyard houses (the so-called "four-room houses"), clustered in groups of two to four, often sharing common walls. The houses have room for animal shelter and storage of provisions on the first floor and ample space for a large extended family on the second floor. These distinctive houses have virtually no precedents in Canaan, but they would be ideal farmhouses. Indeed, almost identical houses are still found all around the eastern Mediterranean in rural areas. No monumental or "elite" structures of any kind have been found in any of these Iron I villages, only clusters of courtyard houses, up to a half dozen or so. Harvard's Lawrence Stager has demonstrated that this unique house form and overall layout of these hill-country villages correspond closely with many narratives of daily life in the period of the Judges in the books of Joshua, Judges, and Samuel, reflecting no doubt a close-knit family and clan structure and an agrarian lifestyle.[19] In Stager's view the single-courtyard house represents the nuclear family dwelling; and the cluster of several such houses would then be the residence of the extended, or multi-generation family equivalent to the biblical *bêt-'āb,* or "house of the father."

I myself have compared this socio-economic structure to the "domestic mode of production," which anthropologist Marshall D. Sahlins has described as "in effect the tribal economy in miniature, so politically it underwrites the condition of primitive society — society without a sovereign."[20] This would seem to be an apt description of both early Israel as described in the Bible and the hill-country archaeological assemblage.

A number of new or more efficiently developed technologies also appear in the hill country at almost the same time — these include, for example, intensive hillside terracing, best suited for small-scale subsistence farming, especially horticulture and viticulture, but also adaptable for cereal production in the small intermountain valleys, and even for herding of animals on many of the drier slopes. Also, plastered cisterns cut into the bedrock are found in many of

19. The literature on Israelite origins has burgeoned in the past decade, too much so to document the following in detail. See, however, with full bibliography, Israel Finkelstein, *The Archaeology of the Israelite Settlement* (Jerusalem: Israel Exploration Society, 1988); Finkelstein and Nadav Na'aman, eds., *From Nomadism to Monarchy: Archaeological and Historical Aspects of Early Israel* (Washington: Biblical Archaeology Society, 1994); William G. Dever, "Unresolved Issues in the Early History of Israel"; "How to Tell a Canaanite from an Israelite," in Shanks, *The Rise of Ancient Israel,* 27-56; "Ceramics, Ethnicity, and the Question of Israel's Origins," *BA* 58 (1995): 200-13; "The Identity of Early Israel: A Rejoinder to Keith W. Whitelam," *JSOT* 72 (1996): 3-24; Shmuel Ahituv and Eliezer D. Oren, eds., *The Origin of Early Israel — Current Debate: Biblical, Historical and Archaeological Perspectives* (Beersheba: Ben-Gurion University Press, 1998); Lawrence E. Stager, "Forging an Identity: The Emergence of Ancient Israel," in Michael D. Coogan, *The Oxford History of the Biblical World,* 123-75. For an overview for nonspecialists, see John J. McDermott, *What Are They Saying about the Formation of Israel?* (New York: Paulist, 1998). The article of Stager referred to here is "The Archaeology of the Family in Ancient Israel," *BASOR* 260 (1985): 1-35.

20. Marshall D. Sahlins, *Stone Age Economics* (Chicago: Aldine, 1972), 95.

the houses. Stone-lined silos for grain storage are still another new feature. These are all relatively rare in preceding periods.

Bronze and flint implements continued in use at this time; but iron, a new technology, appears sporadically, although only in the form of utilitarian objects such as picks or plowpoints. Pottery forms continued generally in the degenerate LB tradition, but wares are now often partly handmade rather than made on a fast wheel.

Nearly all of the traits indicate that the village economy was based on mixed agro-pastoralism, dry farming of cereals, and localized exchange of agricultural surpluses and other products (as well as labor). Large multi-generational families would have been the mainstay and focus of such an economy, the "domestic mode of production" noted above.

Similar agrarian lifestyles have characterized ancient Palestine in the rural areas in many periods, even in the mid-20th century A.D. But one aspect of what archaeologists are now distinguishing as "food systems" is unique: the consistent absence of pig bones in excavated remains. Pork was relatively common in Bronze Age sites, pigs being well adapted to many areas. The statistical rarity of pig bones in Iron I hill-country sites — often absent altogether or comprising only a fraction of a percent — may be an "ethnic marker." In this case, it would be one consistent with later biblical data regarding the prohibition of pork in Israelite society, probably to be understood as a criterion distinguishing "Israelites" from "Canaanites." The presence or absence of pig bones may thus be our best archaeological indicator of the much-debated "ethnic boundaries" and their physical extent.[21] I suspect, however, that many other valid indicators will eventually be discovered.

Politically, there appears to be no central authority, although the inhabitants do seem to be in the process of defining themselves as an ethnic group. Needless to say, this accords well with the statement in Judges: "In those days there was no king in Israel, and every man did what was right in his own eyes" (Judg. 17:6; 21:25).

Religiously, there is a complete absence of temples, sanctuaries, or shrines of any type in these Iron I hill-country villages — in sharp contrast to the proliferation of temples in the preceding Late Bronze Age in Palestine. Currently, we have only one Iron I cult installation of any sort, a small isolated open-air hilltop shrine in the Samaria hills, featuring a low temenos wall, an altarlike platform, and a large standing stone (the biblical *mạṣṣēbā*). A few Iron I pottery

---

21. See Brian Hesse and Paula Wapnish, "Can Pig Remains Be Used for Ethnic Diagnosis in the Ancient Near East?" in Neil A. Silberman and David B. Small, *The Archaeology of Israel*, 238-70.

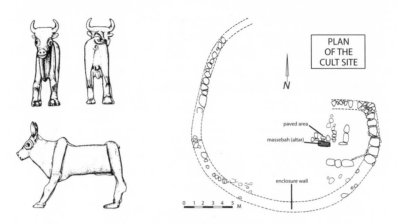

The "Bull Site," 12th century (The Hazor Archaeological Expedition)

sherds, pieces of a terra-cotta cult-stand, some iron fragments, and a well-preserved bronze bull figurine suggest connections with the old Canaanite cult of the male deity El, whose principal epithet was "Bull El." El remained one of the two names of the Israelite national god in many of the early biblical texts, associated particularly with "the god of the fathers." Another putative early Israelite shrine has been found atop Mt. Ebal, the Shechem area; but most authorities regard this installation as an isolated farmhouse or fort.

Otherwise, we have no clear archaeological evidence of Israelite religion and cult before the monarchy in the 10th-9th centuries. The absence of more visible data suggests an extremely simple, aniconic, noninstitutionalized cult, probably based on — and still in the tradition of — the older Canaanite "fertility religions" that would have been well suited to an agrarian lifestyle.

Only a few fragmentary inscriptions have been found in these Iron I villages. A late 13th-/early 12th-century jar handle inscribed with the Proto-Canaanite letters 'aḥl[d], possibly "belonging to Aḥilud," a personal name known from the Bible, was recovered at Radannah, near Ramallah. More important is a four-line ostracon with an abecedary (or list of alphabetic letters), found in an early 11th-century context at 'Izbet Ṣarṭah, possibly biblical Ebenezer, also in Proto-Canaanite letters. While not a literary text with any content, such an abecedary cannot have been an isolated item; it is almost certainly a schoolboy's practice text, and as such it may indicate at least the beginnings of functional literacy.[22]

Pottery reflects many aspects of culture and remains our most sensitive

22. See Aaron Demsky and Moshe Kochavi, "An Alphabet from the Days of the Judges," *BAR* 4/3 (1978): 23-30.

Plan of the Mount Ebal installation, 12th century (Judith Dekel)

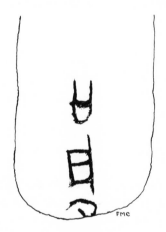

Inscribed 13th-12th-century handle from Khirbet Radannah, reading *'aḥl(d)*, "(Belonging to) Aḥilud" (Frank Moore Cross, Jr.)

index to cultural continuity and change. The Iron I pottery of these hill-country sites, particularly that of the early 12th century, remains strongly in the old LB II local tradition. The direct continuities are clear in nearly all forms, with only the normal, predictable typological developments.

This complex of sites and material culture constitutes a parade example of what archaeologists call an "assemblage" — an assortment of contemporaneous archaeological artifacts and their contexts, found together in a consistent pattern of association and distributed over a particular and well-defined geographic region. Such an assemblage, when documented from enough excavated sites and thereby distinguished from other assemblages, is usually said to denote an "archaeological culture," particularly if the assemblage can be shown to be distinctive, new, or intrusive. The assemblage can then often be confidently attributed to a known "ethnic group," for example, the Philistines of Palestine's

115

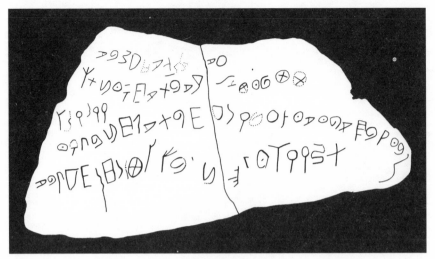

'Izbet Ṣarṭah inscription, with letters of the alphabet; 12th century (Moshe Weinberg)

coastal plain. Similarly we can recognize the remains of the Phoenicians, Aramaeans, Moabites, Ammonites, and Edomites. Why not the Israelites?

A few archaeologists like Israel Finkelstein — who ironically had earlier written *the* book on "Early Israel" — have recently been taken in by the now-fashionable skepticism toward "ethnicity," which is simply part and parcel of the postmodern paradigm already discussed. Since there is so little evidence to support such extreme skepticism, it puzzled me for some time — until I realized that for postmodernists ethnicity is mistakenly equated with racism. The most recent book on archaeology and ethnicity written from this perspective takes as virtually its only case-study of archaeologists improperly identifying "ethnicity" the Nazis and their attempt to use archaeology to distinguish a "Super Race." Surely this is "argumentum ad absurdum."

The same skepticism about our ability, indeed our entitlement, to recognize ethnicity in the archaeological record, is seen among the biblical revisionists. Thompson, for instance, makes the following astonishing claims:

> Ethnicity, however, is an interpretative historiographical fiction: a concept construing human relationships, before it is a term (however conducive to descriptions based on material remains. . . .). Ethnicity is hardly a common aspect of human existence at this very early period.

Thompson thinks that whatever "ethnicity" there might have been dealt only with structures of societal relationships; and "the physical effects of such selective decisions are often arbitrary and are, indeed, always accidental." If that were

116

true, no social science — the study of cultural phenomena that reflect patterned human thought and behavior — would be possible. Other revisionist absurdities are Thompson's statement that "all peoples writ large for purposes fictional"; and Lemche's assertion that "The Canaanites of the ancient Near East did not know that they were themselves Canaanites."[23]

Other biblicists are less doctrinaire, like some of the contributors to the volume edited by Mark G. Brett, *Ethnicity and the Bible*. Yet Brett himself simply accepts at face value the general skepticism of the revisionists, even stating that the failure to locate "Israelites" in the archaeological record would come as no surprise to most anthropologists, a gross over-simplification. Diana V. Edelman, an American scholar often associated with the revisionists and now also at Sheffield, has a long chapter in which she identifies several "ethnic markers," in accordance with myself and other archaeologists who may follow Fredrik Barth's pioneering ethnographic work. These include such material culture traits as settlement type and pattern, architecture, pottery, burial customs, and the like. She denies, however, that these are distinctively new in the archaeology of the early Iron Age, or that even if present in some way would tell us anything about ethnicity. Edelman argues that ethnic identity is complex and dynamic, that ethnic markers cannot be predicted, that no single list of traits can be generated, and that material culture traits alone are not definitive. What archaeologist has ever said *otherwise?* Edelman, not surprisingly, concludes that "given the present state of textual and artifactual evidence, nothing definitive can be said about the ethnicity of premonarchic Israel." Underlying all this skepticism, it seems to me, is not only a regrettable lack of knowledge of the actual LB-Iron archaeological record, but the dubious assumption that because ethnic consciousness and boundaries are flexible they are fictional.[24]

Has archaeology brought to light an entity that we can legitimately call "early Israel"? Consider the "assemblage" described above. It is demonstrably a

23. See Thompson, "Defining History and Ethnicity," 175; Niels Peter Lemche, *The Canaanites and Their Land*, JSOTSup 110 (Sheffield: JSOT, 1991), 152.

24. Mark G. Brett, ed., *Ethnicity and the Bible* (Leiden: Brill, 1996); cf. Siân Jones, *The Archaeology of Ethnicity* (London: Routledge, 1977); Diana Edelman, "Ethnicity and Early Israel," in Brett, *Ethnicity and the Bible*, 54, 55; Niels Peter Lemche, "Clio," 154; Thomas L. Thompson, "Ethnicity and the Bible: Multiple Judaisms or the 'New Israel'" (unpublished manuscript, courtesy of the author). Kenton L. Sparks, *Ethnicity and Identity in Ancient Israel* (Winona Lake: Eisenbrauns, 1999), has nothing to do with archaeology. For the differences between Finkelstein's more negative views on "ethnicity" and my more positive views, see Israel Finkelstein, "Ethnicity and Origin of the Iron I Settlers in the Highlands of Canaan: Can the Real Israel Stand Up?," *BA* 59 (1996): 198-212, an answer to my "'Will the Real Israel Please Stand Up?'" *BASOR* 297 (1995): 61-80.

new phenomenon at the dawn of the Iron Age ca. 1200, despite a few continuities with the Late Bronze Age. This village culture is also intrusive, at least in the previously underpopulated hill country with its few urban centers. And the overall assemblage is sufficiently homogeneous and distinctive to warrant *some* label. The only remaining question is: What label?

We could of course call them "the early Iron Age hill-country settlers." Then there is Thompson's term, "the Iron Age population of Syria's marginal southern fringe" (evidently the very term "Israel" is an embarrassment to him). But even minimalist designations presume a chronological, cultural-evolutionary, and functionalist distinction; and these too are "ethnic markers." So it seems that one cannot avoid a judgment. After much reflection on the archaeological data, I have suggested that we go further, adopting the term "Proto-Israelite" to designate this 12th-11th century complex.

At least two additional pieces of evidence justify this proposal. The well-known "Victory stele" of the 19th-Dynasty Egyptian pharaoh Merneptah, erected at Thebes in about his third year (ca. 1210), celebrates victories over a number of real or perceived enemies in Canaan.[25] The text lists several defeated peoples and then mentions "Israel," who "is laid waste; its seed is not." All scholars would agree that the date is fixed within a margin of less than five years by astronomical reckoning; that the reading "Israel" is certain; that "Israel" is followed by the Egyptian plural gentilic or determinative sign for "peoples," rather than a kingdom, city-state, or the like, and must therefore designate some ethnic group; and that this entity, whatever it is, was distinct in the minds of the Egyptians from Canaanites, Hurrians, Shasu-bedouin, or other groups in Canaan well known to Egyptian intelligence and mentioned in this and other Egyptian texts. Yet despite this fortuitous text — our earliest and most secure extrabiblical textual reference to "Israel" — the revisionists have turned somersaults to avoid the obvious implications. They argue, for instance, that the mention of an "Israel" tells us nothing about its nature or location. Or they denigrate the reference as our "only" known reference.

But one unimpeachable witness in the court of history is sufficient. The only thing we really need to know at this point, the Merneptah stele tells us unequivocally: There does exist in Canaan a people calling themselves "Israel," and thus called "Israel" by the Egyptians — who, after all, are hardly biblically

---

25. The definitive study is now that of my student Michael G. Hasel, *Domination and Resistance: Egyptian Military Activity in the Southern Levant, ca. 1300-1185 B.C.* (Leiden: Brill, 1998). For a map of Canaan at the time of the Merneptah raid, see Frank J. Yurco, "3,200-Year-Old Pictures of Israelites Found in Egypt," *BAR* 16/5 (1990): 34. See also Chapter 3, n. 60.

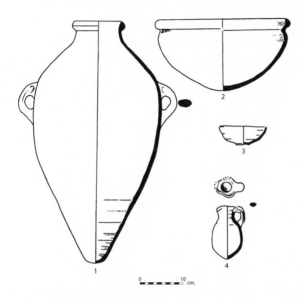

Typical 12th-century
Israelite hill-country
pottery, from Giloh
(Israel Finkelstein and
Nadav Na'aman, *From
Nomadism to Monarchy*)

biased, and they cannot have invented such a specific and unique people as "Israel" for their own propaganda purposes. Moreover, if we look at a map based on the Merneptah stele, we see that the Egyptian-held territory is clear. The "Hurrians" are located in the north; the Shasu-bedouin are to be located in the Negev desert and Transjordan; and in less than a generation the Philistines and other "Sea Peoples" will be entrenched along the coast. What is left in Canaan ca. 1200 as an "Israelite" enclave except the central hill country? If Merneptah's "Israel" was not here, where was it?

I stress that our conclusions at this point do not depend in any sense on a particular reading of the biblical texts, or even on the existence of a "Bible," much less on the need to defend theological positions. The Israeli archaeologists involved in producing most of the above data are all secularists, from many backgrounds but in no case theologically or nationalistically motivated — simply professionals who specialize in the analysis of material culture remains. On the other hand, a number of American archaeologists of conservative religious background, who undertook archaeological research no doubt hoping to be able to defend "invasion theories" like those of the book of Joshua, must have found the overwhelming evidence of the "indigenous origins" of most early Israelites hard to accept. But one and all they did so. As Joseph A. Callaway of Southern Baptist Theological Seminary concluded, henceforth it is the archaeological evidence, not the textual, that will be decisive in understanding Israelite origins.[26]

26. Joseph A. Callaway, "Response," in *Biblical Archaeology Today: Proceedings of the*

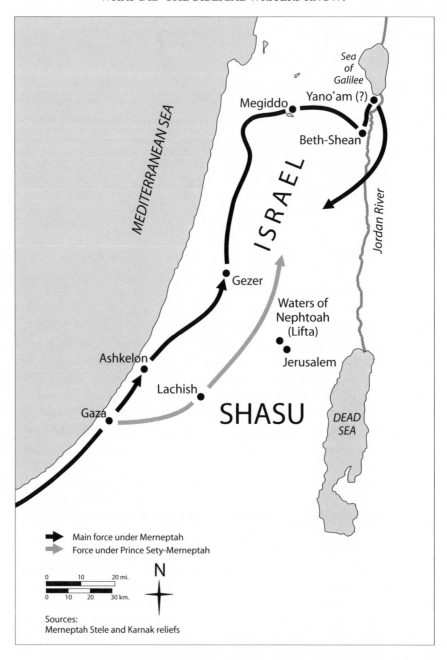

Map of Merneptah's campaign to Palestine, with his "Israel" located in the central
hill country, in accord with the Iron I settlements now known there
(Biblical Archaeology Society)

So much for the revisionists' charge of "biblical bias." For those who seem to know nothing whatsoever about archaeology to malign these archaeologists, myself included, as "biblicists" and "Zionists" is absurd. It certainly does little to inspire our confidence in them as historians.[27]

Now let us turn to the biblical data. If we look at the biblical texts describing the origins of Israel, we see at once that the traditional account contained in Genesis through Joshua simply cannot be reconciled with the picture derived above from archaeological investigation. The whole "Exodus-Conquest" cycle of stories must now be set aside as largely mythical, but in the proper sense of the term "myth": perhaps "historical fiction," but tales told primarily to validate religious beliefs. In my view, these stories are still "true" in that they convey forcefully later Israel's self-awareness as a "liberated people." I have even argued that there may be some actual historical truth here, since among the southern groups whom we know to have written much of the Hebrew Bible there is known a "House (tribe) of Joseph," many of whom may indeed have stemmed originally from Egypt. When they told the story of Israel's origins, they assumed naturally that they spoke for "all Israel" (as the Bible uses the term), even though most of the latter's ancestors had been local Canaanites. In struggling to explain what it means to be an "American," we do the same thing. At the great national holiday of Thanksgiving, we all patriotically identify with those Pilgrims who came over on the *Mayflower* (as though we were all card-carrying members of the Daughters of the American Revolution). But in fact, my ancestors came as dirt-poor Irish farmers from County Donegal in the potato famine of the 1840s; and others may have come from Africa, Mexico, or elsewhere. The revisionists like to stress the *variety* of meanings attached to "ethnicity"; but ethnicity is simply a deep sense of *belonging* that cannot be gainsaid by overlooking the fact of our unity in diversity, or that of any ethnic group. The Jewish community — surely as diverse as any in the world, but no less an ethnic group — understands all this instinctively. At Passover, Jews all over the world solemnly commemorate the Exodus story by reciting: "It is as though *we* had come out of Egypt this night." Precisely. The "Exodus story" is a really a Passover Haggadah, partly fanciful, partly humorous, a hyperbole to be sure, but *profoundly* true as a "story about who we are."

Yet however we attempt to "salvage" much of the biblical narratives about the origins of Israel, we may be limited. We cannot make the Bible what it is not. Fortunately, the writers and editors of the Hebrew Bible, being far more so-

---

International Congress on Biblical Archaeology, Jerusalem, April, 1989, ed. J. Amitai (Jerusalem: Israel Exploration Society, 1985), 72-78.

27. See further Chapter 1, n. 14; Chapter 2, n. 47.

phisticated and better historians than some would have us believe, placed in their final edition *another* version, back-to-back with Joshua, the book of Judges. Many scholars, puzzled by the two often differing versions of events, have attempted to harmonize them, but the obvious contradictions are too great. Joshua, written largely to glorify a great hero of early Israel, credits him with sweeping rapid military victories over most of Canaan, vanquishing the whole land. Judges, however, begins its story with Joshua's death in Judg. 1:1, then goes on to weave a 200-year-long tale of some 12 "judges," or charismatic figures raised up by Yahweh to deal with the very threat that Joshua has disposed of, namely the continuing presence of Canaanites and of Canaanite culture. Then later in ch. 1 we find a "negative list" of the supposed "conquest," cities that were not taken, some of them like Hazor the very same cities that Joshua was said to have utterly destroyed. To explain the continuous struggle and the chaos, the authors or editors of Judges repeat the refrain: "In those days there was no king in Israel, and every man did what was right in his own eyes" (Judg. 21:25).

The modern biblical historian, or even the thoughtful lay person, might observe at once the "anti-royalist" bias of those who produced the book of Judges. But the point here is that recognition of this bias should not obscure the fact that the writers of Judges have described much of the actual historical process accurately. Their rationalization, developed perhaps centuries after the fact, may be suspect; but many essential facts remain. The Iron I period, as we would call it, was not characterized by decisive military battles, the wholesale destruction of the Canaanite urban centers and the annihilation of the populace, and the triumph by brute force of a group of outsiders. It was characterized, rather, as we now know from intense archaeological investigation, by large-scale socio-economic disruption, major demographic shifts to the hill-country frontiers, and by life-and-death struggles between competing ethnic and cultural groups that lasted anywhere from one to two centuries. Among the elements in this "multi-ethnic" society in Palestine and southern Syria in Iron I, scholars have confidently identified "Egyptians," "Canaanites," "Philistines," "neo-Hittites," "Aramaeans," and "Phoenicians." I have argued that there is at least as much evidence for our "Proto-Israelites" as for any of these other well-known ethnic groups.[28] It would seem that arbitrarily eliminating them can only be the result of a prejudice, conscious or otherwise. And the positive evidence for early "Israelites" at this point comes not from the biblical accounts alone, or even primarily — certainly not from the mainstream of the biblical

---

28. Dever, *NEA* 61 (1998): 39-52 and literature there.

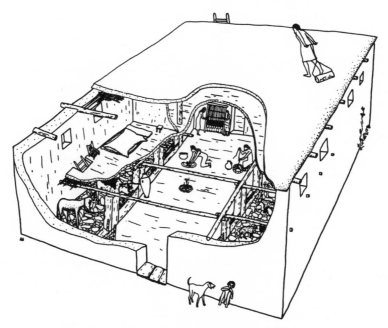

Typical Iron I village house, as reconstructed by Lawrence E. Stager
(Drawing by Abbas Alizadeh)

narrative — but from the convergence of archaeological and textual data, care-fully sifted through, mostly in the book of Judges.

It is not, however, only the *general* cultural situation presumed in the nar-rations of Judges which "rings true" in the light of what we actually know. Stager took notice of the new archaeological data from Israeli surveys in the West Bank at about the same time as I did. His brilliant 1985 article "The Ar-chaeology of the Family in Ancient Israel" outlined exactly the sort of detailed convergences that I have in mind here.[29] These are archaeological "facts on the ground" that correspond astonishingly well with descriptions of daily life and overall socio-economic conditions in the book of Judges that purport to be "factual." But they also converge in some degree with texts in 1-2 Samuel and even in parts of Joshua.

(1) The individual dwelling, with living and storage accommodation for foodstuffs, several animals, and up to a dozen people would represent the *bêt-'āb,* the biblical "house of the father," or patriarchal figure, the nuclear family to which every *geber,* or individual, belonged. (2) The cluster of several

29. *BASOR* 260 (1985): 1-35.

houses, sharing common walls, courtyards, and other features, would then be the biblical *mišpāḥâ,* or "family," in reality a multi-generation extended family (the typical Middle Eastern "stem family" today. (3) At the next higher level of organization, the entire village, consisting of several such clusters, would be the biblical *šebet,* or "clan, tribe." (4) The entire complex of many villages would be the *benê-Yisrael,* or "sons of Israel," that is, the ethnic group as a whole. These striking analogies between new and definitive archaeological data and a sophisticated socio-anthropological reading of the older, folkloric strata of the biblical texts — my "convergence" — suggest to me that at last archaeology has brought to light the actual remains of "earliest Israel." If so, this is one of the most striking success stories in the 100-year history of "biblical archaeology."

It may be significant that none of the revisionists ever refers to Stager's much-quoted article on early Israel. To summarize the convergences at which they might look if they were so inclined, let us put what we can know independently from our two sources in simple chart form (see p. 125).

Convergences in the Biblical Period of the United Monarchy

As we saw above, the revisionists vociferously deny that there ever was any such entity as the Hebrew Bible's "United Monarchy," or the reigns of Saul, David, and Solomon. There was no Israelite "state" in the north, with its capital in Samaria, until the mid-9th century; and no southern or Judean state, with its capital in Jerusalem, until the mid-late 7th century.[30] What is conspicuously absent in their repeated assertions is not only lack of any evidence, but even more damaging, the absence of critical discussion of the voluminous literature on what are called "state-formation processes." This phenomenon has been one of the most discussed topics among socio-anthropologists and scholars in numerous other disciplines for over 20 years. One of the recent revisionists and a student of Ahlstrom, Margaret M. Gelinas comments that "scholars have yet to reach consensus on the definition of 'statehood' as it would be applied to the regions of Palestine during the period of early first millennium BCE," but that

---

30. See references in nn. 31, 32 below; also Chapter 2, nn. 38, 40. Cf. Christa Schäfer-Lichtenberger, "Sociological and Biblical Views of the Early State," in Fritz and Davies, *Origins of the Israelite States,* 78-105. By contrast, see the extensive discussion of the literature on "statehood" in William G. Dever, "Archaeology and the 'Age of Solomon,'" with full references. Also Carol Meyers, "Kinship and Kingship: The Early Monarchy," in Coogan, *The Oxford History of the Biblical World,* 221-71.

"Early Israel"	Iron I highland villages
Source: Biblical texts, chiefly Judges, Samuel	*Source: Archaeological data, 12th-11th cents. B.C.*
Settled mostly in hill country, but in contact with lowlands; cf. "boundary lists"	Sites newly established in formerly sparsely-occupied hill-country frontier
Dated by references to incoming Philistines	Contemporary with new Philistine settlements in Iron I
The metaphor of "tents"; "every man to his own tent." Gideon has only 300 men	Small, simple villages; population of 100-300
Gideon called while plowing in his father's field; the "Nazarite" vow as rejection of urban values	Agrarian economy and lifestyle, based partly on new agricultural technologies
Households, tribes, and clans predominate; endogamous marriage, patrilocal society, individual identities within "father's house"; some Levites are "house priests"	House plan and layout reflect kin-based social structure; villages are homogenous and clustered; some differences between north and south. Socio-economic structure best seen as "domestic mode of production"
"No king in Israel in those days"; battle cry or rally is "Every man to his own tent"	In anthropological terms, an "egalitarian," or better "acephalous," society
The "Israelites" constitute an "ethnic minority," but complex process of working out an identity under way	The village complex is relatively isolated, self-sufficient economically; house-form, ceramic repertoire, few cult sites all indicate some continuities with, but increasing diversion from, LB Canaanite culture
Border wars with Moab and Ammon	Some general cultural similarities to Iron I sites now known in southern Transjordan
Skirmishes with local Canaanites, Philistines, often indecisive. "Canaanite" culture generally prevails	Settlements generally peaceful, few destruction layers; some sites border on Philistia, but have little or no Philistine pottery
Scant literature, but "early poems" reflect some oral traditions; "Shibboleth/Sibboleth" story indicates local dialects; no "national" language and script yet	A few inscriptions in old Canaanite script, including an abecedary; personal names that will appear in later Hebrew

"Thompson has taken this question seriously and started to identify the necessary socioeconomic data to be examined."[31]

This is the danger of scholarly inbreeding. Despite their pronouncements about "states," one searches recent revisionist writing in vain for an awareness of the basic theoretical literature on state formation processes. Again, Finkelstein distinguishes himself from them by a rather thorough acquaintance with the general literature; so although he may differ with me on the date of the emergence of the Israelite states, at least he is knowledgeable when he discusses "states."[32] I can easily cite two dozen leading authorities who have analyzed states and their evolution worldwide, over many millennia. Without exception, they all point out that the single most significant criterion for defining "statehood" is centralization of power.[33] It is that phenomenon, not size, much less urbanization, that characterizes statehood, as we shall see presently.

In the light of competent critical scholarship on the issue of "state-formation," how do the revisionists fare? Not very well. Only Lemche and Thompson have advanced any so-called evidence, and that is bogus. They have declared:

> In the history of Palestine that we have presented, there is no room for a historical United Monarchy, or for such kings as those presented in the biblical stories of Saul, David or Solomon. The early period in which the traditions have set their narrative is an imaginary world of long ago that never existed as such. In the real world of that time, for instance, only a few dozen villagers lived as farmers in all of the Judaean highlands. Timber, grazing lands and steppe were all marginal possibilities. There could not have been a kingdom for any Saul or David to be king of, simply because there were not enough people.[34]

In my opinion, those who so blatantly ignore the facts, even in a single such statement, forfeit any credibility as discriminating scholars. Lemche and Thompson cite no evidence whatsoever for their "few dozen villagers" in the 10th century. But Finkelstein, Adam Zertal, Avi Ophir, the late Yigael Shiloh, I,

---

31. Margaret M. Gelinas, "United Monarchy — Divided Monarchy: Fact or Fiction?" in *The Pitcher Is Broken: Memorial Essays for Gösta W. Ahlstrom*, ed. Steven W. Holloway and Lowell K. Handy. JSOT Sup 190 (Sheffield: Sheffield Academic, 1995), 228. Nowhere has Thompson shown significant acquaintance with the vast literature on "state formation processes" in archaeology and anthropology, nor have most of the other revisionists; see n. 30 above.

32. See *NEA* 62 (1999): 35-52.

33. See n. 31 above.

34. Niels Peter Lemche and Thomas L. Thompson, *JSOT* 64 (1994): 19.

and other archaeologists have shown on the basis of extensive surveys and well-documented demographic projections that the population of the late 13th-century highlands was ca. 12 to 15 thousand. By the 12th century, it had grown to ca. 50 thousand, by the 11th century to ca. 80 thousand, and in all likelihood to ca. 100 thousand by the mid-late 10th century. Finkelstein's estimate of "*ca. 2,200*," which Thompson claims as the basis for his figures, was clearly for the *few villages around* Jerusalem in the 10th century, not the entire Judean highlands, much less Israel and Judah together. Elsewhere Finkelstein's estimate for the population of the hill country — i.e., the territory that would have constituted the heartland of the biblical "United Monarchy" — is ca. 65 thousand. In oral communication Finkelstein says that he agrees with me that ca. 100 thousand is not too high a figure for *all* of "Israel" and "Judah" in the 10th century.[35]

Even if Thompson could cut our 10th-century population to one-half, or possibly one-quarter, he would still have no case against Israelite statehood. The lowland Maya state of Tikal, recognized as such by anthropologists, had a population of only some 50 thousand, and several multi-valley Andean states had a population of 15 to 16 thousand. Other authorities would suggest a threshold of about 20 thousand, beyond which a society may be said to develop a degree of centralization and statehood almost inevitably.[36] As for the "urbanization" that Thompson seems to think essential but lacking in 10th-century Palestine, the anthropological and archaeological literature demonstrates differently. The distinguished authorities Vere Gordon Childe and Robert McCormick Adams have shown independently that often it is not urbanization that "causes" states to form, but the other way around. And some early societies achieved statehood without ever experiencing a truly urban stage of evolution, among them the Han Dynasty in China, one of the half-dozen or so examples of "pristine" (independently evolving) states regularly cited in the literature on statehood.[37]

Quite apart from that consideration, I have recently summarized the available archaeological data in detail, showing that at least a dozen sites in 10th-century Palestine would qualify as "cities" by clear-cut criteria that have been de-

35. Cf. Thompson in Hershel Shanks, *BAR* 23 (1997): 35, obviously referring to Israel Finkelstein, *Levant* 28 (1996): 181, 182. Earlier Finkelstein had estimated the 10th-century hill-country population at ca. 65 thousand, and the population of all of Palestine west of the Jordan at ca. 150 thousand; cf. Magen Broshi and Israel Finkelstein, "The Population of Palestine in Iron Age II," *BASOR* 287 (1992): 55; cf. Dever, "Archaeology and the 'Age of Solomon,'" 221, 222 and references there, esp. Finkelstein, *The Archaeology of the Israelite Settlement*.

36. Dever, "Archaeology and the 'Age of Solomon,'" 243-51 and references there.

37. See "Archaeology and the 'Age of Solomon,'" 245-50 and references there.

veloped for the small-scale entities of the southern Levant in the Iron Age. Even 9th-century Moab in sparsely-populated Transjordan is now being character- ized by archaeologists as a state, at least of the "tribal" type that Philip S. Khoury and Joseph Kostiner have documented so thoroughly in *Tribes and State Forma- tion in the Middle East*.[38] In this case, the term "tribal state" seems to be favored by more and more, rather than the "chiefdom" model that the former generation preferred. The essential point is this: today nearly all archaeologists recognize a small-scale but authentic "state" in central Palestine in the mid-late 10th cen- tury, or the beginning of Iron II, on archaeological grounds alone. Even our label "Israelite" could be extrapolated from the Egyptian reference on the inscription of Pharaoh Merneptah to an "Israel" in Canaan ca. 1210, in connection with the continuity of Iron I-II material culture that all archaeologists acknowledge.[39] It is not we archaeologists and students of the cultural process who need the Bible, but the revisionists, whose point of departure is nevertheless biblical: they rec- ognize an "Israel" not when the biblical text says it develops, but in the mid-9th century when the first references known to us *outside* the Bible occur, namely in the Neo-Assyrian and Moabite texts (below). How is it that the biblical texts are always approached with postmodernism's typical "hermeneutics of suspicion," but the nonbiblical texts are taken at face value? It seems to be that the Bible is automatically held guilty unless proven innocent.

If there were any doubt about the revisionists' presupposition that there cannot have been an early Israel, one has only to look at their summary rejec- tion of the 9th-century Tel Dan inscription mentioning "a king of Israel" and the "House of David," now confidently dated by additional fragments to the reign of Joram ("Jehoram") of Judah, who ruled ca. 847-842. On the "positiv- ist" side of the controversy, regarding the authenticity of the inscription, we

---

38. (Berkeley: University of California Press, 1990). On Western Palestine, see nn. 36, 37 above. For Amman in Transjordan, see Burton MacDonald and Randall W. Younker, eds., *Ancient Ammon* (Leiden: Brill, 1999). On Phoenicia in the 10th century as consisting already of "city-states ruled by monarchies," see Lowell K. Handy, "Phoenicians in the Tenth Century BCE: A Sketch of an Outline," in *The Age of Solomon*, 154-66. On the Ara- maean city-states of the same area, see Mark W. Chavalas, "Inland Syria and the East-of- Jordan Region in the First Millennium BCE Before the Assyrian Intrusions," in Handy, *The Age of Solomon*, 167-78.

39. For the agreement of Finkelstein that there was a "United Monarchy" in the 10th century, however small, see "The Great Transformation: The 'Conquest' of the Highlands Frontier and the Rise of the Territorial States," in Thomas E. Levy, *The Archaeology of Soci- ety in the Holy Land*, 362; also *Levant* 28 (1996): 185. The revisionists never cite this opin- ion of "their" archaeologist; like most of the mainstream literature, it is inconvenient for their scenario.

The 9th-century Aramaic inscription from Tel Dan, mentioning a "King of Israel,"
probably Joram, 847-842 (line 8), and the "House (i.e., dynasty) of David" (line 9)
(Tel Dan Excavations, Hebrew Union College)

now have published opinions by most of the world's leading epigraphers (none
of whom is a "biblicist" in Thompson's sense): the inscription means exactly
what it says. On the "negativist" side, we have the opinions of Thompson,
Lemche, and Cryer of the Copenhagen school. The reader may choose.[40]

A final point should be made in this connection. Thompson and Lemche
must deny that there was any parallel course of development in the two states,
Israel and Judah in the 10th-8th/7th centuries, because they recognize only *one*
— what Thompson calls the state of Samaria or "Samarina" (a strangely pan-
Assyrian notion), that is, the biblical northern kingdom.[41] There are, however,
clear indications of a north-south division by the 9th-8th centuries, on strictly
archaeological grounds. Ruth Amiran's classic *Ancient Pottery of the Holy Land*

40. See references in Chapter 2, nn. 10, 11.
41. See Chapter 1.

Distribution of the late 8th-7th-century Judean inscribed sheqel-weights, corresponding with the political borders of Judah (Raz Kletter, following Nadav Na'aman)

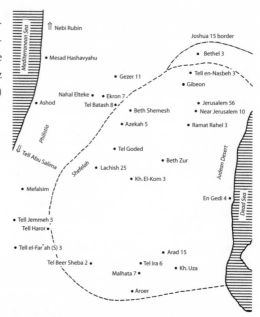

already organized the analysis of much of the Iron Age pottery in terms of northern and southern "families."[42] It is also well known that the late 8th- and 7th-century inscribed sheqel-weights and pillar-base figurines, as well as the late 8th-century "royal stamped jarhandles," so common in Judah, are almost never found in the north. Thus there exists just north of Jerusalem, along the Gezer-Bethel line, what archaeologists would call a "shatter-zone," implying a cultural and thus a *political* border at that point.[43] Biblical scholars themselves have known for a century or more that there are even consistent dialectical differences between Israel and Judah, differences in orthography in general, and specifically in personal names compounded with the name of the deity that end in the north in -*yaw* but in the south in the long form -*yāhu*.[44] Again, these differences are archaeological and linguistic *facts,* not "biblical fancies."

As for Thompson's refusal to acknowledge Jerusalem as a state capital before the 7th century, that is entirely an argument from silence, as Nadav Na'aman has recently pointed out. Na'aman's treatments of Israelite history

42. (Jerusalem: Masada, 1969), 191-265.

43. See most recently the overwhelming evidence in Raz Kletter, "Pots and Polities: Material Remains of Late Iron Age Judah in Relation to Its Political Borders," *BASOR* 314 (1999): 19-54.

44. See Jeffrey H. Tigay, *You Shall Have No Other Gods Before Me: Israelite Religion in the Light of Hebrew Inscriptions.* HSS 31 (Atlanta: Scholars, 1986).

elsewhere have hardly been conservative, but on the contrary rather radical. Yet he easily demonstrates the fallacy of Thompson's (and Lemche's) arguments. Few 10th-century archaeological levels have been *exposed* in the deeply stratified and largely inaccessible ruins of ancient Jerusalem, so the paucity of finds means nothing. Yet there is growing evidence of extensive occupation.[45]

The Gates of Gezer

One "case-study" in the possibilities of a dialogue between texts and artifacts is especially relevant, namely the well-known city gate and walls at Gezer. These were excavated first by R. A. S. Macalister in 1902-9. It was the late Yigael Yadin — widely experienced in matters of both statecraft and military strategy — who first drew attention in modern times to the distinctive four-entryway gate and casemate (or double) city walls at Gezer, after he recognized almost identical gates and walls in his excavations at Hazor in the 1950s and later on at Megiddo in the central Jezreel valley. Yadin, "biblical archaeologist" or not, knew his Hebrew Bible, so in a brief 1958 article he cited 1 Kgs. 9:15-17.[46] This text basically describes how Gezer was ceded by the Egyptians to Solomon after the pharaoh had destroyed the city "by fire"; and how Solomon subsequently "built the wall" at Gezer, along with walls at Hazor, Megiddo, and Jerusalem. Yadin observed that the discovery of nearly identical 10th-century city walls and gates at three of the four sites listed in 1 Kgs. 9:15-17 (and now probably 8th-7th century parallels from Jerusalem itself) could hardly be a coincidence. Indeed, he took the convergence, as we would call it here, to imply that all these defenses could only have been constructed by a sort of "Royal Corps of Engineers" under Solomon's highly centralized administration.

Between 1967 and 1971 the Hebrew Union College–Harvard Semitic Museum excavations at Gezer relocated the long-buried gate and city wall and excavated the portions that Macalister had left uncleared. We had already discovered in Field II that the casemate wall was founded above a deep destruction layer dated by the pottery to about the mid-10th century, the latter possibly the earlier Egyptian destruction in question. In Field III, the city gate associated with the wall turned

---

45. See the optimistic view of Na'aman in "Cow Town or Royal Capital? Evidence for Iron Age Jerusalem," *BAR* 23/4 (1997): 43-47, 67; "It Is There: Ancient Texts Prove It," *BAR* 24/4 (1998): 42-44; cf. Jane Cahill, "It Is There: The Archaeological Evidence Proves It," *BAR* 24/4 (1998): 34-41, 63, all with reference to the principal "minimalist" dissenting view, that of Margaret L. Steiner. Naturally the revisionists cite only the minority view.

46. "Solomon's City Wall and Gate at Gezer," *IEJ* 8 (1958): 80-86.

Plan of several four-
entryway gates, probably
all 10th century (Ze'ev
Herzog, *The City-Gate in
Eretz-Israel*)

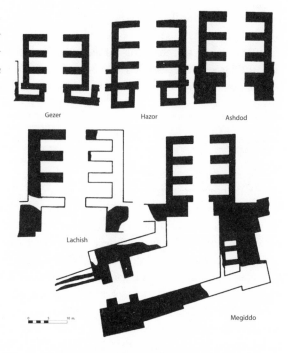

Gezer   Hazor   Ashdod

Lachish

Megiddo

out to be exceptionally well engineered and beautifully preserved. The upper four-entryway gate, founded again on deep fills, had a complex history, with more than a dozen successive street levels. After the third repaving, the outer two-entryway gatehouse (and probably the rebuild of Macalister's "Outer Wall") was added. Then shortly after that, the whole area, including adjoining "Palace 10,000," suffered a major destruction, after which buttresses were required to shore up the weakened western portion of the upper gate. The pottery from this destruction layer included distinctive forms of red-slipped and slipped and hand-burnished (polished) pottery, which have always been dated to the late 10th century. The equally distinctive wheel-burnished pottery characteristic of the early 9th century at all known sites was conspicuously absent. Thus, on commonly accepted *ceramic* grounds — not on naïve acceptance of the Bible's stories about "Solomon in all his glory" — we dated the Gezer Field III city walls and gates to the mid-late 10th century. In addition to the ceramic evidence, we used the datum provided by the well-known campaigns of the Egyptian Pharaoh Sheshonq, ca. 925 (below), to fix the date of the destruction, and thus place the construction and major use-phases somewhat earlier. These would then fall within the ca. 970-930 date that the biblical accounts would give for Solomon's reign.[47] We did not *create* this "conver-

47. For an orientation to the problem, see Dever, "Archaeology and the 'Age of Solo-

The 10th-century four-entryway gate in Field III at Gezer (Stratum VIII), looking
outside the city (Photo by R. B. Wright)

gence"; we simply observed it and thought to use it as a proper source for history-
writing. If the biblical Solomon had not constructed the Gezer gate and city walls,
then we would have to invent a similar king by another name.

We have used this evidence of centralization at Gezer, as well as at Hazor
and Megiddo, as proof of a Solomonic "state" in the 10th century, the heated
denial of which is one of the basic building-blocks of the revisionist agenda.

---

mon,'" 225-35 and full literature, pro and con, cited there, esp. John S. Holladay, "The
Kingdoms of Israel and Judah: Political and Economic Centralization in the Iron IIA-B," in
Levy, *The Archaeology of Society in the Holy Land,* 369-98. Cf. Niels Peter Lemche's effort at
rebuttal of Holladay's arguments, "On Doing Sociology With 'Solomon,'" in Handy, *The
Age of Solomon,* 321-25. Lemche dismisses Holladay's exhaustive analysis of the *archaeological* data, which begins by showing why the biblical texts do not constitute data and
must be discarded, as just another example of biblical archaeology's "contaminated methodology" (332). For a sober critical evaluation of the biblical sources, see Nadav Na'aman,
"Sources and Composition in the History of Solomon," in Handy, *The Age of Solomon,* 57-
80; Na'aman concludes that Solomon was a historical character, despite the skepticism of
some. See the excellent résumé in Gary N. Knoppers, "The Vanishing Solomon: The Disappearance of the United Monarchy from Recent Histories of Ancient Israel," *JBL* 116
(1997): 19-44.

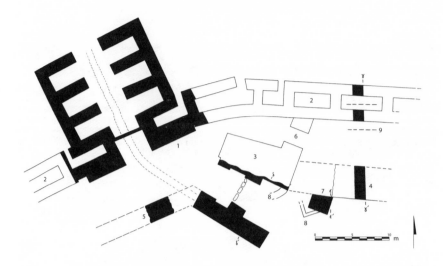

Plan of the Gezer Field III gate

Thompson has recently accused me of going to Gezer in the Spring of 1969, when no one living had seen the partially-excavated and reburied gate of Macalister (his "Maccabean Castle"), to "prove the historicity of the Bible." He even charges that I deliberately removed inconvenient stones from the gate and rolled them down the hill, as well as discarding any of the pottery that might challenge my hypothesis of a 10th-century date.[48] What is one to make of such slander, similar to Thompson's implication that the Tel Dan inscription is a forgery? Is the revisionists' case so weak that they must resort to falsification of the evidence and impugning the integrity of any scholars who differ with them?

Again, I suggest that the archaeological data are *not* "mute," but that some historians cannot bear to listen. Even Thompson's concession that there was a city gate at Gezer, but that it dates to the 9th century (i.e., "non-Solomonic"), is not reassuring. He completely ignores the fact that our 10th-century date derives not from any "biblical connection," but rather from the fact that the foundation and early use levels of the gate and its streets are characterized by a unique style of hand-burnished pottery. Here and elsewhere this pottery is found only in occupational deposits *pre*-dating the destructions accompanying Sheshonq's campaigns. This is the "Shishak" of 1 Kgs. 11:40 and 2 Chr. 12:2-4 (and of Egyptian annals), texts that provide us with the necessary synchronism and thus a *terminus ante quem* for the Gezer gate ca. 925. The latter text does so by noting that Shishak's raid took place "in the fifth year of King Rehoboam,"

48. "Historiography of Ancient Palestine," 30, 31.

Solomon's son and successor, and thus five years after Solomon's death. Solomon then would have reigned ca. 970-930, if the Bible's "forty years" is correct. In any case, the destruction of Solomon's Gezer is closely fixed by *extra*-biblical evidence at ca. 925.[49]

Concerning the Shishak raid, it should be noted that earlier scholars like William F. Albright, Benjamin Mazar, and Yohanan Aharoni worked out a map of the Shishak raid a generation ago, with many sites suggested as candidates for Egyptian destructions. Today the list and the map can be considerably expanded. It would include, at minimum, the following sites and strata (from north to south; *= named on the Shishak list):[50]

Hazor IX	Tel Michal
Tel Abu Hawan III	Tel Qasile VIII
Tell Keisan VIII-A	*Gezer VIII (reading now uncertain)
*Megiddo V-A/IV-B	Tell Batash/Timnah IV
*Ta'anach II-B	Tell el-Hama
*Beth-shan Upper V	Tell es-Saidiyeh XI
Tel Mevorakh VII	Tell Mazar

49. See further the detailed discussion of the Shishak-Solomon correlation in Dever, "Archaeology and the 'Age of Solomon,'" 239-43 and references there. Cf. two other essays in the same volume: Lemche, "On Doing Sociology With 'Solomon,'" which never once *mentions* this fundamental, nonbiblical datum; and the careful analysis of Na'aman, "Sources and Composition," which points out that the biblical writers' use of the Shishak data shows that, while writing later, they had authentic, contemporary sources, perhaps such as the lost work the "Acts of Solomon" mentioned in the biblical texts (59-64, 77). In *The Israelites in History and Tradition*, Lemche discusses the Shishak inscription briefly, but only for its possible chronological value, concluding that "none of the places mentioned by Shoshenq [= Shishak] in his list, however, refer to the central part of either Israel and Judah," so this text constitutes "absolute silence" (56, 57). What about Megiddo, Ta'anakh, Beth-shan, Gezer, and at least 10 other sites? Similarly, Thompson, who will accept nothing other than extrabiblical texts, does not even mention the Shishak datum in *The Mythic Past*. A coincidence? Cf. also n. 51 below, on Gelinas, who simply manipulates the Shishak data out of existence.

50. See further Dever, "Archaeology and the 'Age of Solomon,'" 238-39; and add the newer data in Amihai Mazar, *IEJ* 49 (1999): 1-42. Mazar has a huge destruction layer in his lower city Stratum I that is dated by Carbon 14 analyses to ca. 915-832 (98 percent reliability), which he thinks may be Shishak. But the next lower destruction, being excavated in the summer of 2000, which is also impressive, will probably prove to be Shishak. That would make the upper one due to Aramaean disturbances ca. 840, in keeping with the Tel Dan stele and other evidence long known for this horizon. Cf. Chapter 2, nn. 10, 11.

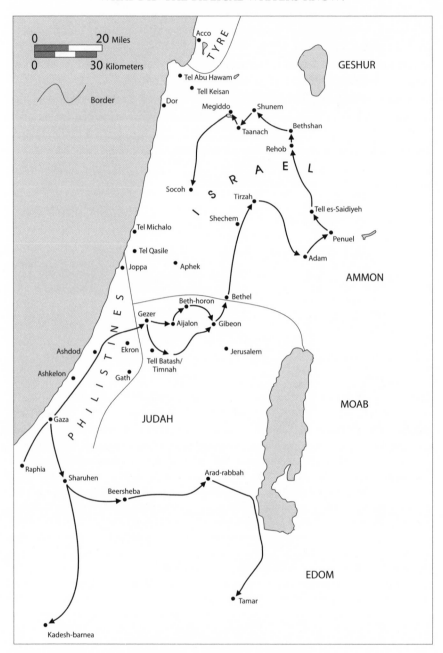

The campaign of Shishak. Note Gezer, Tirzah, Rehob, Bethshan, and Megiddo, all of
which (along with other sites) witness to a late-10th-century destruction
(Yohanan Aharoni, *The Land of the Bible*)

The critical reader will grasp at once the importance of this Solomon-Shishak synchronism. Readers are also likely to sense instinctively that there is simply no way that a biblical writer or editor living in the Persian-Hellenistic-Roman era — when Pharaonic Egypt had long since sunk into oblivion and its literature was largely lost — could have known about such a synchronism. Later compilers also could not have known about specific destructions at the sites noted above, since the ancient remains of these cities had long been buried under the sands of time. The Solomon-Shishak destruction-layer synchronism is so secure that most archaeologists take it for granted, arguing at most over exactly which layer in a given mound is the best candidate for Shishak's raid. Yet biblical scholars, especially the revisionists, are curiously blasé. Recent standard histories of ancient Israel pass over it with a few remarks, but not one goes into the archaeological evidence and its significance. Gelinas, in treating the evidence for a Solomonic kingdom, mentions the Shishak raid once in passing, only to dismiss it because "there is no Egyptian narrative of the account." But what are the battle-itinerary, list of destroyed sites, and registers of booty in the text of the Shishak stele? She simply says that this text does not prove the existence of a "state" of Israel or Judah. Again, does she suppose that an Egyptian pharaoh launched a far-away campaign, of which he later boasted, simply against Thompson's "few dozen villagers in all of the Judaean highlands"? Significantly, Gelinas, along with the other revisionists, is totally silent concerning the well-published archaeological data on the several Shishak destructions in Palestine.[51]

The considerable archaeological evidence that I have summarized here regarding centralized planning and administration reflects what is regarded in the literature as the *principal* trait of state-level organization. Even if one is cautious, however, about drawing such a specific conclusion at this point, the Hazor, Megiddo, and Gezer evidence does not stand alone. The evidence presented here is only the tip of the archaeological iceberg for the 10th century.[52] Before going into detail on some other specific data, I would stress again that the city defenses and all the rest are part of a dramatic, large-scale process of organization and centralization that utterly transformed the landscape of most of Palestine in the period from the early 10th to early 9th century. It is such shifts in settlement type and distributions together with marked demographic changes that signal most clearly a new archaeological and thus new cultural phase, in this case the transition from Iron I to Iron II.

51. Gelinas, "United Monarchy — Divided Monarchy: Fact or Fiction?" 230.

52. When recently confronted by the larger evidence face-to-face in an informational magazine, Thompson remarked that the Bible is not about history, only "about traditions, . . . a collection of traditions"; Shanks, *BAR* 23/4 (1997): 32.

The revisionists simply ignore the data on the Iron I-II transition (Thompson's "few dozen villagers"), but *all* archaeologists are in absolute agreement that the phenomena of urbanization and centralization characterize this horizon accurately. The only differences, even among "extremists," have to do with the precise dating of phases *within* the century noted here: i.e., are the city defenses late 10th century or early 9th century? The revisionists scarcely cite these dates at all, and they refer to archaeologists' differing views on inner phasing only selectively, as though to buttress their own opinions; they have no understanding of the complexities involved, for instance, in ceramic dating.[53]

"Administrative Lists"

Among other specific cases of state-formation, let me turn now to the well-known lists of Solomon's "administrative districts" in 1 Kgs. 4. One of the principal aspects of statehood stressed above is centralization, direct evidence for which we should expect to find in the 10th century if Israel did indeed constitute by then a real state, not merely some sort of a "chiefdom." In this case-study, let me begin with the biblical evidence *per se,* not because it determines our agenda, but simply because it is clearly organized and thus provides a convenient framework for our analysis. According to 1 Kgs. 4:7-19, one of Solomon's major administrative policies was to organize the entire area under his control into 12 districts, each with its own "high official" (Heb. *niṭār*) or governor. One may suspect that this is all much later propaganda on the part of the biblical editors, designed to enhance Solomon's reputation as the "ideal king," and based on the older and possibly nonhistorical notion of the "12 tribes." On the other hand, since each district was to provide for the royal court's needs for one month, one does not have to seek very far for another, nonbiblical rationale.

53. For the pontification of several revisionists on ceramic typology and chronology, see Thompson, "Defining History and Ethnicity," 177; Herrmann M. Niemann, "The Socio-Political Shadow Cast by the Biblical Solomon," in Handy, *The Age of Solomon,* 263. On the revisionists' skepticism about archaeological chronology in general — based on their false accusation that our archaeological chronology is based on "*biblical* schemes" — see e.g., Thompson, *The Mythic Past,* 8, 39; Keith W. Whitelam, *The Invention of Ancient Israel,* 62-64; Niemann, 260-62. Such statements make it painfully clear that the revisionists are not even *amateur* archaeologists. The opinion of any of the revisionists on the pottery of ancient Palestine (or its chronology, for that matter) carries about as much weight as my opinion on the Hebrew imperfect verb.

Our concern here, however, is only the question of whether or not the compilers of this list in 1 Kgs. 4, working at whatever date and for whatever reasons, had actual historical documents upon which to draw. The revisionists would reject such a suggestion out of hand; but fairness requires us to ask whether an original *Sitz im Leben* can be recovered for this passage. That is, does the list of districts and principal cities correlate in any way with "the facts on the ground" — does it make *topographical sense?* Again, a simple chart (see p. 140) can be used to summarize the biblical data (anticipating for the moment possible archaeological correlations by suggesting identifications).[54]

The first and most obvious comment to make about this supposedly historical list is that it is clearly not a first-hand account, nor is it necessarily consistent with other biblical materials. For one thing, the list does not really come out to a number "12" that corresponds exactly with other lists of the "12 tribes." (The identification of districts in our column 1 depends partly on Yohanan Aharoni's correlations.) The biblical text in 1 Kgs. 4 yields at face value the names of only seven of the traditional 12 tribes (although the lists vary), omitting in particular Dan, Manasseh, and Zebulun, but including other areas not in fact controlled by Israel, such as Dor on the coast (probably Philistine or Phoenician) and Bashan and Gilead in Transjordan (certainly not Israelite at this time, if ever). Thus we cannot claim simply that the "administrative list" in 1 Kgs. 4:1-17 is a valid historical document as it stands. In its present highly edited form, it is clearly part of the Deuteronomistic history and its panorama of Israel's history, dating from the late preexilic or postexilic period. That does not necessarily mean, however, as the revisionists maintain in all such cases, that there is no earlier, probably archival, material here. On the contrary, I would argue that some aspects of this list not only fit very well with what we know of the 10th century from extrabiblical sources, but they can scarcely be placed anywhere else.

54. For older literature, see Yohanan Aharoni, *The Land of the Bible: A Historical Geography,* 2nd ed. (Philadelphia: Westminister, 1979), 309-17. Most recently, cf. Niemann, 280-88; Nadav Na'aman, "The District System in the Time of the United Monarchy (1 Kings 4:7-19)," in *Borders and Districts in Biblical Historiography* (Jerusalem: Sinor, 1984), 167-201; Paul S. Ash, "Solomon's? District? List," *JSOT* 67 (1995): 67-86. None of these scholars, however, attempts to correlate the district lists with the archaeology now at our disposal. Surely that would provide our only control.

Number (Aharoni)	District and old "tribal" name	Governor's name	Likely administrative center	Proposed archaeological identification
1.	Ephraim	Ben-hur	Shechem Tirzah?	Tell Balâṭah Tell el-Farʾah (North)
2.	Benjamin	Ben-deker	Beth-shemesh? Gezer?	Tell el-Rumeileh Tell el-Jezer
3.	"Aruboth" (southern coast)	Ben-ḥesed	Hepher? Socoh?	Tell Ifshar Kh. ʿAbbâd?
4.	"Dor" (northern coast)	Ben-abinadab	Dor	Tel Dor
5.	Issac	Baʿna, son of Ahilud	Megiddo	Tell el-Mutesellim
6.	Bashan/Gilead	Ben-geber	Ramoth-gilead	Tell er-Rumeith
7.	Gilead	Aḥinadab	Maḥanaim	Tell edh-Dhab?
8.	Naphtali	Aḥimaʾaz	Hazor	Tell el-Qedaḥ
9.	Asher, Zebulon	Baʿana	Yoqneam	Tell Qeimûn
10.	Issachar	Jehoshaphat	Jezreel?	Zerʿîn
11.	Benjamin	Shimei	Gibeon	Tell el-Jîb
12.	Judah/Gad	"one officer"	Jerusalem	—

Archaeological Correlations

A preliminary consideration might be that five of the 12 governor's names (or six, if one includes Baʿana) are compounded with Heb. *ben,* "Son of," which would be expected in an early society still close to its kin-based roots (and such names are, in fact, relatively rare in later Iron Age contexts). The same could be said for two more governor's names, Aḥinadab and Aḥimaʾaz, which are compounded with *ʾāḥî,* "My brother (is)," another type of name characteristic of "tribal" societies. One of these very personal names in 1 Kgs. 4, "Aḥilud," father of the governor of Megiddo, occurs in all probability on one of our earliest Hebrew inscriptions (although partially broken), a 12th-century inscribed jar handle found at Raddana, possibly biblical Beeroth.[55]

55. See Frank M. Cross, Jr., and David Noel Freedman, "An Inscribed Jar Handle from Raddana," *BASOR* 201 (1971): 19-22.

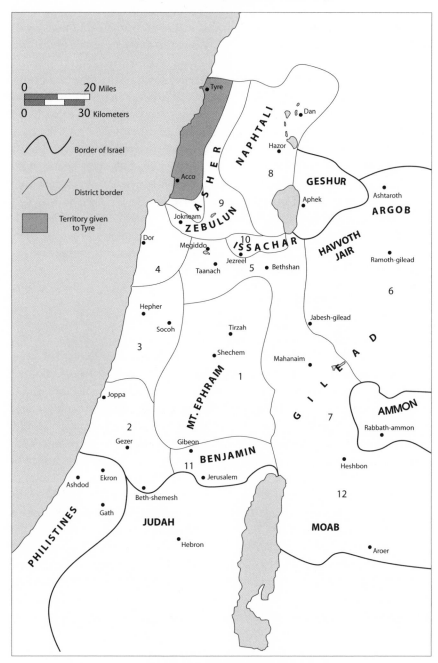

Map of proposed Solomonic districts, with principal towns
(Yohanan Aharoni, *The Land of the Bible*)

141

More compelling, however, than this evidence, which could be considered circumstantial, is the evidence concerning the district capitals in this list. While more than one possible center is listed for some districts (up to three), I have suggested (as others) the larger and better-known town as the best candidate. It is worth noting that of the 15 likely "candidates" on p. 140, all but two can be identified with known ancient sites with some certainty. Of these 15, 13 have been reasonably well excavated, several quite extensively. And what have archaeologists found in the way of 10th-century material that might qualify any of these 12 towns to have served as "district capitals," presumably with some evidence of larger-scale, centralized planning? The answers might surprise the revisionists and other historians of their ilk. We have already discussed 10th-century Megiddo, Hazor, and Gezer in looking at the evidence for state-formation; all three would likely have been the capitals of their districts in the list. But let us add several more similar sites, some with impressive archaeological remains (moving from north to south).

Tirzah

Biblical Tirzah is certainly to be identified with Tell el-Farʿah (North), a large, prominent mound 15 miles northeast of Shechem, situated at the head of the ʿAin Farʿah spring where it begins its steep descent all the way to the Jordan valley. It was excavated in the 1940s-1960s by the great French archaeologist and biblical scholar Père Roland de Vaux.[56] An important and strategic Middle Bronze town, it was refounded as biblical Tirzah sometime in the mid-10th century. Tirzah then served in the 9th century as the capital of the northern kingdom, replacing Shechem (1 Kgs. 14:17), until Omri moved the capital to Samaria after having reigned at Tirzah for seven years (16:17, 18). The 10th-century level in question if Tirzah had in fact served as a district administrative center for Solomon would be Level VII-A. This stratum, securely dated to the 10th century by its pottery, incorporated an offset-inset city wall; a two-entry-way city gate; a large public place near the gate with a shrine; and several contiguous blocks of four-room courtyard houses, so well laid out that they reflect a measure of urban planning. Thus Tirzah may well have been the administrative capital of Solomon's northern district of Ephraim.

---

56. On Tirzah, see Alain Chambon, "Farʿah, Tell el- (North): Late Bronze Age to the Roman Period," *NEAEHL* 2:439-40.

Beth-shemesh

I have suggested that Gezer, a prime example of an urbanized and strongly fortified city of the 10th century, might well have been the administrative center of
the Benjamin district (see p. 140). But an equally good candidate would be
Beth-shemesh, which is in fact named in 1 Kgs. 4:9, whereas Gezer is not. Beth-
shemesh was excavated in 1911-13 and again in 1928-1933 by British and
American archaeologists, but the results remained controversial. In 1990
Shlomo Bunimovitz and Zvi Lederman returned to the city for a new series of
campaigns using much more precise modern methods.[57] The older "Stratum
II-A" was long thought by leading authorities to date roughly to the era of David and Solomon, but it appeared that the site was unfortified during this period, leaving Beth-shemesh in limbo. The current excavations, however, have
already proven that Mackenzie's "Strong Wall" dates not to the Canaanite era,
as he thought, but to the 10th century. Furthermore, it is but one feature of a
major changeover from a rather typical "Proto-Israelite" village of the 11th century to a well-laid-out urban center with a large storehouse, a spacious public
building, and a massive underground water system that is an engineering mar-
vel. One find among the 10th-century materials is especially intriguing: a piece
of a double-sided game board inscribed with the name of the owner, "Ḥanan,"
in an early script dated by the leading authority, Frank M. Cross, to the late 10th
century. Not only does this corroborate our arguments above for Hebrew writing as early as the 10th century, but the inscribed game board is particularly significant at Beth-shemesh since its sister site, as listed next in 1 Kgs. 4:9, is "Elon
Beth-ḥanan," a nearby village named "Oak of the Ḥanan family." The name
Ḥanan also appears now on a 10th-century bowl fragment found at Tel Baṭash,
biblical Timnah, only 5 miles away. The striking convergence here suggests
again that the biblical writers and editors drew on very ancient sources in compiling the Deuteronomistic history in Kings. We now know, at last, what they
knew: Beth-shemesh in the days of the United Monarchy was not an obscure,
undefended village, but a major urban center. In the words of Bunimovitz and
Lederman, two young archaeologists of the "Tel Aviv School," "Beth-shemesh
was completely reshaped into a fortified administrative center." They conclude
of the major building:

> This public building had been constructed by the tenth century B.C.E.,
> probably during the period of the United Monarchy. Thus Beth-shemesh

---

57. See Shlomo Bunimovitz and Zvi Lederman, "Beth-Shemesh: Culture Conflict
on Judah's Frontier," *BAR* 23/1 (1997): 42-49, 75-77.

A reconstruction of the Solomonic temple, following Albright and Wright
(Othmar Keel, *The Symbolism of the Biblical World*)

adds to the evidence of a centralized administration during the period of David and Solomon.[58]

The revisionists will no doubt attempt to discredit this new evidence against Thompson's "few dozen villagers in all of the Judaean highlands." However, Thompson himself has cited the Tel Aviv group of archaeologists *approvingly,* as the direct opposite methodologically of myself and the other supposedly "biblical archaeologists."[59] The simple fact is that *all* professional Israeli, European, and North American archaeologists operate with virtually the same field and analytical methods, differences of final interpretation notwithstanding.

The Temple in Jerusalem

One of Solomon's achievements that the Hebrew Bible regards as most fabulous was his construction of a great national shrine, a monumental temple in Jerusalem. Traditional biblical scholarship has been willing to take the rather elaborate description of the Solomonic temple in 1 Kgs. 6–8 somewhat seriously, but many of the technical terms of the plan, construction, and furnishings have remained enigmatic until fairly recently for want of any external cor-

58. Bunimovitz and Lederman, *BAR* 23/1 (1997): 75, 77.
59. See Thompson, *JBL* 114 (1995): 696, and elsewhere.

roboration. The revisionists, of course, need no evidence to dismiss the descriptions in Kings as completely fanciful. But let us keep an open mind, as good historians should, and see once again whether there is any convergence between texts and artifacts.

The salient features of the Solomonic temple, based at this point solely on the biblical accounts in 1 Kings and 2 Chronicles, can be represented in chart form (see p. 146).

It is important to consider these "data," if they are such, separate from any external data that we may have, in the interest of a dispassionate, honest inquiry. A few philologians and biblical historians have attempted to do that, but most have given up due to the difficulty of several technical terms, as well as their unfamiliarity with the nonbiblical parallels. The point is that the biblical descriptions alone, however we understand the Hebrew, and however consistent the language may appear to be, seem "fantastic," literally unbelievable. Indeed, the "fabulous" nature of Solomon's temple in the Bible is largely what prompts the revisionists and others to dismiss it as a figment of later writers' and editors' imaginations, fired by the old legends of the "Golden Age of Solomon." But is the biblical temple really "fabulous," that is, nothing but a fable? Hardly. It might have been so regarded a generation ago; but the fact is that we now have direct Bronze and Iron Age parallels for *every single feature* of the "Solomonic temple" as described in the Hebrew Bible; and the best parallels come from, and only from, the Canaanite-Phoenician world of the 15th-9th centuries. Few biblical scholars, however, seem aware of these parallels.

Here I can only mention in passing the wealth of archaeological corroboration that we now possess for the Solomonic temple (listed here in reference to the features as numbered in the chart above).[60]

(1) The supposedly enigmatic tripartite or "long room" temple plan turns out to be the standard LB and early Iron temple plan throughout Syria and Palestine, with nearly 30 examples now archaeologically attested. Even the dimensions, proportions, and details fit the norm. The "Phoenician" derivation in Kings and Chronicles thus turns out to be quite correct; there was no native tradition of monumental architecture in Israel's earliest phases of urbanization in

---

60. The literature on the Solomonic temple is vast; but for orientation see William G. Dever, "Were There Temples in Ancient Israel? The Archaeological Evidence," in *Text, Artifact and Image: Revealing Ancient Israelite Religion*, ed. Theodore J. Lewis (forthcoming, 2001), and full citation there of the documentation for the following. See also, provisionally, Volkmar Fritz, "What Archaeology Can Tell Us About Solomon's Temple," *BAR* 13/4 (1987): 38-49; Elizabeth Bloch-Smith, "'Who Is the King of Glory?' Solomon's Temple and Its Symbolism," in Michael D. Coogan, J. Cheryl Exum, and Lawrence E. Stager, *Scripture and Other Artifacts*, 18-31.

1. Tripartite plan, with three successive rooms along a single axis	1 Kgs. 6:3; 2 Chr. 3:3, 4
2. Construction in Phoenician style	1 Kgs. 7:13, 18; 2 Chr. 2:1-16
3. Overall dimensions ca. 30 × 90 ft., 45 ft. high; vestibule and inner sanctum 20 × 20 ft., nave 50 × 20 ft.	1 Kgs. 6:2, 16, 17; 7:9, 10; 2 Chr. 3:3, 4
4. Foundation walls ca. 8 ft. thick	1 Kgs. 6:2
5. Construction of fitted, quarry-dressed foundation stones; reinforcing wood beams inserted every three courses in superstructure; inner walls lined with decorated cedar panels, cedar roof beams	1 Kgs. 6:6-18, 36
6. Two bronze columns with capitals flanking entrance of vestibule, elaborately decorated (pomegranates, lilies)	1 Kgs. 7:15-22; 2 Chr. 3:15-17
7. Interior decoration of wooden panels carved with gourds, palm trees, cherubs, open flowers, and chains, some overlaid with gold leaf	1 Kgs. 6:15-22; 2 Chr. 3:5-9
8. Two carved olivewood, gold-overlaid cherubs in the inner sanctum, 15 ft. high and 15 ft. from wingtip to wingtip	1 Kgs. 6:23-28; 2 Chr. 3:10-14
9. Furnishings of building and forecourt include cast bronze paneled and spoke-wheeled braziers, some with open top ca. 4 ft. high; decorated with wreaths, lions, oxen, cherubs, and palm trees	1 Kgs. 7:27-37; 2 Chr. 4:6
10. Pots, shovels, basins, firepans, and snuffers for offerings	1 Kgs. 7:48-50; 2 Chr. 4:11-22

Iron IIA, so models had to be borrowed from neighboring peoples in the centuries-old Canaanite tradition.

(2) The dressed masonry with interlaced wooden beam construction seems odd at first glance; but we now know that it was typical of MB-LB construction in monumental buildings throughout Canaan, with particularly close parallels coming from palatial buildings at Alalakh and Ugarit, as well as at LB Hazor in northern Palestine. As for the biblical description of "sawn" or chisel-dressed masonry blocks, produced in finished form at the quarries and fitted together at the site "without the sound of a hammer," that also seems odd. So it is, unless one happens to know that *precisely* such dressed, pre-fitted masonry

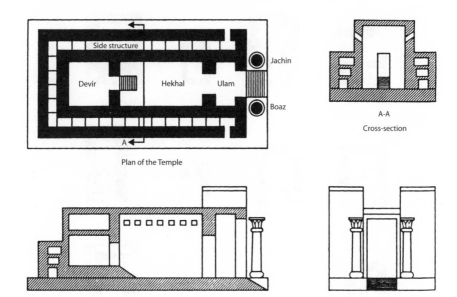

Schematic plan and section of the Solomonic temple
(*Interpreter's Dictionary of the Bible*, 4:537)

— known as "ashlar" to archaeologists — has been found by archaeologists to characterize monumental or "royal" constructions in Israel *precisely* in, and only in, the 10th-9th centuries. The finest examples of such ashlar masonry come from Dan, Hazor, Megiddo, Samaria, Gezer, and Jerusalem, all of which were probably administrative centers in some sense in the 10th-9th centuries, and thus under royal administration (above). The introduction of such ashlar masonry into Israel is now thought by some to have been due to the "Sea Peoples," Philistines and others, who brought (or at least were acquainted with) Mycenaean-style ashlar masonry to Cyprus in the late 13th century, and thence it came to the Phoenician coast where it was probably adopted locally. Once again, the Hebrew Bible's allusion to "Phoenician" artisans and craftsmen in stone makes perfect sense; and the 10th-century date is just what we would expect for early Phoenician-Israel contacts. As for the implication of an unusual style of pre-fitting the stones at the quarry, one must cite ashlar blocks discovered at Megiddo and Gezer, precisely in 10th-century contexts in monumental buildings and the city gates, which exhibit *identical* geometric masons' marks and even traces of red-chalk lines, that is, evidence of advance quarry-fitting.

(5) The description of wooden beams inserted into every third course of masonry may also seem mysterious; but it is a standard device, not only in royal

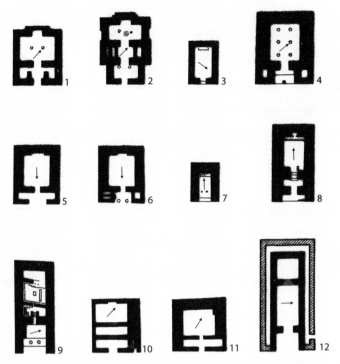

Middle Bronze and Late Bronze Age temples. 1. Hazor, Area H, Stratum III; 2. Hazor, Area H, Stratum IB; 3. Hazor, Area A; 4. Tell Balâṭah (Shechem); 5. Megiddo, Temple 2048, Stratum X, early phase, reconstruction; 6. Megiddo, Temple 2048, Stratum VIII; 7. Tell Mardikh (Ebla); 8. Tell Mardikh (Aharon Kempinski and Ronny Reich, *The Architecture of Ancient Israel*)

constructions at other sites in Israel such as Dan, but especially at sites in Syria — and precisely those where ashlar masonry is featured, as in the great palace at Ugarit. Such construction was apparently a practical device for protecting large heavy walls from earthquake damage by providing them with "break-joints," as in modern construction.

The biblical description of lower courses of masonry combined with upper courses overlaid with wooden panels remained mysterious, unparalleled until modern archaeological discoveries provided the answer. At MB Ebla and at LB Alalakh in Syria, as well as now at LB Hazor in northern Palestine, we have examples of monumental architecture featuring lower dadoes of black basalt (volcanic) stone orthostats (upright blocks), with regularly-spaced drilled holes on the upper sides that are mortises for tenons on the end of wooden panels that were once attached to the orthostats. Once again, the biblical de-

Mason's marks on stone blocks from the Outer Wall and Gatehouse in Field III at
Gezer (Photo by William G. Dever)

Lower courses of 9th-century wall at Samaria, showing groove for
interlaced wooden beams (Photo by William G. Dever)

149

scriptions, though thought to be later, are uncannily accurate for the late LB–early Iron Age. A coincidence?

(6) The two columns with elaborate capitals at the entrance of the Solomonic temple, so prominent that they receive the names Boaz and Jachin in the Hebrew Bible, are also not unique. The standard MB, LB, and Iron bipartite and tripartite temples now known throughout Canaan exhibit just such columns, as revealed by two typical surviving column bases flanking the entrance at the vestibule or entrance-porch (the "temple-in-antis" plan that is well known even down to Classical times). The description of the elaborate decoration of the capitals is not entirely clear, but the motifs fit with the rest of the decor (see 7 below). Elsewhere, in simpler 10th-9th century royal constructions, the carved "palmette" capital (previously called "proto-Aeolic"), usually not free-standing but engaged, is typical; it is almost certainly the stylized "tree-of-life" that goes back to common LB motifs.

(7) All the motifs of the interior decoration of the temple and its furnishings, formerly subject only to speculation, are now well attested in Canaanite art and iconography of the Late Bronze-Iron Ages. The reference to "chains" is not entirely clear, but it recalls the familiar LB Minoan *guilloche* design, featuring a running row of spirals turning back upon themselves, as for instance on a basalt offering basin from the Area H temple at Hazor. "Open flowers" almost certainly refer to lilies or papyrus blossoms, both of which are exceedingly common motifs in the Late Bronze Age. They are also well represented on numerous Iron Age ivories, such as those from 9th-8th century Samaria; on many seals; and on the painted storejars from the 8th-century sanctuary at Kuntillet ʿAjrûd in the Sinai. "Pomegranates," commonly associated with fertility in the ancient Near East, have LB-Iron parallels such as pendants on bronze braziers (below), on a cultic bowl from Lahav, and on seals. They also appear on ivory priests' wands from several sites, including the now famous 8th-century example from chance finds in Jerusalem, bearing the Hebrew inscription "Set apart for the priests of the temple of . . . h" (restore "Yahweh"), which in all probability comes from the temple of Solomon.

(8) The term "cherub" now presents no problem whatsoever, although long misunderstood as some sort of chubby, lovable winged creature shooting darts into lovers. The biblical "cherub" is simply a "mixed creature" of the sort widely known from the 3rd millennium onward in the ancient Near East, usually with the body of a lion, a human head, and wings. From early times the cherub is one of the principal iconographic representations of deities, often occurring in pairs bearing the king seated on his throne on their backs. Such "lion-thrones" occur in Palestine on a well-known 12th-century ivory panel

Typical 9th-8th century Phoenician-style "palmette" (older "Proto-Aeolic") capitals, usually accompanying ashlar masonry (Amnon Ben-Tor, *Archaeology of Ancient Israel*)

Inscribed ivory pomegranate, probably from the Jerusalem temple, ca. 8th century (P. Kyle McCarter, *Ancient Inscriptions*)

from Megiddo, showing a Canaanite king receiving a procession. Later Iron Age examples of cherubs include those on one register of the 10th-century terra cotta cult stand from Taʿanach; on one of the painted storejars from ʿAjrûd (a seated female figure, in my judgment Asherah; below); on the Samaria and other ivories; and on numerous seals. The symbolism of a *pair* of cherubs, a "pagan" motif, in the Jerusalem temple is now clear; Israel's national god Yahweh sat enthroned on a lion-throne just like all the other deities of the ancient Near East, except that he was invisible.

(9) The references to "lions," of course, overlap with references to cherubs, but the lion often appears in its own right in the Late Bronze and Iron Ages, often carrying a nude female deity riding on its back, almost certainly Asherah. She is widely known in ancient texts as the "Lion Lady" and is much favored in iconography from Egypt all the way to Mesopotamia. Iron Age examples of the lion motif would include an ivory box from Megiddo; both 10th-century cult stands from Taʿanach; the storejars at Kuntillet ʿAjrûd; several Samaria ivories; and many seals, especially the well-known Megiddo seal of "the servant of Jeroboam," now thought to be Jeroboam I, ca. early 9th century. "Oxen" may refer to bulls or bull calves. The bull was commonly associated in the Levant with the preeminent Canaanite male deity El, whose titles and imagery were borrowed in early Israel and associated with the new national god Yahweh, as Cross and others have shown. One recalls the famous "golden calf" set up at Mt. Sinai, and again at Bethel when the northern kingdom seceded. Actual Iron Age examples of bulls in cultic context in Palestine include a beautiful bronze bull from a 12th-century Israelite open cult place (the biblical "high place"; below) in the territory of Manasseh; one on the Taʿanach stand (some think it a horse), carrying a winged sun-disk on his back and many examples on 8th-6th century seals.

In the biblical descriptions of the temple, the building and its courtyard were said to have been lighted and heated as well by cast bronze "open-work" braziers. These were as much as 4 ft. high, some with wheels, and decorated with such motifs as cherubs, lions, oxen, and palm trees. Very similar bronze braziers have been found on Cyprus from the 12th century onward, as well as in Phoenicia.

Finally, the reference to "palm trees" is clear, as we have seen in discussing the temple's columns and capitals above. Following Yigal Shiloh's work on "palmette" capitals, as well as that of Ruth Hestrin and others, the meaning of the familiar "tree" imagery is now beyond doubt. We finally understand its frequent prohibition in the prophetic and Deuteronomistic literature and the denunciation of Asherah and her hilltop "groves," vividly expressed in the descriptions of Israel's fornication with strange gods "under every green tree and

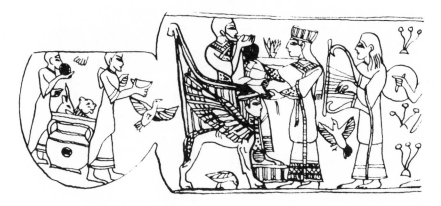

"Lion-throne," 12th-century ivory panel from Megiddo
(Gordon Loud, *The Megiddo Ivories,* No. 2)

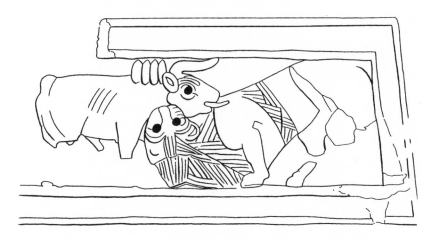

Ivory carving from Samaria, 8th century (Sylvia Schroer, *In Israel Gab es Bilder?*)

on every high hill" (Isa. 57:3-5). Given the capitals that depict the drooping fronds of the palm tree's crown, the columns themselves are clearly stylized palm trees. Indeed, we have several Iron Age *naoi,* or terra cotta temple models, that have just such a pair of trees — columns flanking the entrance, complete with palmette capitals. One comes from 10th-century levels at Tell el-Far'ah (North). Others are known from Transjordan. All have other related temple motifs as well, especially the dove, associated with Asherah/Tanit in the Phoenician world; or the "stars of the Pleiades," again an Asherah-symbol. A clear example of a Phoenician *naos* is the one from Idalion in Cyprus, probably 7th-6th

153

Bronze wheeled brazier from Cyprus (Sylvia Schroer, *In Israel Gab es Bilder?*)

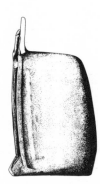

Terra-cotta model temple *(naos)* from Tell el-Far'ah (North), biblical Tirzah, ca. 10th-9th century (Louvre AO.21689; Alain Chambon, *Tell el-Fâr'ah I*)

Royal palace and tripartite temple from Tell Ta'yinat in north Syria, ca. 10th-9th century (Amnon Ben-Tor, *Archaeology of Ancient Israel*)

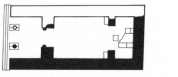

century, which has two fully-represented palm-capitals flanking the doorway and a nude female standing in the doorway, no doubt Asherah (identified with Astarte in Cyprus and associated with Adonis, Semitic *'adôn*, "Lord," or the equivalent of Canaanite-Israelite Ba'al).

I have presented a relatively small sampling of archaeological examples of the individual motifs of the Solomonic temple enumerated in Kings and Chronicles, but we have a number of more or less complete Iron Age temples that may provide even more instructive comparisons. The one usually cited (but ignored by the revisionists) is the small 9th-8th century temple at Tell Tayinat in northern Syria, excavated by the University of Chicago in the 1930s. It is a tripartite building, similar to the biblical description in both plan and size, exhibiting two columns with lion-bases at the portico. The inner sanctum (the biblical *debîr*, or "Holy of Holies") has a podium on the rear wall for a representation of the deity. The excavators presented evidence for ashlar construction, as shown in some reconstructions. Other examples of Syrian temples from the 9th-8th centuries include the recently discovered and marvelous acropolis temple at the Aramaic capital of 'Ain Der'a, in northern Syria near the Turkish border. Few archaeologists or biblical scholars are aware of this temple. It is of tripartite style, decorated in and out with carved basalt orthostats featuring lions and cherubs. The most stunning feature is the four giant footsteps carved into the threshold and then the entrance into the main hall — first one foot, then higher up a pair, and finally one striding across the threshold — the god entering "his house." The effect is overpowering.[61]

Other acropolis temples come from Zinjirli (now in Turkey; the ancient Aramaean capital of Sam'al) and from Tell Halaf. Both these small temples are part of an entire royal complex that incorporates a fortified citadel, a palace, and other monumental structures. The overall resemblance to Solomon's "upper city," with its temple, palace, harem, and administrative complex, is striking. The conclusion we must draw is that Solomon, far from being the bold originator that the biblical authors thought him to be, was little more than an Oriental potentate in the typical Iron Age Levantine style. His "genius" lay in the fact that he got away with it.

Before leaving Solomon, perhaps a bit diminished now, let me emphasize that *every single detail* of the Bible's complicated description of the Jerusalem temple can now be corroborated by archaeological examples from the Late Bronze and Iron Ages. There is nothing "fanciful" about 1 Kgs. 6–8.

---

61. See John Monson, "The New 'Ain Dara Temple: Closest Solomonic Comparison," *BAR* 26/3 (2000): 20-36, 67.

The Aramaean tripartite temple at ʿAin Derʾa in north Syria, ca. 10th-9th century
(Photo by William G. Dever)

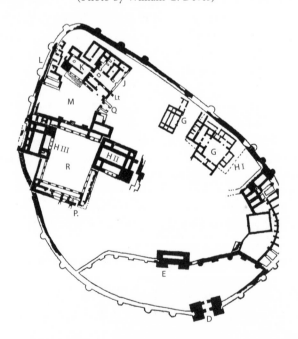

Plan of the 9th-century acropolis at Zinjirli in Turkey, ancient Samʾal
(Felix von Luschan)

What *is* truly fanciful is the notion of the revisionists that a writer in Babylon in the 6th century, much less in Palestine in the Hellenistic-Roman era, could have "invented" such detailed descriptions, which by coincidence happened to fit exactly with Iron Age temples in Syria-Palestine hundreds of years earlier — temples that had long disappeared and had been forgotten. The point is simple: the *only* life-setting for "Solomon's temple," whether there was a biblical Solomon or not, is to be found in the Iron Age, and in the 10th-8th centuries at *latest*. Perhaps the question is simply this. Which strains the reader's credulity more: the supposedly "fanciful" descriptions of the temple in the Hebrew Bible; or the revisionists' scenario of its "total invention" by writers living centuries later?[62]

62. For a portrait of a more modest, but real, historical Solomon similar to that here, cf. the view of Ernst Axel Knauf, "Le Roi est mort, vive le roi! A Biblical Argument for the Historicity of Solomon," in Handy, *The Age of Solomon*, 81-95, esp. 95: "He did not rule from the Euphrates to the Brook of Egypt, but rather from Gezer to Thamar, if not from Gibeon to Hebron. But he did exist, after all." Cf. also the more mainstream but similar treatment of J. Maxwell Miller in the same volume, "Separating the Solomon of History from the Solomon of Legend," 1-24, with full references to the literature. It is precisely this sensible middle ground from which the revisionists' dogmatic extremism excludes them.

CHAPTER 5

Daily Life in Israel in the Time
of the Divided Monarchy

According to the historical framework of those who compiled the Hebrew Bible, Israel's history was divided into two eras by the death of Solomon and what amounted to civil war over the question of dynastic succession, since the issue was considered still unsettled. We have already looked at some of the "convergences" suggesting that the biblical notion of a United Monarchy — or at least an early "state" — ca. 1020-925 B.C. is not a figment of the biblical writers' imaginations, but is based on a fundamental reality.

We turn now to the "Divided Monarchy," ca. 925-586. This era sees a long line of kings of the "house of David" on the throne in Jerusalem, which remained the capital in Judah, while the northern kingdom was ruled by a succession of unstable "royal houses" from capitals at Shechem and Tirzah, then principally at Samaria under Omri and his successors. The secessionist northern kingdom of Israel, supposedly incorporating 10 of the old "tribes," fell to the Neo-Assyrian advance in 735-721. The southern kingdom of Judah, however, whose history is strongly favored by the biblical writers and editors, persisted until the fall of Jerusalem in 587/586 to Nebuchadnezzar II and the Neo-Babylonians.[1]

We have noted the skepticism of the "revisionists" and others about the existence of a pan-Israelite "state" at all in the 10th century, and about a "state"

---

1. Any standard history of ancient Israel will cover this period in some detail — e.g., J. Maxwell Miller and John H. Hayes, *A History of Ancient Israel and Judah* (Philadelphia: Westminster, 1991), 218-436. Cf. nn. 2, 5 below. For the correlations of the biblical kinglists with Neo-Assyrian and Neo-Babylonian texts, see references in Chapter 2, n. 57.

in Judah before the mid-7th century. But just as I have rejected their view on the first issue for lack of any real evidence, I shall now dispose of the latter — again by pointing to a series of remarkable convergences between some of the biblical texts and recent archaeological discoveries.

To be sure, the revisionists do accept the reality of a northern state of Israel with its capital at Samaria after the mid-9th century; but that is *only* because the extrabiblical Neo-Assyrian annals now mention such an entity for the first time. Again, however, the biblical texts are regarded with suspicion, while the Neo-Assyrian texts are accepted at face value as a properly "historical" witness. In any case, the revisionists admit to little more than a skeletal outline of the history of a northern Israelite state, in practice only a bare king-list where there are Neo-Assyrian and Neo-Babylonian synchronisms. But there is *much* more evidence, which the revisionists routinely ignore. Why is that? The archaeological data are summarized in standard handbooks such those as by Helga Weippert, Amihai Mazar, and Amnon Ben-Tor, in hundreds of pages of detailed information.[2]

Rather than repeating the rich data presented in the above reference works, here I shall select only a few convergences to show that they establish a firm Iron Age context for the core of the biblical narratives in Kings and the Prophetic literature, while at the same time they unequivocally rule out a Hellenistic-Roman context.

King-lists and International Synchronisms

A working outline of the supposedly historical narratives of 1-2 Kings (and of 1-2 Chronicles, largely dependent upon Kings) can be developed initially by compiling a list of the Judean and Israelite kings mentioned in the book of Kings. The biblical writers mention all the kings of these two principalities from beginning to end, in successive order, giving the length of their respective reigns, usually cross-indexing them, for instance with such formulae as "King A of Judah began his reign in the ——th year of King B of Israel." These complete and elaborate king-lists can hardly be a late invention but must have come down to the final editors from much older, often contemporary court records, annals, and the like.

2. Cf. Helga Weippert, *Palästina in vorhellenistischer Zeit*, 344-681; Amihai Mazar, *Archaeology of the Land of the Bible, 10,000-586 B.C.E.*, 295-530; Amnon Ben-Tor, *Archaeology of Ancient Israel*, 258-373. Add now Larry G. Herr, "The Iron Age II Period: Emerging Nations," *BA* 60 (1997): 114-83.

In this regard, the biblical king-lists are not unusual, certainly not unique. Elsewhere in the ancient Near East we have, for instance, the well-known Sumerian king-list, a chronicle that purports to go all the way back to antediluvian times (like the biblical genealogies). There is also an Egyptian king-list that covers 30 dynasties and some 3000 years. Both these king-lists in their present form have been in a sense created by scholars, i.e., pieced together from many surviving fragments, some quite late. Nevertheless, it is still possible thereby to produce a more or less coherent and correct ordering, or what we call a "relative chronology." The "absolute" or calendrical dates for such king-lists in the 3rd millennium, however, are still lacking in precision, despite modern corrective tools like carbon 14 dating. Thus dates for the beginning of the 1st Dynasty in Egypt vary according to different authorities from ca. 3200 to ca. 3000 [3]

By the time we reach the 2nd millennium, however, the reigns of kings, particularly those in Egypt, can be fixed often within a margin of error of 10-20 years or so. Such precision is made possible by the fortunate practice of the ancients in observing the heavens for "signs," and particularly their frequent coordination of important political events such as the accession of a king with an astronomical event like a solar eclipse. Modern astronomy can fix the occurrence of an eclipse to the very day. Thus we can often obtain a fixed date upon the basis of which an entire portion of a king-list, like a particular dynasty, can be worked out in detail — a sort of "chronological peg" upon which to hang the whole sequence. The absolute dates for Egyptian chronology in the first half of the 2nd millennium can still vary by as much as some 20 years, due to uncertainty as to exactly how and from where the ancient astronomers made their observations. Thus in both Egypt and Mesopotamia early to mid-2nd millennium dates are given in various sources using so-called "high," "middle," or "low" systems. By the 1st millennium, however, both Egyptian and Mesopotamian chronologies have now been fixed within a margin of error of no more than a very few years, and often are precise to the very year. Thus we know for certain the names and exact dates of a long series of Neo-Assyrian and Neo-Babylonian kings, from before 900 to the founding of the Persian Empire in 539 by Cyrus the Great.[4]

Piecing together this story has taken a century and a half of archaeological discovery, plus painstaking detective work by scholars in many disciplines, including astronomy and the natural sciences. But thanks to those efforts we

3. For general orientation, see William A. Ward, "The Present Status of Egyptian Chronology," *BASOR* 288 (1992): 53-66.
4. See conveniently William W. Hallo and William Kelly Simpson, *The Ancient Near East: A History*, 2nd ed. (Fort Worth: Harcourt Brace, 1998).

now have a fairly reliable chronological framework for ancient Near Eastern history, especially for the 1st millennium, or our Iron Age in Palestine. Such a "framework," however reliable and detailed, does not constitute in itself a proper history, even an episodic "history of events." Yet it provides a beginning, because chronology is the essential foundation upon which any history must be built. The chronological framework gives us a structure into which we can place persons and events in a context that can give them meaning. Without a reliable chronology, history appears to be completely chaotic.

The enormous implications of well-established international synchronisms will be obvious to any reader. As our ancient Near Eastern chronologies began to take shape in the 20th century, biblical scholars quickly seized upon them in the attempt to correct the chronology of the book of Kings by means of *external* data. It must be recalled that until the mid-late 19th century no one had a fixed date at which to *begin* the biblical king-lists, much less any way of knowing whether any of the information was reliable. Real control over the biblical data through the correlation of the king-lists with Assyrian and Babylonian king-lists began with such early works as Edwin R. Thiele's *The Mysterious Numbers of the Hebrew Kings*[5] and continues in the most recent handbooks.

Biblical chronology is an enormously complex subject, and there is a vast literature.[6] The details, however, need not concern us here. For simplicity's sake we can set forth in chart form all the Israelite and Judean kings mentioned in the Bible who can be correlated directly through both biblical and nonbiblical texts with known Assyrian and Babylonian kings, giving the dates for all.

I cannot discuss here all the textual data that make these synchronisms relevant, but some key historical correlations may be mentioned. The first direct Neo-Assyrian references to Israel occur in the annals of Assur-nasir-pal II and of succeeding kings, who will soon refer to Israel as "the house of Omri," the first king they encountered in pushing their increasingly frequent campaigns westward through Syria toward the Mediterranean. The revisionists make much of the fact that the first Assyrian references occur only in the 9th century; indeed, much of their argument that "Israel" was not a "state" at all before then rests solely upon this datum. Not only is this obviously an argument from silence, but the revisionists neglect to tell their readers that the reason why Assyrian references commence only in the early-mid 9th century is simple.

---

5. (Chicago: University of Chicago Press, 1951); 3rd ed. (Grand Rapids: Zondervan, 1983).

6. See most recently William H. Barnes, *Studies in the Chronology of the Divided Monarchy in Israel*. HSM 48 (Atlanta: Scholars, 1991); Gershon Galil, *The Chronology of the Kings of Israel and Judah*. SHANE 9 (Leiden: Brill, 1996).

Israel	Judah	Mesopotamia
Omri, 876-869		Assur-nasir-pal II, 883-859
Ahab, 869-850		
Jehoram, 849-842		Shalmaneser III, 859-824
Jehu, 842-815		
Menahem, 745-738		Tiglath-pileser III, 745-727
Pekah, 737-732		Shalmaneser V, 727-722
Hoshea, 732-724 (fall of Samaria, 722/721)		Sargon II, 722-705
	Hezekiah, 715-680	Sennacherib, 705-681
	Josiah, 640-609	Nebuchadnezzar, 605-562
	Jehoiachin, 598 (died in exile)	

Their western campaigns began only then, so they could scarcely have known or cared about any of the petty states in the west, such as the Aramaean and Israelite states. The Assyrian texts do not mention Judah either in the 10th or even the 9th century for the same reason. That does not mean that Judah did not exist as a state, but only that the Assyrians did not first encounter Judah, so far south, until after the destruction of the northern kingdom in the campaigns of ca. 735-721, in the time of Sennacherib's famous campaign in 701.

Omri's son Ahab, correctly regarded by the Assyrian texts as of "the house (dynasty) of Omri," joined a coalition of western kings and met the Assyrian king Shalmaneser III in 853 at the well-documented Battle of Qarqar, in the Beq'a valley in Syria. The Assyrian annals report that Ahab contributed more forces than any other king, even Ben-Hadad I of Damascus — 2000 chariots and 10 thousand infantry. It happens that archaeologists have now correctly dated the famous "Solomonic stables" at Megiddo, the regional capital, to the 9th century, or the reign of Ahab (although some scholars suggest that they may have been royal storehouses). The great water tunnel, dug deep through the bedrock to convey the water of the nearby springs safely within the city walls, also dates to this period.[7] At Hazor, another district administrative center,

7. Yigael Yadin, "Megiddo of the Kings of Israel," *BA* 33 (1970): 66-96.

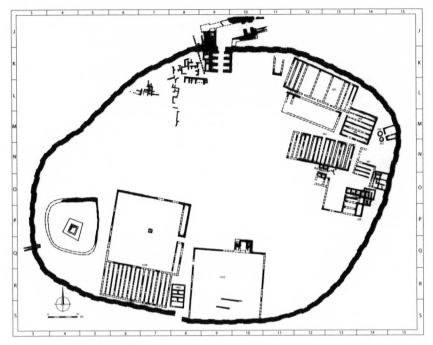

Plan of Megiddo in Stratum IV-A, ca. 9th century, perhaps a "chariot-city" of Ahab
(Aharon Kempinski and Ronny Reich, *The Architecture of Ancient Israel*)

the remains of Ahab's royal constructions include massive structures on the fortified citadel, both a large administrative complex and a series of magazines or storehouses, as well as a water shaft and tunnel that surely rank as ancient Israel's most spectacular engineering feat.[8] And at Samaria, the capital, most of the impressive royal buildings on the acropolis, including double defense walls and a multi-roomed palace, are probably to be attributed to Ahab, since his father Omri, the founder of the dynasty, ruled only seven years. It is likely that some of the beautiful ivory inlays, imports from Phoenicia, found in the final destruction layers, originated in the 9th century.[9]

It is worth noting at this point that Ahab was one of Israel's most capable rulers, to judge from both the impressive remains that he has left us, as well as the respect accorded to him and his dynasty by his Assyrian enemies. Yet the

8. Yigael Yadin, *Hazor, The Head of All Those Kingdoms* (London: Oxford, 1972).

9. See Richard D. Barnett, *Ancient Ivories in the Middle East.* Qedem 14 (Jerusalem: Hebrew University, 1982); Harold A. Liebowitz, "Ivories," *ABD* (1992), 3:584-87; Eleanor Ferris Beach, "The Samaria Ivories, *Marzeaḥ* and Biblical Texts," *BA* 55 (1992): 130-39.

Hazor water tunnel, ca. 9th century (Photo by William G. Dever)

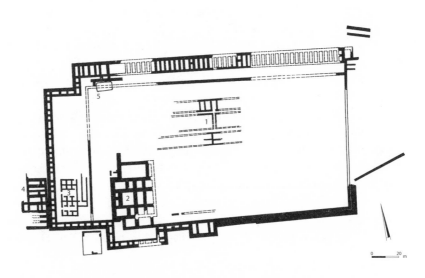

Plan of the acropolis at Samaria in the 9th century (Aharon Kempinski and Ronny Reich, *The Architecture of Ancient Israel*)

writers of the Hebrew Bible, faithful to their southern loyalties and to the Deuteronomistic theological reform movement, treat Ahab and his Phoenician wife with a contempt and loathing reserved for no other king, and attribute his downfall to his apostasy. While these stories may well be legendary as they have been utilized by the compilers of Kings in writing their history, the salient facts of Ahab's long rule are not thereby necessarily obscured — especially if the archaeological data and extrabiblical texts tend to corroborate them, as they do. In particular, the biblical writers' condemnation of such aspects of Ahab's reign as his construction of a temple of Ba'al at Samaria is, ironically, our best proof that just such a temple really did exist. In short, even the heavy overlay of propaganda does not exclude some real history. On the method of "reading between the lines" in the biblical texts we shall see more below, when we come to discuss "popular religion."

Jehu, although the biblical writers approve of the religious fervor that brought him to power, was by contrast a hapless king. He has the dubious honor of being the only king of Israel or Judah whose actual portrait has survived to come down to us. Having just acceded to the throne, he capitulated to the Assyrian Shalmaneser III in 841 and was forced to pay heavy tribute. Thus he is portrayed on the famous Black Obelisk of Shalmaneser, now in the British Museum, bowing in humiliation before the Assyrian king and kissing his feet.[10] The biblical writers do not mention Jehu's paying tribute, either because they did not know about it or possibly because they were hesitant to reject a one-time revolutionary of whom they had originally approved. 2 Kgs. 10:28-32 reports only that "in those days the Lord began to trim off parts of Israel," blaming the attrition on Jehu's abandonment of the "Yahweh only" policies that in their view had brought him to power.

Jehoram, Jehu's short-lived predecessor, is not mentioned in Assyrian records, at least those that are extant. His name, however, can now be restored with certainty from additional fragments of the Aramaic victory stele from Tel Dan, discussed above. The revisionists, as we have seen, deny the reading "the king of Israel," and especially the phrase "the house of David," even suggesting that the inscription is a forgery (Chapter 4, p. 134). Their motives, however, are suspect; and virtually all other scholars would place the Tel Dan inscription alongside the Neo-Assyrian texts, as a historical datum.[11] It is particularly important because this datum appears to confirm the correlation of Jehoram of Israel with the king of Damascus (Hazael, as 2 Kgs. 9:14-16; but possibly Ben Hadad I,

---

10. For the text and an illustration of the obelisk itself, see iller and Hayes, 286, 287.

11. Cf. Niels Peter Lemche and Thomas L. Thompson, *JSOT* 64 (1994): 3-22; and for critical discussion and later literature, see Gary N. Knoppers, *JBL* 116 (1997): 19-44.

since the year 842, Jehoram's last year, marked the succession of the two Aramaean kings). It must be cautioned, however, that the Tel Dan inscription cannot be taken simply as confirmation of the biblical accounts of Aramaean contacts, since it supplies new information that seems to differ with the biblical accounts. Yet it does confirm significant Aramaean victories over northern Israel in the mid-9th century, of which the southern writers and editors seem to have been aware, however sketchy the accounts finally produced for their own purposes in 2 Kings.

The last Israelite kings that we can correlate with the available Neo-Assyrian texts are listed in Fig. 1 above, all of whom encountered first Tiglath-pileser III in his western campaigns, and then in the fatal final siege of Samaria, which lasted perhaps a year and a half or more, Shalmaneser V and Sargon II.

The brief biblical accounts of the destruction of Samaria and the Assyrian annals may seem to contradict each other, since 2 Kgs. 18:9 attributes the victory to Shalmaneser, whereas in the Assyrian accounts it is Sargon who claims to have captured Samaria. But it is clear from the Assyrian king-lists that Sargon succeeded Shalmaneser in 722, no doubt while the siege was in progress. Thus the difficulty is easily resolved. That the biblical account provides so few specifics for such a momentous event as the fall of the northern kingdom, while Sargon supplies much more detail, also poses no problem for the historian. Each party is interpreting events to glorify its own exploits; and from the point of view of the Judean editors of Kings, apostate Israel got just what it deserved and needed no further mention.

Again, the bias of the biblical writers and editors is obvious; but because of its obviousness the bias can be easily eliminated so as to clarify underlying events that really did happen. It is worth noting here that on their own methodological postulates the revisionists would be required, in the name of consistency, to deny the fall of the northern kingdom, were it not for the *extra*-biblical accounts. Their principle is: "One witness is no witness." Yet on that ground one could deny the existence of most great individuals and events of antiquity. For instance, outside the New Testament there are almost no extant references to the earliest Christian movements, not even to the person of Jesus himself. We shall return to this methodological issue somewhat later.

Sennacherib and Hezekiah

The most widely discussed convergence between our several sources of history-writing is the well-documented campaign of a later Neo-Assyrian king, Sennacherib, against Judah in 701. Here the *divergences* may be as instructive as the convergences, remarkable as the latter are. The pertinent sources for Sennacherib's campaign of 701 are: the long passage in 2 Kgs. 18:13–19:37 (paralleled in Isa. 36–37 and supplemented by 2 Chr. 32:1-31); the Assyrian annals of Sennacherib describing the capture of 46 towns in Judah and the siege of Jerusalem; the series of monumental stone reliefs depicting the siege and capture of Lachish, found in Sennacherib's palace at Nineveh and now in the British Museum; and the extensive excavations of Lachish carried out by British archaeologists in 1935-38 and by Israeli archaeologists under David Ussishkin and others in 1973-1987.[12]

It is noteworthy, but not surprising, that the biblical editors barely mention Lachish, Kings noting in a single verse only that Sennacherib had "been" at Lachish at one time, and Chronicles adding only a single reference to a "siege" there. No destruction of the site whatsoever is alluded to in the Bible. The Assyrian annals, however, boast of the fall of Lachish as a great victory — indeed, one important enough to be commemorated by having an entire hall of Sennacherib's palace at Nineveh dedicated to it, featuring some of the finest Assyrian art ever discovered, and portraying the battle of Lachish in graphic and often horrifying detail.

What is even more remarkable is that the archaeological excavations at Lachish have corroborated the Assyrian reliefs to an astonishing degree. The evidence of it is all there: the enormous sloping siege ramp thrown up against the city walls south of the gate; the double line of defense walls, upslope and downslope; the iron-shod Assyrian battering rams that breached the city wall at its highest point; the massive destruction within the fallen city; the refugees streaming out of the destroyed gate and the burning city, headed for exile; the brutal slaughter of resisters, some depicted as having been beheaded and others staked out on the ground and flayed alive; and the abandonment of the city to Assyrian garrisons.

Virtually all the details of the Assyrian reliefs have been confirmed by archaeology, even the hilltop vantage-point from which Sennacherib must have watched the battle and from which artists made their original sketches. Also brought to light by the excavators were the double city walls; the complex siege ramp, embedded with hundreds of iron arrowheads and stone ballistae; the counter-ramp inside the city; the destroyed gate, covered by up to 6 ft. of destruction debris; huge boulders from the city wall, burned almost to lime and

---

12. Cf. *ANET*, 287, 288; David Ussishkin, *The Conquest of Lachish by Sennacherib* (Tel Aviv: Tel Aviv University, 1982); "Answers at Lachish," *BAR* 5/6 (1979): 16-39; "The Assyrian Attack on Lachish: The Archaeological Evidence from the Southwest Corner of the Site," *TA* 17 (1990): 53-86.

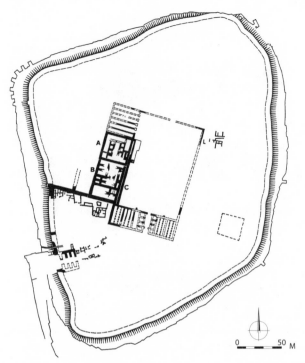

Plan of Stratum III at Lachish, late 8th century (David Ussishkin, *NEAEHL*)

fallen far down the slope; some 1500 skeletons from the cleanup of the city, thrown into a deep water-shaft; well-preserved Assyrian-style helmets; and even layers of pig bones indicating the Assyrians' love of pork, forbidden to Jews. One can only suppose that the Assyrian kings took along on their foreign campaigns an ancient version of "war correspondents," scribes who took notes and artists who made accompanying sketches. This strategy must have been designed to enhance stories back home later of the mighty king's prowess in battle — and of the fact of his being favored by the national god, now proven more powerful than the gods of all the other nations. The Assyrian texts and battle-reliefs are thus without doubt "propaganda," and of the most blatant sort. Yet they nonetheless convey an account of events that actually did happen, and moreover are now known to have happened in very much the way that the story implies.

If we turn to the unusually long and detailed accounts of the same events in the Hebrew Bible, we are struck by how obviously they are propaganda as well. The entire account in both Kings and Chronicles is obviously shaped by the Deuteronomistic historians' overriding "Jerusalem temple theology." The story

Main siege ramp and assault on the town of Lachish under Sennacherib, 701
(David Ussishkin, *The Conquest of Lachish by Sennacherib*)

Destruction debris fallen down from western gateway of Lachish into the valley below
(Photo by William G. Dever)

celebrates the miraculous delivery of Jerusalem from Sennacherib's siege when Yahweh sends a plague on the Assyrian camp, and the decimated army (2 Kgs. 19:35 specifies 185 thousand dead) retreats in defeat. According to both the Kings and Chronicles versions, blasphemous Sennacherib is not only humiliated, but upon his return to Assyria he is assassinated by his own sons while worshipping in the temple of his god Nisroch. Hezekiah does not even have to pay tribute to get the Assyrians to withdraw; the temple is saved, and its treasures are intact. All that matters is that Yahweh has triumphed over the mighty Assyrian armies and their impotent gods. Of the other sites in Judah that were threatened, only Lachish and Libnah are even mentioned, and that only in passing.[13]

I can think of no more telling demonstration of the biblical writers' and editors' single-minded preoccupation with theocratic history than their rendering of the campaign of Sennacherib. This campaign was undoubtedly the most significant event in the life of Judah in the last quarter of the 8th century, as well as the beginning of the series of disasters that finally overtook Judah and brought it to an end a century later. Yet the biblical "history" is oblivious to all but the deliverance of Jerusalem. Nevertheless, once again there is some real history that one can glean from the narrative, especially when the biases of the biblical texts can be corrected by extrabiblical evidence, as we shall see. This much is clear, even from the biblical text alone, when read with some sophistication: (1) Lachish, presumed to be the most strategic fortress in all Judah, was besieged. (2) Jerusalem was also besieged and severely threatened by Sennacherib, but for some reason it was not conquered. (3) The Assyrians did retreat, and somewhat later Sennacherib died and was succeeded by his son Esarhaddon (681-669).[14]

It is interesting to see that these "bare facts" gleaned from the biblical accounts do not necessarily contradict the version of Sennacherib's campaign of 701 in Assyrian records. There are, as would be expected, a number of differing interpretations of the events in the Assyrian version. For one thing, we learn that as many as 46 Judean towns and cities were threatened in one way or another, not just Jerusalem, Lachish, and Libnah. In addition, the Assyrian records do narrate a determined siege of Jerusalem — Sennacherib boasts "Hezekiah, the Jew (i.e., Judean), I shut up like a bird in a cage"; but the texts pointedly do not claim an actual destruction of the city. Finally, Assyrian records note that Sennacherib did die subsequently at the hands of assassins, his own sons, although 20 years later (ca. 681) rather than almost immediately as

---

13. On Lachish, see n. 12 above. The location of Libnah is not certain, but it is often identified with nearby Tell Bornât, which remains unexcavated.

14. See further Miller and Hayes, 353-65 and references there.

the biblical story implies (i.e., as prompt, divine retribution). Yet none of these interpretations of events in the Assyrian sources contradicts the essential facts of the biblical account, only their interpretation by the Deuteronomists — whose biases are so well known that they can rather easily be stripped away from the story. When we add the unequivocal evidence of the reliefs and the archaeological discoveries at Lachish (and Jerusalem), a reasonably accurate and believable history of Sennacherib's invasion emerges. Again, the best possibility for history lies in the convergences, divergences, and the "balance of probability."

The Last Days of Judah

Between a century and a century-and-a-half later, we meet the last Judean kings who are mentioned in Mesopotamian texts, especially the ill-fated reformer Josiah, and the last independent king of Judah, Jehoiachin. Josiah's fatal involvement in the Battle of Carchemish, and his death at Megiddo while attempting to block the advance of an Egyptian relief column in 609, can be correlated with both the rise of the Neo-Babylonian Empire under Nebuchadnezzar II, beginning in 605, and the reign of the Egyptian 26th-Dynasty pharaoh Neco II (609-593). The accounts of Josiah's last days in 2 Kgs. 23:29, 30 and 2 Chr. 35:20-24 make perfect sense in the light of what we know from other sources about the turbulent transfer of power from Neo-Assyria to Neo-Babylonia in the mid- to late 7th century, as well as Egypt's attempts to intervene and thus stave off an invasion of Egypt itself by either power. Josiah, caught hopelessly in the middle of the conflict, forfeited his life and his kingdom. Here the biblical narrators have got it right, despite the fact that the tragedy destroys *their* history, rather than validating it. They solemnly record all the portentous events at face value, even though they lionized Josiah and mourned the fall of Jerusalem a few years later, with little or no editorializing.

The last real king of Judah, Jehoiachin, is known to us in the Hebrew Bible only from brief accounts. He gained the throne at 18 after the Babylonians' first siege in 598/597, then three months later was deposed and sent to Babylon in exile, where he eventually died. Seal impressions of a certain Jehoiakin, no doubt this very king, have been found. Moreover, the Babylonian chronicles from the year of 562 refer to rations provided for an exiled king "Jehoiakin."[15] *Sic transit gloria mundi.*

---

15. *ANET,* 308; on the last days of Judah, see Miller and Hayes, 377-436.

Religion and Cult in the Divided Monarchy

I have argued thus far that at least an outline of what might be called a "political history" of Israel and Judah in the 300-year period of the Divided Monarchy emerges from the core material of Kings, despite its overarching, tendentious Deuteronomistic framework. Now we must begin to fill in that outline by expanding beyond Kings to the broader Deuteronomistic and prophetic literature and turning then to archaeological discoveries. The latter, and the latter alone, can "flesh out" a history of ancient Israel, precisely because of archaeology's unique ability, as we saw above, to supplement the elitist approach of the "great tradition" of the classic literature. Archaeology at its best provides a graphic illustration of the everyday masses, the vast majority of ordinary folk, their brief lives forgotten by the biblical writers in their obsession with eternity, their voices long muted until modern archaeology allows them to speak again to us. It was these anonymous folk — not just kings and priests and prophets whom we know by name — -who made Israel what it was. Their world, their situations, are different from those who wrote the Bible, but no less important for that. Indeed, the *lack* of convergences here may be the most revealing of all the data that we have now for writing a realistic history of Israel — not the "ideal Israel" of the imaginations of the biblical writers, but an "Israel, warts and all."

Let us begin to listen to the lost voices by focusing first on religion and cult in the Divided Monarchy. In doing so, we must recognize, as one of my theologian friends reminds me, that the Hebrew Bible is "a minority report." Largely written by priests, prophets, and scribes who were intellectuals, above all religious reformers, the Bible is highly idealistic. It presents us not so much with a picture of what Israelite religion really was, but of what it should have been — and would have been, had the biblical writers only been in charge. Furthermore, the Bible is an elitist document in another sense, because it was written and edited exclusively by men. It therefore represents their concerns — those of the Establishment of the time — to the virtual exclusion of all else. In particular, the focus is on "political history," the deeds of great men, "public events," affairs of state, and the great ideas and institutions. The Bible almost totally ignores private and family religion, women's cults and "folk religion," and indeed the religious practices of the *majority* in ancient Israel and Judah.

If the biblical texts alone are an inadequate witness to ancient Israelite religion, where else could we turn for information? Modern archaeology can be an excellent source, for many reasons. First, archaeology has brought to light a mass of new, factual, tangible information about the long-lost biblical world, and the history and religion of ancient Israel in particular. Second, this new information is incredibly varied, almost unlimited in quantity, and has the further advantage of being more "objective" than texts in some ways, that is, less deliberately edited. Finally, archaeology possesses unique potential for illuminating "folk religion," in contrast to the "official religion" of the texts, because material remains reflect the masses rather than only the elites, and they illustrate concrete religious practices rather than abstract theological formulations. Thus, if "religion" is what the majority of people actually *do* in the name of the deity or deities, rather than what priests and clerics say they *should* do, then archaeology can give us a different and perhaps more realistic picture of Israelite religion (although not one that is necessarily "truer" in the theological sense).

In what follows I shall review some of the recent archaeological data, which I believe force us to rewrite all previous histories of ancient Israelite religion, and in particular to address the issue of whether Israel in the monarchical period was truly monotheistic.[16]

A Survey of Cult-Places Brought to Light by Archaeology

Let us look now at a number of recently excavated sites in Israel that have produced materials that are clearly cultic in nature, some of them no doubt what the Bible means by references to condemned *bāmôt,* or "high places." We shall move from north to south and from the period of the judges to the Monarchy, or the Iron I-II periods.

16. For details and further documentation, see my extensive treatments elsewhere, including "'Will the Real Israel Please Stand Up': Part II: Archaeology and the Religions of Ancient Israel," *BASOR* 298 (1995): 37-58; "Folk Religion in Early Israel: Did Yahweh Have a Consort?" in *Aspects of Monotheism — How God Is One,* ed. Hershel Shanks (Washington: Biblical Archaeology Society, 1997), 27-56. A useful account of popular or "folk" religion from a textual perspective is Karel van der Toorn, *From Her Cradle to Her Grave: The Role of Religion in the Life of the Israelite and Babylonian Woman.* Biblical Seminar 23 (Sheffield: Sheffield Academic, 1994). See also Susan Ackerman, *"Under Every Green Tree": Popular Religion in Sixth-Century Judah.* HSM 46 (Atlanta: Scholars, 1992). The latest works are again by van der Toorn, *Family Religion in Babylonia, Syria and Israel: Continuity and Change in the Forms of Religious Life.* SHANE 7 (Leiden: Brill, 1996); *The Image and the Book: Iconic Cults, Aniconism, and the Rise of Book Religion in Israel and the Ancient Near East* (Leuven: Peeters, 1997). Finally, see the seminal treatment of Jacques Berlinerblau, *The Vow and the "Popular Religious Groups" of Ancient Israel.* JSOTSup 210 (Sheffield: Sheffield Academic, 1996). The best all-round work is that of Rainer Albertz, *A History of Israelite Religion in the Old Testament Period,* 1: *From the Beginnings to the End of the Monarchy* (Louisville: Westminster John Knox, 1994). See now the magisterial work of Ziony Zevit, *The Religions of Ancient Israel: A Synthesis of Parallelactic Approaches* (New York: Continuum, 2001).

The "high place at Tel Dan," ca. 9th century (Abraham Biran, *EAEHL*)

(1) A small open-air hilltop sanctuary in the tribal territory of Manasseh, dating to the 12th century, was excavated in 1981 by Amihai Mazar. It features a central paved area with a large standing-stone (the biblical *māṣṣēbâ*) and an altarlike installation, the whole surrounded by an enclosure wall. The only material recovered consisted of a few early Iron I sherds; some fragments of metal and of a terra-cotta offering stand; and a splendidly preserved bronze zebu bull. The bull, possibly a votive, is matched almost precisely by another bronze bull found by Yadin at Hazor in a Late Bronze context some two centuries earlier. It must be recalled that the principal epithet of El, the chief male deity of the Canaanite pantheon in pre-Israelite times, was "Bull." Thus the Manasseh shrine or sanctuary — the only clear Israelite cultic installation yet found from the period of the judges — was probably associated not with Yahweh, but with the old Canaanite deity El (although in the earliest period Yahweh appears as an El-like figure).[17]

(2) Tel Dan on the Lebanon border, one of the early centers of the northern kingdom of Israel, has been excavated since 1966 by Avraham Biran. At the highest point on the northern end of the mound there is an impressive 10th-9th-century installation. It consists of a large podium or altar; an approach in the form of a monumental flight of steps, all in fine ashlar (chisel-dressed) masonry; and an adjoining three-room sanctuary, in one room of which was found a low stone altar, a nearby ash-pit, and three iron shovels. The latter is probably an example of the biblical *liškâ*, or sanctuary; and the whole installation is probably best understood as an example of the enigmatic Canaanite-style *bāmâ*, or "high place," that is condemned in the Hebrew Bible. We may have here, in fact, the very "house/temple 'on' high places" that is mentioned in 1 Kgs. 12:31. Related materials brought to light within the precinct include an olive oil–pressing

17. Amihai Mazar, "The 'Bull Site' — An Iron Age I Open Cult Place," *BASOR* 247 (1982): 27-42.

installation, for liturgical purposes; large and small four-horned altars of the types alluded to in several biblical passages; a bronze-working installation and several implements such as a fine priestly scepter; seven-spouted lamps; a *naos*, or household temple model/shrine; several dice; both male and female figurines; and other items. This cult installation lasted from the 10th/9th century into the 8th/7th century. If we attempt to coordinate text and artifact, it is evident that most of the features of the Dan "high place" are misunderstood by the southern writers and editors of the Hebrew Bible — loyal to the temple in Jerusalem — or not mentioned at all. The installation in general, however, is condemned as a prime example of the worship of "foreign gods" — in this case, no doubt the Canaanite-Phoenician deities Ba'al and his consort Asherah. Nevertheless, despite the disapproval of the biblical writers, the archaeological evidence from Dan illustrates dramatically that "non-Establishment" cults did exist, in the early Monarchy as well as throughout Israel's and Judah's history.[18]

(3) Tell el-Far'ah (North), biblical Tirzah, the temporary capital of northern Israel in the early 9th century, was excavated by Père Roland de Vaux in 1946-1960. Just inside the city gate is a *māṣṣēbâ* and an olive-press, very similar to installations at Dan — no doubt a "gate-shrine" like those of which the Bible hints. In addition, there were found at Tell el-Far'ah (North) numerous 10th/9th-century female figurines (some of the earliest known "Asherah" figurines; below); and in particular a rare terra-cotta *naos*, which to judge from comparative examples typically had a deity, or pair of deities, standing in the doorway, one of them certainly Asherah, the old Canaanite Mother Goddess (above, p. 152). This Stratum VII-B Canaanite temple model is roughly contemporary with the Solomonic temple in Jerusalem, which according to the biblical writers centralized all worship in Jerusalem.[19]

(4) Another example of supposedly prohibited local worship is a household shrine found in 10th-century levels at Megiddo, a Solomonic regional capital in the north. The shrine consists of several cult vessels and small four-horned limestone altars, of the type found at many Israelite sites. They were probably used for incense-offerings, which are integral to official worship in the biblical texts, although the horned altars are not specifically referred to (only much larger examples are mentioned, as in 1 Kgs. 1:50, 51).[20]

---

18. See conveniently Avraham Biran, *Biblical Dan* (Jerusalem: Israel Exploration Society, 1994), 159-233.

19. Alain Chambon, *Tell el-Fâr'ah*, 1: *L'Âge de Fer* (Paris: Éditions Recherche sur les civilisations, 1984), 66.

20. See Gordon Loud, *Megiddo II* (Chicago: University of Chicago Press, 1948), 45, 46, figs. 100-2.

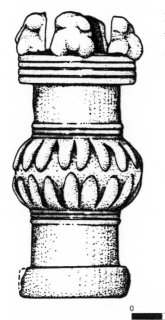

Bronze priestly scepter-head found near
the altar at Tel Dan, ca. 9th century
(Abraham Biran, *Biblical Dan*)

0   3

Plan of Tell el-Far'ah, biblical Tirzah,
ca. 10th century (Stratum VIII)
(Helga Weippert, *Palästina in
vorhellenisticher Zeit*)

(5) A few miles east of Megiddo lies its sister city Ta'anach, where even more substantial 10th-century cultic remains have come to light.[21] A shrine there consists again of a large olive press; a mold for making terra-cotta female figurines like those at Tell el-Far'ah (North), probably as votives; and a hoard of astragali, or knuckle-bones, for use in divination rites. More remarkable were two large, multi-tiered terra-cotta offering stands. One, found long ago in the German excavations, depicts ranks of lions. The other, from the American excavations of Paul W. Lapp, has four tiers. This stand is probably best understood as a temple model. The top row or story shows a quadruped carrying a winged sun-disk on its back. The next row down depicts the doorway of the "temple," which however stands empty, perhaps to signify that the male deity presupposed here in the door of his "house" (in Hebrew, *bêt*, "house," means "temple" when used of a deity) is invisible. The third row down has a pair of sphinxes, or winged lions, one on each side, examples of the biblical "cherubim" that are located in the Solomonic temple. The bottom row is startling, for it has two similar flanking lions, with a smiling nude female figure standing between them, holding them by the ears. Who is this enigmatic figure? I have suggested elsewhere that she can be no other than the Canaanite Asherah.[22] She is known throughout the Levant in this period as "the Lion Lady," often depicted nude, riding on the back of a lion. A 12th-11th century inscribed arrowhead from the Jerusalem area reads on one side in the Canaanite or Old Hebrew script "Servant of the Lion Lady," probably the title of a professional archer, naming his patroness. On the other side we read his own name, "Ben-'Anat" or "son of 'Anat," 'Anat being the old Canaanite war goddess.[23] We can only wonder what a model temple depicting possibly an invisible Yahweh and a *very* visible Asherah is doing at Israelite Ta'anach in the days of Solomon and the Jerusalem temple. This is a remarkable piece of ancient Israelite iconography. As we shall see, however, there is much more evidence today for the cult of Asherah in Israel in the biblical period.

(6) Among the many pieces of archaeological evidence of religion from Jerusalem, I single out only a few here. A monumental rock-cut tomb on the grounds of the Dominican École Biblique, long known but only recently dated correctly to the 8th-7th century, has benches for the bodies that feature

---

21. Paul W. Lapp, "Taanach by the Waters of Megiddo," *BA* 30 (1967): 2-27; for a good drawing of the stand see Weippert, 472, fig. 4:31.

22. William G. Dever, "Asherah, Consort of Yahweh? New Evidence from Kuntillet 'Ajrûd," *BASOR* 255 (1984): 21-37.

23. Frank Moore Cross, "Newly Found Inscriptions in Old Canaanite and Early Phoenician Scripts," *BASOR* 238 (1980): 1-20.

Terra-cotta cult stand from Taʿanach, ca. 10th century, showing Asherah the "Lion Lady" on the bottom register (Helga Weippert, *Palästina in vorhellenisticher Zeit*)

The "Lion Lady," Egyptian New Kingdom plaque, with all three of her names: Qudšu, Astarte, Anat (Collection of Winchester College)

179

headrests carved in the shape of the well-known Hathor wig. This distinctive bouffant wig is worn in New Kingdom Egypt by Qudshu, "the Holy One," who is the Egyptian cow-goddess now identified with the popular Canaanite goddess Asherah. The point is that even in Jerusalem, the spiritual center, a pious Judean woman could be buried with her head resting in the representation of a wig that was everywhere associated with the Canaanite goddess Asherah.[24]

Another tomb, of the late 7th century, found near St. Andrew's Scots Church, produced similar benches with headrests, as well as two silver amulets. One amulet is particularly interesting, since it is inscribed with the Priestly Blessing of Num. 6:24-27. Its date ca. 600 makes it by far our oldest surviving fragment of a biblical text — at least four centuries older, for instance, than any manuscripts from the Dead Sea caves. Furthermore, this bit of Scripture is not being used for edification, as the priests would no doubt have prescribed, but as "magic," which was strictly forbidden in orthodox Israelite religion. What we have here is a biblical text engraved on silver, rolled up and worn around the neck on a string as an amulet, a good-luck charm.[25] And there are many more archaeological examples of such magical or superstitious rituals, from Israelite and Judean contexts, some of them invoking foreign deities like the Egyptian gods Bes and Osiris. Biblical scholars have paid little attention to archaeological finds of this sort, but they should, because they illustrate the prevalent "folk religion" that the biblical writers condemn so vigorously — apparently without really understanding themselves what they were dealing with. A prime example of such elite misunderstanding of "folk religion" is 1 Kgs. 15:13 (2 Chr. 15:16), which condemns a *mipleṣet*, "an abominable thing" of some sort, made for Asherah. That word occurs only here in the Hebrew Bible, and we are not sure of its meaning. The later biblical writers probably weren't sure either; they only knew that one shouldn't have the "abominable thing," whatever it was.

(7) Beersheba, marking the southern limits of the settled zone in monarchical times (the borders "from Dan to Beersheba"), was excavated by Yohanan Aharoni in 1969-1975. Among the most spectacular finds were several large, dressed blocks of stone that make up a monumental four-horned altar like those that perhaps stood in the Levitical "cities of refuge" (especially in Jerusalem; 1 Kgs. 1:50-53), where one could seek asylum by clinging symbolically to

---

24. Gabriel Barkay and Amos Kloner, "Jerusalem Tombs from the Days of the First Temple," *BAR* 12/2 (1986): 22-39.

25. Gabriel Barkay, *Ketef Hinnom: A Treasure Facing Jerusalem's Walls* (Jerusalem: The Israel Museum, 1986). On magic, see Marvin Meyer and Paul Mirecki, eds., *Ancient Magic and Ritual Power* (Leiden: Brill, 1995); Ann Jeffers, *Magic and Divination in Ancient Palestine and Syria.* SHANE 8 (Leiden: Brill, 1996).

the horns of the altar. This is one of only two examples of such large altars that archaeologists have brought to light (the other being at Dan). Its stones, however, were not recovered *in situ,* but were found built into the rubble walls of the later "storehouses" near the city gate — stones from a *dismantled* horned altar, thrown out and picked up later for building material. Where had that altar originally stood, and why had it been dismantled? Aharoni argued that his "basement building" — a large structure set into an unusually deep foundation trench that obliterated lower levels — was the site of what had once been a large temple. There the altar had originally stood. In that case, the temple had perhaps been destroyed in the religious reforms of Hezekiah in the 8th century, among whose measures was pulling down the "high places" and their altars. As though to confirm Aharoni's theory, a large krater or two-handled pot found nearby is inscribed in Hebrew *qōdeš,* "sacred/set apart" (for cultic use). Here at Beersheba we have perhaps the first actual archaeological evidence confirming the reforms of various Judean kings — and the need for such, just as the biblical prophets complained in denouncing what they call the worship of "foreign gods."[26]

(8) Not far east from Beersheba is Arad, a small Judean hilltop fortress and sanctuary also excavated by Aharoni. The dating and interpretation of the various 10th-6th-century phases remain controversial because of faulty excavation methods and the lack of final reports. Yet the main points for our purpose are clear. One corner of the walled citadel of the 9th-8th centuries is occupied by a tripartite (or three-room) temple, very similar to the plan of the partly contemporary temple in Jerusalem. The outer area (the biblical *'ûlām,* "vestibule") is actually an open-air courtyard with a large stone altar, at the base of which there were found burned animal bones; a terra-cotta offering stand; a fine crouching bronze lion; and two shallow platters inscribed with the Hebrew letters *qōp kāp,* probably an abbreviation for *qōdeš hā-kōhānîm,* "sacred/set apart for the priests." And several priestly families at Arad, with names identical to such families in the Bible, are in fact known from the ostraca, or inscribed potsherds, one of which (no. 18) also mentions the "house/temple of Yahweh." The middle chamber (the biblical *hêkāl,* or main room) is a smaller room, its main feature being low benches, undoubtedly for the presentation of offerings. The inner chamber (the biblical *debîr,* or "Holy of Holies") is a still smaller niche. It features two stylized horned altars at the approach steps, found with an oily organic substance on top that suggests incense; and against the back wall, two stone stelae (the biblical *māṣṣēbôt,* "sacred standing stones") with traces of red paint, one of them conspicuously smaller than the other. Since

26. Yohanan Aharoni, "The Horned Altar of Beer-sheba," *BA* 37 (1979): 2-6.

An unrolled silver foil amulet from
a Jerusalem tomb, ca. 600
(Gabriel Barkay)

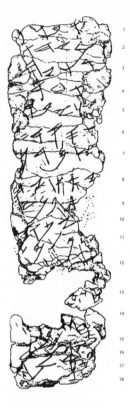

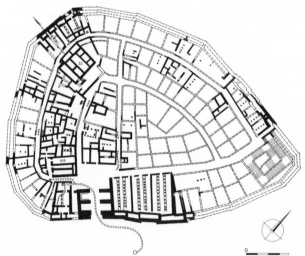

Plan of Stratum III at Beersheba, ca. 8th century (Aharon Kempinski and Ronny Reich,
The Architecture of Ancient Israel)

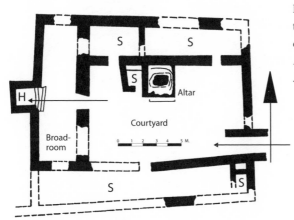

Plan of Israelite fort and temple at Arad, ca. 8th century (Helga Weippert, *Palästina in vorhellenisticher Zeit*)

these altars and standing stones had been carefully laid down and floored over in a later stage of this building, Aharoni argued that here again we have archaeological evidence of the reforms of Hezekiah (others said Josiah), who abolished local sanctuaries in order to favor the Jerusalem temple. I would go further to suggest that both the bronze lion and the pair of standing stones show that Asherah, the "Lion Lady," was worshipped *alongside* Yahweh at Arad, and for perhaps a century or more before this became a problem for religious reformers. Do we confront here the sort of "syncretism" that the prophets decried; or was Asherah so thoroughly assimilated into the Israelite cult from early times that she was thought by most Israelites to be "native" to their belief and practice, i.e., associated with Yahweh, perhaps even his consort?[27]

(9) As though to answer this question, dramatic textual evidence of Asherah has recently come to light at two sites. Kuntillet ʿAjrûd is a hilltop caravanserai, or stop-over station, in the remote eastern Sinai desert, discovered by the British explorer Edward Palmer in 1878 and excavated in 1978 by the Israeli archaeologist Zeʾev Meshel. Again the finds are controversial and published only in preliminary reports.[28] Yet the impact of the material known so far is

27. Yohanan Aharoni, "Arad: Its Inscriptions and Temple," *BA* 31 (1968): 2-32; Zeʾev Herzog, Miriam Aharoni, and Anson F. Rainey, "Arad — An Ancient Israelite Fortress with a Temple to Yahweh," *BAR* 13/2 (1987): 16-35; Herzog et al., "The Israelite Fortress at Arad," *BASOR* 254 (1984): 1-34.

28. See Zeʾev Meshel, *Kuntillet Ajrud: A Religious Centre from the Time of the Judean Monarchy* (Jerusalem: Israel Museum, 1978). See my early interpretation in *BASOR* 255 (1984): 21-37. There is now a considerable secondary literature, as for instance in many of the chapters in Patrick D. Miller, Paul D. Hanson, and S. Dean McBride, eds., *Ancient Israelite Religion: Essays in Honor of Frank Moore Cross* (Philadelphia: Fortress, 1987).

Platter/bowl from Arad, with the Hebrew letters *qôp-kâp*, probably an abbreviation for "sanctified for the priests" (Yohanan Aharoni, *Arad Inscriptions*)

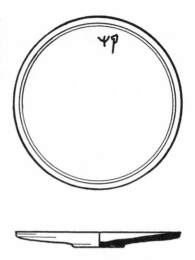

revolutionary for our understanding of ancient Israelite and Judean religion. The main structure, from the 8th century, is a large rectangular fort with double walls, towers at the corners, and an open courtyard in the center, similar to other known Iron Age fortresses in the Negev. The entrance area, however, is unique. It is approached through a white plaster esplanade that leads into a passageway flanked by two plastered siderooms with low benches, behind which are cupboard-like chambers. The latter are clearly *favissae,* or storage areas for discarded votives and cult offerings, such as are known at many Bronze-Iron Age sanctuaries; and the benches are not for sitting but for placing offerings, again with many parallels. If there were any doubt about the existence of a shrine here in the ʿAjrûd gateway (and surprisingly enough, some scholars do doubt it), it is removed by even a cursory examination of the finds. These include a large stone votive bowl inscribed in Hebrew: "(Belonging) to Obadaiah, Son of Adnah; may he be blessed by Yahweh." On several large storejars there are painted motifs and scenes: a processional of strangely garbed individuals; the familiar "tree of life" with flanking ibexes; lions; and especially a striking scene with two representations of the Egyptian good-luck god Bes and a seated half-nude female figure playing a lyre, whose distinctive lion-throne suggests to me that she is a goddess (as we find seated on lion-thrones, along with kings, elsewhere in the ancient Near East). A Hebrew inscription on this storejar is a blessing-formula, ending with "May X be blessed by Yahweh of Samaria and by his Asherah." Other Hebrew inscriptions also mention Asherah, as well as El and Baʿal, alongside Yahweh. Some biblical scholars take a "minimalist" view of the appearance of the Hebrew word *ʾăšērâ* here, which occurs some 40 times in the Hebrew Bible and often appears to refer only to a wooden image of some

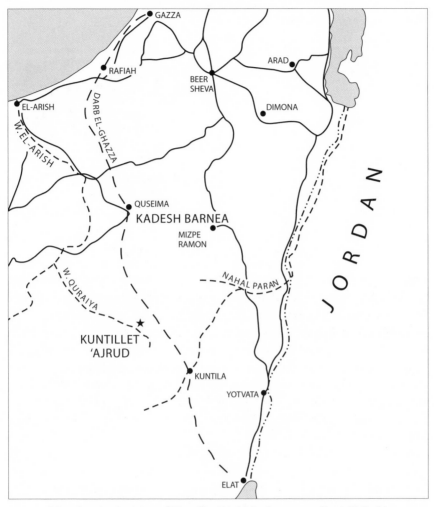

Map showing location of Kuntillet 'Ajrûd in the eastern Sinai (P. Peck)

kind, a pole or tree, commonly associated with the well-known goddess of the same name.[29] Yet a growing number of scholars begin to recognize the point: whether "a/Asherah" at 'Ajrûd means the goddess herself or merely her symbol as an "agent of blessing" that could be invoked alongside Yahweh, it was the widespread perception of the goddess's *reality* in ancient Israel that gave the

29. For the textual evidence, see Saul M. Olyan, *Asherah and the Cult of Yahweh in Israel.* SBLMS 34 (Atlanta: Scholars, 1988); and also Ackerman. For the association of Asherah with trees, see the pioneering study of Ruth Hestrin, "The Lachish Ewer and the 'Asherah," *IEJ* 37 (1987): 212-21.

Painted scene and Hebrew inscription mentioning "Asherah" on a storejar from Kuntillet ʿAjrûd, ca. 9th-8th century (Zeʾev Meshel, *Kuntillet ʿAjrûd*)

symbolism its efficacy. Either way, old Canaanite Asherah was not dead and gone in many circles in Israel, but was alive and well — despite the abhorrence of some prophets and priests by the 8th-7th centuries, when attempts to discredit her began. The archaeological evidence at Kuntillet ʿAjrûd alone, even on a minimalist interpretation, would in my opinion force us to rethink much of what scholars have written about "normative" religion, about monotheism, in ancient Israel. The ideal of the later formulations of the Hebrew Bible is one thing; actual religious practice was another, reflecting a popular religion that we would scarcely have known about apart from the accidents of archaeological preservation and discovery.[30]

(10) The ʿAjrûd texts do not stand alone, but actually corroborate the meaning of an 8th-century Judean tomb inscription at Khirbet el-Qôm near Hebron that I discovered in 1968. Although parts of the reading are difficult and controversial, the best reading goes something like this:

> ʿUriyahu, the Prince; this is his inscription.
> May ʿUriyahu be blessed by Yahweh,
> For from his enemies he has saved him by his Asherah.

Virtually all scholars now agree that the reading "by his a/Asherah" in line 3 is certain — and *identical* to that at ʿAjrûd, and with the same problems of interpretation. Nevertheless, considering that we have literally only a handful of ancient Hebrew inscriptions from tombs or cultic contexts, the fact that two of

---

30. See works cited in nn. 16, 29.

Inscription no. III from Khirbet el-Qôm, ca. 8th century (William G. Dever)

them mention "a/Asherah" in a context of blessing is statistically striking. It would appear that in *non*-biblical texts such an expression was common, an acceptable expression of Israelite-Judean Yahwism throughout much of the Monarchy. Thus Asherah was thought of as the consort of Yahweh, or at least as a "hypostasis" of him, a personified aspect (as "Sophia," Wisdom, became later; or the "Shekinah," God's "effective presence" in the world of medieval Kabbalistic Judaism). I would argue that the orthodox textual tradition has, in effect, purged the Bible of many original references to the Goddess Asherah, as well as downplaying the remaining references to the point where many are scarcely intelligible.[31]

31. For the original publication, see William G. Dever, "Iron Age Epigraphic Material from the Area of Khirbet el-Kôm," *HUCA* 40-41 (1969-1970): 139-204. For more recent bibliography and interpretation, see "Archaeology and the Ancient Israelite Cult: How the Khirbet el Qôm and Kuntillet ʿAjrûd Texts Have Changed the Picture," *ErIsr* 26 (1999): 9*-15*.

Artifactual Data and Israelite Cult

In addition to the cult-places discussed above (and a number of other similar examples), we now have many individual artifacts that reflect the variety of religious beliefs and practices in ancient Israel and Judah.

(1) We have dozens of terra-cotta offering-stands from ancient Israel, dating to the 12th-7th centuries. They continue a long Bronze Age tradition of offering-stands throughout the ancient Near East, which as we know from seal impressions and paintings were used to present gifts of food and drink to the gods, as well as perhaps to offer incense. Such rituals also became part of the standard cult in ancient Israel, as we know from many biblical texts, so there must have been at one time a fairly elaborate paraphernalia. Yet it is a curious fact that *nowhere* in the Hebrew Bible are offering-stands even hinted at, as though the writers were unaware of them — or perhaps disapproved? (The text is also silent concerning other cult artifacts that we now have.)

Some of the Israelite-Judean offering-stands are rather plain, with no obvious symbolic significance. But others, like the 10th-century Taʿanach stand discussed above, are full of "Canaanite" religious imagery. One of the most enigmatic is a 12th-century stand from ʿAi, certainly an Israelite site of the period of the judges, that has numerous fenestrations or "windows," probably for use in incense-burning, but also features a curious row of well-modeled, protruding human feet around the bottom. A foot-fetish cult? In any case, the omission of any reference whatsoever in the Hebrew Bible to these common offering-stands, when the texts are so preoccupied with sacrificial rituals, should give us pause. What *are* the biblical writers and editors describing: actual religious practices in ancient Israel, or their own idealistic, theologized reconstruction of what should have taken place?[32]

(2) We have noted above some of the four-horned limestone altars, including the one life-sized example we have from Beersheba. Most examples, however — and at least 40 are now known — are of the miniature variety, from about 1 to 3 ft. high. These small horned altars, ranging from the 10th to the 6th centuries, are found all over Israel and Judah, in many contexts, cultic, domestic, and even industrial.[33] The significance of the four hornlike projections at the corner (sometimes stylized) is uncertain, but the symbolism may be connected with the older Bronze Age "bull cults" well known throughout the Eastern Mediterranean world. We

---

32. See conveniently, LaMoine F. DeVries, "Cult Stands: A Bewildering Variety of Shapes and Sizes," *BAR* 13/4 (1987): 27-37.

33. For a complete typology, see Seymour Gitin, "Incense Altars from Ekron, Israel and Judah: Context and Typology," *ErIsr* 20 (1989): 52*-67*.

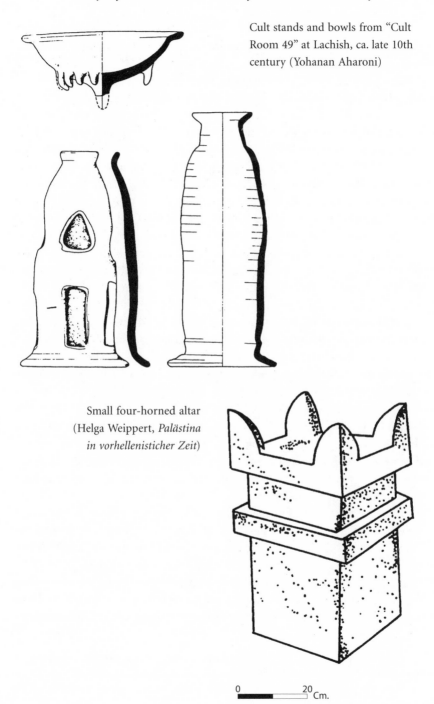

Cult stands and bowls from "Cult Room 49" at Lachish, ca. late 10th century (Yohanan Aharoni)

Small four-horned altar (Helga Weippert, *Palästina in vorhellenisticher Zeit*)

have noted above the title "Bull" used of El in the Canaanite pantheon. It is also significant that when the biblical writers want to speak of apostasy among the Israelites, they tell stories of the setting up of a bronze calf at Mt. Sinai, or the golden calf that Jeroboam erected in his newly established royal sanctuary at Dan (1 Kgs. 12:28, 29) after the death of Solomon and the secession of the northern tribes.

In any case, once again the biblical writers and editors are completely silent. There is not even a hint in the texts of these small horned altars, despite the fact that they were probably used for burning incense, and incense offerings are often described in some detail in the biblical text. Again, we must ask, What is going on? When the Bible describes local altars being "torn down" in religious reforms, it surely does not refer to these small, portable monoliths. But in that case, what is being referred to, and why do the texts not give us any details? If they had, we might have identified more monumental altars, of which we have so few certain examples, as well as the miniature varieties. As it is, the "facts on the ground" do not coincide entirely with the biblical descriptions, indicating at the very least two differing perceptions, if not religious realities, where texts and artifacts are concerned.

(3) We have many archaeological examples of various exotic terra-cotta vessels and implements, often one of a kind, that are probably best understood as "cultic" in nature. That is, they were no doubt used for ritual purposes, even though the exact manner in which they were employed, as well as the rationale, may elude us. One class of such cultic vessels would be the *naoi*, or model temples, discussed above, of which we have several Israelite examples.[34] They continue a long Bronze Age tradition of model shrines for household usage, often with a deity or pair of deities depicted standing in the doorway. The frequent association with lions, doves, and Hathor wigs suggests that these model shrines were used in the veneration of Asherah, perhaps by women at local shrines and in domestic cults.

Another class of cult vessel is the *kernos* (pl. *kernoi*), or "trick-vessel," closely connected with Cyprus and perhaps introduced into Israel by the "Sea Peoples" or the Phoenicians. These are usually small bowls with a hollow rim that conducts fluid and communicates with hollow animal heads perched on the rim at the top. When filled with something like olive oil or wine, these bowls can be tilted and manipulated so as to make the heads drink and/or pour. While some scholars seem to think that the *kernoi* were simply toys, it is more reason-

---

34. A large corpus of ancient Near Eastern examples is assembled in J. Bretschneider, *Architekturmodelle in Vorderasien und der östlichen Agäis vom Neolithikum bis in das 1. Jahrtausend.* AOAT 229 (Neukirchen-Vluyn: Neukirchener, 1991). There is no English equivalent.

Kernos from Khirbet el-Qôm, ca. 8th century (Photo by Theodore Rosen)

able to presume that these complex, exotic vessels were used in the cult, no doubt for libation offerings. Such offerings are frequently mentioned in biblical texts; but again there is no hint of *kernoi* or of any other libation vessels that we can actually identify archaeologically.[35]

Next we may note the very common terra-cotta zoomorphic figurines, especially from 8th-7th century Judean tombs. Most are quadrupeds like horses (sometimes with riders), cows, or bulls, but other common farm animals are portrayed as well (in one case an amusing three-legged chicken). Some of these animal figurines are hollow and could have served as libation vessels, but others are enigmatic. The horse-and-rider figurines or quadrupeds with sun-discs on their heads have been connected with references such as those in 2 Kgs. 23:11, 12 describing Josiah's cleansing the Jerusalem temple of the "horses" and "chariots of the sun." This is an obvious allusion to the Assyrian and Babylonian solar and astral cults that probably made serious inroads into Israelite and Judean religion in the 8th-6th centuries and which met with prophetic condemnation.[36]

---

35. See William G. Dever, "Iron Age *Kernoi* and the Israelite Cult," forthcoming in *Studies in the Archaeology of Israel and Neighboring Lands in Memory of Douglas L. Esse*, ed. Samuel R. Wolff (Chicago: University of Chicago Press, 2001). Cf. Menahem Haran, *Temples and Temple-Service in Ancient Israel: An Inquiry Into Biblical Cult Phenomena and the Historical Setting of the Priestly School* (1978, repr. Winona Lake: Eisenbrauns, 1985), 216-22. Haran does not even allude to any possible archaeological evidence for libation offerings.

36. J. Glen Taylor, *Yahweh and the Sun: Biblical and Archaeological Evidence for Sun*

Zoomorphic figurines from
Cave I in Jerusalem, ca. late
7th century (Kathleen M.
Kenyon, *Jerusalem: Exca-
vating 3000 Years of History*)

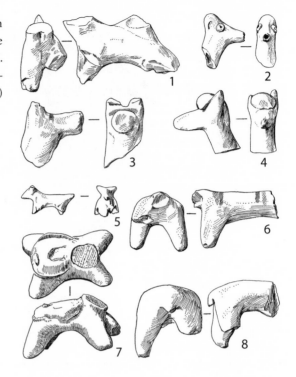

There are many other terra-cotta items now known from archaeology that almost certainly had a cultic function, but I can mention only a few of them here. Particularly common in tombs are miniature models of household furniture, such as chairs, couches, or beds. They undoubtedly were meant to accompany the dead into the afterlife, and thus they must have had some religious ("magical") significance. The same is probably true of the small stone-filled "rattles," but apart from the general connection of music with the cult little can be said of these rattles. All these and other vessels are sometimes interpreted merely as "toys," but it seems to me that such reductionist views simply highlight our ignorance (or lack of imagination?) in dealing with the ancient cult. On the other hand, some clay vessels, like the perforated tripod censers, have an obvious cultic function, and we must try to understand what that was.[37]

(4) By far the most intriguing cultic artifacts that archaeologists have re-

---

Worship in Ancient Israel. JSOTSup 111 (Sheffield: JSOT, 1993); and cf. Morton Cogan, *Imperialism and Religion: Assyria, Judah and Israel in the Eighth and Seventh Centuries B.C.E.* SBLMS 19 (Missoula: Scholars, 1974).

37. Elizabeth Bloch-Smith, *Judahite Burial Practices and Beliefs about the Dead.* JSOTSup 123 (Sheffield: JSOT, 1992), 101-3.

covered are the 2000 or more mold-made terra-cotta female figurines, found in all sorts of contexts. They depict a nude female *en face*, the earlier examples often clutching a tambourine (or bread-mold) or occasionally an infant to the upper body, the later Judean ones prominently emphasizing the breasts. In contrast to the typical LB plaques depicting the Mother Goddess with large hips and exaggerated pubic triangle, the Israelite figurines usually show the lower body stylistically, the body only a pillar possibly representing the tree symbolism often connected with Asherah (giving them the name "pillar-base" figurines). These comparatively "chaste" portrayals may indicate that Asherah/ 'Anat, the old consort of the male deity in Canaan, with her more blatantly sexual characteristics, has now been supplanted by a concept of the female deity principally as Mother and patroness of mothers. William F. Albright's designation of these as "*dea nutrix* figurines" may be close to the mark. More recently, Ziony Zevit has aptly termed the female figurines "prayers in clay" — in this case, invocations to Asherah.[38]

In view of the obvious imagery of these female figurines, it is surprising that so many biblical scholars and archaeologists are reluctant to conclude *anything* about them. Some think them merely "toys" — what I call the "Barbie doll syndrome." Others think that we simply do not and cannot know what they are. To me, however, their cultic connotations are obvious. I would argue that in ancient Israel most women, excluded from public life and the conduct of "official" political and religious functions, necessarily occupied themselves with domestic concerns. Predominant among these concerns were those connected specifically with reproduction — conception, childbirth, lactation — but also those connected with rites of passage, such as marriages, funerals, and all the other practical matters that insured the maintenance and survival of the family. To be sure, men were probably involved in some of these domestic activities as well, but "the religion of hearth and home" fell mainly to women in Israel, as it did everywhere in the ancient world. It would not be surprising if Yahweh — portrayed almost exclusively as a male deity, involved in the "political history" of the nation — seemed remote, unconcerned with women's needs, or even hostile. Thus one-half of the population of ancient Israel, women, may have felt closer to a female deity, identified more easily with her. In this case, it would

---

38. See Zevit, *The Religions of Ancient Israel.* The most recent catalog and analysis of the "pillar-base" figurines is that of Raz Kletter, *The Judean Pillar-Figurines and the Archaeology of Asherah* (Oxford: Tempus Reparatum, 1996), and full literature cited there. Kletter's interpretations, however, must be used with caution; he is ambivalent on the association with Asherah, but in the end he does accept it. For more astute comparison of the archaeological and biblical textual materials, see John Barclay Burns, "Female Pillar Figurines of the Iron Age: A Study in Text and Artifact," *AUSS* 36 (1998): 23-49.

Female mold-made terra-cotta figurines of (a) the "tambourine" style, Taʿanach, 10th century (Sylvia Schroer, *In Israel Gab es Bilder?*); and (b) the "pillar-base" style, Jerusalem, 8th century (Urs Winter, *Frau und Göttin*)

have been Asherah, who was still widely venerated in many guises in the Levantine Iron Age (and even much later). To this and other aspects of popular religion we now turn.

Toward a Definition of "Popular Religion"

At the outset of this chapter, I noted that nearly all commentators on ancient Israelite religion have based themselves on what we may call texts of the "Great Tradition." In this case, the evidence comes from the official, or canonical, texts of the Hebrew Bible, which as we have shown are thoroughly elitist. That version of the religion of ancient Israel — the "orthodox" one — may have been the one intended by the final editors of the Hebrew Bible. Certainly it has been the one congenial to most of the theologians and clerics who have commented on the biblical text over the centuries. But such a portrait is artificial, even arbitrary; and it scarcely does justice to the rich variety and vitality of the actual religious practices of the majority in ancient Israel. It is only recent *archaeological* discoveries that have enabled us to balance this portrait, by giving attention to "folk" or "popular religion," usually not directly reflected in the written sources.

But what *is* popular religion? A number of recent studies have approached the subject, but none in my opinion even offers a working definition. That would include works like Susan Ackerman's *"Under Every Green Tree": Popular Religion in Sixth-Century Judah* and Karel van der Toorn's *From Her Cradle to Her Grave: The Role of Religion in the Life of the Israelite and the Babylonian Woman.*[39]

One way to define popular religion would be to look not only at the archaeological evidence, which may differ radically from official texts, but also to look closely at the *condemnation* of religious practices in the texts of the Hebrew Bible. In doing so we are making a practical and legitimate assumption, namely that prophets, priests, and reformers "knew what they were talking about." That is, the religious situation about which they complained was real, not invented by them as a foil for their revisionist message. The irony is that in condemning popular religious practices, the biblical writers have unwittingly preserved chance descriptions of such practices, of which formerly the "archaeological revolution" constituted our only witness. (That is not to say, however, that the same writers and editors in their zeal for orthodoxy did not deliberately suppress much information about popular religion that we should like to have.) Fortunately, archaeology has supplied not only much supplementary information, but in doing so it has given us some valuable clues as to how to "read between the lines" in the biblical texts.

As examples of how we might read the textual and the archaeological records together, each illuminating the other on popular religion, I would suggest the following. In Jer. 7:18 there is a telling description of what must have been a common *family* ritual, although one decried by the prophet: "The children gather wood, the fathers kindle fire, and the women knead dough, to make cakes for the Queen of Heaven." The latter is either Asherah or her counterpart ʿAstarte; the two often coalesced in the Iron Age. An even fuller example of what was really going on in Judean times is the lengthy description in 2 Kgs. 23 of King Josiah's reform measures in the late 7th century. Most biblical scholars have taken this famous passage largely as a piece of "Deuteronomistic propaganda," not an accurate historical account. But apart from the question of whether the supposed "reform" was successful, there is the question of whether the purported *need* for such a reform is based on an eye-witness, realistic appraisal of the actual religious situation. It appears that it was; indeed, as I have shown recently, every single religious object and/or practice that is proscribed in 2 Kgs. 23 can readily be illustrated by archaeological discoveries. The terminology of the

39. See n. 16 above. Van der Toorn's more recent work *The Image and the Book* coins the term "book religion" in contrast to "popular religion," which I find useful.

text is not at all "enigmatic," as has usually been supposed by textual scholars, but is a clear reflection of the religious reality in monarchical times.[40]

I would argue that all of the following features are now well known archaeologically and give us an accurate picture of what may be called "popular religion." Popular religion is an alternate, nonorthodox, nonconformist mode of religious expression. It is largely noncentralized, noninstitutional, lying outside state priests or state sponsorship. Because it is nonauthoritarian, popular religion is inclusive rather than exclusive; it appeals especially to minorities and to the disenfranchised (in the case of ancient Israel, most women); in both belief and practice it tends to be eclectic and syncretistic. Popular religion focuses more on individual piety and informal practice than on elaborate public ritual, more on cult than on intellectual formulations (i.e., theology). By definition, popular religion is less literate (not by that token any less complex or sophisticated) and thus may be inclined to leave behind more traces in the archaeological record than in the literary record, more ostraca and graffiti than classical texts, more cult and other symbolic paraphernalia than Scripture. Nevertheless, despite these apparent dichotomies, popular religion overlaps significantly with official religion, if only by sheer force of numbers of practitioners; it often sees itself as equally legitimate; and it attempts to secure the same benefits as all religion, i.e., the individual's sense of integration with nature and society, of health and prosperity, and of ultimate well-being.

The major elements of popular religion in ancient Israel, as we can gather both from substrata of the biblical text and archaeology, probably included: frequenting *bāmôt* and other local shrines; the making of images; veneration of *'ăšērîm* (whether sacred-trees or iconographic images) and the worship of Asherah the Great Lady herself; rituals having to do with childbirth and children; pilgrimages and saints' festivals; planting and harvest festivals of many kinds; *mārzēaḥ* feasts (sacred banquets); various funerary rites, such as libations for the dead; baking cakes for the "Queen of Heaven" (probably 'Astarte); wailing over Tammuz; various aspects of solar and astral worship; divination and sorcery; and perhaps child sacrifice. These and other elements of "folk" religion are often assumed to have characterized the religion of "hearth and home," and thus to have been almost the exclusive province of women. That assumption, typically made by male scholars, inevitably carries with it a note of condescension. After all, women in ancient Israel were largely illiterate and marginalized; they played an insignificant role in the socio-political processes that shaped Israelite life and institutions.[41] Nevertheless, I think that family re-

---

40. William G. Dever, "The Silence of the Text," 105-17.

41. There is now a vast literature on women in ancient Israel. On women and the

ligion in ancient Israel involved many men as well, especially in rural areas far from the influence of elite circles in Jerusalem. Asherah, who brought life, could be the patroness of men as well as women.

Asherah Abscondita

Why has the role of popular religion and the cult of the Mother Goddess in ancient Israel been neglected, misunderstood, or downplayed by the majority of biblical scholars? There are many reasons, including the male, Establishment, elitist bias of most students of the subject, agreeing (not coincidentally) with the biases of the biblical writers themselves; the typical preference of the Protestant scholars, who have dominated the study, for theology rather than cult (i.e., religious *practice*) in any form; and the notion that texts alone can inform us adequately on religious matters — that philology, rather than archaeology or the study of material remains, should prevail. Yet archaeology is literally forcing us to revise our basic notion of what ancient Israelite religion was. In particular, we now know that the old Mother Goddess Asherah — virtually expunged from the texts of the Hebrew Bible, and all but forgotten by rabbinical times — never died out, but enjoyed a vigorous life throughout the Monarchy. This is not really surprising, since most biblical scholars now agree that true monotheism (i.e., not merely "henotheism") arose only in the period of the Exile and beyond.[42]

There are even later reflexes of the cult of the Great Mother: the personification of divine Wisdom *(Ḥokmah)* in later Judaism; and the conception of the Shekinah, or effective divine presence in the world, sometimes called the Matronit or even the Bride of God, in medieval texts of the Kabbalist sect of Judaism. In the Christian Church, parallel doctrines that may go back to a primitive memory of feminine manifestations of the deity may be seen in the development of the doctrine of the Holy Spirit, a more immanent, nurturing aspect of the transcendent God. Especially relevant in this connection is the later ele-

---

cult specifically, among the best studies are those of Phyllis A. Bird, "The Place of Women in the Israelite Cultus," in Miller, Hanson, and McBride, *Ancient Israelite Religion,* 397-419; Carol Meyers, "'To Her Mother's House' — Considering a Counterpart to the Israelite Bêt-ʾāb," in Jobling, Day, and Sheppard, *The Bible and the Politics of Exegesis,* 39-51, 304-7.

42. See, e.g., Mark S. Smith, *The Early History of God: Yahweh and the Other Deities in Ancient Israel* (San Francisco: Harper and Row, 1990); and cf. the essays by Michael David Coogan, John S. Holladay, Jr., and P. Kyle McCarter, Jr., in *Ancient Israelite Religion* (above, n. 28). Also Johannes C. de Moor, *The Rise of Yahwism: The Roots of Israelite Monotheism.* BETL 91 (Leuven: Leuven University Press, 1990).

vation of Mary to the position of Mother of God, a feminine intermediary through whom many Christians pray, rather than directly to God himself. Mainstream, more orthodox clergy, both Jewish and Christian, have always resisted these "pagan" influences in what are ostensibly rigorously monotheistic religions. In popular religion, however, the old cults die hard. But when they do, archaeology sometimes rescues them and thus writes a better balanced history of religion.[43]

The point of all the foregoing résumé is simply that the biblical writers and editors were once again not so much "wrong" in many of the facts of their history of Israel's religious development as they were one-sided in their *interpretation* of the facts. Yet despite their own partisan, rigorously orthodox outlook, they nevertheless give us many clues as to what the "real" religions of ancient Israel were. Perhaps they do this unwittingly; but nevertheless by their very condemnation of pagan beliefs and rites they confirm their widespread existence. Otherwise, there would have been no point to the repeated condemnations by prophets and reformers like the Deuteronomists. Here is where we might agree with the new literary critics and revisionists and do a little deconstruction of our own. It is by reading many of the biblical texts "against the grain," or *despite* their idealistic pretensions, that we may best get at the truth about ancient Israelite religions. This may not be the religious "truth" that the biblical writers had in mind, but it is historical truth, and that is our proper goal as archaeologists and historians. Even *without* the archaeological evidence sketched here (and there is much more) we might, however, have grasped this truth long ago, were it not for the fact that too many of us, Jews and Christians, have sided perhaps unconsciously with one particular biblical worldview, that of the late Deuteronomists and reformist prophets. Yet there were many *other* worldviews that were once part of Israel's Yahwistic religion, however unorthodox they came to be seen in time. How the recognition of the actual diversity and vitality of religion in ancient Israel may contribute to our own religious thinking is a topic that we will explore further in the final chapter.

Daily Life in Biblical Times: Fortifications

I have argued in Chapter 4 that ancient Israel had achieved statehood already by the 10th century, and even the revisionists would grant as much by the 9th century, for the northern kingdom at least. I based my case for statehood, for both the northern and the southern kingdoms, on the strong archaeological evi-

43. See Dever, "Folk Religion in Early Israel," 56.

dence for several developments by the late 10th century: a pronounced shift to an urban settlement pattern; evidence for highly centralized administration; and the emergence of Israel as a major international and economic power among the nascent states and peoples of the southern Levant by the time of the fully developed Iron Age.

Apart from the difference of opinion among scholars about the date of the first unequivocal evidence of statehood, we need to inquire now whether the writers and editors of the Hebrew Bible had any real knowledge of such typical features of statehood as city fortifications in the Iron II period, or the Divided Monarchy, in which their history is set. In short, what convergences may there be between the biblical texts and what we now know archaeologically? Honoring our principle of independent sources and inquiries, let us look first at what we might learn from the biblical texts alone.

City walls are rather "generic," lacking in specific features. Thus, while they are archaeologically well enough known, they cannot be expected to be described in detail in the biblical texts. Let us look rather at city gates, which exhibit many diagnostic features. Numerous such features are mentioned in biblical texts. (1) General descriptions of city gates appear in several texts, such as 2 Sam. 18:4, 24, a passage that refers to a lower and an upper gate, an inner chamber, and two towers. This, of course, fits precisely the plan of the 10th-century city gates of Hazor, Megiddo, and Gezer (discussed above, pp. 131-34), and also a few 9th-8th-century gates, such as the ones at Lachish and at Assyrian-period Gezer. It is worth noting that none of the city gates of this type excavated thus far postdates the 8th century, so it is hard to see how much later writers could have "invented" them.

(2) Specific aspects of city gates mentioned in the Hebrew Bible include several features. (a) Swinging wooden doors (Heb. *delet*), usually with metal bars, are mentioned in texts such as Deut. 3:5 (Bashan); 1 Kgs. 16:34 (Jericho); Judg. 16:3 (Samson, in Gaza). Actual sockets for such swinging doors can still be seen today in the excavated city gates at 10th-8th-century Gezer and at 9th-8th-century Dan.[44] (b) The iron bolts (*manʿûl*) that were needed to secure these doors in place are mentioned in Neh. 3:3-15, beams (*qôrâ) and bars (beriyaḥ)* that would have been used for reinforcement are noted in texts like 2 Kgs. 6:2, 5; 2 Chr. 3:7; and Deut. 3:5; Judg. 16:3; 1 Sam. 23:7; and 2 Chr. 8:5, 14:7. The holes in the threshold stone of the city gate, where the iron bolts were shot home, can still be seen in the gate at Gezer. (c) The fact that city gates served for more than defensive purposes, and could also have economic, juridi-

---

44. Cf. R. A. S. Macalister, *The Excavation of Gezer* (London: Palestine Exploration Fund, 1911), 218; Biran, *Biblical Dan*, 276.

Foundation stones of the Gezer Field III gate, where an iron bolt and socket once were; ca. 10th century (Photo by William G. Dever)

cal, and ceremonial usages, is indicated by such biblical passages as 2 Kgs. 7:1, 18 (a "marketplace"); Deut. 21:19, 20; Ruth 4:1, 11; Isa. 29:21; Amos 5:12, 15 ("justice," "retribution," and "charity" dispensed in the gate). Several excavated 10th-7th-century gates have produced unique ceramic grain-scoops, large storejars, bronze balance-scales, and inscribed stone sheqel-weights — all clear evidence of commercial activities. In addition, there have been found benches lining the walls of the inner rooms of the gateway complex at Gezer and elsewhere — so basic that they were rebuilt and reused in every successive stratum.[45] These benches would have been suitable for local judges sitting in tribunal in the gate area. Ceremonial functions of gate complexes are illustrated in particular by the gate at Tel Dan, which has in the outer courtyard a prominent low podium of dressed ashlar masonry, no doubt for a wooden throne, with four surrounding recessed stone column bases that served originally as sup-

45. Cf. William G. Dever et al., "Further Excavations at Gezer, 1967-1971," *BA* 34 (1971): 94-132. On the grain-scoops, see now the full typology and analysis of Seymour Gitin "Scoops: Corpus, Function and Typology," in *Studies in the Archaeology and History of Ancient Israel in Honour of Moshe Dothan,* ed. Michael Heltzer, Arthur Segal, and Daniel Kaufman (Haifa: Haifa University, 1993), 99-126. For sheqel weights from gate areas, see Kletter (nn. 74, 75 below). For an example of balances from the gate area at Lachish, see Gabriel Barkay, "A Balance Beam from Tel Lachish," *Tel Aviv* 23 (1996): 75-82.

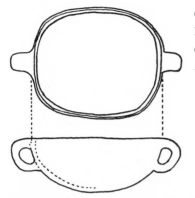

Ceramic grain-scoop from
Lachish Level III, late 8th
century (Olga Tufnell,
Lachish III)

Benches running around the three walls of the "guard rooms" of the Field III
city gate at Gezer, ca. 10th century (Photo by R. B. Wright)

ports for wooden beams which would have upheld an overhead canopy. That would explain a passage like Josh. 20:4, which prescribes that an accused person can flee to a designated "city of refuge" and there "stand at the entrance of the gate of the city, and explain his case to the elders of that city." Other texts refer to the custom of the city elders sitting in judgment in the city gate (Deut. 21:19, 20; Ruth 4:1, 11), reproving in the gate (Isa. 29:21), and hearing the claims of the needy in the gate (Amos 5:12). Above all, one recalls Amos's impassioned plea: "Hate evil and love good; and establish justice in the gate" (5:15). In addi-

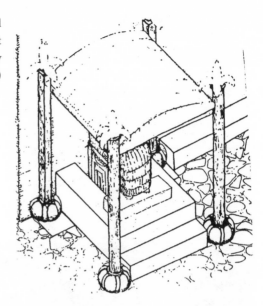

Reconstruction of the canopied "throne" in the inner gate plaza at Tel Dan, ca. 9th-8th century (Abraham Biran, *Biblical Dan*)

tion, the 9th-8th-century Tel Dan gate had in the outer courtyard area several unique structures that suggest the "bazaars" or extramural marketplaces (*ḥuṣṣôt,* or "outer installations") that Ahab was given permission to construct in Aramaean Damascus, and that the Aramaeans were granted reciprocally in Samaria (cf. 1 Kgs. 20:34).[46]

In conclusion, the many biblical passages that mention city gates — not as part of any deliberate propaganda, but simply offhand — fit remarkably well with excavated gates at a number of sites of the 10th-7th centuries, and *only* of this period. In the Persian-Hellenistic-Roman period such gates had long since passed out of existence and memory, as archaeological evidence has shown. No writer living then could have "invented" city gates like ours, known only long before in the Iron Age.

Literacy in Ancient Israel

One of the revisionists' principal objections to Israel's having been a centralized state in the 10th century is that writing would have been a bureaucratic necessity, but we have little if any 10th-century evidence. I have mentioned that the few early Hebrew texts that we do happen to have, however, include an

46. Avraham Biran, "Two Bronze Plaques and the *Ḥuṣṣot* of Dan," *IEJ* 49 (1999): 43-54. On the "throne platform," see Biran, *Biblical Dan*, 238-43.

abcedary, or list of the letters of the alphabet (ʿIzbet Ṣarṭah; 12th-11th century), and a poem giving the agricultural seasons (Gezer, 10th century).[47] Both are almost certainly schoolboys' practice texts. Students and others were now learning to write, adapting the Old Canaanite alphabet and script as Hebrew developed into a national language and instrument of cultural expression. We may assume that writing, and even what we may call "functional" literacy, was reasonably widespread by the 10th century, and certainly by the 9th century when even the revisionists must concede that an Israelite state did exist.[48]

It remains true, however, that we have relatively few examples of Hebrew writing of any kind from the 9th century and have produced no extrabiblical texts that could be considered real "literature." The problem becomes particularly acute if we consider the Yahwist and Elohist sources or "schools" that began the literary tradition which later grew into the Pentateuch and other historical works to have emerged as early as the 10th-9th century, as most biblical scholars have argued until recently. Could there possibly have been written sources that early, given our lack of any significant literary remains except the Hebrew Bible (which in its present form is later than the Iron Age)?

There is considerably more written evidence from Iron Age Palestine than the revisionists and other minimalists know or are willing to take seriously.[49]

47. See Aaron Demsky and Moshe Kochavi, *BAR* 4/3 (1978): 23-30; Daniel Sivan, "The Gezer Calendar and Northwest Semitic Linguistics," *IEJ* 48 (1998): 101-05 and literature cited there. For an excellent argument for widespread literary in early Israel, see Alan R. Millard, "The Question of Israelite Literacy," *BR* 3/3 (1987): 22-31; "The Knowledge of Writing in Iron Age Palestine," *TynBul* 46 (1995): 207-17 and literature cited there. See also Ian M. Young, "Israelite Literacy: Interpreting the Evidence, Parts I-II," *VT* 48 (1998): 239-53, 408-22. In addition, see the fundamental study of Susan Niditch, *Oral World and Written Word: Ancient Israelite Literature* (Louisville: Westminster John Knox, 1996).

48. Cf. further Chapter 2.

49. Consider, for example, the attempt of Philip R. Davies to redate the late 8th-century Siloam tunnel inscription to the 2nd century — immediately and decisively refuted by a number of the world's leading epigraphers. See John Rogerson and Philip R. Davies, "Was the Siloam Tunnel Built by Hezekiah?" *BA* 59 (1996): 138-49; and cf. the devastating replies in the articles by leading epigraphers Frank Moore Cross, Esther Eshel, Jo Ann Hackett, Avi Hurvitz, André Lemaire, P. Kyle McCarter, Jr., and Ada Yardeni in "Defusing Pseudo-Scholarship: The Siloam Inscription Ain't Hasmonean," *BAR* 23/2 (1997): 41-50, 68. Can there be any doubt that the repudiation of an absolutely dated Iron Age inscription — the very foundation of our paleographical sequence — is the result not merely of scholarly incompetence, but also of an ideological predisposition against there having been a real Israel in the Iron Age?

But before turning to this evidence, let us begin, as before, by looking at the evidence for writing in the Hebrew Bible itself.

Many scholars have suggested that biblical texts such as Deut. 6:6-9 — God instructing the Israelites to "write (the commandments) on your doorposts" — indicate early and widespread literacy. But this passage, although set by the Deuteronomistic editors in the "Mosaic era," is almost certainly quite late, probably postexilic, and offers no real evidence for the early Iron Age. In fact, the text actually implies that the *oral* tradition was still the primary means for transmitting knowledge. Many of the other allusions to writing in the biblical "Patriarchal" and "Mosaic" eras reflect the same preliterate stage of cultural evolution, such as Exod. 17:14. This passage relates how, after the Battle of Amalek, God said to Moses: "Write this as a memorial in a book and *recite* it in the ears of Joshua." Thus the mention of "writing" in these and related texts is really an anachronism, not historical evidence.[50]

Seals and Sealings

There are several other biblical texts that offer more possibilities, especially for archaeological commentary. One category of Hebrew inscriptions that is well illustrated is the practice of writing on a gemstone for a signet-ring or seals, which could be worn on a finger or hung around the neck. The Hebrew word for "seal" (*ḥôtām*) occurs a number of times in the Bible. In Gen. 38:18, 25 Tamar demands from Judah his "seal and cord" as a pledge that he will keep his promise of a gift. Signet rings themselves are described as gifts or offerings to God in Exod. 35:22; Num. 31:50. According to Exod. 28:11, 21, 36; 39:6, 14, 30, priests serving in the temple possessed "engraved seals," some with "the names of the sons of Israel." The king and other high state officials in ancient Israel had seals as symbols of their authority, worn on the right hand (Jer. 22:24).

Seals could be and often were not only symbols of wealth or authority, but were used in a practical way to designate ownership. In 1 Kgs. 21:8 Jezebel seals Ahab's documents, that is, she affixes a signet-ring to a wax or clay patty that binds the strings and knots surrounding a rolled-up papyrus or parchment document. Jer. 32:10-44 refers several times to "sealing" deeds of purchase. In Neh.

50. In short, *oral* tradition dominated in premonarchic Israel, as would be expected. It is significant that the revisionists never even consider oral tradition in their numerous attempts to discredit any real historical foundations of the later written traditions. They completely ignore the massive evidence that Niditch, e.g., documents in *Oral World and Written Word*.

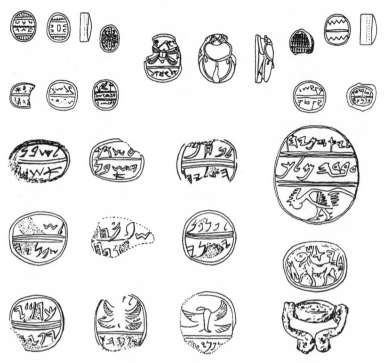

A selection of Israelite and Judean seals of the 8th-7th century (John W. Crowfoot, Grace M. Crowfoot, and Kathleen M. Kenyon, *The Objects from Samaria*)

9:38; 10:1 the priests "seal" a covenant document. Certainly seals were intended for making seal-impressions, as proven by the fact that all the hundreds of examples we possess are engraved in the negative, even though that was technically difficult. Both Cant. 8:6 and Isa. 8:16 use the term "seal" as a metaphor (the latter in reference to a *megillah,* or scroll), referring to God's promise to "bind up my testimony, seal my teachings." While these and a few other passages in the Bible attest to the rather widespread ownership of seals, many of the texts themselves cannot be dated precisely. Nor can it be assumed necessarily that everyone who possessed and used a seal could read or write — indeed, the inability to do so might be one reason for having a seal, although *someone* must be presumed to have been literate or the whole business of sealing something would have been pointless.

There are so many known Iron Age seals — perhaps a thousand or more, to judge from many recent publications and an Israel Museum Catalogue — that I can note here only a few of the most significant convergences with biblical texts.[51]

51. Nahman Avigad, "The Contribution of Hebrew Seals to an Understanding of Israelite Religion and Society," in Miller, Hanson, and McBride, *Ancient Israelite Religion,*

If space permitted, I could cite hundreds of 9th-6th-century seals inscribed with Hebrew personal names, the vast majority of which occur also in the Hebrew Bible, including the supposedly "Hellenistic-Roman" Deuteronomistic materials. A number of seals and seal impressions, however, have such specific connections with individual biblical texts that they must be singled out here. One of our best collections of bullae — or clay patties from papyrus scrolls, with seal impressions in them — is the group of more than 300 7th-6th-century examples published in 1976 and 1986 by Israeli epigrapher Nahman Avigad.[52] Many of them bear ordinary Hebrew personal names well known from the Hebrew Bible (more than 140 different names); but at least some have the names and titles of high-ranking officials, since this is an archive of important documents. Three of this group of bullae feature the title "who is over the house," identical to the phrase in Isa. 22:15, identifying one Shebna as "the royal chamberlain." The same phrase — indeed with the same name, Shebna — occurs in another extrabiblical text, the famous Royal Steward Inscription (below). Two other bullae in the Avigad group feature the title "servant of the king," and three others belonged to "sons of the king" or royal princes (in this case, Neriyahu and Yeraḥme'el). The most interesting bulla, however, is that of "Berakyahu, son of Neriyahu the scribe." This is only the second Hebrew seal of a "scribe" to be published, and is thus unusual in itself. Moreover, as Avigad points out, this must be the seal of none other than "Baruch (the short form of the name), the son of Neriyahu," whom the Hebrew Bible identifies as the amanuensis of the prophet Jeremiah (Jer. 36:4-32).[53] So important was this Baruch that some scholars think he was the real author not only of the book of Jeremiah, but perhaps of the first version of the Deuteronomistic history. Richard E. Friedman's book, *Who Wrote the Bible?* even argues that much of the Hebrew Bible in its present form is the work of this very

---

195-208; P. Kyle McCarter, Jr., *Ancient Inscriptions: Voices from the Biblical World* (Washington: Biblical Archaeology Society, 1996), 142-50; and for recently published seals, see André Lemaire, "Royal Signature — Name of Israel's Last King Surfaces in a Private Collection," *BAR* 21/6 (1995): 48-52; Robert Deutsch, "First Impression — What We Learn from King Ahaz's Seal," *BAR* 24/3 (1998): 54-56, 62. For the definitive catalogue of Hebrew (and other) seals, still in progress, see Benjamin Sass and Christoph Uehlinger, *Studies in the Iconography of Northwest Semitic Inscribed Seals.* OBO 125 (Fribourg: University of Fribourg Press, 1993); Othmar Keel, *Corpus der Stempelsiegel-Amulette aus Palästina/ Israel.* OBO Series archaeologica 10 (Fribourg: University of Fribourg Press, 1995).

52. Nahman Avigad, *Bullae and Seals from a Post-Exilic Judean Archive* (Jerusalem: Hebrew University, 1976); *Hebrew Bullae from the Time of Jeremiah: Remnants of a Burnt Archive* (Jerusalem: Israel Exploration Society, 1986).

53. Avigad, *Hebrew Bullae from the Time of Jeremiah,* 120-30.

Seal impression of "Hanan, son of Hilkiah the Priest," ca. 600 (P. Kyle McCarter, *Ancient Inscriptions*)

Seal impression of "Yeraḥme'el, son of the King," ca. 600 (Original drawing by Nahman Avigad, courtesy Israel Exploration Society)

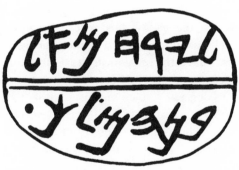

Baruch. The bulla of Baruch in the Avigad archive bears a fingerprint on the clay patty. Is this the "signature" of the man who wrote the Bible? Possibly! And more recently a bulla bearing the name of the great reformer King Hezekiah has appeared.

An even more intriguing possibility, however, involves another biblical convergence. According to the biblical sources (Jer. 36:1ff.), in the fourth year of King Jehoiakim of Judah, or 605/604), Baruch wrote down on a scroll an oracle of Jeremiah concerning the imminent destruction of Jerusalem. The king, incensed, ordered the scroll burnt; but, forewarned, Baruch and Jeremiah re-

Seal impression of "Berakyahu
(Baruch), son of Neriyahu the
Scribe," ca. 600 (Original drawing
by Nahman Avigad, courtesy Israel
Exploration Society)

wrote the scroll. On another occasion, Baruch was witness to a symbolic land
purchase made by Jeremiah, who entrusted the "sealed deed of purchase" to
Baruch with the request that he put it in a jar for safekeeping (Jer. 32:1-15). Was
it sealed with the *same* signet-ring that produced the Avigad bulla? Perhaps. In
any case, the seal was used repeatedly; we even have another bulla, now in the
Israel Museum, impressed by the *same* signet-ring that made the Avigad bulla.
Now what is the revisionists' reaction to this rather striking convergence, even
if taken minimally? Thomas L. Thompson and Niels Peter Lemche have recently suggested, in all seriousness, that the *bulla* is a fake![54] We now have at
least 65 other late Iron Age bullae, however, some from well-controlled archaeological contexts, like those from Jerusalem and Lachish. It would be almost
impossible for a modern forger to duplicate bullae like these, not only because
there is no way that a forger could *know* the authentic early scripts that well, not
to mention "inventing" nonbiblical personal names that are precisely of biblical
type, but because of technological difficulties. Where would a modern forger
get the right kind of papyrus to make the papyrus impressions that are clearly
visible on the backs of the bullae? What can one say when scholars resort to

54. Thompson and Lemche also doubt the Tel Dan inscription's authenticity; see
Chapter 2, nn. 10, 11. For a charge that many of the recently published seals and bullae are
fakes, see Robert P. Carroll, "Madonna of Silences," in Lester L. Grabbe, *Can a "History of
Israel" Be Written?* 84-103. Carroll says of the distinguished epigrapher Nahman Avigad
that "from such bits of clay he reconstructs the world" (100). For further discussion of the
problem of possible forgeries, see Lemche, P. Kyle McCarter, and Thompson in *BAR* 23/4
(1997): 36-38 (Lemche suggesting specifically that the "Barukh" *bulla* is a forgery).

Reconstruction of a sealed papyrus document, with three bullae attached (Original drawing by Nahman Avigad, courtesy Israel Exploration Society)

such desperate measures to deny or to suppress evidence that may threaten their cherished theories?

One other point deserves mention here. While it is obvious that the more than 300 Hebrew bullae that we now possess were once attached to papyrus scrolls as seals, we have found only *one* fragment of an actual Iron Age papyrus scroll. It survived among the much later Wadi Murabbaʿat texts only because of the extremely arid conditions at the Dead Sea area.[55] Does the present lack of any written remains on papyrus scrolls from the Iron Age mean that they never existed? To be consistent, and to protect their theories, the revisionists would have to say: Yes. But again, this is strictly an argument from silence — and in this case, manifestly absurd. It is obvious that at least a rudimentary or "functional" form of literacy was widespread in ancient Israel, and it could not have developed overnight only in the late 7th century, at the very end of the Monarchy. If much of the writing was done on papyrus, as both the textual and archaeological evidence demonstrate, we should not expect to recover very much. The fact, as all archaeologists know, is that in the damp winter climate of most of Palestine, organic materials like fragile papyrus simply do not survive. Fortunately, other written materials do.

Ostraca

From all appearances it seems that the more important documents in ancient Israel — such as official decrees, land deeds and other records of legal transactions, and whatever literature that may have been produced — were written on papyrus, even though it was perishable. Simpler transactions, however, were often recorded by writing in ink or scratching on the broken pieces of pottery

---

55. Niditch, *Oral World and Written Word*, 50.

Ostraca no. 17 from Samaria,
"from 'Azoh to Gaddiyaw," and
dealing with "refined oil," early
8th century (G. A. Reisner,
C. S. Fisher, and D. G. Lyon,
*Harvard Excavations at
Samaria*)

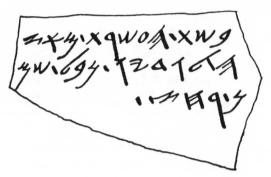

(potsherds) that were lying about everywhere on the ground (Isa. 45:9) and
came conveniently to hand. It is often implied that Hebrew ostraca (sg.
ostracon) are as rare as other epigraphic materials. In the early days of archaeology they were indeed relatively unknown. But the Harvard excavations at Samaria in 1908-1910 discovered an archive of some 102 ostraca from the early
8th century — our earliest such archive (dating probably to the reign of Jeroboam II, 785-740, to judge from year-formulae of the ostraca themselves). They
were found on the floor at an administrative complex attached to the palace
built by Omri and Ahab a century earlier. These ostraca, written or scratched in
cursive Hebrew on large potsherds, are mostly receipts for taxes paid by wealthy
landholders in various commodities, such as oil or wine.[56]

Here we have clear evidence of centralized administration in the capital
of the northern kingdom. Moreover, there are several interesting convergences
with biblical texts. The personal names are usually similar to those known in
the Hebrew Bible, consistent even to the short form of the divine name, -*yaw*
in northern compound names, compared with -*yāhū* in Judah. Scholars have
observed, however, that the proportion of personal names compounded with
the name of Ba'al here in the "pagan" north, rather than with Yahweh, is
higher than the ratio in the Bible: 6 of 15 compound names feature Ba'al, 9
Yahweh. That datum, however, accords well with the biblical portrait, biased
or not, of the northern kingdom as much more heavily influenced by Phoenician religion. Another convergence lies in the fact that a relatively few taxpay-

---

56. On written materials generally, see André Lemaire, "Writing and Writing Materials," *ABD* 6:999-1008; K. A. D. Smelik, *Writings from Ancient Israel* (Louisville: Westminster John Knox, 1991); McCarter, *Ancient Inscriptions;* and cf. Niditch, *Oral World and
Written Word.* Cf. also references in n. 57 below. On Samaria specifically, see conveniently
Gabriel Barkay, "The Iron Age II-III," in Ben-Tor, *Archaeology of Ancient Israel,* 319-23. For
translations of the ostraca, see *ANET,* 321; Smelik, 51-62.

ers show up again and again on the Samaria receipts, no doubt evidence of large agricultural estates being owned and managed by landed gentry. Such a socio-economic situation provides us with a setting into which we can place the protest of the prophet Amos against the idle nobles who feel secure in "the mountain of Samaria"; who "trample on the poor and take from them extractions of wheat" (Amos 5:11; 6:1-6). And Micah complains of those who "covet fields, and seize them; houses, and take them away" (Mic. 2:2).

The second major find of Hebrew ostraca was made by British excavators in 1935-38 at the great Judean border fortress of Lachish. There an archive of 23 ostraca was found on the floor of the guardroom of the city gate, among the ashes of the Babylonian destruction wrought by Nebuchadnezzar in 587/586. These ostraca are letters written to Lachish on the eve of its destruction. Letter no. 4 is particularly poignant; it is a last-minute plea for help from an outlying village, saying that they can no longer see the fire-signals of nearby Azekah but are watching desperately for a signal from Lachish. Letter no. 4 also refers to an unnamed prophet; and letter 6 alludes to a prophet who "weakens the hand," i.e., gives a discouraging oracle — the latter phrase exactly the same as a contemporary expression in Jeremiah (38:4). Letter no. 3 is also pertinent to our discussion of literacy, since in it one Hawshi'yahu expresses his hurt feelings over the fact that his correspondent, Ya'ush, has accused him of "not knowing how to read a letter." He protests that not only does he read every letter without any assistance ("nobody has ever tried to read *me* a letter!"), but he reads it immediately and remembers everything in it.[57]

A third major discovery of ostraca, the largest archive yet, with more than 100 8th-6th-century letters, was made by the Israeli archaeologist Yohanan Aharoni at Arad, near Beersheba.[58] Mostly in Hebrew, but a few written in Aramaic, the Arad ostraca are painted in ink on sherds of large jars. All those from Stratum VI belong to an archive of correspondence of "Eliashib, son of Ishyahu," apparently commander of the garrison in the late 7th century, stationed here to guard the desert borders with Edom. Many of these ostraca are rather banal, having to do with the transfer of various provisions. One, how-

---

57. For the Lachish and other Hebrew letters on ostraca, see Dennis Pardee, "Letters (Hebrew)," *ABD* 4:282-85; and in much more detail, *Handbook of Ancient Hebrew Letters: A Study Edition.* SBLSBS 15 (Chico: Scholars, 1982). Good translations of the Lachish letters will be found in *ANET,* 321, 322; McCarter, *Ancient Inscriptions,* 116-18; Smelik, 116-31.

58. For the original publication, see Yohanan Aharoni, *Arad Inscriptions* (Jerusalem: Israel Exploration Society, 1981), and cf. Pardee, *Handbook of Ancient Hebrew Letters,* 28; Niditch, *Oral World and Written Word,* 52; McCarter, *Ancient Inscriptions,* 105-9; Smelik, 101-15.

Ostracon no. 4 from Lachish, early 6th century (*Inscriptions Reveal,* Israel Museum)

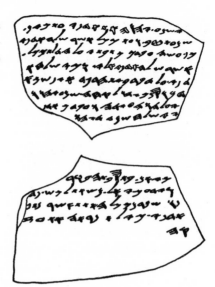

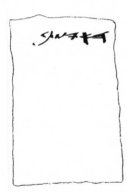
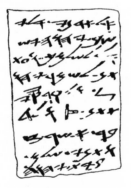

Ostracon no. 18 from Arad, mentioning the House of "Yahweh," ca. 7th century (Yohanan Aharoni, *Arad Inscriptions*)

ever, no. 18, is of unusual interest in that it assures the reader that "the house (i.e., temple) of Yahweh is well; it endures." This may be a reference to the earlier tripartite temple of Arad brought to light by Aharoni, or it may refer to the temple in Jerusalem. If the latter is the case, we have here the only surviving nonbiblical reference to Solomon's temple apart from the broken ivory pomegranate mentioned above (the name "Yahweh" partly missing).[59]

59. Aharoni, *Arad Inscriptions,* 35-38. For the pomegranate, see André Lemaire, "Probable Head of Priestly Scepter from Solomon's Temple Surfaces in Jerusalem," *BAR* 10/1 (1984): 24-29.

A number of individual ostraca are also now known, enough to show beyond doubt that extensive written materials did exist in ancient Israel besides official archives, that is, that many besides elites could read and write. Particularly significant are the 8th-century inscriptions painted on pottery (although not strictly "ostraca") discussed above.[60] The 8th-century fortress at ʿAjrûd was really out in the boondocks, miles away from civilization. Yet people residing there, or frequenting the place as travelers, left behind quite a corpus of written material. Some of the short messages written on the plastered walls of the gate shrine may be considered more "graffiti" than the work of a trained hand; but that confirms my suspicion that even many ordinary folk in ancient Israel were at least "functionally literate," that is, they could manage simple business transactions and the like.

One isolated ostracon deserves special mention here. It was found by Itzhaq Beit-Arieh in his 1982-88 excavations at Ḥorvat ʿUza in the eastern Negev desert. Dating to the 7th century, it is written in Hebrew but also contains a list of Egyptian hieratic signs for numbers. Many of these same Egyptian hieratic numerals are found in other 8th-7th Hebrew inscriptions, even on sheqel-weights (below), indicating that for some reason an Egyptian system of numerals was preferred and used throughout Israel and Judah. Nadav Naʾaman has recently suggested that this system must have been adopted from Egypt by the 10th century; it cannot have been borrowed from Israel's Semitic neighbors, since none used it. And it is conspicuously unattested in Egypt itself in the 8th-7th centuries, so it must derive from an earlier time. Finally, the Egyptian system is used in both the northern and the southern kingdoms. Thus Naʾaman concludes: "These hieratic signs must have entered the Hebrew script before the division of the monarchy — namely in the tenth century B.C.E." Naʾaman — a highly critical, at times radical, historian who cannot be dismissed as a "biblicist" — concludes overall that the historical, written, and archaeological evidence now at hand requires the historian to take seriously the biblical concept of a Davidic-Solomonic "kingdom," in the 10th century, complete with a temple in Jerusalem.[61]

Inscribed Objects

The reader will have noted that much of the inscribed material I have discussed thus far has been brought to light relatively recently. Before such discoveries,

---

60. See also n. 28.

61. See Itzhaq Beit-Arieh, "A Literary Ostracon from Ḥorvat ʿUza," *TA* 20 (1993): 55-65; and cf. Nadav Naʾaman, *BAR* 23 (1997): 43-47, 67.

Inscribed 8th-century water decanter
from Khirbet el-Qôm (William G.
Dever, *HUCA* 40-41 [1969-1970]:
139-204)

2:5   1:5

biblical scholars like the revisionists might have gotten by with arguments from silence, but no longer. One very important category of inscribed objects was not known at all until about 30 years ago, and not well understood until the past decade. I refer to pottery vessels that are inscribed with the name of the individual owner — a practice that is inexplicable unless we assume at least rudimentary literacy. One of the first inscribed 8th-century Judean water decanters to be discovered is the vessel that I recovered in 1968 from Iron Age tombs at Khirbet el-Qôm (discussed above for the tomb inscription mentioning "Asherah").[62] Its owner's Hebrew name, Yaḥmol, is not a careless graffito of some sort, but was carefully carved onto the upper shoulder after firing with a vee-shaped chisel — a technically demanding technique. When I published the el-Qôm decanter in 1970 it was a rare example, paralleled only by one found earlier by Kathleen M. Kenyon in Jerusalem (reading "Belonging to ʿEliyahu [Elijah]"), so I did not realize the importance of the chisel-carved technique. In 1972, however, Avigad pointed out other examples of this technique in publishing another Judean decanter that read "Belonging to Yeḥazyāhū; dark (?) wine." Then in 1981 a well-stratified 8th/7th-century water decanter was published by Aharoni from his excavations at Arad, reading "Belonging to Zadok."[63]

Still more recently, Robert Deutsch and Michael Heltzer have published a typical *northern* or Israelite example of an 8th-century decanter bearing a most interesting phrase: "Belonging to Mattanyāhū; wine for libation, one-fourth."

62. See Dever, *HUCA* 40-41 (1969-1970): 139-204; *ErIsr* 26 (1999): 9*-15*.
63. Cf. Nahman Avigad, "Two Hebrew Inscriptions on Wine-Jars," *IEJ* 22 (1972): 1-9; Aharoni, *Arad Inscriptions*, 107.

First, the Hebrew word *nesek,* "libation," is the same term that is used in several biblical passages for the libation offerings that are prescribed for the temple.[64] The libation vessels, however, that were to be used have not yet been convincingly identified with any surviving vessel known to us. That may be because those made specifically for temple-service were of precious gold and silver (as some texts specify), and so would long ago have been looted and melted down. We must suppose, on the other hand, that many ordinary folk also made libation offerings at local sanctuaries or at household shrines. Such rites are not alluded to directly by the biblical writers, of course (particularly the Deuteronomists), because they were considered "non-Yahwistic." But if such rites did exist, what vessels did most people use for libation offerings of oil or wine? The answer is obvious: ordinary household ceramic vessels, perhaps set aside or "consecrated" for special use by being inscribed. Now we actually have just such a libation vessel, specifying wine-libations. But there is more information on the new decanter: the liquid measure of the wine to be offered, "one-quarter." The larger unit is not noted, probably because it was so well known that it was assumed. Here we have, however, a direct convergence with such biblical texts as Exod. 29:40 and Lev. 23:13, which specifically state that the libation offering is to be "a quarter of a *hin* of wine." From other texts, as well as from excavated ceramic vessels and their evidence, we can calculate that the biblical liquid measure *hin* was equal to one-sixth of a *bath.* Thus, since the *bath* equaled about 5.5 gal., the *hin* was a little less than 1 gal. Deutsch and Heltzer report that their "one-quarter" decanter has a liquid capacity when full of 1270 cm., or about 1.3 l. (a little more than 5 cups). "One-fourth" of a *hin* of ca. 1 gal. would be about a quart — not only within the range of a 5-cup decanter, but a suitable amount for a small libation, especially if we are dealing with the daily offerings of poor folk. Once again, we must pose some hard questions for the revisionists. Are these and the other Iron Age decanters "fakes" too? If not, how can we explain their use of "Biblical" Hebrew in the 8th-7th centuries, if such Hebrew is a "late, artificial, scribal" language invented by the literati who wrote the Bible in the Hellenistic-Roman period? A final ostracon for our purposes here is the late 7th-century letter found in 1960 at Meṣad Ḥashavyahu, a small fortress on the coast south of Tel Aviv, near ancient Jamnia.[65] The text, which is

---

64. Robert Deutsch and Michael Heltzer, *Forty New Ancient West Semitic Inscriptions* (Tel Aviv: Archaeological Center, 1994), 23-26.

65. Joseph Naveh, "A Hebrew Letter from the Seventh Century B.C.," *IEJ* 10 (1960): 129-39; "More Hebrew Inscriptions from Mesad Hashavyahu," *IEJ* 12 (1962): 27-32; and cf. Pardee, *Handbook of Ancient Hebrew Letters,* 15-20; McCarter, *Ancient Inscriptions,* 116. Add now K. A. D. Smelik, "The Literary Structure of the Yabneh-Yam Ostracon," *IEJ* 42 (1992): 55-61.

The "Yavneh Yam" ostracon, from Meṣad Ḥashavyahu (Joseph Naveh, *Early History of the Hebrew Alphabet*)

complete, is a complaint dictated to a scribe by a poor field laborer whose outer garment or cloak (Heb. *beged*) has been seized because of his alleged theft of goods or poor performance. This letter is to be sent to the local governor in hopes of redress of this injustice. One is struck, of course, by the similarity of this case to what must have been frequent practice, which the 8th-century prophet Amos denounced bitterly, pronouncing doom upon those who "lay themselves down beside every altar upon clothes (pl. *begādîm*) taken in pledge" (2:8).

Tomb Inscriptions

Hebrew inscriptions somewhat more monumental than those discussed thus far have been found in several Iron Age tombs. One of the 8th-century tombs that I excavated at Khirbet el-Qôm, biblical Makkedah, has been discussed above because of its inscription referring to "Yahweh and his Asherah."[66] Tomb I also had two Hebrew inscriptions, both around the doorway of one of the three burial chambers. The first read: "Belonging to 'Ophai, the son of Nethanyahu. This is his tomb chamber." The second, over the doorway, read: "Belonging to 'Uzzah, the daughter of Nethanyahu." Not only are these all good Judean names, well

---

66. See n. 31 above and references there to other tomb inscriptions. On Iron Age tombs in general, see Bloch-Smith, *Judahite Burial Practices*.

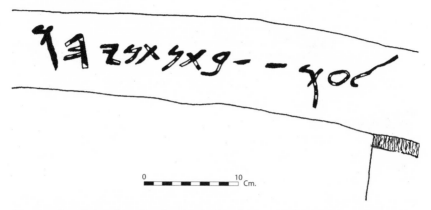

0   10 Cm.

Doorway inscription from Tomb 1 at Khirbet el-Qôm, reading "Belonging to 'Uzzah, the daughter of Nethanyahu" (William G. Dever, *HUCA* 40-41 [1969-1970]: 139-204)

known from the Hebrew Bible (Ophai means "swarthy one," or "Blacky"), but this is an excellent example of a typical Judean bench-style tomb that was used by a single family over an extended period of time, sometimes producing dozens of successive burials over a century or so. Under the back bench of each chamber is a large recess cut into the rock, where the bones of earlier burials were deposited in large piles. This recalls, of course, the common Israelite practice of referring to the death of an individual as being "gathered to the fathers," or joining one's ancestors. "Minimalists" might attempt to explain away such a phrase by saying that it is simply a general metaphor for the afterlife of the deceased. It is absolutely clear, however, that there was no such belief in Israel in biblical times, only some dim notion of Sheol. The doctrine of the "immortality of the soul" is the direct result of Greek influence and appears in the Hebrew Bible only perhaps in the book of Daniel, one of the latest books and probably Hellenistic in date.[67] Being "gathered to the fathers" means just what it says: having one's remains interred in an ancestral tomb that was designed specifically to receive and perpetuate them. Such tombs with communal repositories are typical in the Iron Age, but to my knowledge they do not appear in Palestine in the Hellenistic-Roman period. Again, we have an exclusively Iron Age setting for a biblical practice and form of speech.

A curious footnote can now be added to my publication of the Khirbet el-Qôm material nearly 30 years ago. In 1994, Deutsch and Heltzer included in their publication of a group of antiquities a stone slab that had come originally from el-Qôm at the time I was attempting to stop tomb robbing there, but lay unknown for

67. John J. Collins, "Daniel, Book of," *ABD* 2:29-37; J. Edward Wright, *The Early History of Heaven* (New York: Oxford University Press, 2000), 85-88.

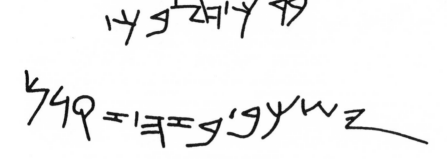

Stonecutter's inscription from Khirbet el-Qôm (Robert Deutsch and Michael Heltzer, *Forty New Ancient West Semitic Inscriptions*)

years in a private collection.[68] Written in nearly the same hand on this stone was the phrase: "Blessed be your stonecutter; may he lay old people to rest in this!" This stone, like all the other stonework in the el-Qôm tombs, shows excellent masonry skills. More to the point, however, is that here we have unusual evidence of the high esteem in which those who carved rock-cut tombs were held — a further manifestation of the respect for the dead that is implied in many biblical texts.

A Judean bench tomb very similar to the one I excavated at el-Qôm was found in 1961 by Joseph Naveh at Khirbet Beit Lei, some 7 miles east of Lachish in the Judean Shephelah. The tomb was a typical late Iron Age bench tomb, re-used in the Persian period but no doubt originally dug in the 7th/6th century or so. There were several fragmentary inscriptions, really graffiti; but the main inscription is complete and reasonably well executed in a cursive Hebrew script. Naveh translates it:

> Yahweh (is) the God of the whole earth; the mountains of
>   Judah belong to him, to the God of Jerusalem.
> The (Mount of) Moriah Thou hast favored, the dwelling of
>   Yah, Yahweh.

What is noteworthy about this tomb inscription is that it is not a banal blessing formula, as expected, but has a truly literary quality. Furthermore, its "Jerusalem temple theology" is fully consistent with that of the Deuteronomistic history in Kings, with which the inscription is contemporary.[69]

68. *Forty New Ancient West Semitic Inscriptions*, 29-30; cf. McCarter, *Ancient Inscriptions*, 111, 112.

69. See Joseph Naveh, "Old Hebrew Inscriptions in a Burial Cave," *IEJ* 13 (1963): 74-92; cf. Niditch, *Oral World and Written Word*, 47, 48 and references there.

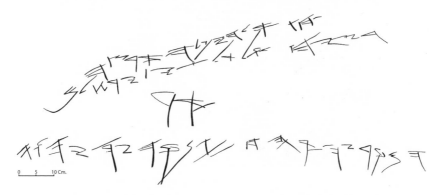

Khirbet Beit Lei inscription, ca. 7th-6th century (Joseph Naveh)

One of the best-known Judean tombs is a monumental rock-cut tomb of elaborate architectural style that is still visible in the Arab village of Silwan (biblical Siloam), just across the Kidron valley southeast of the Temple Mount. In 1870 a badly damaged inscribed stone was cut out and removed to the British Museum. It lay there collecting dust until it was brilliantly deciphered in 1953 by Avigad.[70] The inscription reads:

1. "This is [the sepulchre of . . .] yahu who is over the house.
   There is no silver and no gold here
2. but [his bones] and the bones of his slave-wife with him.
   Cursed be the man
3. who will open this!

Avigad dated the inscription to the late 8th century on the basis of paleography (the comparative shape of the letters). He saw at once the connection of the phrase "who is over the house" (Heb. *'ašer 'al-habbāyit*) with the identical phrase in 1 Kgs. 4:6; 16:9; 18:3, etc., clearly a technical term for "royal chamberlain." In Isa. 22:15-19 we meet a certain "Shebna, who is over the house" in Hezekiah's time, succeeded by Eliakim son of Hilkiah (Isa. 22:20-25; 36:3; 37:2). Avigad suggested that the broken Hebrew name of the beginning of the inscription should be restored as "Shebnayahu" (the typical Judean long-form of names compounded with the name of the deity), and all subsequent scholars have agreed. In that case, the impressive Siloam tomb is the very tomb of Shebna, King Hezekiah's royal chamberlain. As though that were not convergence enough, we apparently have a direct biblical reference to this tomb in Isa.

70. Nahman Avigad, "The Epitaph of a Royal Steward from Siloam Village," *IEJ* 3 (1953): 137-53.

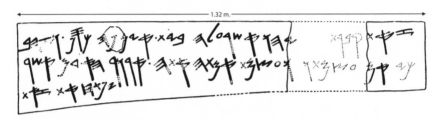

The "Royal Steward" tomb and inscription, late 8th century
(Amnon Ben-Tor, *Archaeology of Ancient Israel*)

22:15, 16, where the prophet rebukes this same Shebna for having himself such a visible and ostentatious tomb in the cliffside, in full view of the temple — "a sepulchre on high." Shebna's tomb is still visible there today; but the Arab villagers of Silwan use it as a garbage dump. Isaiah would no doubt think this appropriate divine retribution.

When Avigad published the "Royal Steward" inscription in 1953 it stood alone, both in coming from the first preexilic inscribed tomb to be dated accurately, and also in exhibiting for the first time outside the Bible the title "who is over the house." Today we have a number of seals with Hebrew personal names and that title. Avigad himself has adduced several from the hoard of bullae he published in 1986, with such well-known biblical names as Adoniyahu (three examples, two by the same engraver) and Natan. Needless to say, this hitherto rare title "royal chamberlain," now so well attested in both our biblical and archaeological sources, occurs exclusively in the Iron Age, and it could not possibly have been known to biblical writers in the Hellenistic-Roman period unless they were working with very ancient records.[71]

There is a final inscription to be considered here, although it is from a ref-

71. See further Avigad, *Bullae and Seals*, 21, 22.

uge cave rather than a burial cave. It was discovered in 1974 by Pesah Bar-Adon, written elegantly in ink on a huge stalactite-like stone column on an isolated cliff overlooking the Dead Sea near 'Ein-gedi, and dating to ca. 700. It is not all legible, but much of it clearly has to do with formulaic curses and blessings, including the phrase "blessed be Yahweh." What is significant here is the curious circumstance (a refugee, fleeing to the wilderness, seeking salvation?), but also the fact that here in the most remote area imaginable some anonymous Judean in dire circumstances was capable of such elegant handwriting. An "illiterate" society?[72]

Commerce and the Economy: Weights

One does not have to be a Marxist, or a "vulgar materialist," to recognize the fact that economic concerns are paramount in any human society. Collective ideology may help to shape history; but unless individuals can shelter, and clothe, and feed themselves, there *is* no history, since no one will survive to write it. As one distinguished contemporary, Norman K. Gottwald, put it in his *The Tribes of Yahweh: A Sociology of the Religion of Liberated Israel, ca. 1250-1050* B.C.E.: "Only as the full *materiality* of ancient Israel is more securely grasped will we be able to make proper sense of its *spirituality*."[73]

We shall look at ancient Israel's economy from the vantage point of our two usual sources, texts and artifacts. The biblical sources on the overall economy are, however, too numerous and too diffuse for us to summarize all the data here. I have chosen therefore to focus on two classes of basic data that may have archaeological correlations, namely the evidence for commerce that weights and measures may provide.

The basic unit of currency in the Hebrew Bible is the sheqel, the Hebrew term deriving from a root meaning "to weigh," that is, to pay by weighing out silver. Sheqel units are mentioned in many biblical passages. The booty from the Israelite conquest of 'Ai was reckoned in sheqels (Josh. 7:21). Similarly, Goliath's armor is evaluated in sheqels (1 Sam. 17:5; cf. 2 Sam. 21:16), as is Absalom's hair (14:26). The prices of various commodities are also given in sheqels: fields (1 Chr. 21:25; Jer. 32:9), oxen (2 Sam. 24:24), measures of barley (2 Kgs. 7:18), and daily rations of food (Ezek. 4:10; 45:12). When an ox gores a slave, recompense is figured in sheqels (Exod. 21:32). In addition, tribute in given in

72. Pesah Bar-Adon, "An Early Hebrew Graffito in a Judean Desert Cave," *ErIsr* 12 (1975): 77-80; cf. Niditch, *Oral World and Written Word*, 47.

73. (Maryknoll: Orbis, 1979), xxv.

units of sheqels (2 Kgs. 15:20; Assyrian tribute). Sheqel weights of varying systems are mentioned, such as "gold" sheqels (2 Chr. 3:9). Sheqel weights could be altered; Amos (8:5) protests the "enlarging" of weights in the merchants' favor. Special sheqel weights "of the sanctuary" are mentioned (Exod. 30:13, 24; Lev. 5:15; Num. 3:47, 50; 7:13).

Sheqel fraction weights are also mentioned in the Hebrew Bible, that is, specific weights smaller than 1 sheqel. Thus we have references to weights of a half-sheqel (Exod. 30:13-15; 38:26), of a one-third sheqel (Neh. 10:32), and of a one-quarter sheqel (1 Sam. 9:8). Smaller fractions are also mentioned, or gerahs, of which there were 20 to the sheqel (Exod. 30:13; Lev. 27:25; Ezek. 45:12). Several specific fraction-weights are mentioned by name in biblical texts: the *beqaʿ*, or half-sheqel (Heb. *beqaʿā*, "to split"), and the *pîm* (only in 1 Sam. 13:21, etymology unknown).

In addition to references mentioning sheqels, we have, as expected, texts referring to the balances with which the sheqel weights were used. The Hebrew term for balance is *meʾōznāyim*, a dual noun which really means "ears" — apparently from the fact that the flanking balance-pans could be seen as resembling two ears. A number of biblical passages refer to balances in general, such as Ezek. 5:1, describing how the prophet's severed hair was weighed. Lev. 19:36 mentions balances in connection with sheqel weights, and Prov. 16:11 mentions "balances" in parallel with "scales." Some biblical passages, however, refer specifically to "false balances," that is, balances that were tampered with in order to favor the merchant. Thus Prov. 11:1 compares both "just" and "unjust" balances *and* weights; and 20:23 protests "false scales" and "diverse weights." Mic. 6:10-11 denounces mercantile practices that were corrupted by "wicked scales" and "a bag of deceitful weights."

The above texts reflect a consistent system of sheqel weights, fraction weights, and balances in the Hebrew Bible. Now let us turn to archaeology to see whether there are any convergences with the biblical texts. If the revisionists are right, we should expect to find coins but no evidence of sheqel weights and balances: they, like all the rest, are literary "inventions" of writers in the Hellenistic-Roman period. In fact, we now have more than 350 Iron Age sheqel weights and fraction weights, as well as a number of balances and parts of balances, all from late 8th-7th-centuries Judah.[74]

The larger sheqel weights are dome-shaped, carved usually in soft lime-

---

74. See now the definitive work of Raz Kletter, *Economic Keystones: The Weight System of the Kingdom of Judah*. JSOTSup 176 (Sheffield: Sheffield Academic, 1998). I disagree, however, that these standardized inscribed weights have nothing to do with reform measures of the late Judean monarchy. See nn. 76, 77 below.

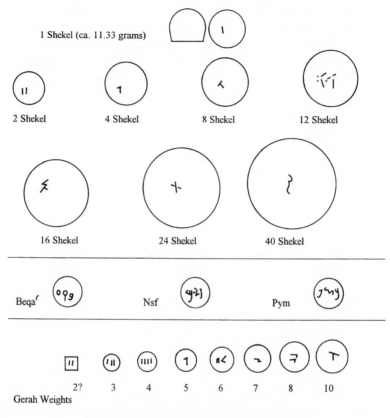

The Judean sheqel-weight system (Raz Kletter)

stone, and inscribed with both a symbol that obviously denotes "sheqel" (re-sembling a small pouch, in which silver was carried) and Egyptian hieratic symbols for numbers. At present, we have examples of inscribed stone sheqel weights in denominations that we can distinguish as 1, 2, 4, 8, 12, 16, 24, and 40 — that is, mostly in multiples of 4 or 8. As noted above, the numerical system is undoubtedly Egyptian, and it may have been introduced into Israel as early as the 10th century. Inscribed sheqel weights that we actually possess, however, all date from the mid-8th to early 6th century, or the Divided Monarchy, to judge from the stratified examples. Numerous studies of these sheqel weights have been undertaken, including my own based on 10 weights from Khirbet el-Qôm. It appears that the "standard" sheqel was equivalent to ca. 11.35 grams; but there is some evidence for a parallel "heavy" (possibly royal) system of weight. Similar inconsistencies exist with dry and liquid measures, so we cannot en-tirely fathom the "logic" of the overall system of weights and measures in ancient Israelite commerce. Part of the difficulty may be due to the fact that both Egyptian and Mesopotamian schemes, and even numerical signs, were borrowed, but never consistently applied in practice or fully standardized. Finally, ancient "science" was not all that precise, and especially with weights and capacities and the like there was much room for unintentional error, not to mention manipulation of the system (which the prophets thought not so "innocent"). One interesting fact is that some weights are "chiseled" (below).

Denomination	Number of examples	Egyptian sign
1 sheqel	34	I
2 sheqel	34	II
4 sheqel	47	٦
8 sheqel	42	∧
12 sheqel	1	ᐵᒣ
16 sheqel	3	⨎
24 sheqel	2	⼁⼂
40 sheqel	2	⁷

Most of the known examples are, not surprisingly, the smaller 1 to 8 sheqel weights, which would obviously have been much more common in daily use. It is by weighing and comparing the hundreds of weights now known that scholars have been able to work out how the system once functioned. The most recent study by Raz Kletter has shown that while the overall system has a ca. 3 percent deviation from the projected standard, the deviation of the more common 1 to 8 sheqel weights is a mere 0.5 percent — an astonishing uniformity, indicating almost certainly royal supervision of the system. On the basis of the careful comparisons made by Kletter, an average for the standard sheqel comes out to 11.33 gm. (11.33249 gm. to be exact).[75]

Three units of fraction-sheqel weights are known: the *neṣep, pîm,* and *beqʿa,* the latter two of which are mentioned in the Hebrew Bible (above). The *neṣep* weights, of which 46 are known, average 9.659 gm., or about 5/6 of a sheqel. The *pîm* weights, 42 in all, average 7.815 gm., or ⅔ of a sheqel. The *beqʿa* weights (Heb. "half"), some 29 known, should represent a half-sheqel,

---

75. See the earlier study of Raz Kletter, "The Inscribed Weights of the Kingdom of Judah," *TA* 18 (1991): 121-63.

and at an average of 6.003 gm. they are reasonably close. Smaller denominations, or *gerah* weights, are known from biblical references (20 to the sheqel) as well as in some 70 archaeological examples, but they are less well understood. For instance, the numerical signs differ somewhat, still Egyptian-based, but perhaps now more "Hebraized." Also, the *gerah* weights deviate considerably from the ½₀ of 11.33 gm., or ca. .57 gm. that they ideally should weigh, often being heavier. Kletter has suggested that while a 20-*gerah* system could have been in operation, a 24-*gerah* system, analogous to that of Mesopotamia, could also have been in use.[76]

What are the implications of the textual and artifactual data above, that is, what convergences do we see, and what do they imply? Here Kletter's exhaustive analysis makes things clear beyond doubt. (1) In the first place, it is obvious that the sheqel system emerged only in the 8th century in *Judah*. All but five of the 353 known weights come from there; and those that are well stratified cannot antedate the 8th century, most being in fact mid-8th to 7th century in date. (2) The overall system now appears to be far more standardized than formerly thought, with relatively few "exceptions" and only rare glimpses of another "royal" weight system. (3) The numerical signs were borrowed from Egypt, partly due to strong Egyptian influence in Judah in this period, and partly to facilitate international trade. (4) Royal initiation and supervision of such a standardized system must be presumed, beginning probably under Hezekiah in the mid-late 8th century in Judah, i.e., after the fall of the northern kingdom. (5) The continuing and widespread use of the sheqel weight system in Judah throughout the 7th century indicates use not only by a centralized government but by the entire population of Judah.

Kletter observes, as others before him, that some convergence might be sought between data provided by the sheqel weights and biblical notions of "reforms" and "justice." However, like so many Israeli (hardly "biblical") archaeologists, he declines to enter the discussion of biblical parallels. He does note, however, that "as relatively little is known from biblical sources, the weights actually aid in elucidating the biblical text, rather than *vice versa*." He thinks that is partly because the biblical writers are biased in favor of elites, international relations, and political history, whereas "the Judean weights, on the other hand, reflect daily trade and economy."[77] Precisely my point. But *what* do they reflect? And do the now precise date and well-established context of the sheqel weights tell us anything about an actual, Iron Age historical setting for the biblical texts? Here Kletter's reticence robs him of a golden opportunity; and, unfortunately,

76. *TA* 18 (1991): 135-37.
77. *TA* 18 (1991): 135-37; cf. also 137-39.

it indicates once again how little dialogue there has been between archaeologists and biblical scholars.

I would argue that it cannot be a mere coincidence that a standardized system of weights based on a "royal sheqel" emerges exclusively in Judah, precisely in the long reign of Hezekiah (715-686), then peaks in the reign of Josiah (640-609). These are the two "reform" kings of whom the prophets and the Deuteronomistic writers approve — indeed, the only two in all of Israel's and Judah's later history. Presuming that the biblical descriptions of the reigns of these two kings are not altogether "propaganda," is it not likely that basic to any reform measures would have been the attempt to eliminate corrupt business practices by standardizing weights and measures under royal administration? Certainly that is what prophetic protests such as those of Hosea, Amos, and Micah are all about — all of them reformist figures who were active in the 8th-7th centuries. Micah, a Judean prophet who lived during the reign of Hezekiah and probably advised the king on religious matters, thundered (6:11): "Shall I acquit the man with wicked scales, and with a bag of deceitful weights?"

Kletter brushes aside such clear reference to deceitful weights (Heb. 'eben we-'eben, or "stones and stones") by asserting that in an individual community "any deviation is neutralized if the same weights are consistently used: one wins as one buys, then loses as one sells."[78] Of Mic. 6:11 specifically, he says that any cheating implied there lay in using different, not "false," weights. Yet he himself has shown that the actual weights we have do not differ significantly within each category. Did the unwary buyer not know the difference between a 1-sheqel weight marked "1" and a 2-sheqel weight marked "11" in the balance pan? Not only is Kletter's notion of local trade facile, but he neglects to mention the fact that a number of the known sheqel weights show chisel-marks on the underside, as I pointed out in publishing the el-Qôm weights.[79] Why is that? The explanation is quite simple: the stone weights were probably cut slightly oversized, then adjusted to conform to the standard as necessary by shaving off the bottom a bit. However, a "heavy" weight that would be to the merchants' advantage — the old "butcher's thumb on the scale" — could easily be produced by not shaving off quite enough. The fact that ancient weights were often altered is exactly the source of our English term "to chisel" someone. This practice in ancient Judah is surely what Micah is referring to: not "different" or various weights, but "differing" or altered weights. Does this prove that Hezekiah's or Josiah's reforms actually took place, and that the standardized sheqel system was part of their economic policies? No; but it does

---

78. *TA* 18 (1991): 135-37.
79. Dever, *HUCA* 40-41 (1969-1970): 139-204.

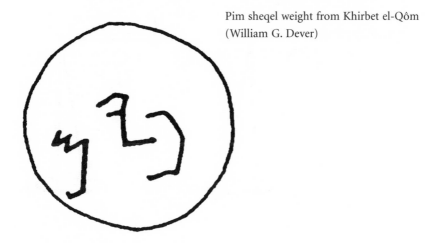

Pim sheqel weight from Khirbet el-Qôm
(William G. Dever)

provide a very plausible setting and thus lends historical credibility to the biblical narratives, whatever their theological agenda may have been.

Another significant datum is overlooked by Kletter, namely the fact that the biblical reference to a *pîm* weight in 1 Sam. 13:21 is the only occurrence of this term in the Hebrew Bible. It therefore gives us a *terminus post quem* (or "date after which") for the final editing, if not the composition, of this passage: it cannot be earlier than the 8th century, although the story is set in the Philistine era. On the other hand, 1 Sam. 13:21 cannot be much later, for the simple reason that the sheqel system of which it was an integral part went out of use completely with the fall of the Judean kingdom in 587/586 (as Kletter has shown), presumably replaced by a Babylonian/Persian system. The point for our purposes here is that the story about a *pîm* weight in 1 Sam. 13:21, told almost nonchalantly because everyone knew what a *pîm* weight was, cannot possibly have been "invented" by writers living in the Hellenistic-Roman period several centuries after these weights had disappeared and had been forgotten. In fact, this bit of biblical text from an original Iron Age setting was handed down intact, although the unique, enigmatic reference to a *pîm* was no longer understood — indeed, would not be understood until the early 20th century A.D., when the first actual archaeological examples turned up, reading *pîm* in Hebrew. If the biblical stories are all "literary inventions" of the Hellenistic-Roman era, how did this particular story come to be in the Hebrew Bible? One may object, of course, that the *pîm* incident is "only a detail." To be sure; but as is well known, "history is in the details."

Before leaving our discussion of the sheqel weight system in ancient Israel, we need to note that fragments of the scales or balances that were used with them

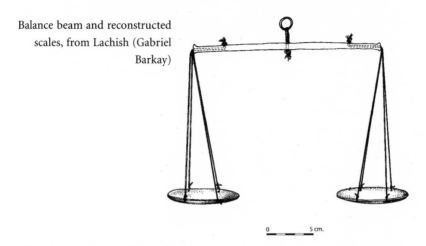

Balance beam and reconstructed scales, from Lachish (Gabriel Barkay)

0   5 cm.

have also been found. One of the best pieces of evidence comes from Lachish, where a well-stratified mid-8th-century ivory balance beam was found in 1972 among the remains in a residential unit. Significantly, it is clearly of an Egyptian type that was used throughout the New Kingdom and the Iron Age — another example of Egyptian influence on the Judean system of weights and measures. A similar ivory (or bone) balance beam was found long ago at Megiddo, dating in all probability to the 10th-9th centuries. At a number of other sites remains of Iron Age scales have been brought to light, especially bronze (or bone) scale-pans, as well as bits of chains, at sites such as Megiddo, 'Ein-gedi, Ashdod, and elsewhere.[80] Thus the 14 references to "balances" in the Hebrew Bible (above). It is clear that silver was the preferred medium of exchange, usually in the form of scraps (Judg. 5:19) that were "paid/weighed" out in one balance-pan, the stone weight or weights being placed in the other (Jer. 32:9-10). The merchant held the scales in one hand and adjusted them with the other, just as street peddlers still do in Jerusalem today. It was easy, as the biblical prophets knew, to cheat and be cheated (as in the "chiselling" of weights noted above).

Measures of Volume in the Divided Monarchy

Many references in the Hebrew Bible mention various units of liquid and dry measures, if only in passing, since the biblical writers are interested primarily in the larger picture, not daily life. In principle, we might isolate and quantify a "vocabulary of measures," then determine whether the Hebrew terminology in

80. See n. 45 above.

the Bible would fit better, for instance, in a preexilic or a postexilic setting. In practice, however, this is difficult. For one thing, the terminology of measurements is universally conservative by definition, and thus it may not change significantly over long periods of time. When we come to our question here — "What did the biblical writers know; and when did they know it?" — we face a peculiar difficulty. It is likely that the latest editors did have some older archives to draw upon. But ironically, they did not have our modern advantage: they had no extant examples of measures to reconstruct how the system worked. The ancients possessed traditions, but they did not have access to the complex set of information and techniques that would make it possible for the modern scholar to make history, rather than "story," out of the ancient evidence.[81]

The question is whether we *can* make history out of the biblical data. I would argue that it is only with the assistance that archaeology can provide that we stand any chance of doing that. Before citing that evidence, let us give a sort of consensus view that represents what we can reasonably reconstruct of the system of liquid and dry measurements from the biblical sources alone (using typical modern American, rather than metric, values).

Liquid measures:

Unit	Other Information	Approx. Capacity
hin	¹⁄₁₀ of an issaron	1 qt.
bath		5½ gal.
log		½-⅔ pint
cor/homer		50-60 gal.?

Dry measures:

Unit	Other Information	Approx. Capacity
kab		1 qt. plus
omer/issaron	¹⁄₁₀ of an ephah	2 qt.
seah		⅔ peck
ephah		½ bushel
dethech	½ of a homer	2½ bushels
homer/cor		5 bushels (an "assload")

It must be acknowledged that actual surviving examples of the vessels that were used in making these measurements are rare. That is to be expected, however, since many of the containers may have been perishables like baskets.

81. See generally Ovid R. Sellers, "Weights and Measures," *IDB* 4:828-39; Marvin A. Powell, "Weights and Measures," *ABD* (1992), 6:897-908.

Storejar neck from Lachish Stratum III, reading "royal bath" (Drawn from Olga Tufnell,
Lachish IV)

Others, mostly common pottery vessels used to measure, were probably not inscribed with the name of the unit in question, since it was familiar and taken
for granted. In short, we confront again a relative lack of written evidence. Yet
there is some.

Long ago Albright found at Tell Beit Mirsim in southern Judah a fragment of a large storejar inscribed in Hebrew *bt*, "bath," a unit of liquid measure
mentioned in such passages as Ezek. 45:11, 14, which was equal to the *ephah*
and equivalent to about 5½ gal. Another, reading "royal bath," comes from
Level III in Lachish, dated now precisely to the destruction of Sennacherib in
701; this is either an "official" or a somewhat larger unit of measure. The
issaron, equivalent to an *omer*, can be illustrated by the discovery of a storejar at
Arad (and Beersheba) inscribed *omer*, which has a capacity of just over 2 qts.
That would fit approximately with the note in Ezek. 45:11-14 that an *omer* is
equivalent to "¹/₁₀ of an *ephah*," the latter being approximately ½ bushel.[82]

Pottery in Ancient Israel

Archaeologists everywhere seem preoccupied with the study of pottery. Their
fascination, however, is easily explainable. Pottery was almost universally used
in antiquity and is abundant at every site. It broke easily, but if fired was virtually indestructible, so it provides us with thousands and thousands of little con-

82. On weights and measures generally, see Kletter (above, nn. 74-75); Sellers;
Powell. For the Tell Beit Mirsim and Lachish data, see William F. Albright, *The Excavation
of Tell Beit Mirsim*, 1: *The Pottery of the First Three Campaigns*. AASOR 12 (New Haven:
Yale University Press, 1932), 77, fig. 12; Olga Tufnell et al., *Lachish III: The Iron Age* (London: Oxford University Press, 1953), 356, 357. For an analysis of the Arad and Beersheba
"bath" inscriptions, see Joseph Naveh, "The Numbers of *Bat* in the Arad Ostraca," *IEJ* 42
(1992): 52-54.

temporary "time-capsules." Finally pottery's very plasticity made it an ideal vehicle for expressing technological innovations, aesthetic norms, various functional ideas, and even religious notions. Pottery, as one distinguished archaeologist put it, "is our most sensitive medium for perceiving shared aesthetic traditions in the sense that they define ethnic groups, for recognizing culture contact and change, and for following migration and trade patterns."[83]

To begin with biblical texts that mention ceramics in general, I would note frequent references to clays (Heb. *ḥōmer*) and clay processing for making pottery (e.g., Isa. 41:25, the "potter treading, kneading, clay"); potter's wheels (*'ābnayîm,* the dual form, because of the upper and lower wheel), like the one in the famous parable of the potter's workshop in Jer. 18:3-6; pottery molds (*ḥôtām,* lit., "seal," but here something carved, engraved); pottery kilns (*tannûr,* "oven"), as in Neh. 3:11; 12:38; and broken potsherds (*ḥeres*) strewn on the ground, as in Isa. 45:9, or even a gate in Jerusalem named the "potsherd gate" (Jer. 19:2). In these and other biblical passages, however, it must be acknowledged that there is little that can be related to pottery and ceramic production in general, that is, nothing that could place these texts in a specifically Iron Age context. For instance, dual pottery wheels, with a lower kick-wheel and an upper forming wheel, are known from ca. 3000 on.

A more fruitful avenue of inquiry does exist, however, namely the analysis of particular Hebrew terms for various kinds of ceramic vessels. It may surprise many readers (and most biblical scholars as well) to learn that there are more than 30 such Hebrew terms in the Bible. Here we have a challenge that would seem obvious, indeed irresistible, namely to do a careful analysis of these terms and their etymologies, as well as a detailed exegesis of all the passages where they occur. It would then be pertinent to see whether any connection can be made between these technical terms for ceramic vessels and the actual pottery we have excavated from Iron Age (or later) Palestine. Obvious or not, it has never been done — perhaps because once again there has been so little dialogue between specialists in biblical and in archaeological studies. The only attempt ever made was by James L. Kelso, a seminary professor who worked both with Albright at Tell Beit Mirsim in 1920-1932 and then collaborated later (1948) with a professional potter in studying the Tell Beit Mirsim Iron Age pottery.[84] Kelso, however, was not a professional archaeologist, and his work was done long before the Iron Age pottery of Palestine was well understood.

83. Robert W. Ehrich, *Chronologies in Old World Archaeology,* 3rd ed. (Chicago: University of Chicago Press, 1992), vii, viii. The standard handbook on Palestinian pottery is still Ruth Amiran, *Ancient Pottery of the Holy Land.*

84. The results summarized in James L. Kelso, "Pottery," *IDB* 3:846-53.

What I have done in the following is based on the philological and exegetical analysis recommended above. To summarize the results in a non-technical way, I have put them in chart form, giving the Hebrew term; the general functional description apparent from a composite of all the references; and, most important for our purposes here, an example of a typical Iron Age vessel that I think the term may refer to. I stress that this analysis, while original, is still speculative and preliminary; I certainly do not claim that by this use of a certain Hebrew term the writers of the Hebrew Bible meant this actual vessel and no other. Again, we are trying simply to deduce, from all the evidence available, how much the writers of the Hebrew Bible actually *knew* about daily life in the Iron Age — how much, and perhaps how little.

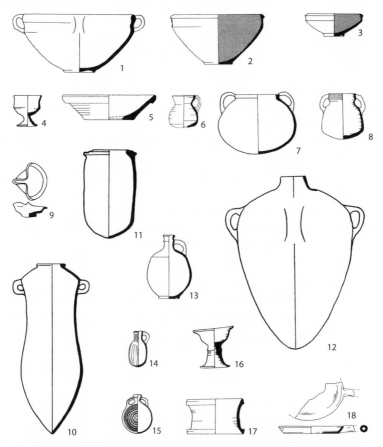

Sources: 1-4, 7-16 (Ruth Amiran, *Ancient Pottery of the Holy Land*);
5 (Moshe Dothan, *Ashdod II-III*, 6, 17 (Yohanan Aharoni, *Beer-sheba*);
18 (Ze'ev Herzog et al., *Excavations at Tel Michal, Israel*)

232

Hebrew term	General description, function	Possible example (Fig. XX)
'agān	A large krater with handles, used as a bowl for dining in general	1
sēpel	A large bowl, perhaps with or without handles, used for eating or drinking	2
ṣallaḥat	A bowl or dish used for eating and drinking	3
kôs	A small bowl or cup for drinking	4
miš'eret	A large bowl for kneading dough	5
pîyōr	A jug used for cooking	6
sîr	A large cooking pot	7
dûd	A smaller, narrow-mouthed cooking pot	8
nēr	An oil lamp	9
nēbel	A large jar for storing oil, wine, etc. (perhaps = 2 "baths")	10
kad	A smaller jar for drawing water; storing water or oil, dry meal	11
'āsîd	A large oil-jar	12
baqbūq	A decanter for liquids	13
pak	A small juglet for oil or perfume	14
ṣappaḥat	A "canteen" for water	15
gābî'a	A chalice for wine	16
kîrayim	A ring-base for cooking pots	17
	A "skillet"	18

It is significant that all the best ceramic parallels above come from well-dated 8th-7th century sites, almost all in Judah. This strongly corroborates mainstream scholarly opinion that the biblical texts that mention these vessels — mostly the J, E, and D sources — were largely composed and edited in penultimate fashion precisely in that period, i.e., in the late Monarchy. It is noteworthy that a few rare and enigmatic biblical terms, such as those for "frying-pan," are attested only in Late Hebrew or in Aramaic parallels, and also occur only in the P or "Priestly" source, the final editing of which scholars have dated late. And it is precisely these forms that are completely and conspicuously absent from the earlier Iron Age ceramic repertoire. Such forms do occur, however, in the Hellenistic period, confirming the late editing of the references in the P materials. Once again, the ceramic repertoire with which the *original* writers of the J, E, and D traditions were familiar is that of the Iron Age or Monarchy — and no *other* period.[85] The text may have been *edited* late, but most of its contents are early.

Art in Ancient Israel

Discussing art in ancient Israel, according to most biblical scholars until recently, should be relatively easy: there was none. The attitude of most biblicists may have been unduly influenced by a naive presupposition that the Second Commandment — "You shall have no images" — should be and was taken seriously as "historical fact." Nevertheless, the presupposition is wrong.[86] But what does "Israelite art" consist of? And why would more conventional biblical scholars not be aware of its existence?

In answer to the first question, Israelite art of the period of the Divided Monarchy consisted primarily of engraved seals, some of which have been discussed above, although largely for their onomastic information (personal names); and carved ivory panels, mostly inlays for wooden furniture, of both Syrian and Phoenician styles.

85. Examples shown are based on Amiran. For the late terms here, cf. e.g. *marḥešet*, a "frying-pan for meat," only in Lev. 2:7; 7:9, obviously P material; *maḥăbāt*, a "pan for frying flat cakes," only in Lev. 2:5; 6:14; 7:9, again P; and *pārûr*, a "pan for baking manna-bread," only in Num. 11:8; 1 Sam. 2:14, both probably P. For examples of ceramic one-handled skillets from the Hellenistic period, see Paul W. Lapp, *Palestinian Ceramic Chronology*. Such vessels are absolutely unknown anywhere in the Iron Age (cf. p. 232, no. 18).

86. A German biblical scholar and art historian, Sylvia Schroer, has recently published a book with which few American biblical scholars seem to be familiar: *In Israel Gab es Bilder?* (in English, *Was There Art in Israel?*). OBO 74 (Göttingen: Vandenhoeck & Ruprecht, 1987).

Seals

Much more could be said about the seals, or "glyptic art," beyond the onomastic evidence discussed above, important though that is. Biblical scholars, however, philologically (and theologically) oriented, have rarely had much interest in or empathy with art history. A notable exception is the group of European biblical scholars headed by Othmar Keel of Fribourg University in Switzerland. The "Fribourg school" has created an impressive body of works intending to illuminate the history and religions of ancient Israel by studying ideology through its art and iconography, situating them in the broader context of ancient Near Eastern art and iconography. In addition to Sylvia Schroer's volume on ancient Israelite art in general, distinguished recent books in this genre include Urs Winter, *Frau und Göttin* (English, *Woman and Goddess*).[87] Especially noteworthy are a number of works by Keel himself: several large volumes on seals, in German, as well as synthetic works including *The Symbolism of the Biblical World*.[88] A basic handbook is that by Keel and his student Christoph Uehlinger, *Gods, Goddesses, and Images of God in Ancient Israel*.[89]

The corpus of artistic motifs in common use in ancient Israel and her neighbors that the Fribourg school has brought to our attention is so vast and so rich in parallels that I can only allude to some items here. In particular, Keel and Uehlinger have shown us how the several thousand seals they have collected can help to illuminate ancient Israelite religion. They have demonstrated, for instance, that most of the motifs of the 10th-8th-century seals are borrowed, either directly from Egypt, or more often via the medium of Phoenician art, which was characterized by a mixture of Egyptian and Mesopotamian themes. Later on, in the late 8th-6th centuries, Neo-Assyrian and Neo-Babylonian motifs predominate, as expected. Common motifs on the Phoenicianizing seals include lions, bulls, sacred trees, dung-beetles, and other themes from nature, most with known religious connotations. The later group features much more astral imagery — sun, moon, stars of the heavens — as well as specifically Mesopotamian themes.

Here we have both convergences and divergences with the biblical texts. On the one hand, such art ought not to have existed *at all* in light of the Second Commandment: "You shall not make for yourself a graven image, or any likeness

---

87. *Exegetische und ikonographische Studien zum weiblichen Gottesbild im alten Israel und in dessen Umwelt.* OBO 53 (Göttingen: Vandenhoeck & Ruprecht, 1983).

88. *Ancient Near Eastern Iconography and the Book of Psalms* (1978, repr. Winona Lake: Eisenbrauns, 1997).

89. (Minneapolis: Fortress, 1996).

A typical Late Judean seal bearing only a personal name, "Hoshiyahu, son of Shelmiyahu" (Helga Weippert, *Palästina in vorhellenisticher Zeit*)

of anything that is in heaven above, or that is on the earth beneath, or that is in the water under the earth" (Exod. 20:4). On the other hand, a number of the motifs are found in the biblical descriptions of the temple and its furnishings, which I have argued above should be taken quite literally. I suspect that whatever date one assigns to the Ten Commandments in their present form (many scholars think they date roughly to the 8th century), there was *always* a certain ambivalence about representative art in ancient Israel. This was especially because Israel had no native artistic traditions and thus usually borrowed art from its "pagan" neighbors, which led to conflicting associations and ultimately to the religious syncretism that the later Yahwistic parties so vigorously denounced.

However uncertain much of the picture of Israelite art may be, I find two aspects of our data on seals suggestive. (1) The early period is heavily influenced by Syrian, specifically Phoenician, art, and most of it is found in the north. That is entirely in keeping with the main biblical tradition, which condemns the north for succumbing to "foreign gods." One recalls in particular the vehement opposition of the Deuteronomists to Ahab, and especially to his Phoenician queen Jezebel, who brought with her to Samaria an entire Ba'al cult and its entourage of priests and priestesses. Of course our view of this single-minded wrath must be tempered by the acknowledged Phoenician influence on the construction and furnishings of the Solomonic temple, of which the editors of Kings do not disapprove. (2) It also strikes me as significant that by the 7th-6th century the vast majority of Israelite (now really Judean) seals have no symbols or artistic motifs at all, only personal names. In short, they, like the later "official" tradition of the Deuteronomistic school, are now severely aniconic. Is this merely coincidence? I doubt it. Such an overwhelming change to an austere, "anti-representational" style on the engraved seals of the late period suggests to me that the "religious reforms" claimed by the Deuteronomists are not wholly propagandistic. There does seem to be a tendency to purge Israelite art, if it can still be called that, of foreign elements, particularly in the late 7th/early 6th century. The Avigad and Shiloh hoards of bullae alone would confirm that; the seals used to make these bullae are almost all severely aniconic (and the personal names, as well, are mostly compounded with the name of Yahweh). I do not take this necessarily to mean that there was a sweeping "religious revival" in Josiah's time, much less that it succeeded, since many of the seals and bullae may represent only the elites in Jerusalem and in other royal centers. Popular religion in the countryside probably remained highly syncretistic, as I have argued above.[90]

Ivories and Ivory-carving

The second major class of ancient Israelite art, again strongly Phoenician in character, consists of a series of carved ivory inlays of the 9th-8th centuries. These are found mostly in the northern kingdom, at administrative centers such as Hazor, and especially at Samaria, the capital. The large collection of burned fragments found on the floors of the palace at Samaria was undoubtedly what remained from booty taken in the Assryian destruction in 722/721. Ivory fragments in the same style, some with Hebrew letters engraved on the back, have been found at the Assyrian capital at Nimrud.

The carved ivory panels found in Israel all belong to an international style of art, mostly of north Syrian and Phoenician manufacture or style, that spread all over the Mediterranean world in the 9th-8th centuries. Large hoards have been discovered at Arslan Tash, Til Barsip, and other sites in Syria, as well as at sites from Carmona in Spain to the Neo-Assyrian capital at Nimrud and elsewhere.[91]

The group of ivories known from Israel comes mostly from Samaria (over 500 fragments), some 9th-century pieces kept as heirlooms, others closer in date to the final destruction of the Israelite palace in 722/721. It is clear that most of these small, individual low-relief carvings, some partially inlaid or gilded, were designed to make up attached panels for costly wooden furniture. Many of the panels are half-scenes, or one of a matching pair, and others have tabs at the top and bottom for attaching them. That they are inlays is now shown from well-preserved examples of just such ivory-inlaid wooden beds and chairs from Phoenician tombs at Salamis in Cyprus, of the late 9th or early

90. This is shown as well by Ackerman.
91. For orientation to the ivories, see works in n. 9 above.

Carved ivory inlays from Samaria, with lion and stylized "sacred tree" (John W. Crowfoot and Grace M. Crowfoot, *Early Ivories from Samaria*)

8th century. The major artistic motifs of most of the Israelite ivories known are typically Phoenician: lions, bulls, cherubs, palmettes, lilies, lotus blossoms, etc. As with the seals, we have here a convergence with the candid biblical notion that there was little native Israelite art, so that Solomon had to resort to Hiram, king of Tyre on the Phoenician coast, to design, build, and furnish his temple in Jerusalem. Phoenician influence also continued later, as reflected in the stories of Ahab, Jezebel, and the temple of Baʿal at Samaria.

It is in fact at Samaria that we find the most instructive convergence of the ivories with biblical texts. In a passage that remained enigmatic until the discovery of the ivories in modern times, the prophet Amos rebukes the idle rich who live in "great houses," "houses of ivory" (3:15). 1 Kgs. 22:39 specifies that the "house or palace" of Ahab at Samaria was built of ivory (cf. Ps. 45:8), where in fact most of the ivories were found. These references as they stand make little sense, since one could not possibly construct a house of the small ivory panels that elephant or boar tusks would yield. The writers or editors of 2 Kings do not mention ivory-decorated couches and armchairs, or the elephant hides and tusks given to Sennacherib as bounty by Hezekiah in 701 in order to spare the temple, but we know of these from Sennacherib's own tribute lists.[92] These latter references obviously denote smaller items, for which ivory

92. *ANET,* 321; 287, 288.

inlays would indeed be suitable. We also read in 1 Kgs. 10:18 (cf. 2 Chr. 9:17) of Solomon's "great ivory throne." And again a passage from Amos (6:4) comes to mind: "Woe to those who lie upon beds of ivory!" An even more striking convergence, just because it is such a seemingly casual footnote, is found in Amos 3:12, in which the prophet refers to the "remnant" that will be saved from Yahweh's wrath in the coming destruction of Samaria, "rescued, with the corner of a couch and part of a *bed*." This text has little meaning unless Amos is speaking of luxury items that may be valuable enough to be salvaged, like ivory-inlaid furniture — and the "beds" we have noted above.

The relevance of the 9th-8th-century ivories for our purposes here is obvious. The passages we have cited from such biblical sources as the prophets and the Deuteronomistic editors of Kings find astonishingly close and detailed convergences in the ivories that archaeology has brought to light — of the 9th-8th centuries — and *only* then. These distinctive Levantine Iron Age ivories passed out of use by the 7th-6th centuries, as did the custom of inlaying wooden furniture. It would be incredible to suggest that the biblical references were "invented" by writers living in the Hellenistic or Roman period. They *must* have had ancient sources, in this case records going back at least to the 8th century, if not earlier.

Secondary "Royal Residences"

In any discussion of convergences between biblical texts and archaeological artifacts, it would be particularly desirable, of course, to investigate the two ancient capitals, Jerusalem and Samaria. Of Iron Age Jerusalem we admittedly know very little (but see above); and we have already discussed the palace of Omri and Ahab, the ostraca, and the ivories from Samaria. The kings of both Israel and Judah, however, had not only a principal palace in their capital, but also smaller summer and winter residences elsewhere. Two of them are relevant to our discussion here.

Jezreel

A story of the type routinely dismissed by the revisionists as fiction is the well-known account of Naboth's vineyard in 1 Kgs. 21. The story recounts how Ahab, taunted by Jezebel, conspired to seize a vineyard of a small landowner, one Naboth, at Jezreel where the kings of Samaria had an auxiliary residence. This was probably a winter palace, since the high hill of Samaria can be bitterly cold in winter, but Jezreel, beautifully situated on the south rim of the Jezreel valley at a lower altitude, enjoys a mild winter climate. As we have already seen, Amos says in the same breath as his denunciation of "the houses of ivory" that Yahweh will "tear down the winter house as well as the summer house" (Amos 3:15).

The ancient site of Jezreel, presuming that the story in 1 Kings may have had a historical background, has long been identified with a small but strategic mound near the modern Arab village of Zer'in, on the southern heights overlooking the Jezreel valley. The Jezreel references in the Hebrew Bible have been much discussed by biblical scholars, but the proposed site was never extensively investigated until salvage excavations were carried out by Ussishkin and colleagues in 1990-91. The results provide another remarkable convergence with biblical accounts.[93]

There is some scattered occupation of the hilltop of Jezreel and in the vicinity in the 10th century, just as we now know was the case at Samaria. The major construction, however — an enclosure of ca. 10 acres surrounded by casemate walls with corner towers — dates to a single phase of use, in the 9th century. This fortified acropolis was destroyed sometime later, and the site of Jezreel was never again extensively built up.

The remarkable size of the enclosures, the deep, elaborate constructional fills on which it was erected, the casemate defense walls, and the use of alternating "pilasters" of dressed ashlar masonry are all typical features that would be found only in royal constructions. Indeed, similar architecture has been brought to light thus far only at Hazor, Megiddo, and Samaria in the north, and at Gezer and Ramat Raḥel in the south — all but Ramat Raḥel royal constructions of the 10th-9th centuries. Ussishkin modestly (and correctly) postpones direct connections with the specific biblical texts. As an archaeologist (and one praised by the revisionists, for his separation of biblical and archaeological data), Ussishkin concludes:

> It would appear that the enclosure at Jezreel was built either by Omri (882-871 B.C.E.) or by Ahab (873-852), and was then used by Ahab's sons Ahaziah (852-851) and Jehoram (851-842). The destruction of the enclosure should be assigned to Jehu's *coup d'état* in 842 B.C.E. and is probably reflected in Hosea 1:4.[94]

93. David Ussishkin and John Woodhead, "Excavations at Tel Jezreel 1990-1991: Preliminary Report," *TA* 19 (1992): 3-55; "Excavations at Tel Jezreel 1994-1996: Third Preliminary Report," *TA* 24 (1997): 6-72; and cf. Nadav Na'aman, "Historical and Literary Notes on the Excavations of Tel Jezreel," *TA* 24 (1997): 122-28.

94. Ussishkin and Woodhead, *TA* 19 (1992): 53.

My point in adducing the data here is simple. Once again, the direct correspondences indicate that the final editors of the Deuteronomistic history in Kings did not imagine a "winter palace" at Jezreel in Ahab's time; they *knew* about it from much earlier sources, in this case sources that can scarcely be much later than the 9th century.

Ramat Raḥel

Another example of a royal palatial estate is biblical Beth-Haccherem, or "The house/palace of the vineyards," identified with the small mound of Ramat Raḥel just north of Bethlehem. Beth-Haccherem is not mentioned by name but is apparently alluded to in Jer. 22:13-19, where the prophet denounces Jehoiakim, the son of Josiah, for defrauding the poor to "build his house by un-righteousness." This palace does not appear, however, to be the main palace in Jerusalem; but it may be, like Jezreel, a country estate or retreat. This palace is described as "a great house, with spacious upper rooms," having "cut-out windows" and paneled with cedar and "painted with vermillion" (Jer. 22:14).

The site of Ramat Raḥel, on a prominent hilltop overlooking terraced vineyards with Jerusalem visible on the horizon, was excavated by Yohanan Aharoni between 1954 and 1962.[95] The site was founded in the 9th century and was then occupied principally in the later Iron Age and the Persian periods. The major structures belonged to Stratum V-B of the 8th century, and Stratum V-A of the late 7th/early 6th century. A large perimeter wall with its own gate enclosed an area of ca. 800 sq. m., most of it apparently not built up. The single structure inside the walls was a large multi-roomed citadel with its own casemate walls, a large central court, and many adjoining rooms. The construction was unusually fine, featuring dressed ashlar masonry laid in header-stretcher style — the only known example of such royal masonry after the 10th-9th century. As with ashlar buildings elsewhere, at Ramat Raḥel there were palmette or "Proto-Aeolic" capitals. A unique find was a stone window balustrade with several short palmette-columns with drooping fronds, topped with stylized palmette capitals joined to form a continuous window rail. That this was originally a window balustrade is shown by almost identical windows and balustrades on typical 8th-7th-century Phoenician ivories — often with a woman leaning over the balustrade, which is apparently meant to depict the second-story window of a palace or temple. Significantly, the columns and capitals bore traces of red paint.

95. See conveniently Yohanan Aharoni, "Ramat Raḥel," *NEAEHL* 4:1261-67.

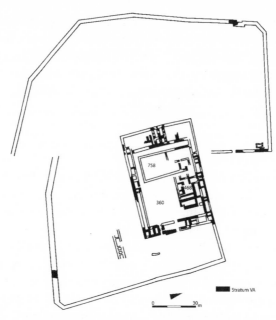

Plan of the "Palace" and enclosure at Ramat Raḥel, ca. 7th-6th century
(Helga Weippert, *Palästina in vorhellenisticher Zeit*)

Reconstruction of a stone balustrade from
fragments found at Ramat Raḥel (Original
drawing by Leen Ritmeyer, courtesy
Simon & Schuster)

A carved ivory from Nimrud,
8th century (Othmar Keel,
The Symbolism of the Biblical World)

242

Here the convergence between the description of a royal palace in Jer. 22 and the archaeological evidence from Ramat Raḥel is striking. The Stratum V B-A enclosure and principal structure are certainly palatial, built on far too grand a scale and embodying too costly construction to be of domestic character. The ashlar masonry alone makes this a "royal" establishment. The fenestrated window and balustrade fit the biblical description of a "cut-out window" astonishingly well, just as the traces of red paint correspond to the house "painted in vermillion." All these architectural features had disappeared, were buried and long forgotten, after the destruction at Ramat Raḥel by the Babylonians in the early 6th century. A Persian administrative building occupied the hilltop later, but it cannot have given rise to the detailed biblical description of a "great palace" of the kings of Judah. Once again, it defies credulity to suppose that the biblical writers or editors in the Hellenistic or Persian period "invented" the Iron Age palace at Ramat Raḥel.

CHAPTER 6

What Is Left of the History of Ancient Israel, and Why Should It Matter to Anyone Anymore?

It has been my contention thus far that there is a crisis in the current study of the history of ancient Israel. The implication is that this crisis should be of concern not only to theologians and clerics, but also to intelligent lay folk, and indeed to all who cherish the Western cultural tradition, which in large part derives from values enshrined in the Bible. Yet the gravity of this particular crisis can be appreciated only by seeing it as part of a *larger* dilemma that characterizes modern intellectual and social life in every area, particularly in the Western world.

The Western Tradition and the Enlightenment under Attack

The modern dilemma may be described most simply by regarding it as the "loss of innocence." This stage of consciousness represents the denouement of a long process. The opening up of the vast frontiers of knowledge that began with the Age of Reason in the 17th-18th centuries swept away the old order of credulity, of naïveté, forever, but what has it left in its place? Richard Tarnas, in his sweeping survey, *The Passion of the Western Mind,* remarks:

> Perhaps the most momentous paradox concerning the character of the modern era was the curious manner in which its progress during the centuries following the Scientific Revolution and the Enlightenment brought Western man unprecedented freedom, power, expansion, breadth of knowledge, depth of insight, and concrete success, and yet simultaneously

245

served — first subtly and later critically — to undermine the human being's existential situation on virtually every front: metaphysical and cosmo-
logical, epistemological, psychological, and finally even biological.[1]

In short, our long quest for objective knowledge of the nature of the universe and of the human condition has, despite measurable progress, brought us
not to the point of confidence, but of increasing skepticism and even despair.
What *can* we know? And, moreover, what can we *trust* as "true," whether for our
own sense of self or for the foundations of society? These are the fundamental
doubts that plague what is called the "postmodern condition," which we examined briefly in Chapter 2 above — "modern" meaning up to about the mid-
20th century, and "post" everything thereafter.

The postmodern malaise that seems to grip intellectuals is seldom felt by
most people, for whom daily life goes on marked by countless nagging little
worries, but scarcely any overwhelming, cosmic *Angst*. This apparent normalcy,
this ordinariness, may, however, be deceptive. The old order, on which our familiar civilization was founded, really *is* gone — and with it, the certainties that
most people still take for granted and in which they presume to find comfort.

Even though "postmodernism" never makes headlines, there are signs
that the public is becoming more aware of changes it has brought about. While
I was completing this book, the *Atlantic Monthly* published an excellent article
on "The Academy vs. the Humanities,"[2] in which Frank Kermode reviewed
John M. Ellis' *Literature Lost: Social Agendas and the Corruption of the Humanities*.[3] Both here and in his previous work, *Against Deconstruction*,[4] Ellis expresses his alarm at the extraordinary changes that various "post-Enlightenment" ideologies have wrought in American universities. The "disinterested"
study of literature for its intrinsic values is now "politically incorrect," subject
to incredible abuse. The traditional curriculum must be replaced by one that
advocates that the ultimate purpose of all inquiry is political, that the *proper*
objects of study must be race, gender, and class. Academics now routinely rail
against "the Western tradition" in thought and literature, often without any real
credentials in the requisite disciplines, full of anti-establishment and Utopian
fantasies. One simply mines the literature looking for evidence of oppression,
which Ellis finds a corruption of the very idea of disinterested inquiry and criti-

---

1. P. 325. This masterful intellectual history of the Western cultural tradition puts
postmodernism in context better than any work I know. Anyone reading it will understand that revisionism really does share in postmodernism's inherent nihilism.

2. (August, 1997): 93-96.

3. (New Haven: Yale University Press, 1997).

4. (Princeton: Princeton University Press, 1989).

cal dialogue. Of one of the leading architects of the modern academy, Fredric Jameson, Ellis states that he "appears to lack any moral sensibility." Jameson's influence, despite outrageous pronouncements, "derives neither from the power of his argument nor from the moral force of his position but only from his having furnished what seems to those who use it a serviceable underpinning for the victim-centered criticism that has overtaken university literature departments."[5] In short, I would say, honest inquiry, scholarly documentation, and reasoned discourse have been replaced by ideology and politics in many social science disciplines. And that is precisely what I am arguing here has happened in many seminary and university departments of religion and theology. I invite the reader to go back now and read Davies, Thompson, and Whitelam; it will be obvious where they are coming from.

Even *Time* magazine has taken notice of the corrosive effects of post-

---

5. Kermode, a distinguished retired professor of English and literary critic, regards all of this as an intellectual catastrophe: "There have been fads and fashions before, and they have passed, but this one has resulted in the creation of new, self-perpetuating university departments and has packed existing departments with sympathizers"; *Atlantic Monthly* (August, 1997): 96. Kermode hopes that "the practitioners of race-class-gender criticism will grow discontented with their sterility, and not wishing to seem dull and ridiculous, seek to regain contact with the fine things," but he does not think this very likely. My complaint against the revisionists and their Bible-bashing is similar, and for good reason. For some hope that many university faculty and leading intellectuals are fed up with "political correctness" and the resultant "culture wars," see J. Engell and A. Dangerfield, "The Market-Model University: Humanities in the Age of Money," *Harvard Magazine* (May, 1998): 48-55, 111. The authors warn of the consequences of raising a new generation who have never learned from the past and have never "witnessed the treacheries and glories of human experience profoundly revealed by writers and artists" (111) — and, I would say, by the Hebrew Bible *par excellence.* See also D. K. Magner, "10 Years of Defending the Classics and Fighting Political Correctness," *Chronicle of Higher Education* (December 12, 1997): A12-A14, a spirited defense of the recently created "National Association of Scholars," whose goal is "to reclaim the academy" and reaffirm the Classical tradition. The notorious deconstructionist Stanley Fish, of Duke University, has dismissed the group as "racist, sexist, and homophobic." Note also the resurgence of "Neo-conservatives" (read "traditionalists") at Harvard, as reported by J. Tassel, "The 30 Years' War: Cultural Conservatives Struggle With the Harvard They Love," *Harvard Magazine* (September-October, 1992): 57-99. Jon D. Levenson, Lisht Professor of Jewish Studies at Harvard, is quoted as saying: "Harvard Divinity School prides itself on its liberalism and open-mindedness, its embrace of diversity, but in fact there is no diversity in these issues. Political correctness is the new orthodoxy" (61). Similarly, I regard revisionism as in danger of becoming the new orthodoxy. See further Paul R. Gross and Norman Levitt, *Higher Superstition: The Academic Left and Its Quarrels with Science* (Baltimore: Johns Hopkins University Press, 1998); and especially Keith Windschuttle, *The Killing of History.*

modernism in the academy. The July 7, 1997 issue carried an article on Robert Alter, a distinguished Hebraist and pioneer in newer literary critical approaches to the Hebrew Bible. Alter, now at Berkeley and president of the recently formed Association of Literary Scholars and Critics, is opposing the powerful professional Modern Language Association (30 thousand members) for turning "grievance politics" into a method. Alter's group has set out to defend traditional academic and literary values against the prevailing trends of deconstruction, multicultural studies, and gender studies. Alter and his colleagues, including many distinguished writers, believe according to *Time* that "obsessions with race, gender and sexuality reduce imaginative writing to the sum of its crimes against humanity, losing sight of the ambiguous and magical ways in which novels, poems and plays really operate."[6] Yet Alter may be a voice crying in the wilderness. The newer generation of academics seems totally committed to the "politics of dissent" in the academy, to what *Time* labels "ideological lit-crit."

Also, the *New York Times* carried a review by Michik Kakutani of Alvin Kernan's edited volume, *What's Happened to the Humanities?*[7] It is no secret by now that support for and interest in the humanities — literature, classics, art history, philosophy, and religion — has been waning for nearly a generation. Kernan's distinguished collaborators all tend to connect this decline with the fact that "the humanities have become a noisy battleground in the culture wars, a battlefield on which debates over deconstruction, multiculturism and gender studies continue to rage," as Kakutani puts it. The younger generation of academics, raised on the radical politicization of scholarship that began with the Vietnam War in the 1960s, is committed to the proposition that "all choices are political choices, that every intellectual interest serves some social end," as one of the authors, Yale's David Bromwich, says. Bromwich says further that it has now become fashionable for radical historians not only to question "consensus history," but also to "pardon the defeated conspicuously and withhold all pardon from the victors."[8] (Perhaps it is pertinent to note here that, perhaps not by coincidence, Thompson has attacked me specifically as one who "does history by committee," who practices a form of "Harvard censorship" to suppress him and other "liberation historians.") Finally, in this volume another writer, Gertrude Himmelfarb, author of *On Looking Into the Abyss,*[9] argues that empow-

6. "War of Words," *Time* (July 7, 1997): 92.

7. (Princeton: Princeton University Press, 1997).

8. David Bromwich, "Scholarship as Social Action," in Alvin Kernan, *What's Happened to the Humanities?* 220-43 (quotes from 221, 224, 225).

9. Gertrude Himmelfarb, *On Looking Into the Abyss: Untimely Thoughts on Culture and Society* (New York: Knopf, 1994).

ered by deconstruction's emphasis on the indeterminacy of texts and Michel Foucault's theory of hegemonic power, the "new historians" enshrined subjectivity over objectivity, and in the process they made relativism more and more an end in itself (in Kakutani's summary).[10]

The Impact of Postmodernism

The sheer ambiguity, indeterminacy, and relativism that characterize the postmodern mind have affected every field of inquiry today, every discipline both practical and professional, not just the humanities. To take but one discipline in more detail, we might note the revealing self-analysis of anthropologists George E. Marcus and Michael M. J. Fischer, in *Anthropology as Cultural Critique*. While their primary concern is the epistemological crisis in current anthropology, they observe that other disciplines are also in crisis, indeed essentially the same crisis. As they say at the outset:

> At the broadest level, the contemporary debate is about how an emergent postmodern world is to be represented as an object for social thought in its various contemporary disciplinary manifestations.[11]

In Chapter 1 they characterize an identity crisis — their rather optimistic "experimental moment" — in many disciplines. We have already noted the radical challenge of New Literary Criticism. In philosophy, one sees a turning away from the centuries-old discussion of abstract, universal systems of knowledge, discourse, or morality to a preoccupation with "epistemology": not *what* can we know, but *how* we can know anything at all. In art, music, and architecture, we have moved far beyond even surrealism: *nothing* is real, not even in terms of shock value, so without any consensus the "postmodernist aesthetic" is endlessly and tiresomely debated. In law, traditional and authoritative models of legal reasoning are subjected to withering critique by the Critical Legal Movement. In linguistics, the very nature of language is held by many authorities to be indeterminate, so that one focuses rather on "language games." Even the natural sciences have been affected, as witness the currency of Werner Heisenberg's "principle of indeterminacy" in physics, or "chaos theory" in mathematics. Of anthropology itself — perhaps the discipline closest to archaeology — Marcus and Fischer comment on "the extreme fragmentation of research interests and the theoretical eclecticism of the best work, which seem to us to be the most

10. Michik Kakutani, *New York Times,* July 15, 1997.
11. *Anthropology as Cultural Critique,* vii.

compelling traits of anthropology today." But they also note that anthropology as a discipline is in crisis, a crisis of uncertainty about how to "represent social reality," as with many other disciplines.[12]

Another anthropologist, David I. Kertzer of Brown University, declares:

Doubting objectivity, disdaining objectivism, and not knowing what to make of the other, American anthropologists have recently suffered from a self-absorption bred of epistemological malaise. The crisis of ethnographic authority threatens to turn ethnography into a denial of anthropology's claim to be anything more than either conduits for more authentic (native) voices or simply an exotic locus for psychoanalysis. The malaise, though, goes beyond epistemology into *Politics,* for the *cris de coeur* that punctuate any gathering of anthropologists these days stem less from questions of epistemology than from issues of power and morality.[13]

All those disciplines in crisis — including archaeology and biblical studies — have two things in common: a loss of confidence in their ability to "represent" in any convincing way the reality with which they supposedly deal — indeed, doubts about whether there *is* any objective reality "out there"; and fundamental distrust of all "metanarrative" discourse, of all "totalizing visions." What I would call the fundamentally "nihilistic" thrust in all the fields of inquiry is implied in Marcus and Fischer's perceptive comment: "Present conditions of knowledge are defined not so much by what they *are* as by what they come *after*."[14] Thus we confront the postmodern mind, i.e., post-Enlightenment, post-positivist, now even post-Marxist.

Yet the very term "postmodern" is disturbing to me. The mindset here is reactionary, negative, and finally impotent. We know what postmodernism is *against;* but what is it *for?* Furthermore, there is a lamentable tendency to narcissism in postmodernism. Having rejected the possibility of any vision of objective reality, the observer becomes preoccupied with his own "way of seeing"; in the end, it is only the individual's perception of self in a text (for instance) that matters. We have observed above, with others, that such a celebration of subjectivity soon mires one in the morass of relativism (see further below). Finally, I am offended by the arrogance that is implied in the postmodernist stance. Having outgrown all previous pretense to knowledge (for so it was), *we* have finally arrived at the apogee of human intellectual and social evolution.

---

12. *Anthropology as Cultural Critique,* 7-16.

13. David I. Kertzer, "Representing Italy," in *Europe in the Anthropological Imagination,* ed. Susan Parman (Upper Saddle River, N.J.: Prentice-Hall, 1998), 70.

14. Marcus and Fischer, 8.

Presumably "*post*-modern" is about as *avant garde* as one can get! (Or is it "radical chic"?)

Since the "post" in "postmodern" takes as its point of departure the Enlightenment, we need to examine further the *causes* of the disillusionment. If the Enlightenment enshrined reason, the postmodern era dethrones it — constitutes, in fact, a "flight from reason and science," as Harvard's Administrative Dean of Arts and Sciences Nancy Maull recently put it in a review-article entitled "Science Under Scrutiny: Can Pure Knowledge and Democracy Beneficially Coexist." The new "antirealists" — "social constructivists," as she terms them — address as their main question precisely the issue posed throughout our discussion: "whether the cognitive content of science is determined by nature *out there,* or is merely the temporary construction of social entities and processes." Maull thinks that "controversy invoked by these new sociologists of science has turned out, rather surprisingly, to be the major preoccupation of *fin de siècle* metascience." She quotes Paul R. Gross, one of the editors of *The Flight from Science and Reason,* as saying that "rejection of reason is now a pattern to be found in most branches of scholarship and in all the learned professions." Yet I would ask: What is there to *be* learned, if there are no *facts?* In any case, Maull concludes:

> The social constructivists are quite hard to pin down: either they are saying that science is influenced by social forces (ho-hum) or that scientific knowledge is only the product of social forces, and therefore "relative" (wait a minute). As the volume's philosophers of science point out, no acceptable defense of the relativist implications of social constructivism has, so far, been made.[15]

In fact, one of the philosophers of science in the volume under review, Harvard's Mallinckrodt Professor of the History of Science and of Physics, Peter Galison, has written a devastating empirical critique of relativism, *How Experiments End.*[16] They end by invalidating *some* theories, but nonetheless confirming *others* — not by denying that any empirical knowledge is possible, as the postmodernists' caricature of any science would have it, including their own "pseudo-science."

One of the most amusing and devastating spoofs of postmodernist pretensions was a fabricated, nonsensical "scientific" article planted by Alan Sokal

---

15. Nancy Maull, "Science Under Scrutiny," *American Antiquity* (March-April, 1997): 23; Paul R. Gross, Norman Levitt, and Martin W. Lewis, eds., *The Flight from Science and Reason* (New York: New York Academy of Sciences, 1996).

16. (Chicago: University of Chicago Press, 1987).

and Jean Bricmont in the Spring/Summer 1996 issue of the trendy postmodern journal *Social Text*. The article was apparently accepted by the journal's reviewers and editors because its authors expressed a politically correct view with which they agreed, namely cultural and even scientific relativism. The article, replete with scholarly citations, "proved" that the physical laws of science are historically and culturally contingent, and therefore subject to criticism and rejection from any position, say, for example, a feminist or minority point of view. Subsequently there appeared Sokal and Bricmont's popular exposé of their prank, entitled *Fashionable Nonsense: Postmodern Intellectuals' Abuse of Science*.[17] According to one reviewer, Columbia University's Alexander Alland, the primary purpose of the book was:

> to awaken American intellectuals and their students who, the authors feel, have been seduced away from clear thinking by a group of naïve postmoderns. The message to these readers is clear: don't let obscurantist prose replete with esoteric citations buffalo you into accepting a dangerous version of radical relativism that denies the possibility of any stable reality.[18]

Alland, who entitled his review "Don't Cut the Pi Yet!" applauds Sokal and Bricmont's hope that, in place of faddish postmodern "discourse," there will be the development of a truly intellectual culture that will stick to the rules of rationalism but will eschew dogmatism; that will be scientifically rigorous but capable of avoiding scientism; that will be open-minded but not frivolous; that will be politically progressive without committing the sins of sectarianism.[19] I concur. It is precisely this *balance* that extreme postmodernism and biblical "revisionism" lack.

Part of the extremism is the love of "word-games," which often obscures any sensible point postmodernists might wish to make. For example, one of the leading postmodernist thinkers, whom Sokal and Bricmont quote, is the French social theorist Jean-François Lyotard, who in *The Postmodern Condition* defines his position as follows:

> The conclusion we can draw from this research . . . is that the continuous differential function is losing its preeminence as a paradigm of knowledge and prediction. Postmodern science — by concerning itself with such things as undecidables, the limits of precise control, conflicts characterized

17. (New York: Picador USA, 1998).
18. Alexander Alland, *American Antiquity* 100 (1999): 1036.
19. Alland, *American Antiquity* 100 (1999): 1029.

by incomplete information, *"fracta"* catastrophes, and pragmatic paradoxes — is theorizing its own evolution as discontinuous, catastrophic, nonrectifiable, and paradoxical. It is changing the meaning of the word *knowledge,* while expressing how such a change can take place. It is producing not the known, but the unknown. And it suggests a model of legitimation that has nothing to do with maximized performance, but has as its basis difference understood as paralogy.[20]

This is a good example of what Sokal and Bricmont mean by "fashionable nonsense." An example closer to home is the definition of postmodernism recently adopted approvingly by the American biblical scholar George Aichele, again from Lyotard:

> The postmodern would be that which, in the modern, puts forward the unpresentable in presentation itself; that which denies itself the solace of good forms, the consensus of a taste which would make it possible to share collectively the nostalgia for the unattainable; that which searches for new presentations, not in order to enjoy them but in order to impart a stronger sense of the unpresentable.[21]

In his work *Sign, Text, Scripture: Semiotics and the Bible,* Aichele thinks that he can "deconstruct" the Gospel of Mark and thereby enhance its theological significance. His definition of theology, a typical "postmodern statement," is instructive:

> Concrete theology as a deconstructive theology must reveal its proper nonpresence in the dispersed materiality and violence of inscription, in a dissemination beyond historical univocity or structural polysemy, in a fundamental (but never original) undecidability. . . . In order to exceed the limits, theology must uncover the not-itself which lies unnamed at its center, its hidden eccentricity and non-identity: it must become concrete.[22]

I'm not sure what any of this means, but then if "postmodernists" are right there is no "meaning."

I agree with Oxford's Oriel and Laing Professor John Barton at the conclusion of his book *Reading the Old Testament:*

---

20. Jean-François Lyotard, *The Post-Modern Condition: A Report on Knowledge* (Minneapolis: University of Minnesota Press, 1984), 60.

21. Lyotard, 81.

22. Interventions 1 (Sheffield: Sheffield Academic, 1997), 19, quoting Aichele, *The Limits of Story.* Semeia Studies (Chico: Scholars, 1985), 138-39.

I find postmodernism absurd, rather despicable in its delight in debunking all serious beliefs, decadent and corrupt in its indifference to questions of truth; I do not believe in it for a moment. But as a game, a set of *jeux d'esprit*, a way of having fun with words, I find it diverting and entertaining: I enjoy the absurd and the surreal, and postmodernism supplies this in ample measure. Postmodernist theory is much like postmodernist knitting. You begin to make a sock, but having turned the heel you continue with a neckband; then you add two (or three) arms of unequal length, and finish not by casting off but simply by removing the needles, so that the whole garment slowly unravels. Provided you don't want to *wear* a postmodern garment, nothing could be more entertaining. But when the knitter tells us that garments don't really exist anyway, we should probably suspend our belief in postmodernist theory, and get back to our socks.[23]

As I have observed elsewhere, all this "postmodern piffle" leaves "revisionist" biblical scholars like Davies, Thompson, Lemche, Whitelam, and other historians without any history; philologians without any texts that are pertinent; would-be archaeologists with no comprehension of material culture; ethnographers with no field experience; anthropologists with no theoretical framework; and, finally, social engineers with no blueprint. In an age of skepticism and relativism, it is tempting to flirt with nihilism, but this is where it must always end: If we can know nothing, then we cannot even know that we know *that*. I will settle for the "happy delusion" that there are such things as facts; that they do not always deceive us; that some facts matter; and that on such facts we can gradually build cumulative knowledge.

The Biblical Revisionists as Postmodernists

What I suggest in all moral earnestness is that the revisionist historians of ancient Israel with whom we have dealt here are best understood as closet "social constructivists," of precisely the type just described above. The *Hebrew Bible* is the "metanarrative" that is to be rejected. The basic premise in treating the biblical texts, as we saw above, is that these texts are not historical at all, only ancient and modern "social constructs"; and furthermore that our supposed knowledge of an ancient Israel in a real time and place is also such a "social construct," and no more. To be sure, most of the revisionists have carefully avoided the term "postmodern" to describe their agenda, for obvious reasons.

23. John Barton, *Reading the Old Testament: Method in Biblical Study,* 2nd ed. (London: Darton, Longman & Todd, 1996), 235.

Yet Thompson has used the term now and then, even if only in an off-hand manner.[24]

What is *more* significant than terminology, however, is the emergence of revisionism as a self-conscious "school," with its own explicit method and agenda, all of it decidedly in the deconstructionist mode. Although Thompson has recently denied that there is such a school, on the ground that its practitioners are not monolithic in their approach, that is disingenuous. Thompson resists labels of any sort (and he and the others have certainly chafed at my label "neonihilist"), but he himself coined the term "revisionist" that I use here.[25]

The new revisionist school even has its own headquarters. The University of Sheffield in England has become a sort of institutional support center for the revisionist school. Several leading revisionists and New Literary Critical practitioners teach in the Department of Biblical Studies there, including Philip R. Davies, J. Cheryl Exum, D. J. A. Clines, and Diana V. Edelman. Davies helped to launch the newer approach with his *In Search of "Ancient Israel"* (1992); and Exum and Clines are editors of the standard handbook, *The New Literary Criticism and the Hebrew Bible* (1993). Sheffield University Press began publishing its seemingly endless series of books in our fields (now nearly 700) in 1985 under the imprint of the Almond Press, dubbed by some the "nut press" for the trendy themes it preferred (now JSOT Press or Sheffield Academic Press). Similarly postmodern is the Press's *Journal for the Study of the Old Testament* (edited for many years by Davies and Clines), begun in 1976. Founded specifically to keep abreast of "state-of-the art" trends in biblical studies is Sheffield's annual journal *Currents in Research: Biblical Studies,* launched in 1993. The press now publishes a number of journals (at least 10 in our field), most recently *Gender, Culture, Theory* (1996), edited by Exum. According to the publisher's announcement, the journal will self-consciously "employ postmodern approaches," including "critical theory, gender studies, cultural criticism, metacommentary and media studies."

24. For a devastating critique of one of postmodernism's most prominent methods — the "deconstruction" of ancient texts and the depreciation of any "meaning" in them, following Jacques Derrida and others — see Ellis, *Against Deconstruction.* Ellis notes that since 1975 the "know-nothing" attitude of deconstructionists, the rejection of reason as a basis of discourse, has meant that there has been little dialogue and that most critiques of deconstructionism have been ignored or suppressed as "politically incorrect."

25. For the term "revisionist," see Lemche and Thompson, *JSOT* 64 (1994): 19; Lemche, *The Israelites in History and Tradition,* 157. For the other labels in this discussion, some quite acrimonious, see Chapter 1, n. 14; Chapter 2, n. 47. Thompson alternately advocates the most outspoken "school" mentality, yet denies that he and the other revisionists constitute a school; see particularly *JBL* 114 (1995): 683-98.

A recent Sheffield catalog reveals an astonishing variety of catchy titles, many of the recent ones having to do with the heavily ideological and programmatic issues that divide our disciplines, issues upon which I have focused here because they are timely. Perhaps a few recent titles will best give the "flavor" of the Sheffield series.

> D. J. A. Clines, *Interested Parties: The Ideology of Writers and Readers of the Hebrew Bible*
>
> Athalya Brenner, ed., *A Feminist Companion to Exodus-Deuteronomy*
>
> Melissa Raphael, *Theology and Embodiment: The Postpatriarchal Reconstruction of Female Sexuality*
>
> J. Cheryl Exum, *Plotted, Shot, and Painted: Cultural Representations of Biblical Women*
>
> Philip R. Davies, *Whose Bible Is It Anyway?*
>
> Lester L. Grabbe, ed., *Can a "History of Israel" Be Written?*
>
> David J. Chalcraft, ed., *Social-Scientific Old Testament Criticism: A Sheffield Reader*
>
> George Aichele, *Sign, Text, Scripture: Semiotics and the Bible*
>
> Lori L. Rowlett, *Joshua and the Rhetoric of Violence*
>
> Michael Prior, *The Bible and Colonialism: A Moral Critique*

I do not mean by this listing of recent Sheffield titles to belittle the press or to depreciate its contribution to our field, for it has consistently published valuable "state-of-the-art" works. I simply point out Sheffield's reputation now as *the* press for trendy stuff. That the press and the University of Sheffield are now widely considered the home of the revisionist school and other radical new approaches to biblical studies may be indicated by the fact that a kind of "intellectual (or 'political'?) history" of the Sheffield group and of "social-scientific" criticism has been put forward by David Gunn.[26]

The secondary institutional home of revisionism is the University of Copenhagen, in whose Department of Theology Niels Peter Lemche and Thomas L. Thompson teach. Colleagues there who are of a similar bent include Frederick H. Cryer in Semitic languages as well as a number of graduate students who are already publishing. Although not as blessed as Sheffield with long momentum and their own press, the "Great Danes" (as they jokingly call themselves) have a more self-conscious and determined agenda, and in Thompson they have the most prolific and doctrinaire spokesman of the revi-

---

26. David Gunn, "Narrative Criticism," in Steven L. McKenzie and Stephen R. Haynes, *To Each Its Own Meaning*, 171-95.

sionist school. Thompson himself, in attempting to define various schools, may have pointed out something significant: the revisionists and their colleagues are *all* European scholars. In North America, only David W. Jamieson-Drake could possibly be identified with this school; but after his book *Scribes and Schools in Monarchic Judah: A Socio-Archaeological Approach* was either largely ignored or unfavorably reviewed, he left university teaching.[27] Thus I would agree with Thompson in suggesting that the heated controversies being aired here in popular format are not only generational, but in large part are transcontinental. That makes dialogue even more difficult; it also makes the attempt more crucial than ever.

The Revisionists as Typical Postmodernists: Ideology, Politics, and Rhetoric

Despite the flood of ink that the revisionists have spilled in the past five or six years, revealing an ever-clearer ideology and agenda, mainstream biblical and especially archaeological scholarship seem almost to have ignored the threat they pose.[28] On the issue of ideology — where I think the revisionists are most vulnerable, yet at the same time most menacing — only one biblical scholar has dared to challenge them directly, Iain Provan. His scathing attack, "Ideologies, Literary and Critical: Reflections on Recent Writing on the History of Israel," was published in the venerable *Journal of Biblical Literature,* which has traditionally stuck to philological and exegetical issues and studiously avoided theological or even broader historical issues. Provan's attack was spirited and correctly focused on ideology, together with related issues of competence and historical method. Nevertheless, I fear that Provan's initial shot across the bow missed the mark. It did, however, provoke a rambling, polemical, often simply bewildering response in the same issue of *JBL* by Thompson, as well as an irate but generally provocative response from Davies, entitled appropriately "Method and Madness: Some Remarks on Doing History with the Bible."[29]

27. JSOTSup 109 (Sheffield: Almond, 1991). Note Lemche's apparent dismissal of Jamieson-Drake; *The Israelites in History and Tradition,* 82; "Clio," 140, 141. The only other American scholar sometimes said to be associated with the revisionist school is John Van Seters, but he himself does not subscribe to either the label or much of the extremist ideology. See his works dating the Pentateuch (not the Deuteronomistic history) to the Persian period or later, e.g., *Prologue to History: The Yahwist as Historian in Genesis* (Louisville: Westminster John Knox, 1992).

28. See virtually the entire literature to date, cited in Chapter 2.

29. Provan, *JBL* 114 (1995): 585-605; Thompson, 683-98; Davies, 699-705.

Provan, to his credit, sees the growing trend to view the Bible merely as "literature" as the crucial issue. As he puts it, this creates a problem, for then "history is played off against ideology." And, as Provan implies, history is always the loser. But Provan is surely wrong in seeing the revisionists as ideologues of the radical right; they are as far to the radical left as one can get. Similarly, they are hardly "positivists," as Provan thinks, but fiercely antipositivist. Yet his conclusion is right to the point when he analyzes the basic contradiction in the work of a "historian" like Davies. Provan points out that in Davies' *In Search for "Ancient Israel"* we find that everyone else's "historical Israel" is rejected as compromised by theological biases, while Davies confidently proclaims his own "Israel" as based on "real historical research." As Provan observes, here "we are encountering a confession of personal faith, lightly disguised as a job description." In short, he asks, is all this a scheme that is "part of an elaborate deception whose purpose is to highlight the ideology of others (i.e., both the biblical and modern interpreters), while concealing one's own?" Even if Provan is accusing the revisionists of bad faith, I fear that here he has hit the nail right on the head. If there were any doubts, Thompson's candid and extremely defensive response in the *Journal* removes them.

Perhaps, then, Provan has done us all a service by "smoking Thompson out." But there is so much *more* evidence of Thompson as an ideologue, a polemicist. His response to Provan is an attempt at self-justification, alternately condescending and vicious. (1) First, it is full of contradictions. Thompson bristles at Provan's raising the issue of scholarly credentials (i.e., Thompson's as a real historian); yet he says "this issue relates to competence." He complains about Provan's "debating style of polemic," but almost immediately concedes of his own writing that it is "often originally designed as much to provoke as to enlighten." He stresses everywhere the "subjective" nature of knowledge, yet he claims himself to be doing *Wissenschaft*, or "scientific" study of the Bible. He implies that Provan's disagreement with him stems from Provan's being a theologian (of the "neofundamentalistic-literary" persuasion and of "church-oriented biblical scholarship"), yet he claims that he and Lemche "both understand ourselves as theologians," and are in fact committed to "a renewal of theological interest in OT studies." As proof of his being a "theologian," Thompson sides with Lemche in quoting a German passage from Schiller, which translates: "For some, it is a matter of heavenly gods; for others, it is the efficient cow who provides them with milk and butter." Somehow, such New Age theo-babble does not give me much confidence in Thompson the theologian.[30]

30. Thompson, *JBL* 114 (1995): 683-98, esp. 695.

(2) Beyond the many contradictions, there are outright dissimulations in Thompson's response to Provan. Of one of his passages cited by Provan, Thompson says that he is certainly capable of writing this, but that he did *not* write it; however, Provan has correctly cited Thompson, word for word. Thompson brings up Clifford Geertz's well-known description of "thick" and "thin" histories and claims that his source is a symposium where he and another panelist had discussed this; however, the published papers show that it was only *my* paper that brings up and discusses Geertz's "thick-thin," and Thompson's never mentions Geertz (nor cites me). In vociferously denying that he and his colleagues constitute a "school," Thompson claims a great diversity for his "group" of "dozens of participants who live and work on four if not five continents." He then proceeds in a long footnote to list many scholars, supposedly of his persuasion — many of whom could not *possibly* be considered revisionists or on Thompson's side at all. (Elsewhere he has claimed a long list of Israeli archaeologists as supporters, most of whom have scarcely heard of Thompson and in any case would be horrified at his misuse of archaeology.)[31]

(3) Throughout his response to Provan, Thompson's arrogance is apparent. Provan is simply "ignorant of the process of scholarly discussion that has occurred in our field," guilty of "bad scholarship," of quoting Thompson "out of context," and so on. Provan and the others who stand in the way of the "revolution" are merely obscurantists or alarmists — "consumers of knowledge or visitors of ideas." Thompson and his colleagues are the "real" historians"; the "objective" scholars, not "ideologues"; the masters of biblical "science"; the ones who are "denying authority to old opinions and institutions"; harbingers of the brave new world, who "never gave up the hope that we could do something positive for this world," especially since "1968" (whatever that means). Thompson closes his rambling diatribe against all who would oppose him with a pronouncement that I find ominous:

> There is no more "ancient Israel." History no longer has room for it. This we do know. And now, as one of the first conclusions of this new knowledge, "biblical Israel" was in its origin a Jewish concept. . . . The field as a whole is no longer in crisis. For *Wissenschaftler,* however, for those committed to science — and this is hardly a naïve use of this term — it is a very exciting time in which to work.[32]

---

31. Thompson, *JBL* 114 (1995): 684, 685, 690, 696; and cf. William G. Dever, "Archaeology, Material Culture and the Early Monarchical Period in Israel," in *The Fabric of History: Text, Artifact and Israel's Past* (Sheffield: Sheffield Academic, 1991), 115.

32. Thompson, *JBL* 114 (1995): 697-98. Perhaps even more ominous is another recent pronouncement of Thompson: "We have already identified 'ancient Israel' as a liter-

Little comment is needed for the reader of any sensibilities. All the hall-marks of the revolutionary ideologue are here in Thompson, as well as in much of the writing of Davies and Whitelam. Without documenting them in detail,[33] I would note the following characteristics of the "ideologue," everywhere present in the works of the revisionists though they decry ideology and usually imply that they have none (are they dishonest, or merely naïve?). Consider these hallmarks:

1. The reaction against the Enlightenment and "positivism" generally, a postmodern stance simply being assumed and no philosophical defense of it offered.
2. The rebellion against the perceived Establishment and indeed against all "authority," all "hegemonic domain assumptions," all "totalizing paradigms and discourse" (in their typical jargon); theirs are beleaguered "voices from the margin," opposing oppression, "patrimony and power."
3. The rejection of "objective," reasoned argument in favor of repeated dogmatic assertions, polarization of issues, demonization of opponents, revolutionary slogans, and claims to represent the triumphant New Order.
4. The radical re-reading of classical texts so as to "interrogate" them and expose their self-contradictions, their ideological biases, and their use to suppress the masses; "social context," not the recovery of what it was really like in the past, is all that matters.
5. The adoption of cultural relativism as the *modus operandi;* there is no "truth" (except ours); we can change our minds about anything at any time, without feeling constrained to explain or even to admit the change.
6. The declaration that in the end the "search for knowledge" is all about ideology, not "facts," always political; scholarship is not "disinterested" but must be political critique, social and ideological warfare.
7. Utopian ideals; liberation rhetoric; claims that victory is imminent.

One of the surest signs that it is ideology that drives the revisionist school is the fact that they frequently change their minds, but rarely with any acknowl-

---

ary construct, and are in the course of identifying ancient Judaism as a religious one." Thompson says further that the Persian-Hellenistic province of Judea (Yehûd) does not reflect a distinct "people" or ethnic group at all; that so-called Judaism was only an "intellectual and philosophical movement of Hellenism itself"; and finally that "until the fourth-fifth centuries Judaism was a philosophy not a religion." See "Defining History and Ethnicity," 185 and n. 48. The first step to denying the people of ancient (or modern Israel) any legitimacy is to make them "nonpeople."

33. See Chapter 2.

edgment that they have done so, and, more to the point, without citing any new evidence that has compelled them to do so. When scholars modify their views and revise a hypothesis on the basis of new data, as archaeologists are constantly doing, that is commendable — indeed essential to ongoing, honest scholarship and rational discourse. But when a scholar does an about-face without citing any new reasons for rejecting a former opinion, much less evidence for the latest argument, we are entitled to suspect that it is not new knowledge that is at work here, but simply new dogma.

Much of the "new knowledge" claimed by the revisionists is transparently ideology. Thus Thompson a decade ago wrote as if there were an "early Israel," even an early state; now neither exists. Lemche wrote two excellent books on "early Israel" in 1985 and 1988, both of which he now repudiates as too dependent upon the biblical text. Whitelam wrote some years ago several studies of early and Monarchical Israel, the very Israel he now says never existed.[34] At least Davies has been *consistently* a minimalist: he was an iconoclast from the beginning, and is quite candid, if sometimes outrageous, about that.

Even the Israeli archaeologist Israel Finkelstein, no revisionist but claimed by them, has fallen into "the latest is the best" mode of argumentation. It was primarily his *Archaeology of the Israelite Settlement* (1988) that produced the hard evidence from extensive surveys in the West Bank that forced most of us to abandon conquest models of Israelite origins and think in terms of indigenous origins. It must be stressed that there have been no significant surveys or excavations in the West Bank since the late 1980s, due to the intifada, so the basic data today remain precisely what they were a decade ago. Yet Finkelstein now maintains that there *was* no "early Israel." What evidence led him to such a radical about-face? Or was it an ideological revelation, as one of his own Israeli archaeological colleagues, Amihai Mazar, has implied recently?[35]

The above cannot be dismissed as caricatures; they are drawn, verbatim, from various of the revisionist manifestoes (although not all would subscribe to all points). The "flight from reason," the "triumph of ideology," the pervasive "political correctness," all will be obvious to most readers. I would simply highlight some of the philosophical contradictions of revisionism, which I think

34. Cf. Thomas L. Thompson, *Early History of the Israelite People*; Niels Peter Lemche, *Early Israel; Ancient Israel*; Keith W. Whitelam, "Israel's Traditions of Origin: Reclaiming the Land," *JSOT* 44 (1989): 19-42. On the revisionists' repudiation of their own earlier works, see Lester L. Grabbe, *Can a "History of Israel" Be Written?* pp. 146-48, 178-79.

35. Amihai Mazar, *Levant* 29 (1997): 164, where he links him with the revisionists. See Finkelstein's reply, suggesting that his Israeli colleague is a "Bible archaeologist" in his "sentimental, somewhat romantic approach to the archaeology of the Iron Age"; *Levant* 30 (1998): 167-74.

pose not only unresolvable intellectual problems but a very real danger to our society, constituted as it has been on the premises of the Enlightenment and the Western tradition.

Deconstructing Deconstructionism

All of the "minimalist" historians I am reviewing here, of whatever school, have in common their rejection of the Hebrew Bible as a source of history-writing for the Iron Age, largely because of its predominantly *theological* character, that is, its basic theme of "salvation-history" (German *Heilsgeschichte*). Yet the deconstructionist and New Literary Critical approaches adopted by *all* the minimalists end up by reading out of the texts the specifically *biblical* "liberation theology," only to replace it with their own, usually quite arbitrary "liberation theologies," often sympathizing with Third World Theology. As we have noted at several points above, minimalist scholarship focuses not on what are supposedly the *historical* issues of the Hebrew Bible, but rather on such *modern* issues as totalitarianism, social justice, economic oppression, gender, race, and above all political power, privilege, and coercion. The "biblical worldview" is portrayed in such a one-sided and exaggerated way as to make it appear to be on the wrong side, the "politically incorrect" side, of *all* these, the "real" issues.

One wonders what would happen if the minimalists would simply forgo their usual hostility to the texts and read the Hebrew Bible with enough empathy to see that its real message is often more pertinent to social justice than their own. The biblical message is also more honest, in that the biblical writers usually do not pretend to be anything but elites, a few prophets like Amos being the exception. Compare this with the sorry spectacle of the revisionists — all highly-educated privileged professors, at prestigious universities, protected by tenure — championing the cause of the disenfranchised of this world. At the very least, such "populism" is hypocrisy. It is also a form of radical social engineering without so much as a blueprint. If everything is "ideology," as the revisionists and others adamantly insist, why is *theirs* any better than the biblical or any other traditional ideology?

The violently antitheological revisionist ideology outlined above is, ironically, itself what Jon D. Levenson of Harvard calls a "secular analogue to religious revelation." His essay "Historical Criticism and the Fate of the Enlightenment Project" points out that secularity is no guarantee of religious neutrality.[36] And despite Thompson's indignant insistence that "we do strive to be objective

---

36. Jon D. Levenson in *The Hebrew Bible, the Old Testament, and Historical Criticism* (Louisville: Westminster John Knox, 1993), 115-17.

scholars and are not ideologues,"[37] I am unconvinced. Their position seems to me like a new quasi-religious vision, and they certainly exhibit all the typical fervor of new converts. Those who know Davies tell me that his sometimes outrageous polemics are best understood as possibly a delayed reaction against his own conservative background. Whitelam's apparent pacifist Quaker background may help to explain his antipathy to the "militant" modern state of Israel. The fact that Thompson is a graduate of the University of Tübingen may account partly for his jaundiced view of Judaism.[38] We *all* have our biases; but honest scholars do not mask theirs as "objectivity," or confuse scholarship with advocacy of social causes.

Finally, there are nagging epistemological issues posed by the revisionist school, not simply the contradictions that abound, but rather what appear to me to be fundamental yet largely unexamined presuppositions. Let me put my misgivings in the form of questions, questions that I do not mean to be simply rhetorical.

1. The revisionists contemptuously dismiss the Enlightenment, yet they presume to be more "enlightened"; but on what basis, since reason is *passé?*

2. They vilify the whole history of biblical interpretation for its privileged and isolated "realms of discourse"; but their whole program consists of an elaborate "realm of discourse," usually inbred to the point of intellectual incest. Why is their "realm" preferable or superior?

3. As postmoderns, they reject "positivism"; yet their pronouncements are at least as dogmatic; they reject "ideology," yet are ponderously ideological, what some have called "secular Fundamentalists."

4. As purists, they protest the "manipulation" of the biblical texts by traditional scholarship; yet they do not hesitate to appropriate the same texts for their program of intellectual and social reform.

5. Since the Hebrew Bible does not reflect the actual reality of life in Palestine in the Iron Age, they intend on their own to "reify" the past (a favorite term of New Literary Critics); but on what basis, except sheer imagination, since there are no "facts"?[39]

---

37. Cf. Thompson, *JBL* 114 (1995): 693.

38. Cf. Thompson's paper on "Hidden Histories and the Problem of Ethnicity in Palestine" read in Amman, Jordan, a copy of which I owe to his courtesy. See further William G. Dever, *NEA* 61 (1998): 39-52.

39. See further Chapter 1.

I do not think that the revisionists and other minimalist biblical scholars can answer these questions — at least, they have not done so thus far. If I am off-base in my indictment, let them show that.

Where the Revisionists and Deconstructionists Are Wrong

Now, to put matters in a more positive way, let me attempt to countermand some of the presuppositions (they would say "conclusions") that the revisionists and their minimalist confreres have put forward in a more or less deliberate way (although not as straightforwardly as they should have).[40]

(1) They contend that texts are not "time-space conditioned," at least in any way we can determine, so they can be interpreted any way we moderns choose. But texts, precisely like archaeological artifacts, are very much "time-space" bound in their original context; and the task of interpretation, while it will always be influenced by "subjective" factors, is to strive to understand that original context as far and as objectively as possible, simply in the interests of honest inquiry.

(2) Language is not "indeterminate," but terribly specific, even if the meaning of words may change, or when our perception may be different from that of those who first used the words. The fact that literary texts may possess a diversity of legitimate meanings for the sensitive reader does not mean that there was no single, original, preferable meaning, or that one implied "meaning" is as good as another. To argue that an author's words did not or do not convey specific intent is absurd, and if true would make sheer chaos of human communication, which does take place by and large despite inherent difficulties. Texts have an intrinsic "meaning," or else the authors were fools, and we are greater fools to pay any attention to them.

(3) The "distance" that is asserted between their world and ours, both objectively and subjectively, does indeed exist, and it poses in some ways a barrier to understanding. The way to deal with that distance, however, is not to ignore it and to coerce ancient texts into saying what we may want them to say, but rather to use the tools of modern critical scholarship — particularly archaeology and its ability to recover original context — to transcend the distance. The hermeneutics of suspicion and hostility — trying to "stand the text on its head" — will never bring us within understanding distance.

(4) To argue that *how* texts "signify" is more important than *what* they signify is nonsense. It certainly would be news to the ancient authors. Here is

40. See p. 51, n. 61.

where the "sophistication" of modern literary critics simply outstrips the evidence. Their theory of literary production (if any) imputes to ancient writers, like the authors of the Bible, a polymorphism, a preoccupation with hidden symbols, that I find incredible. Sometimes, as Freud might have said, "A cigar is just a cigar." A text sometimes means just what it says, no more and no less.

(5) Something of the "semantic universe" of the ancient author may indeed be necessary to know; but if it is unrecoverable, what is the point of the inquiry?

(6) If, as many of the New Literary Critics maintain, it is largely "intertextuality" that sheds light on a given biblical text — the interaction with other earlier and later texts — then we, from our perspective, can know more about what a text "means" than the original author. That seems a curious conceit to me.

(7) The biblical texts, and in particular the history of Jewish-Christian biblical interpretation, are accused of having been "tools of oppression" — the "Great Metanarrative" that must be rejected. Yet I would observe that the misuse of biblical texts by later interpreters is scarcely to be blamed on the biblical writers themselves; and the fact that we have allowed such "domination" by the texts says more about our own insecurities, and about the failure of critical scholarship, than it does about anything in the texts themselves. Now the revisionists declare that "theology must *liberate* itself from history."[41] Exactly where does that leave theology? Perhaps it should, instead, *reclaim* history, even if that is a somewhat truncated, more realistic history (below).

An Indictment

In summary, my own indictment of *all* the "minimalist" approaches to the Hebrew Bible and to the history of ancient Israel is as follows.

(1) The minimalist approach is hardly innovative, much less "revolutionary"; it is simply another of the fads that so often prevail in our uncertain and cynical times — "New Age pap" that stems largely from a failure of intellectual and theological nerve.

(2) It is arrogant and pretentious in its claims to "new knowledge" — not so much "post-Enlightenment" as *anti*-Enlightenment, anti-reason, anti-good sense, and ultimately anti-social despite its Utopian goals. As a supposedly intellectual movement, it is so incestuous that it is breeding simple-mindedness.

41. Cf., e.g., Niels Peter Lemche, *Currents in Research: Biblical Studies* 4 (1996): 9, 10, whose phrase this is, and Thomas L. Thompson, *The Mythic Past*, 386.

(3) It is ultimately frivolous, parroting slogans and exalting cleverness above sensibility (note the catchy titles of publications). Its deliberately provocative style and other outrageous declarations amount to little more than "offing the establishment." It is so lacking in any attempt at serious engagement that it is tempting to dismiss all this as so much "postmodern piffle."

(4) The revisionist agenda masquerades as "progressive" scholarship, but it is really demagoguery.

(5) The minimalist approach in practice does amount to nihilism; this is not name-calling, but simply recognizes that this school has no epistemological foundations, no rational justification for its assertions. But if no objective knowledge is possible, then it is not possible even to know *that*. The fact that nihilism is a "dead-end" with which most people in the real world cannot live (that is, the world outside the academy) is beginning to be recognized. I would go so far as to say that the "revolt against reason," if carried through resolutely, opens the way first to intellectual and social anarchy, then to Fascism. Fascist tendencies are already evident in some of the more extreme polemics of the revisionists, particularly in Thompson's diatribes.

As a leading proponent of biblical deconstruction, William A. Beardslee, recently remarked, in an essay on "Poststructuralist Criticism," "Deconstruction is a particularly rigorous form of poststructuralism, because taken by itself it does not offer any alternative structure to the pattern it deconstructs." Yet, as Beardslee notes, that is becoming increasingly intolerable, even to the most intrepid intellectual and social theoreticians. *Some* framework for human thought and action must be found, even if not an absolute one. Thus Beardslee observes that "a recognition of this is part of the reason that college and university departments of literature and philosophy are moving away from deconstruction toward neopragmatism."[42]

Here is what I would call a wicked irony: *avant-garde* as they fancy themselves, the revisionist school in biblical studies, barely a decade old, is already one fad behind. In the remainder of this chapter, I shall adopt a working model of "neopragmatism" myself, in order to point a better way to approach the reality of "ancient Israel" and to suggest ways of appropriating its meaning for us today. If this is positivism, so be it.

---

42. William A. Beardslee, in Steven L. McKenzie and Stephen R. Haynes, *To Each Its Own Meaning*, 231-32. Beardslee's comprehensive essay, largely on "deconstructionism," is meant to be sympathetic but is in fact devastating.

What Is Left? A Historical "Core" in the Hebrew Bible

The objective throughout this book has been to use the "external data" provided by archaeology as a tool for isolating a reliable "historical core" of events in the narrative of the Hebrew Bible, despite its theocratic nature. These events should enable us to characterize a *real* Israel in the Iron Age, not a "Biblical Israel" that the revisionists claim was conjured up by Jewish scribal schools in the Hellenistic era. Since I have already outlined a historical sketch of several major epochs in Chapters 4-5 above, a brief summary will suffice here.

(1) *Early Israel.* There can be relatively little doubt today that the 12th-11th century B.C. complex of highland villages and agrarian life sketched in Chapter 4 above reflects not only the "Israel" of the late 13th-century Merneptah stele, but also the "Israel" of the Hebrew Bible's "period of the judges," my "Proto-Israelites."[43] Here the "convergences" of the recent archaeological data and the narrative accounts of the book of Judges (and much of 1-2 Samuel) are striking. The parallel account in Joshua, however, is now seen to be based largely on the folktales glorifying a Joshua, which although perhaps of early date are mostly fictitious. Thus archaeology largely confirms one of the two biblical accounts that have come down to us, even if it tends to discredit the other. There *was* an "early Israel"; and we now know that the Hebrew Bible's basic historical framework of an age-old cultural struggle as "Israelites" sought to distinguish themselves from the "Canaanites" is authentic. Whatever late, tendentious, or miraculous elements there may be in the stories of Israel's origins and emergence in Canaan, the actual multi-ethnic and socio-cultural situation of Iron I Palestine — and no *other* era — is faithfully reflected in the Hebrew Bible's overall account.

(2) *The United Monarchy.* Of the reigns of Saul and David, the first two "kings" of Israel in the late 11th and 10th century, we can still say little archaeologically. Yet the revisionists' cavalier dismissal of such early statehood is based either on arguments from silence, which further excavation will likely demolish, or on ignoring what evidence we do have. One thing is self-evident to all archaeologists. By ca. 1000, the highland village culture was rapidly being transformed into a "proto-urban" society that was much more highly centralized. It is enlarging its territory; it is engaging in limited international trade; and it can now be easily recognized by its emerging and increasingly homogeneous material culture, which surely reflects Israelite "peoplehood," if not a full-fledged nation-state.[44]

It may be that David, and particularly the still-shadowy Saul, were in fact

43. See Dever, *NEA* 61 (1998): 39-52 and literature cited there.
44. See Dever, "Archaeology and the 'Age of Solomon.'"

closer to what socio-anthropologists would call "chiefs" than they were kings as we tend to think of the latter. But it is still reasonable to visualize David, and even Saul, as local "kings" of petty states-in-the-making, for which there are innumerable historical and ethnographic parallels. Even if the revisionists were right in their demographic projections (and as we have seen above, they are way off-base), the relatively small-scale nature of the socio-political entity of the early Iron II archaeological period is irrelevant for an analysis of state-formation processes.[45]

I would also note that however folkloric the stories of Saul's and David's amours, wars, misadventures, and heroic deeds may seem to be (and probably are), they nevertheless have the ring of truth about them in many regards. Among the likely historical aspects that we can now place in a comprehensible archaeological context, I would single out the following: (1) Wars against the Philistines, which were devastating at first, but saw the tide gradually turning in Israel's favor, as we know from well-documented destructions at several sites ca. 1000.[46] (2) The ambivalence in early Israel about the institution of kingship, which Samuel and the Deuteronomistic editors faithfully reflect (at least in one strand of the tradition); the potential instability of the incipient monarchy; and the uncertainty about dynastic succession. All these features of the biblical narratives, however late in their present form, are not only credible in themselves, but would fit very well into the stratigraphic sequence and the archaeological data now actually in hand from several late Iron I/early Iron II sites.

In short, there is nothing inherently improbable in the main outline of the biblical story as it now stands. There is no reason, for instance, to dismiss the "era of David" as no more historical than many regard the tales of King Arthur (as Thompson does). Despite many embellishments by the later Deuteronomistic redactors, the main elements of the story probably derive from ancient sources and depict actual conditions at the time.[47] It is difficult, if

45. See Dever, "Archaeology and the 'Age of Solomon,'" 245-50 and references cited there.

46. On the Philistines, see most recently Lawrence E. Stager, "The Impact of the Sea Peoples in Canaan (1185-1050 BCE)," in Thomas E. Levy, *The Archaeology of Society in the Holy Land*, 332-48 and full references there to the earlier literature. For the Philistines and destructions at the end of the period, see Amihai Mazar, *Archaeology of the Land of the Bible, 10,000-586 B.C.E.*, 296-328, 368-75.

47. On David specifically, see the fundamental work of Baruch Halpern, "The Construction of the Davidic State," in Volkmar Fritz and Philip R. Davies, *The Origins of the Ancient Israelite States*, 44-75; Nadav Na'aman, "Sources and Composition in the History of David," 170-86. Both argue, from different perspectives, not only that David was a historical figure, but that the biblical writers' sources for their narratives were roughly contemporary, i.e., dating back to the 10th century.

not impossible, to explain how Jewish writers living in Palestine in the 3rd-2nd centuries, when the remnants of Israel had not experienced kingship for some three or four centuries, could have made up such complex stories about kingship out of whole cloth.

The "Age of Solomon" I have treated in considerable detail in Chapter 4. It is revealing that none of the revisionists has confronted the extensive archaeological evidence now available. They continue to repeat that Solomon had no "empire that stretched from the Mediterranean to the Euphrates." This is disingenuous at the least; I know of no archaeologist (and very few biblical scholars) who ever believed that he *did* amass such an empire. Such hyperbole is all too typical of revisionist arguments. What the majority of archaeologists are now saying is that by the mid-late 10th century Israel had indeed achieved full-fledged statehood, and that a king of "Solomon's" stature and achievements must be presupposed on the basis of the strictly *archaeological* evidence of Israel's increasing centralization and growing prominence. Of the archaeological revisionists, only Finkelstein differs, and that only by down-dating some elements of these changes to the early 9th century. He still speaks, however, of a "United Monarchy" in the 10th century. In short, archaeology cannot comment on the biblical stories about Solomon's fabled wisdom, his coffers of gold, his many wives and concubines, the visit of the Queen of Sheba, or the role of Bathsheba in Solomon's succession. Archaeology *can,* however, document in the mid-late 10th century an era of relative peace with the Philistines, a highly centralized administrative system in operation throughout most of Western Palestine, a growing and increasingly prosperous population, and the construction of such monumental architecture as impressive city fortifications at many sites and in all likelihood a national temple or shrine in Jerusalem that was modeled on similar structures in the surrounding Canaanite-Phoenician regions of the Southern Levant. The biblical writers did not "invent" Solomon, although they have aggrandized him out of their intent to glorify the Davidic line of kings. Nevertheless, if *they* had not described him, we archaeologists would have to imagine a "Solomon by another name," simply to account for the actual evidence of kingship that we now have.

(3) *The Divided Monarchy.* In Chapter 5 I have described some of the archaeological evidence we now possess for the "political history" of the 9th-6th centuries, as well as illustrating patterns of daily life in ancient Israel and Judah in the Iron II period. I must emphasize here that the evidence I have presented is but a fraction of that now well known to archaeologists and to those few biblical scholars who, though nonspecialists, do make an effort to keep up with the burgeoning archaeological literature. Once again, I am not attempting in any way to "defend" the writers and editors of the Hebrew Bible, much

less *their* convoluted "history." All I am arguing is that the overall historical and chronological framework of the books of Kings (perhaps much of Chronicles) and of most of the prophets actually reflects what we know of the archaeological Iron II period — and no other. The physical and cultural setting of the biblical stories, the "life-setting" that we have sought here, is that of the Iron Age in Palestine, and the context cannot be arbitrarily transposed to the Hellenistic, much less the Roman period, and still make any sense at all. Even a now relatively conservative date in the Persian period is ruled out for most of the biblical material in its original form. These are stories *from* the Iron Age, not arbitrarily set there by later writers, although in their final edited form in the Hebrew Bible they are the product of a long history of transmission.

The nature of religion and cult in the Divided Monarchy was surveyed extensively in Chapter 5. Once again, as with the biblical accounts of the settlement process, the Hebrew Bible in its present, composite form contains at least two portraits of ancient Israelite religion. The one that prevails in the minds of the Deuteronomistic editors who shaped the final version of the history sometime after the fall of Jerusalem is the "normative" one — not only for those who produced the Hebrew Bible, but for nearly all Jews and Christians who followed them, and indeed for the vast majority of biblical commentators up until recently. This portrait paints Israelite belief and practice from the beginning as monotheistic, the worship of the one God Yahweh, from the formative age of Moses in pre-Israelite times until the end of the Monarchy (and even beyond). Polytheism was merely a lapse from an original, pure Mosaic monotheism. Yet we now know, largely from archaeological data that enable us to reconstruct "popular religion," that the "official" portrait in the Bible is highly idealistic, reflecting largely the view of the elite, orthodox, nationalistic sects and parties that produced the versions of the traditions that we happen to have in the Hebrew Bible.

Another version, however, far more realistic and more representative of the masses in ancient Israel, can be reconstructed by reading "between the lines" in the Hebrew Bible's denunciation of popular, "pagan" cults. It is that version of ancient Israelite religion which is corroborated by a mass of recent archaeological data, as we have seen. Yet the conventional distortion of the religious reality of ancient Israel is due not principally to the biblical writers' biases, obvious though they are. It derives rather from our own simplistic, and I fear wistful, *reading* of the biblical texts. We have, unwittingly or otherwise, bought into the propaganda of the Deuteronomistic historians; but archaeology can now rescue us from the illusion and force us to confront the reality of the religions of ancient Israel, in all their variety and vitality. If all along we had read the biblical texts with more sophistication, and fewer biases of our own, we might have gained these insights long ago. The prophets knew what they were talking about when they condemned non-Yahwistic practices as wide-spread. That is not a moral judgment on my part, but simply a historical one: it is a fact, one now well established by archaeology.

What Kind of History Does the "Core" Make the Bible?

I have been arguing here that we can isolate a "historical core" in the Hebrew Bible by singling out certain events where the textual and archaeological data happen to "converge." I do not, as Thompson charges in his pejorative term "harmonizing-literary" approach, *create* these "convergences." I merely observe them where they occur, and then try to ask what they mean in terms of evaluating our available sources for history-writing. That is called synthesis, what any good historian does with all his or her sources.

In further pursuit of honest scholarship, we need at this point to look not only at "convergences," but also at *divergences,* or instances in which our best understanding of a particular biblical text seems to be contradicted by the archaeological evidence. We have already acknowledged a number of such instances, where the archaeological data must prevail, so that the biblical account cannot be taken at face value as historical. Indeed, most of the biblical narrative falls without question into this category, consisting as it does of miraculous tales, legends, folktales, sagas, myths, and the like. But even many passages in Joshua-Kings that purport to be straightforward historical accounts must be regarded with some suspicion, because the basic narrative is overlaid with many elements that will appear to most modern readers not only as embellishments, but as fanciful or even totally fantastic. It is for that reason that many biblical scholars of the mainstream — not only radicals like the revisionists — regard the Hebrew Bible as basically "rationalized myth," "fictionalized history," "historicized fiction," "story," or simply "pious fiction."

In Chapter 2 I addressed these issues generally, preferring the term "theocratic history," with many biblical scholars. In that view, the Hebrew Bible is a peculiar kind of history, typical of the premodern world. As Baruch Halpern has shown in *The First Historians,* the biblical writers "had authentic antiquarian intentions" and indeed adhered to the sources they had. We must approach the biblical literature with serious questions, but we cannot legitimately suppose *a priori* that it is all "fiction" or "romance." As I would put it, despite the overriding theological agenda of the final editors of the Hebrew Bible, both the basic framework of the narrative and many of the original sources that lay behind the final redaction may be regarded as "historical," at least within the parameters of the history-writing that prevailed in the ancient world generally.

That is all that we can expect, since it is unreasonable to demand that the ancient writers should have been modern, scientific, and academic historians, or that they should have written the history we want. Judged by the standards of the time, as Halpern argues, the Deuteronomists were every bit as much real "historians" as Herodotus, Thucydides, and other ancient writers — indeed *more* factual when they chose to be.[48]

Such a position on the historiographical issues aired here is neither "minimalist" nor "maximalist" — certainly not the "neo-Fundamentalism" that Thompson charges — but instead conservative in the proper sense: moderate, practical, sensible, middle-of-the-road. This approach can perhaps be described in terms of the recent trend noted above toward "neopragmatism" in literary-critical studies. It might also be compared with certain new "critical-historical" approaches in history. These would include the renewed emphasis of basic field ethnographic work in anthropology, and also the "postprocessual" and new "cognitive-historical" schools in archaeology. Even in the natural sciences, research proceeds in the face of "indeterminacy" theories. The majority of the particles presupposed by theoretical physicists cannot even be shown to exist; but that does not impede pragmatic science. The existence of the planet Mars cannot be demonstrated by the unaided conceptual powers of the human mind; but in the summer of 1997 we landed there anyway. The lack of absolute certainty about many of the details of the history of ancient Israel need not preclude our being confident that there was such a history.

What the revisionists have done is to make a pronouncement that is old-hand and banal — no "objective" history of ancient Israel is possible — and

48. Baruch Halpern, *The First Historians*, 111-13. Halpern develops the notion of "intentionality" as a criterion of genuine history-writing, i.e., did the biblical writers (and later editors) intend to "tell the truth" about the past as they *knew* it? Halpern, along with most biblical scholars, thinks that they did. The revisionists' view of biblical literature, on the other hand, necessarily makes the writers out to be "pious frauds," although they resent that characterization fiercely. But what else can the biblical writers have been, since for the revisionists virtually all their writing is not only "myth" but deliberate "fiction"; and they were obviously pious as well as orthodox? For the revisionists' attack on Halpern, cf. several of the essays in Fritz and Davies, *The Origins of the Ancient Israelite States*, esp. Davies, "Introduction," 30-37; and Thompson, "Historiography," 30-37. See also Keith W. Whitelam, *The Invention of Ancient Israel*, 24-27, 32. Much of this is probably in response to Halpern's exposé and stinging critique in *BR* 11/6 (1995): 26-35, 47. Again and again Halpern deftly skewers the revisionists' presuppositions, superficial arguments, and hypocrisy. He states that "the views of these critics would seem to be an expression of despair over the supposed impossibility of recovering the past from works written in a more recent present — except, of course, that they pretend to provide access to a 'real' past in their own written works in the contemporary present" (31). See further Chapter 2, n. 61.

from that they jump to the extreme and totally unwarranted conclusion that there *was* no "ancient Israel." The "neopragmatic" approach advocated here attempts to counter that extremism, as well as the equally untenable position of Fundamentalism, for which all the biblical history is literally "true." Unfortunately, the moderate position taken here is not likely to satisfy extremists on either side; but in my view it is the *only* sound and sensible way to approach the Hebrew Bible and the problem of writing a history of ancient Israel at the present time. Yet the question of when to date the *writing* of the source-materials on which we must base a history of Israel has yet to be worked out.

Dating the "Historical Core"

The point of the foregoing attempt to outline a "historical core" of the Hebrew Bible in the Iron Age is simply to answer the question of our title: "What *did* the biblical writers know, and *when* did they know it?" They knew a lot; and they knew it early, based on older and genuinely historical accounts, both oral and written. One simply cannot force all the biblical texts down into the Persian, much less the Hellenistic, period.

One of the fundamental flaws of the revisionists' attempt to compress the composition of all the Hebrew Bible into the Persian or Hellenistic period must be pointed out here. They have presented no actual proof for the Persian-Hellenistic period as the only literary setting. They have neither internal evidence, in the form of allusions in the text to actual conditions of that era in Babylon or Palestine (or "anachronisms"), which surely even the most ingenious "forger" could not have avoided, nor external evidence in other texts of the period.[49] Despite the assertion of Thompson that the Hebrew Bible and

---

49. In both public debates and private correspondence, Davies and Thompson have angrily denied that their view of the Hebrew Bible makes it a "pious forgery"; but cf. n. 48 above. As for proof that they might offer of the "late date" of the biblical texts, there simply is none, as several scholars have pointed out. In particular see Avi Hurvitz, "The Historical Quest for 'Ancient Israel' and the Linguistic Evidence of the Hebrew Bible: Some Methodological Observations," *VT* 47 (1997): 301-15; Ziony Zevit, review of Davies, *In Search of "Ancient Israel," American Jewish Studies Review* 20 (1995): 155. Nowhere that I have seen do the revisionists reply to these criticisms, or even acknowledge them. For wide-ranging critiques of the revisionists and their methodology in general, see Chapter 2, n. 61; also n. 47 above. On the problem of anachronisms — which simply could not have been avoided — and the absence of any real knowledge of the Hellenistic world among the biblical writers, see below. For the latest, see Lester L. Grabbe, ed., *Did Moses Speak Attic? Jewish Historiography and Scripture in the Hellenistic Period* (Sheffield: Sheffield Academic, 2000).

"ancient Israel" were in their origin "a Jewish concept" of the Persian-Hellenistic period, he now informs us that there *was* no "Judaism" until the 2nd century A.D.: the many earlier "Judaisms" are all "a literary fiction."[50] Should we then not move the composition of the Hebrew Bible down to the 2nd century A.D., when there *was* a Jewish religious community capable of producing such a literary work? Thompson never really addresses a key problem: the existence of the Septuagint, or Greek translation of much of the Hebrew Bible ca. 200 B.C. — a translation of a nonexistent Hebrew "Bible."

As for Davies, who prefers a Hellenistic date for the composition of the Hebrew Bible (as Thompson also allows most recently), he has neither a *Sitz im Leben* nor a *Sitz in Literatur* (or "setting"). Again, Davies does not show any real familiarity with Hellenism or Judaism in the Hellenistic period (ca. 322-67). He can only speculate that "scribal schools" attached to the "temple in Jerusalem" produced this literary corpus (in effect again a "pious fraud").[51] *What* "temple" in Jerusalem in this era? The only evidence of such a Persian-Hellenistic temple is from such texts as those of 1-2 Maccabees, which surely Davies would trust even less than the biblical texts. And the supposed "temple" of that era is not even counted by the Jewish (or any other) community; it is the later Herodian or Roman temple that is called the "Second Temple." A small sanctuary may have existed in Jerusalem in the Hellenistic period, but there is no evidence whatsoever that it was an "academy" of the sort that Davies' scenario would require. Furthermore, Davies' attempt to characterize the language of the Hebrew Bible as a late, "artificial scribal language" has been shown by competent Hebraists to be absurd. Biblical Hebrew is not "archaizing"; it is genuinely *archaic*.[52]

50. See n. 37 above.

51. Philip R. Davies, *In Search of "Ancient Israel,"* 94-154, esp. 102-5 (Biblical Hebrew as a Persian-Period *Bildungssprache,* a "scholarly construct" as Knauf had maintained) and 106-12 ("scribal schools" in temple circles). Cf. n. 48 above.

52. Scholars like Cross, Eshel, Hackett, Halpern, Hurvitz, Lemaire, McCarter, Rainey, Yardeni, and Zevit — all distinguished epigraphers and Hebraists — have shown that most Biblical Hebrew is not "archaizing," much less an artificial literary argot, but genuinely archaic; and furthermore that it is the language of the hundreds and hundreds of seals, ostraca, and other Hebrew inscriptions from the Iron Age. See references in n. 48 above.

What Would the Hebrew Bible Look Like
If It Had Been Written in the Hellenistic Period?

The revisionists' picture of a Hebrew Bible written almost entirely in the Hellenistic period, the date they now increasingly prefer, is a "scenario." Not only is such a scenario unlikely, indeed wholly imaginary, but the revisionists have never thought through the issue of what the Hebrew Bible would look like if it actually had been a literary product of the Hellenistic–early Roman era in Palestine. The revisionists seem to know very little of such a world — an exceedingly rich mileu that gave rise to Rabbinic Judaism and early Christianity. This complex field is hardly the domain of Old Testament scholars, and it would require at minimum the mastery of Classics, the archaeology of Late Antiquity, Jewish apocryphal and pseudepigraphic ("intertestamental") literature, and New Testament studies. Thompson's *History* does not even cite the basic archaeological handbook, Ephraim Stern's *The Material Culture of the Land of the Bible in the Persian Period, 538-332 B.C.*,[53] or for that matter such standard works as Francis E. Peters' magisterial *Harvest of Hellenism*.[54] Equally conspicuous by their absence from revisionist discussions and citations are fundamental works on the cultural, intellectual, and spiritual milieu of nascent Palestinian Judaism, such as Martin Hengel's monumental *Judaism and Hellenism*.[55]

Let me suggest briefly some aspects of the world of Hellenistic Palestine that would inevitably have been reflected in the biblical literature, had it actually been composed then. (1) The impact of the Greek worldview — rational, empirical, and "Western" — would surely be seen, at least as a backdrop, and probably as a foil for the biblicists' propaganda. Yet the outlook of the Hebrew Bible is pervasively Oriental and "mythopoeic," reflecting an old order unaware of the new order of Hellenism.

(2) The everyday life of 4th-1st century Palestine would also be reflected if the Hebrew Bible stemmed from that period. This was a world of Greek *poleis,* of cities planned *de novo* and their cultural institutions; of cosmopolitan tastes in science, philosophy, literature, religion, and the arts; and, above all, of the spread of the Greek language as a cultural vehicle alongside the commonly spoken Aramaic. Yet the Hebrew Bible betrays no trace of such a world, apart from the book of Daniel (below). Its relatively isolated world is still that of vil-

---

53. (Jerusalem: Israel Exploration Society, 1982).

54. *The Harvest of Hellenism: A History of the Near East from Alexander the Great to the Triumph of Christianity* (New York: Simon & Schuster, 1970).

55. *Judaism and Hellenism: Studies in Their Encounter in Palestine during the Early Hellenistic Period* (Philadelphia: Fortress, 1974). See also n. 49 above.

lages and small walled towns atop the old Bronze Age mounds. The Hebrew Bible knows nothing of the complex multi-ethnic and multicultural mix of Hellenistic Palestine; it reflects rather the old Iron Age population of Israelites, Philistines, Canaanites, Phoenicians, Aramaeans, and finally Samaritans. The starting point for all the revisionists' rejection of the Hebrew Bible as a source for the history of a real Iron Age Israel is that it was written almost entirely later, in the Hellenistic era, and thus yields an accurate portrait of only that period. I challenge the revisionists to show anyone a single fact or facet of life in the Hellenistic world that we can glean from the Hebrew Bible (save one; below).

(3) Most significant of all, if its writers really meant it to be understood in this era, the Hebrew Bible would have been written mostly in Greek, which already in the Persian period had replaced Hebrew as the vernacular language in Palestine, or perhaps in Aramaic. Yet only portions of Ezra and Daniel, admitted as being late by all scholars, are written in Aramaic; and there is no trace whatsoever of Greek. The Hebrew Bible is written almost entirely in Hebrew; and Hebraists have shown convincingly that this is not "late Hebrew," much less Davies' "artificial scribal" language of the Second Temple. It is the standard Hebrew of the Iron Age, as attested in hundreds of archaeologically well-dated ostraca, inscribed objects, seals and seal impressions, and even a few remains of monumental stelae.[56]

(4) Finally, the Persian-Hellenistic temple, and especially the Hasmonean wars, centered around this shrine in the 2nd century B.C., would have provided the religious setting of the Hebrew Bible had it been a product of those times. Yet the "temple" is always Solomon's; and the stories of wars reflect nothing of the Hasmoneans and their struggle against Hellenization.

In asking what the Hebrew Bible would look like if it were really a Hellenistic religious document, we need to recognize that we actually have such literature. First, there is the biblical book of Daniel, almost certainly written in the context of the Hasmonean wars of the 2nd century, although of course artificially set in the Babylonian-Persian period for literary effect, as was customary in much ancient literature. And it is no coincidence that the last chapter of Daniel clearly presupposes the Greek notion of the "immortality of the soul" totally foreign to ancient Israel, and therefore conspicuously absent in all the rest of the Hebrew Bible. Daniel is what a "Hellenistic Bible" might look like; and it is atypical, indeed unique, in the corpus of the Hebrew Bible. The books of 1–2 Maccabees are even better comparisons.

Finally, we must confront the dilemma that the revisionists pose, but have never acknowledged. If the writers of the Hebrew Bible lived in the 4th-1st cen-

56. Cf. e.g., K. A. D. Smelik, *Writings from Ancient Israel;* P. Kyle McCarter, Jr., *Ancient Inscriptions.*

turies, and they succeeded in producing a "story" that was artificially and deliberately projected back into the Iron Age, several conclusions must be drawn. (a) They did so without a trace of any anachronisms that would have given them away, that is, implicit or explicit references to conditions of their own day. (b) They wrote this purportedly historical account without any of the historical records that we take for granted, since most of these had disappeared with the end of the Iron Age (i.e., Assyrian, Babylonian, and Egyptian records) and were not recovered until the 19th-20th centuries A.D. The biblical writers simply "invented" the story of an ancient Israel in the Iron Age and got right virtually every detail that we can now confirm. (c) Finally, if the revisionists' view of the nature and origins of the literary traditions of the Hebrew Bible were correct, the biblical "fiction story" of an ancient Israel would constitute the most astonishing literary hoax of all time and the most successful, too, since it fooled almost everyone for 2000 years. Possible? Yes: but not very likely.

Theories of Literary Production

In fact, one of the weaknesses of Davies' method is that he has no clear and persuasive theory of "literary production" — a must for anyone embracing any aspect of the New Literary Criticism. The same conspicuous lack is seen in the works of the other revisionists. They all simply presume that because the final editors of the Hebrew Bible were *influenced* by the cultural situation of the Jewish community in the Persian-Hellenistic era, that situation — the "social context of knowledge" again — *produced* the overriding ideology of the Hebrew Bible. But "situations" do not produce literature; authors do. Cultural context helps to shape literature; but it does not "cause" it. Here is where the revisionists' arguments are weakest; not only are they over-simplistic, but they fall into the trap of all mechanistic and reductionist schemes: they lack an adequate explanation of "causation." For anthropologists and archaeologists — indeed for all historians who seek to go beyond description — explanation of the historical and cultural process is the ultimate goal. That goal may never be fully achieved, but it certainly cannot be ignored. The irony here is that the revisionists, despite their heavy stress on ideology, minimize the innovative ideology of the original biblical historians, denying to them any truly creative role in the way they shaped their history of ancient Israel. They assume that their own practice is "truer than the practitioners' practice."[57]

---

57. The latter phrase is from Levenson, *The Hebrew Bible*, 115; the result, he says, is a "'new clerisy' of academic theorists."

The revisionists are naïve in another sense. They seem unaware that the formative Jewish community, which did indeed "produce" the Hebrew Bible in its final form, did not spring fully developed out of nowhere. This "New Israel" (a term of which Thompson is fond) evolved directly out of the "Old Israel" sketched here, or it would otherwise have been completely inexplicable. The revisionists, in speaking, as we all do, of "tradition" (something "handed down"), overlook the fact that in a historical or even in a literary tradition, there must be *something* to be handed down. In short, authors and historians never simply invent *de novo*, but draw rather upon long, shared cultural traditions, for this alone gives their work credence and currency. If the Hebrew Bible and its story of ancient Israel had been "invented" out of whole cloth by writers living in the Persian or Hellenistic period, as the revisionists claim, it would have been meaningless to those living at the time, and would shortly have passed into obscurity.

At this point one of Lemche's and Thompson's pronouncements reveals how poorly they understand either the literary or the historical process: "The Bible is not history, and only recently has anyone ever wanted it to be."[58] The fact is that almost *everyone* for the last 2000 years and more wanted it to be, thought it was, and valued it precisely for that reason. If in our sophistication we wish to move *beyond* that point, that is understandable; but first let us understand as well what the Bible was, and what its creators thought it was. Modern critical scholarship, to be progressive, does not need to caricature the Hebrew Bible as a "pious fraud" — for that is what it would be if the revisionists' view of its literary production were correct. Such contempt for ancient histories is neither good historiography nor a very sound basis upon which to build a theology of any sort.

I cannot resist pointing out that here, once again, the revisionists reveal how scarcely innovative they are, indeed how out of touch with developments in many allied fields. For instance, "biblical" archaeology's attempts to deal with the question of the historicity of the Hebrew Bible have often been compared with Classical archaeology's struggle with the "Homeric legends." A generation ago, even a decade ago, Classicists and ancient historians would have dismissed Homer as a mythical figure and would have argued that the tales of the Trojan Wars were mainly "invented" by much later Greek writers. (Sound familiar?) Yet the most recent collection of essays on this topic, by distinguished scholars honoring the retirement of Emily Vermeule from Harvard, shows a rather surprising about-face.[59] It is now thought that those stories of warfare

58. Lemche and Thompson, *JSOT* 64 (1994): 18.
59. Jane B. Carter and Sarah P. Morris, eds., *The Ages of Homer: A Tribute to Emily Townsend Vermeule* (Austin: University of Texas Press, 1995).

do not simply reflect the situation of Greece in the 8th-7th centuries, but go much farther back to a genuine historical situation of the 13th-12th centuries, that is, to the period of the movements of the various "Sea Peoples" across the Mediterranean (including the biblical "Philistines"). Thus, it is now argued, a long oral tradition, preserving many authentic details of earlier Greek history, persisted down until about the 8th century, at which time these traditions were finally reduced to writing. There are indeed many obvious mythological elements in Homer, which no one would wish to deny; but there is also a "core" of genuine history, and it is a history recoverable largely through the progress of archaeology. Two observations may be in order: (1) The Classical authorities here can hardly be dismissed as "Fundamentalists." (2) The parallels with the early history of Israel and the growth of the biblical tradition and literature are clear, even extending to the chronology of events. If Homer can in a sense be "historical," why not the Hebrew Bible?

Oral and Literary Traditions

It is significant that the revisionists totally ignore the role of the oral aspect in the tradition itself and in the creation of the written legacy, even though numerous studies of oral tradition in Israel and in the ancient world generally over the past two generations have shown how significant a factor it was. Recently Susan Niditch has surveyed the extensive evidence. Her arguments alone, neither theological nor archaeological, would demolish the presuppositions of the revisionists regarding literary production.

Niditch takes quite seriously new approaches such as ideological criticism, but she intends as a social historian to shift the focus away from those with power and the events they instigated and to the everyday realities experienced by the vast majority of the population. (The similarity to my approach here is obvious.) In so doing, Niditch deals with the fact that "large, perhaps dominant, threads in Israelite culture were oral, and that literacy in ancient Israel must be understood in terms of its continuity and interaction with the oral world."[60]

Niditch's work then explores in depth the evidence for literacy in ancient Israel; remains of oral style in the biblical literature; attitudes toward writing; evidence for records, annals, and archival sources; and finally the interplay between orality and literacy, or the "oral mentality and the written Bible."

Niditch is exploring an entire "prebiblical" world, where a *real* history of the majority of those living in Iron Age Israel was narrated, preserved, cele-

---

60. Susan Niditch, *Oral World and Written Word*, 1.

brated, and passed on in oral traditions. And these early oral traditions can easily be shown to have survived almost intact for centuries in ancient Israel, as elsewhere in many preliterate cultures. Even if they survived only until the 8th-7th centuries or so, when most scholars believe the Deuteronomistic tradition began to be written down, they would have had a significant if not decisive impact on the story of "ancient Israel" as told in the main strand of the Hebrew Bible.

It seems to me that henceforth the burden of proof in denying the role of earlier oral tradition in biblical historiography must fall on the revisionists and other minimalists. They are fond of saying that ancient Israel was "no different" from other peoples and the ancient world. Precisely; and there, too, narrative history was passed down to subsequent generations largely in the form of oral tradition, whose reliability as "history" cannot be dismissed simply because it was not yet written down. The Bible and Homer do not stand alone in incorporating older oral traditions that have preserved many genuine historical memories and events. Again, the final redactors of the Hebrew Bible did not work in a vacuum. They had much older sources.

Niditch's conclusions are must reading for anyone who wishes to confront issues of literature and history in the Hebrew Bible.

> Recognition of Israelite attitudes to orality and literacy and of the complex interplay between the two forces us to question long-respected theories about the development of the Israelite literary traditions preserved in the Bible. . . . Given this assessment of Israelite aesthetics and the importance placed on the ongoing oral-literate continuum, source-critical theories become suspect, as do other theories about the composition of the Hebrew Bible that are grounded in modern-style notions about Israelites' uses of reading and writing.[61]

Compare this sophisticated theory of literary production, from a scholar well grounded in the original sources, with the facile statements of Thompson and the other revisionists. They mistakenly take the relative scarcity of early Iron Age written remains as evidence that all of the Hebrew Bible was written later, and is therefore "unhistorical." Simply put, they do not understand that late *editing* does not necessarily mean late *composition,* much less a late origin for the *tradition* as a whole.

---

61. Niditch, *Oral World and Written Word,* 134.

Are a "Secular History" of Ancient Israel and a "Nonhistorical Theology" Adequate?

In the foregoing discussion of various topics, I have argued that while the Hebrew Bible is not "history" in the modern sense, it nevertheless contains at least the outline, as well as many details, of a real "ancient Israel" in the Iron Age. Yet my extended defense of a certain kind of "historicity" in the Hebrew Bible admittedly results in what will be a disappointment for some. That is because the "core history" set forth here is not "maximalist" (despite the revisionists' attempt to stick this label on me and other consensus historians); not literalistic ("the Bible is the Word of God, and every word is true"); and especially not theologically motivated, or even necessarily providing a sound basis for any theology (not authoritative Scripture, but simply an outline of the history that produced the literature). The latter — history and theology — is the point at which we now need to draw matters to a conclusion in this final chapter on "why the Bible still matters."

Throughout this book, the question lurking insistently just under the surface has always been: "Is the Bible *true?*" And if so, in what sense? I am arguing that there are historical truths preserved here and there throughout much of the Hebrew Bible. But my definition of "truth" is largely historical, not theological. The result is something like what Robert Oden advocates in his provocative little book, *The Bible without Theology.* But is that possible? Is such a Bible, stripped of its essential proclamation of "God who acts in history," not robbed of all its religious power and moral meaning?

The answer lies partly, I think, in recognizing that theology, religion, and morality are not one and the same — indeed can and should be separated. And all must be separated from the category of "history." History-writing, even when it allows us to reconstruct the past in some detail, even (and especially) when it is biblical history that is at issue, can at best tell us something of what happened in the past. But it cannot tell us what the events meant then, much less what they may mean now, at least beyond mere suggestion. Thus the biblical writers set forth certain "facts of history," based on the experience of events in their time. And sometimes we may be able to confirm that the events actually happened, through independent archaeological or other means of investigation. Yet the major thrust of the Bible is not the "story," but rather the principal actor, God; not "what happened," but rather a certain theocentric interpretation of the events. The biblical writers and editors are making statements of faith. And faith is not knowledge; it cannot by definition be indisputably proven or disproven, and is not so much irrational as supra-rational. As Gertrude Stein might have put it: "Faith is faith is faith." The real question is whether the faith of the writers of the Hebrew Bible can any longer be ours. For some it can be; for others not.

Faith and History

Here we must confront squarely the essential dilemma of the modern reader of the Hebrew Bible, a dilemma that nearly all writers today acknowledge. Does critical study of the Bible inevitably undermine religious faith, perhaps more importantly, diminish the value of the Bible as the basis for cultural and moral values?[62] For Fundamentalists, or even for many conservative Christians, Jews, and others, the answer is: Yes. These folk must then reject modern literary and other critical methods, although I have assumed here that such methods are to be taken for granted by any well-informed reader in the modern world. There is an irony here. In North America and in places in Europe, archaeology is accepted, even enthusiastically embraced, because it is mistakenly thought that it will, after all, "prove that the Bible is true." But in Israel, Orthodox Jews — Israel's Fundamentalists — are violently opposed to archaeology. This is ostensibly because archaeology disturbs what are thought to be (but rarely are) Jewish burials; but I suspect that actually it is because the Orthodox fear any modern scientific investigation of their tradition. The truth of the matter, as I have sought to show throughout this book, is that archaeology by definition cannot "prove" the Bible's theological interpretation of events, can at best only comment on the likelihood of the events in question having happened historically. But, if it is any comfort to believers, archaeology, by the same token, cannot *disprove* the Bible's assertions of the meaning of events.

The "secular" approach to the Bible advocated here may seem radical, even heretical. But it is one taken today by virtually all archaeologists; by most biblical scholars, at least those who teach in universities, rather than in seminaries; and indeed by a surprising number of educated laypeople. Why is that thought to be a problem? What apparently disturbs many is the fear that approaching the Bible with skepticism about it as "history" puts one on a slippery slope, one that inevitably leads to the rejection of the Bible altogether — as, in effect, a "pious fraud." How can such a fraudulent literature be the basis for any system of belief, morality, or cultural value?

Again, I suggest that we may separate history from theology, theology from religion, religion from morality, and perhaps even morality from culture.

62. For orientation to the vast literature, see references in Chapter 1, n. 1; Chapter 2, n. 44; Chapter 4, n. 16.

Such a separation would be, however, partly heuristic — that is, for the practical purposes of honest inquiry and clear articulation of issues. It may be desirable, and perhaps possible in the end, to reintegrate the concerns of all these avenues of knowledge (for that is what they are). But let us assume for the purpose of argument that the separation is valid. Where does that lead us? And how, then, does the core history of ancient Israel, which I have sought to disentangle from the overriding theological framework of the Hebrew Bible, become relevant for the modern critical reader, who wishes to "salvage" something from the Bible?

Here two old notions, which have been around from the very time when the Hebrew Bible was first being composed, may be helpful.

(1) The first notion embraces the possibility that reading the Bible's stories *too* literally may miss the real point. Reading the text simplistically — mechanically, as it were — may enable one to understand individual words, but it may fail to apprehend the message and intent of the text as a whole. Furthermore, such a literalistic approach is superficial: it is not only pedestrian, but it is guilty of the classic fallacy of "reductionism," which errs by not seeing the sum as greater than the whole of its parts. In reading the Bible, as with all great literature, one must see beyond the words, which are, after all, merely imperfect symbols, to the deeper reality of the author's vision of life. That is the level at which the real "meaning" of the text begins to appear. And to grasp it, one must read with empathy, intuition, imagination — and, may I say, with the spirit as well as with the mind.

In the case of stories in the Bible that are obviously myths, most of us intuitively recognize the truth of the foregoing. As we said in Chapter 1, we all understand that Genesis 1-3 are not just naïve, amusing folk-tales about a garden, some fig leaves, a snake, and an apple. Beyond their entertainment value, these are profound and moving descriptions of the universal human condition. To take these stories literally would indeed be to miss the point. And I happen to think that even some of the ancients were sophisticated enough to understand that. Looking for the Garden of Eden on the map is misguided.

But with the later, supposedly "historical" stories of the Hebrew Bible, we sometimes get so bogged down in questions of philology, context, and literal meaning — historical exegesis — that in our myopia we lose sight of the larger truth that the biblical writers ultimately wanted to convey. And this "larger truth" may still be valid even if the biblical writers got some of the details of their story or its chronology wrong, as they exaggerated the events — even if the story's religious "propaganda" seems to overwhelm the history. In short, even a flawed historical narrative can convey moral truths.

Faith and "Meaning"

Let me illustrate what I mean here. Take, for instance, the biblical story of the call of Abraham, a story that attempts to account for the ultimate origin of the Hebrews by relating Abraham's migration from Mesopotamia to Canaan. There is, however, no archaeological or historical proof that such a migration ever took place, or indeed that a historical figure such as Abraham actually lived anywhere back in the Bronze Age. Archaeologists like myself have long since given up the "quest for the historical Abraham." But what is the Genesis story really all about? It wants to portray Abraham not so much as an immigrant, an innocent abroad, but as "the Father of the faithful." It is a universal story about faith as risk — daring to set out for a Promised Land. Again, this Promised Land is not to be found on any map, for it is a condition of the mind and the soul. And I believe that the biblical story was originally read that way by many in ancient Israel — certainly so by the latter rabbis. Is the story "true"? Of course it is, whether literally or not.

Even with accounts that are certainly more historical, or based on some historical events, like the great cycle of dramatic stories about David, we must look past the biblical writers' propaganda. Then, instead of focusing on David "God's Anointed," we are able to see David the man, deeply flawed, a tragic yet heroic figure. And that David teaches us that while the greatest gifts can be squandered, renewal (dare I say redemption?) is possible. Such a reading of the text is morally edifying. Debating endlessly about whether David was a real "king" or merely a "tribal chief" is not, not even for scholars.

Above all, the enduring message of the classical Hebrew prophets of the 8th-6th centuries transcends academic debate about whether individual prophets by such names as Amos or Isaiah actually lived and delivered their oracles in the context that we have in the Bible, or whether later "schools" produced these as composite literary works.[63] There *is* a real history or setting here. The words

---

63. The revisionists deny the Iron Age date of the prophetic literature, as well as the historicity of the prophets themselves. There was no Israelite prophet "Isaiah," because there was no "ancient Israel"; we have only a Hellenistic, fictional literary composition by that name. There is no "real-life" setting. Thus Robert P. Carroll, one of the more strident revisionists, who has devoted a lifetime to the book of Jeremiah, states that "our knowledge of the processes that gave rise to the book of Jeremiah in the first place is absolutely nil"; and furthermore, "Jeremiah studies would certainly benefit greatly from the abandonment of the search for either 'the historical Jeremiah' or 'the author of the book of Jeremiah'. I believe both quests to be doomed to utter failure and also to be a waste of time and energy." Elsewhere Carroll admits, "I still find that that book eludes my reading of it." No wonder! Cf. "Intertextuality and the Book of Jeremiah," 56, 62, 74.

attributed to the prophets may have come to form in part propaganda for the various "Yahweh-alone" movements of late Israel and Judah. But the portentous historical situation and real-life theological crises of the Assyrian and Babylonian era produced an eloquent call for reform — for social justice — that is found nowhere else in the literature of the ancient Near East. In that sense, the prophets were indeed "inspired," and their message remains vital today.

(2) The second notion that may help us to read the Bible intelligently — critically yet sympathetically — is that of "the multiple meanings of Scripture." Earlier orthodoxies had insisted upon a single, all-encompassing, "correct" reading, something that the New Literary Critics rightly questioned. Their challenge was hardly new, however, because there is already an inner dialogue going on among the writers and editors of the Hebrew Bible *within* the biblical period. Later texts do not hesitate to amplify earlier texts, reinterpreting them in the light of new social situations. That such a practice was acceptable, even with Scripture, should not be surprising. All great literature has many "layers" of meaning and is thus rich in possibilities for interpretation, which is why it becomes immortal. That does not mean that there is no intrinsic meaning in texts, as the revisionists insist, but that on the contrary there are many meanings that are both possible and legitimate. Thus the Bible can be "true" on many levels, some not so much ahistorical as supra-historical.

The later Synagogue and Church understood this phenomenon very well and perpetuated the idea of "multiple meanings." The Synagogue proceeded under the guise of constant rabbinical reformulation, which was held to be just as authoritative as Scripture (as in the Talmud and the Mishnah, or halakah), even more so. The Church, both Roman Catholic and Protestant, promulgated the doctrine of "progressive revelation," in which God himself was said to have made possible new meanings to the biblical text, not essentially changing the texts themselves, but revealing new meanings to the sensitive reader of later times.

However salutary these new-old ways of reading the biblical texts may be, it is tempting to ask whether they do not in effect beg the question of "historicity." Moreover, they seem to sink us in the same morass of relativism for which we castigated the New Literary Critic: "the text means whatever I want it to mean." Once again, however, Synagogue and Church long ago faced this dilemma, in the form of the "allegorical meaning," attributed to various difficult biblical texts. In its more extreme form this became "spiritual exegesis," which ignored historical context and meaning altogether and claimed to possess hidden or esoteric insights known only to believers (of one's own persuasion, of course).

The antidote to both relativism and allegorical flights of fancy lies in understanding that, however multifaceted the biblical texts may seem now, they originated in a real *historical* setting, not merely a literary and cultural milieu.

Therefore there are boundaries — or legitimate realms of possibilities — within which biblical hermeneutics must proceed if it is not to violate the integrity of the text. We must grasp what the text *did* mean in its own time and place, before we venture to say what it can and *does* mean for us today. And the juxtaposition of the two interpretations must not be so forced as to strain one's credulity. The Exodus story, for example, may be about "liberation from spiritual bondage," and a re-reading of it may help to sensitize us to the plight of oppressed peoples today. But that is not primarily what the biblical story "means," since it cannot have been what it meant to those who experienced the original events, whatever they were. Yet, because the text is not static but dynamic, it can come to mean that. Here is an illustration of how we must separate history and proper historical interpretation from theology. Both are legitimate avenues to understanding, but they differ, and the integrity of each must be respected.

Toward a Bible without Theology?

At this point, it might be helpful to outline in chart-form the two basic approaches to the Hebrew Bible and its interpretation that I have advocated, one theological, as traditional; the other a more modern, critical "secular" approach. As with all charts, however, juxtaposing the two in such sharp contrast is somewhat overly simplistic; and in doing so I do not wish to imply that an individual must choose. It is likely that many people can and do combine elements of both approaches. More likely, most of us are ambivalent — a theist on some occasions, more an agnostic on others. Perhaps that is because we are dealing here with questions of ultimate concern — the very nature of reality — where there can be little certainty.

Theological	Secular
Confessional	Nonconfessional
Canonical	Noncanonical
Faith community	Academic community
Fideism	Historicism
Absolutism	Relativism
Particular	General
Static	Dynamic
Theism	Humanism

If the above dichotomy represented the only possibilities for approaching the Hebrew Bible, I as an archaeologist, historian, and academic would come

286

down on the side of the right-hand column. Here I would have to agree with Philip R. Davies, one of the principal revisionists, who in his book *Whose Bible Is It Anyway?* describes himself as "humanistic about scriptures; agnostic about deities." Nevertheless, as Davies correctly points out, such a stance *vis-à-vis* the Bible "does not diminish one's joy in reading the Bible," nor does it "deprive one of a sense of right and wrong." Davies then goes on to argue for the strict separation of the two approaches I outline above, even to the extent of regarding them as two distinct (although legitimate) disciplines, one belonging in the Church, the other at home in the academy. In answer to the question in the title of his book, Davies concludes:

> Whose B/bible is it? It is yours — and mine. And theirs. It is especially for anyone who wants to argue about it with *anybody* else — and can use the discourse to do so.[64]

It is astonishing to me that very few biblical scholars have been as candid as Davies. My impression is that many are "closet agnostics," or even atheists; many others have simply never examined their consciences; and a few seem to be schizophrenics. But are we not entitled to know what professional biblical scholars, whether they are clerics or not (most no longer are), after a lifetime of study and reflection have come to *believe* about the Bible, that is, about its ultimate claims? After all, this is precisely the dilemma that has been precipitated by a century-and-a-half of modern critical study of the Bible, and is now widely acknowledged: "What *can* we believe any longer?" Or, to put the question in my deliberately more "secular" language: "What value does the biblical tradition any longer have for the Western cultural tradition?" Then one would have to ask further: "Could that tradition be sustained *without* the Bible, or at least without traditional understandings of the Bible?"

The latter become crucial questions, because it is clear that we cannot turn the clock back; we cannot, out of nostalgia, seek to return to the premodern era, when the literal meaning of the Bible was taken for granted. What then are we to do if we wish to maintain a position of high prestige and value for the Bible in the modern world? (The revisionists, along with other postmodernists, say simply that we cannot.) Finally, of specific concern here, is *archaeology* of any help in this crisis of knowledge, of confidence?

To their credit, a few biblical scholars have addressed the above issues recently. From the conservative or evangelical Christian perspective, one might cite such works as *The Bible in Modern Culture* by two Lutheran theologians, Roy A. Harrisville and Walter Sundberg. Yet for all their courageous attempt to

---

64. Davies, *Whose Bible Is It Anyway?* 16, 10-55.

embrace the historical-critical method — it can "neither destroy nor support faith" — they lose courage in the end. Their final sentences affirm "God's saving act in Christ," then conclude that "insofar as historical-critical method brings us before this central truth of Christian existence, it is not the enemy of the church, but its austere teacher, even its friend."[65] That, it seems to me, is wanting to have it both ways — precisely what I have argued that we can no longer do. It blurs and even obscures the necessary separation of inquiries.

A more critical attempt to defend traditional biblical interpretation is the series of essays edited by Alan R. Millard, James K. Hoffmeier, and David W. Baker, *Faith, Tradition, and History.* Here several of the authors do make use of modern archaeological data, unlike Harrisville and Sundberg, even engaging in dialogue at least with me, if not with many other archaeologists. Particularly noteworthy is the chapter "Story, History, and Theology," by Millard, a well-known British scholar from Liverpool University of evangelical personal persuasion. In a statement not far from mine here, Millard concedes:

> Many of the books (of the Bible) themselves were clearly written to present and explain Israel's history from a particular point of view: they are, therefore, forms of propaganda.[66]

Millard's way out of the dilemma is to distinguish "narrative theology" from "historical narrative proper," only the former being normative for faith. That is not unlike the separation of disciplines that I have proposed, although Millard is a theist and I am not.[67]

In a much more popular vein, and representing the vantage point of liberal Anglican theology, is John Shelby Spong's best-selling *Rescuing the Bible from Fundamentalism: A Bishop Rethinks the Meaning of Scripture.*[68] Whether Spong is successful in "rescuing the Bible," readers will have to judge for themselves. In any case, however radical his approach may seem to many churchgoers, it is still church-centered, a far cry from the "secular humanist" approach that I as an archaeologist and historian take here.

One churchman and Old Testament scholar who has wrestled productively with the "faith and history" issue is James Barr, former Oriel Professor at

65. Roy A. Harrisville and Walter Sundberg, *The Bible in Modern Culture,* 273.

66. Millard, "Story, History, and Theology," in Millard, Hoffmeier, and Baker, *Faith, Tradition, and History,* 51.

67. Millard, "Story, History, and Theology," 37-64; on "narrative theology," see 60-63. Elmer A. Martens provides another thoughtful treatment from a very conservative theological perspective, "The Oscillating Fortunes of 'History' within Old Testament Theology," in Millard, Hoffmeier, and Baker, *Faith, Tradition, and History,* 313-40.

68. (San Francisco: HarperSanFrancisco, 1992).

Oxford. In his seminal book *The Bible in the Modern World,* as well as in more recent works, Barr has battled Fundamentalism eloquently and persuasively, while still trying to retain the Bible as "authoritative" for Christian faith, as well as for the Western cultural tradition. Barr argues frankly for a selective and pluralistic interpretation of the Bible:

> The Bible is not in fact a problem-solver. It seems to me normal that the biblical material bears upon the whole man, his total faith and life, and that out of that total faith and life *he* takes his decisions as a free agent.[69]

In many recent scholarly discussions, the perennial "faith and history" issue has surfaced in the form of the question: "Is a critical and historical biblical theology possible?" One position, very close to mine here, is that of John J. Collins, in a provocative article entitled "Is a Critical Biblical Theology Possible?" Collins, a distinguished Roman Catholic biblical scholar and theologian, says that biblical theology cannot in fact be "historical." That is, not only is the biblical interpretation of "saving events" not historically verifiable, but the modern critical "principle of intellectual autonomy" precludes the church *or* the state prescribing for the scholar which conclusions he or she should reach.[70]

A leading biblical scholar of conservative Jewish persuasion, Jon D. Levenson agrees with Collins that a separation of theology from critical-historical study is desirable — but for an altogether different reason. In his essay "Historical Criticism and the Fate of the Enlightenment Project," written partly to counteract Collins' "Christian" perspective, Levenson rejects the "biblical theology" approach altogether, as a spurious, largely Protestant enterprise. Levenson argues that while scholars in the academy and in modern intellectual life generally must be committed to critical-historical methods, they still should and can be committed to a believing community as well — in his case, Jewish. Yet Levenson candidly acknowledges elsewhere that historical criticism *can* undermine both faith and religious identity. In other words, he too wishes to separate the disciplines of history, biblical studies, and theology. But it is not clear to me, despite Levenson's many incisive and perceptive observations on the use of the Bible in the modern world, whether he is really consistent or, for that matter, how he thinks the separation of inquiries can actually be accomplished. His ba-

---

69. James Barr, *The Bible in the Modern World,* 142. *See also Fundamentalism* (Philadelphia: Westminster, 1978); *Does Biblical Study Still Belong to Theology?* (Oxford: Clarendon, 1978), his inaugural lecture at Oxford; and also "Story and History in Biblical Theology," *JR* 56 (1976): 1-17.

70. *The Hebrew Bible and Its Interpreters,* ed. William H. Propp, Baruch Halpern, and David Noel Freedman (Winona Lake: Eisenbrauns, 1990), 1-17.

sic conclusion is that "the secularity of historical criticism represents not the suppression of commitment, but its relocation." While it is clearly not his own solution to the problem, Levenson does allow for the possibility of substituting "a cultural for a religious motivation." This will "center on the importance of the Bible in Western civilization," a defense of which in the current climate will then become "imperative."[71] I could not agree more. But, unlike Levenson, I believe that a nonconfessional, "secular" approach is not only viable for many, but is the most defensible approach. In that case, Church and Synagogue will be freed to promote their own theological agendas, quite apart from any need for historical proofs, including those thought to derive from archaeological "confirmations of Scripture." This approach recognizes that archaeology may, at its best, be able to answer such historical questions as Who, What, When, and Where. But it *cannot* answer the philosophical and theological question: Why?

Preserving the Bible in the Western Tradition?

If the place of the Bible in the Western cultural tradition is to be considered seriously, as Levenson supposes, it must be acknowledged that the Bible *has* had a place in that tradition. This should be obvious to any but the most radical postmodernist, and that it indeed has had a *central* place. I would suggest that the Western, or so-called "Judaeo-Christian," tradition takes for granted the following notions and cultural values, nearly all of them derived from one or another interpretation of the worldview of the Hebrew Bible (and, to a lesser degree, from the New Testament, much of it dependent upon the Hebrew Bible).

1. The absolute worth of the individual (the right of self-determination)
2. The rule of law and justice (democracy)
3. The immutable authority of morality (virtue)
4. Liberty and justice as the foundations of politics (public morality)
5. A free, entrepreneurial market (capitalism)
6. The power of the mind to dominate nature and grasp truth of a higher order (science)
7. Government as ordained (the rule of law and order)
8. The importance of tradition and its meaning (religious and cultural values)
9. History as purposeful (progress)
10. Universalism as the ultimate goal (triumphalism)

71. Levenson, *The Hebrew Bible*, 106-26.

Perhaps the question is not whether the Western cultural tradition is biblically based, but only whether the above concepts deserve to survive; and whether they can do so without still being undergirded by at least the "history" (if not the theology) set forth in the Bible. Some may regard these as nonissues, certainly the more radical revisionists and other postmodernists, who are in effect social engineers without a blueprint, intent upon overthrowing the Western tradition, which they think has "privileged" itself. It has done so, they say, largely by appealing to traditional readings of the Bible for legitimization, and by having used the Bible's "totalizing discourse" to disenfranchise the masses. Once again, however, as we saw above, the search for the truth of the matter — for a balanced and judicious resolution — is supplanted by ideology, rhetoric, and politics. And in the process, the survival of the Bible in cultural life, the life of Church and Synagogue; the fundamental value of the Western cultural tradition; and indeed all dispassionate and intelligent discourse are threatened. Perhaps the Western tradition is not "superior" in the long run. But it is *our* tradition, at least for the majority of us. It has served us well for centuries, and it has within it the seeds of renewal. To demonize and jettison the Western cultural tradition and offer nothing in its place is irresponsible. The revisionists are not "revolutionaries"; they are demagogues. Their agenda, if it could be carried out, would in my opinion see not the advent of a secular Utopian "Brave New World" but rather of anarchy, chaos, and ultimately those conditions of despair that have often historically led to Fascism. That is why I abhor revisionism in all forms.

One of the most penetrating recent analyses of the history of the Western cultural tradition is that of the Classicist and medievalist David L. Gress, in his book *From Plato to NATO: The Idea of the West and Its Opponents*. Gress eloquently demonstrates that the postmodernists' wholesale rejection of the Western tradition, of its "Grand Narrative," as he phrases it, is based largely on ignorance of the roots of that tradition, i.e., of its complex and multifaceted character; and on caricatures of the tradition, emphasizing only the distortions and excesses.

Gress also exposes the "revolutionary zeal" of postmodernism since the 1960s for what it really is: a thinly-disguised and hypocritical "antinarrative" of the West, compounded with New Left political activism, multiculturalism, communitarianism, and universalism (and, he adds, doctrinaire feminism and environmentalism). Above all, Gress points out, the postmodernists were not the emancipated social commentators that they claimed to be, "liberated from all political narratives," but were in fact moralists of the very sort that they themselves decried.

> The late liberal and multiculturalist heirs of the radical Enlightenment did not throw out the Columbia model of the Grand Narrative because there

was no truth, but because they believed they had a higher and fairer truth than the allegedly Eurocentric and biased version of the Grand Narrative. That was not a postmodernist argument, but a highly moralistic modern argument.[72]

Gress concludes: "Postmodernists pretended to be the ultimate skeptics; in fact, most of the leading spokesmen of the movement were moralists in the tradition of Voltaire and Rousseau." To this radical legacy they added only a touch of nihilism. Yet, as Gress puts it:

> But if postmodernism was merely nihilism, it offered nothing other than a new name to distinguish itself from the far more serious and better-defined nihilism analyzed by Nietzsche and Spengler. . . . If postmodernism concealed, under a façade of nihilism, yet another version of the radical attack on the legitimacy of the West, that again was nothing new, merely a tedious and repetitive recital of the same grievances and errors denounced by Rousseau, Marx, and their followers for two centuries. The sole contribution of postmodernism as a label or a movement was to sow further confusion by combining anticapitalist and antimodern resentments.[73]

Gress's prescription for the ailing Western tradition is partly to recognize that "what was at bottom a struggle to enforce, or condemn, the legacy of the radical Enlightenment became in 1980s and 1990s America a fight within moral and religious traditions."[74]

I could not agree more wholeheartedly, but curiously enough, Gress does not see that the "moral and religious traditions" of the West rest upon *biblical*, as well as Classical and Enlightenment foundations. The presumption is that there was a "biblical world" that really existed, in whose actual experiences in history these traditions are rooted, a *history* that alone gives them any "meaning" they may have. Take away the historicity of the central events narrated in the Bible — our "core history" here — and you undermine the foundations of the Western cultural tradition.

Gress's own hope is that the best of the Western tradition can somehow be salvaged, although radically reformulated. For him, relativism is "a cultural luxury, not a genuine philosophical choice." He ends his book by observing:

> The skeptical Enlightenment needs to be protected against its radical, impatient, and moralistic counterpart. And in the age of illusory universalism,

72. David Gress, *From Plato to NATO*, 476.
73. Gress, *From Plato to NATO*, 477.
74. Gress, *From Plato to NATO*, 495.

the way to restore that balance is to recover the Old West in its full color and passion, not as a caricature to be rejected, but as the source of one's social and cultural being.[75]

Gress ends by quoting Virgil; I agree with his diagnosis, even his prescription, but I would prefer to quote biblical philosophers who preceded Virgil by centuries.

In Defense of "Secular Humanism" — with the Bible

In many ways, what I am advocating here is a kind of "secular humanism," which, however: (1) takes the Bible seriously, as both a historical and a cultural tradition; and (2) does not deny the transcendent and its role in human life, but rather celebrates it. If the reader thinks these two tenets self-contradictory, let me refer to the perceptive essays of a distinguished Harvard historian of comparative religion, and nominal Christian, Wilfred Cantwell Smith. In his essay "Shall the Next Century Be Secular or Religious?" Smith points out that "secularism" as a concept originated only about 150 years ago; that it is often misconstrued as being the antithesis of "religion" and as opposed to the concept of a transcendent realm; and that it can be nihilist. Smith argues, however, that our choice in future is not between a naïve "religiousness" or a nihilist "secularism." He concludes:

> It is because I am a secular humanist — but not in the nihilist or any negative sense — that I have come to recognize that we are, and the world is, in profound trouble unless we are also and deeply what my fellow secular humanists call religious.[76]

Another vision — this time that of a scientist, rather than a humanist — at the turn of the millennium is similar. Harvard's eminent Research Professor, Curator in Entomology, and two-time Pulitzer Prize winner Edward O. Wilson recently published a provocative work entitled *Consilience: The Unity of Knowledge*. Wilson observes that Enlightenment thinkers knew a lot about everything, today's specialists know a lot about a little, and postmodernists doubt that we can know anything at all. Wilson believes, however, that "it is worth asking, particularly in this winter of our cultural discontent, whether the origi-

---

75. Gress, *From Plato to NATO*, 559.
76. Wilfred Cantwell Smith, *Modern Culture from a Comparative Perspective* (Albany: State University of New York Press, 1997), 83.

nal spirit of the Enlightenment — confidence, optimism, eyes to the horizon — can be regained." He thinks that it can and must be, because "a vision of secular knowledge in the service of human rights and human progress . . . was the West's greatest contribution to civilization." Wilson offers a bold and refreshing vision of the future by concluding that knowledge is not a "social construct"; that we can know what we need to know; and that our new knowledge in future will lead us to the discovery that underlying all forms of truth, scientific *and* humanistic, there lies a fundamental unity (thus his "consilience."). Wilson is that rare scientist who also values the humanities — including the creative arts, philosophy, and religion — which he thinks *together* with science will be the "two domains (that) will continue to be the two great branches of learning in the twenty-first century."[77]

Is this vision of a natural scientist not better than the atomistic, fractious, and tiresome rhetoric that currently infects the social sciences, and which in the form of biblical "revisionism" threatens to undermine one of the pillars of the Western cultural tradition?[78]

77. Edward O. Wilson, *Consilience: The Unity of Knowledge* (New York: Knopf, 1998). Many of Wilson's most perceptive observations are most easily accessible in his excerpt from the book, "Back From Chaos," published in *Atlantic Monthly* 28/3 (March, 1998), 41-62.

78. As this book was going to press, the revisionist controversy broke out in the media even more openly than it had in the previous year or two. Ze'ev Herzog, a colleague of Finkelstein at Tel Aviv University, published an article in the major Israeli newspaper *Ha'aretz* (October 29, 1999) in which he claimed that archaeology had "proven" that the biblical patriarchs, exodus, conquest, period of the judges, early monarchy, Israelite monotheism, the exile and reform, etc., were all fictitious. Henceforth, Israelis who have seen in their "history" some legitimization for their claims to the land would have to give this all up. Earlier, the *Jerusalem Post* (October 11, 1997) had already broken the story of "Historical Battleground," documenting how the newly-constituted Palestine Authority in the West Bank had begun to use archaeology to establish *its* claims to the land, even issuing revisionist elementary school textbooks to augment the "arsenal of historical weaponry." This was followed by a much more detailed and explicit report by Netty Gross of a clash between Israeli and Palestinian archaeologists at a symposium in Gaza on "Who Got Here First, and Does It Matter?"; "Demolishing David," *Jerusalem Report* (September 11, 2000). Whitelam should be pleased; he and other meddling revisionists have succeeded in undoing the efforts of two generations of Palestinian archaeologists — of *all* nationalities and persuasions — to keep Middle Eastern nationalism and religious fanaticism out of archaeology. Earlier, the magazine *Science* (287 [January 7, 2000]: 28-35) carried an excellent series of stories by Michael Balter with ample quotations from myself and other American archaeologists, from Israelis, and from Palestinians. Unfortunately, much of the rhetoric is like shouting "fire" in a crowded theater. See Gustav Niebuhr, "The Bible, as History, Flunks New Archaeological Tests," *New York Times* (July 29, 2000).

Conclusion

My intent in writing this book was not to save the Hebrew Bible from its many detractors in our postmodern era, not least from the "revisionists," although I believe that we must take seriously their attempt to undermine the Bible's credibility as a source of historical facts and moral truths. The Hebrew Bible, however, will be read and cherished long after these "troublers of Zion" (if one will forgive a biblical phrase) are gone and forgotten.

What I have attempted to do throughout this book is twofold. First, I have focused on *methodology,* in order to unmask the revisionists' ideology and the postmodernist paradigm that lies partly hidden behind it, and in so doing to expose their faulty methodology in approaching the texts of the Hebrew Bible. Second, I have sought to counter the revisionists' minimalist conclusions by showing how archaeology uniquely provides a *context* for many of the narratives in the Hebrew Bible. It thus makes them not just "stories" arising out of later Judaism's identity crisis, but part of the history of a real people of Israel in the Iron Age of ancient Palestine. As the title puts it: "What did the biblical writers know, and when did they know it?" They knew a *lot,* and they knew it early.

My method in going about the inquiry here has been that of good historians everywhere, namely to sift through all the available data, however limited and faulty they may seem, in search of facts — especially those that can be established as such by "convergences." These convergences can be seen wherever the textual and the archaeological data, viewed independently, run along the same lines and point ultimately to the same conclusions. This is not old-fashioned "biblical archaeology," as the revisionists charge, nor does it presume to "prove" the Bible's historical claims, much less its theological propositions. It is simply sound historiographical method, which always depends upon the critical evaluation of *numerous* potential sources for history-writing and seeks to isolate a "core history" that is beyond reasonable doubt.

My chief complaint is that the revisionists tend to distort or even ignore what many now see as our *primary* source for writing history of ancient Israel, namely modern archaeology. At the same time, they approach their only source of data, the texts of the Hebrew Bible, with such overwhelming suspicion that they end up seeing the Hebrew Bible's narratives and ancient Israel largely as "fictions." As an archaeologist, I could easily write a 1000-page, richly documented history of an "ancient Israel" in the Iron Age and early Persian period. None of the revisionists, working with their methodology and data, could produce more than a handful of pages. That is why I say that they are, practically speaking, nihilists.

I suggest that the revisionists are nihilist not only in the historical sense, but also in the philosophical and moral sense. Here their basic approach to the texts of the Hebrew Bible gives them away as all-too-typical postmodernists.

One of postmodernism's fundamental devices is seen in the way in which the classical texts of the Western cultural tradition, including the Bible, are approached. To use typical language, this employs the "hermeneutics of suspicion." The texts are to be read as "metanarratives" that are subversive and must be resisted; as nothing more than "social constructs" that must be *de*-constructed. In postmodernism's extreme forms the texts are analyzed only to expose their ideology and to delegitimize their claims to knowledge and power. To use a typical slogan, "all readings are political." There is no truth or beauty to be found here; these are "texts of terror."

The revisionists read the Hebrew texts of the Hebrew Bible in much the same way. For them, the Hebrew Bible is only "literature"; but they have a tin ear and a foggy lens. They read the *entire* Hebrew Bible — not just the obvious mythological literature — as flat, monolithic, all the product of a brief time period and an extremely narrow cultural context. It is all a "social construct" of Hellenistic Judaism, little more than pious "survival literature," as Thomas L. Thompson calls it.

Nowhere in the revisionist literature do I find any appreciation of the sheer literary beauty or the lofty moral aspirations of the Hebrew Bible *at its best*. If the revisionists had their way, if the "indeterminacy" of the Bible texts were always highlighted, virtually no one except a few religious fanatics would bother to *read* the Hebrew Bible anymore. It is what seems to me the revisionists' latent(?) hostility to the Hebrew Bible and its worldview that troubles me most, not only because it inhibits critical inquiry and honest scholarship, but because it leads to aesthetic and moral devaluation.

Several of those who have waded through the flood of revisionist litera-ture have observed an overall methodology that might be described as "creep-ing skepticism." I have noted this as well, in pointing out that nearly all the revi-sionists had written more or less confidently about an "early Israel" a few years ago, but have now repudiated their own works. Since there are few new data in the last decade (none textual), this seems clearly to mark an *ideological* shift, not any genuine progress of knowledge. But *skepticism* does not constitute a scholarly method, especially when it involves one in dubious presuppositions and leads to consistently negative results.[1] Skepticism should be no more than one aspect of a scholar's general attitude toward data, namely the desire to be "critical" in the proper sense, that is, discriminating. It may be unfair, but I can-not escape the feeling in reading revisionist treatments of ancient Israel that the conclusion is foregone: there cannot have *been* an "ancient Israel," because that would be inconvenient for the theory. "Special pleading" for such an Israel is bad scholarship; but so is "special pleading" against it, and for the same reasons.

Throughout this book, as well as in much of my writing elsewhere over the past 35 years, I have sought to find and defend a middle ground. By temper-ament and conviction I am neither a positivist nor a nihilist; neither a credulist nor an atheist; neither a maximalist nor a minimalist. Where the progress of our knowledge of ancient Israel and a more enlightened and humane view of the Hebrew Bible are concerned, I am a "modest optimist" rather than a "creep*ing skeptic." Although common in today's climate of skepticism, the picture of "scholars" vying with each other as to who knows and believes the *least* about the past is to me a sorry spectacle. Would you consult a physician who thought good health only a "social construct"? Or a lawyer who was intent only upon overthrowing the legal establishment? There was a time when pro-fessional biblical scholars — those presumably best qualified to read and un-derstand the texts handed down to us — could be looked to for some sort of moral enlightenment and leadership. The revisionists, even when they presume to be constructive, are not able to make much sense of the biblical texts or of ar-chaeology. Instead, they have become demagogues. They do not grasp a simple truth: the Hebrew Bible does not have to be *literally* true, in every historical de-tail, to be morally true or edifying.

One contention of the revisionists, however, is true, although banal. "An-cient Israel" is indeed in some ways a "social construct," of both the writers and editors of the Hebrew Bible, as well as of later Jewish and Christian commenta-

---

1. See William W. Hallo, "The Limits of Skepticism," *JAOS* 110 (1990): 187-99. This reference and the phrase "creeping skepticism" I owe to Marc Brettler; see Brettler, "The Copenhagen School" (forthcoming).

tors, and indeed of modern scholars of any persuasion. But that is true of *all* claims to knowledge; the only question is whether such claims rest on some objective facts or are entirely fanciful. We may even grant the revisionists one of their favorite terms, "invention," as in Keith W. Whitelam's *The Invention of Ancient Israel.* But one should be reminded of the etymology of the English verb "to invent"; it is from the Latin *invenire,* "to come upon, to meet with" (Note: not to "make up" something that is *not* there, but to "discover" something that *is*).

Ancient Israel *is* there, a reality perhaps often hidden in the idealistic portraits of the Hebrew Bible or obscured by its overriding theocratic version of history, and also hidden in the dirt awaiting the discoveries of the archaeologist. It is *archaeology,* and only archaeology, that gives back to all those ordinary, anonymous folk of the past — those who "sleep in the dust of the earth" (Dan. 12:2) — their long-lost voice, allowing them to speak to us today. Their knowledge of the larger world around them was circumscribed; and their experience of truth was limited, even if some of the more literate among them thought that in that experience they had heard the Word of the Lord. But these people, this Israel, must not be written out of history.

For Further Reading

Ackerman, Susan. *"Under Every Green Tree": Popular Religion in Sixth-Century Judah.* HSM 46. Atlanta: Scholars, 1992.

Amiran, Ruth. *Ancient Pottery of the Holy Land.* Jerusalem: Masada, 1969.

Ben-Tor, Amnon, ed. *Archaeology of Ancient Israel.* New Haven: Yale University Press, 1992.

Bunimovitz, Shlomo. "How Mute Stones Speak: Interpreting What We Dig Up." *BAR* 21/2 (1995): 58-67, 96.

Coogan, Michael D., J. Cheryl Exum, and Lawrence E. Stager, eds. *Scripture and Other Artifacts: Essays on the Bible and Archaeology in Honor of Philip J. King.* Louisville: Westminster John Knox, 1994.

Coote, Robert B., and Keith W. Whitelam, eds. *The Emergence of Early Israel in Historical Perspective.* Social World of Biblical Antiquity 5. Sheffield: Sheffield Academic, 1987.

Davies, Philip R. *In Search of "Ancient Israel."* JSOTSup 148. Sheffield: JSOT, 1992.

————. *Whose Bible Is It Anyway?* JSOTSup 204. Sheffield: Sheffield Academic, 1995.

————. "Whose History? Whose Israel? Whose Bible? Biblical Histories, Ancient and Modern." In *Can a "History of Israel" Be Written?*, ed. Lester L. Grabbe, 104-22.

Dever, William G. "Archaeology and the 'Age of Solomon': A Case-Study in Archaeology and Historiography." In *The Age of Solomon,* ed. Lowell K. Handy, 217-51.

————. "Archaeology, Ideology, and the Quest for an 'Ancient' or 'Biblical' Israel." *NEA* 61 (1998): 39-52.

————. "Biblical Archaeology: Death and Rebirth." In *Biblical Archaeology Today, 1988,* ed. Avraham Biran and Joseph Aviram. Jerusalem: Israel Exploration Society, 1993, 706-22.

————. "Histories and Nonhistories of 'Ancient Israel.'" *BASOR* 316 (1999): 89-105.

————. "Impact of the 'New Archaeology.'" In *Benchmarks in Time and Culture: An Introduction to Palestinian Archaeology,* ed. Joel F. Drinkard, Gerald L. Mattingly, and J. Maxwell Miller. SBL Archaeology and Biblical Studies 1. Atlanta: Scholars, 1988, 337-52.

————. "On Listening to the Text — and the Artifacts." In *The Echoes of Many Texts: Reflections on Jewish and Christian Traditions,* ed. Dever and J. Edward Wright. Brown Judaic Studies 313. Atlanta: Scholars, 1997, 1-23.

————. *Recent Archaeological Discoveries and Biblical Research.* Seattle: University of Washington Press, 1990.

————. "Syro-Palestinian and Biblical Archaeology." In *The Hebrew Bible and Its Modern Interpreters,* ed. Douglas Knight and Gene M. Tucker. Chico: Scholars, 1985, 31-74.

————. "Unresolved Issues in the Early History of Israel: Toward a Synthesis of Archaeological and Textual Reconstructions." In *The Bible and the Politics of Exegesis,* ed. David Jobling, Peggy Lynne Day, and Gerald T. Sheppard. Cleveland: Pilgrim, 1991, 195-208.

————. "'Will the Real Israel Please Stand Up?' Archaeology and Israelite Historiography: Part I." *BASOR* 297 (1995): 61-80.

————. "'Will the Real Israel Please Stand Up': Part II: Archaeology and the Religions of Ancient Israel." *BASOR* 298 (1995): 37-58.

Exum, J. Cheryl, and D. J. A. Clines. *The New Literary Criticism and the Hebrew Bible.* JSOTSup 143. Sheffield: Sheffield Academic, 1993.

Finkelstein, Israel. *The Archaeology of the Israelite Settlement.* Jerusalem: Israel Exploration Society, 1988.

————. "Bible Archaeology or Archaeology of Palestine in the Iron Age? A Rejoinder." *Levant* 30 (1998): 167-74.

Friedman, Richard E. *Who Wrote the Bible?* Englewood Cliffs: Prentice Hall, 1987.

Fritz, Volkmar, and Philip R. Davies, eds. *The Origins of the Ancient Israelite States.*OTSup 228. Sheffield: Sheffield Academic, 1996.

Garbini, Giovanni. *History and Ideology in Ancient Israel.* New York: Crossroads, 1988.

Gelinas, Margaret M. "United Monarchy — Divided Monarchy: Fact or Fiction?" In *The Pitcher Is Broken,* ed. Steven W. Holloway and Lowell K. Handy. JSOT Sup 190. Sheffield: Sheffield Academic, 1995.

Grabbe, Lester L., ed. *Can a "History of Israel" Be Written?* JSOTSup 245. Sheffield: Sheffield Academic, 1997.

Halpern, Baruch. "The Construction of the Davidic State: An Exercise in Historiography." In *The Origins of the Ancient Israelite States,* ed. Fritz and Davies, 44-75.

————. "Erasing History: The Minimalist Assault on Ancient Israel." *BR* 11/6 (1995): 26-35, 47.

————. *The First Historians: The Hebrew Bible and History.* San Francisco: Harper & Row, 1988. Repr. University Park: Penn State University Press, 1996.

Handy, Lowell K., ed. *The Age of Solomon: Scholarship at the Turn of the Millennium.* Leiden: Brill, 1997.

Hodder, Ian. *Reading the Past: Current Approaches to Interpretation in Archaeology.* Cambridge: Cambridge University Press, 1986.

King, Philip J. *American Archaeology in the Mideast: A History of the American Schools of Oriental Research.* Philadelphia: American Schools of Oriental Research, 1983.

Knauf, Ernst Axel. "From History to Interpretation." In *The Fabric of History: Text, Artifact and Israel's Past,* ed. Diana V. Edelman. Sheffield: JSOT, 1991, 26-64.

Lemche, Niels Peter. *Ancient Israel: A New History of Israelite Society.* Sheffield: JSOT, 1988.

————. "Clio Is Also Among the Muses! Keith W. Whitelam and the History of Palestine: A Review and a Commentary." In *Can a "History of Israel" Be Written?,* ed. Lester L. Grabbe, 123-55.

————. "Early Israel Revisited." *Currents in Research: Biblical Studies* 4 (1996): 9-34.

————. *The Israelites in History and Tradition.* Louisville: Westminster John Knox, 1998.

———— and Thomas L. Thompson. "Did Biran Kill David? The Bible in the Light of Archaeology." *JSOT* 64 (1994): 3-22.

Levenson, Jon D. *The Hebrew Bible, the Old Testament, and Historical Criticism.* Louisville: Westminster John Knox, 1993.

Levy, Thomas E., ed. *The Archaeology of Society in the Holy Land,* 2nd ed. London: Leicester University Press, 1998.

McKenzie, Steven L., and Stephen R. Haynes, eds. *To Each Its Own Meaning: An Introduction to Biblical Criticisms and Their Application.* Louisville: Westminster John Knox, 1993.

McNutt, Paula M. *Reconstructing the Society of Ancient Israel.* Library of Ancient Israel. Louisville: Westminster John Knox, 1999.

Miller, J. Maxwell. "Is It Possible to Write a History of Israel Without Relying on the Hebrew Bible?" In *The Fabric of History*, ed. Edelman, 93-102.

———. "Reading the Bible Historically: The Historian's Approach." In *To Each Its Own Meaning*, ed. McKenzie and Haynes, 11-28.

——— and John H. Hayes. *A History of Ancient Israel and Judah*. Philadelphia: Westminster, 1991.

Moorey, P. R. S. *A Century of Biblical Archaeology*. Louisville: Westminster John Knox, 1991.

Niditch, Susan. *Oral World and Written Word: Ancient Israelite Literature*. Louisville: Westminster John Knox, 1996.

Provan, Iain W. "Ideologies, Literary and Critical: Reflections on Recent Writing on the History of Israel." *JBL* 114 (1995): 585-606.

Shanks, Hershel. "Face to Face: Biblical Minimalists Meet Their Challengers." *BAR* 23/4 (1997): 26-42, 66.

Thompson, Thomas L. "Defining History and Ethnicity in the South Levant." In *Can a "History of Israel" Be Written?*, ed. Grabbe, 166-87.

———. *Early History of the Israelite People from the Written and Archaeological Sources*. SHANE 11. Leiden: Brill, 1992.

———. "Historiography of Ancient Palestine and Early Jewish Historiography: W. G. Dever and the Not So New Biblical Archaeology." In *The Origins of the Ancient Israelite States*, ed. Fritz and Davies, 26-43.

———. *The Mythic Past: Biblical Archaeology and the Myth of Israel*. London: Basic Books, 1999.

———. "A Neo-Albrightian School in History and Biblical Scholarship?" *JBL* 114 (1995): 683-98.

Van Seters, John. *In Search of History: History and Historiography in the Ancient World and the Origins of Biblical History*. New Haven: Yale University Press, 1983; repr. Winona Lake: Eisenbrauns, 1997.

de Vaux, Roland. "On Right and Wrong Uses of Archaeology." In *Near Eastern Archaeology in the Twentieth Century*, ed. James A. Sanders. Garden City: Doubleday, 1970, 64-80.

Weippert, Helga. *Palästina in vorhellenistischer Zeit*. Munich: C. H. Beck, 1988.

Whitelam, Keith W. *The Invention of Ancient Israel: The Silencing of Palestinian History*. New York: Routledge, 1996.

Wright, George Ernest. "What Archaeology Can and Cannot Do." *BA* 34 (1971): 70-76.

Zevit, Ziony. *The Religions of Ancient Israel: A Synthesis of Parallelactic Approaches*. New York: Continuum, 2001.

Index of Names

Index of Scripture References

Index of Subjects

agrarian (lifestyle), 110, 125
Ahab, 50, 163-66, 210, 236, 239
'Ai ('Ay), 110, 188
'Ain Der'a, 155, 156
Albright, W. F., 31, 56-58, 61, 69, 70, 75
altar, 175, 176, 180, 181, 188, 190. *See also* four-horned altars
amulet, 180
anachronism, 277
'Anat, 178, 179, 192
anthropology, 43, 60, 64, 105, 249, 250
anti-Semitism, 9, 37, 260
Arad, 181-84, 211, 212, 230
Aramaeans, 128, 163, 167, 202
archaeology: biblical, 6, 20, 21, 33, 44, 48, 56-59, 73, 106, 124, 144; definitions of, 54, 55, 62; as a discipline, 26, 61-62; and historiography, 6, 7, 26, 40, 62-66, 79-81, 88, 90; history of, 54-62; Israeli, 7, 27, 35, 80, 119, 143, 144, 225, 259; limits of, 78; methods of, 58, 59, 69; names of, 60-62; "New," 34, 59-65, 76; "Post-processual," 65-68; and reasoning, 77, 78; record, 81, 82, 89; theory, 59, 63-65, 72, 73, 76, 77
art, 234-39
artifact. *See* sources for history writing, archaeological

Asherah, 152, 153, 175-80, 183-88, 190, 192-97, 216
Astarte, 195-96

Ba'al, 155, 156, 166, 184, 210, 230
balances (for weights), 222, 228
Baruch, the scribe, 206-8
beam, wooden, 147, 148
Beersheba, 180-82, 188, 230
Beit Mirsim, Tell, 230, 231
Beth-shan, 43
Beth-shemesh, 143
Bes (god), 184
Bible, Hebrew: as history, 3, 4, 10, 14, 20; late composition of, 4, 26, 29, 32, 50, 227, 243, 273-76; as literature, 2, 10-14, 17, 18, 39; as "pious fiction," 4; as theology, 19, 20. *See also* criticism, biblical
Braudel, F., 74, 86, 105
brazier, 152, 154
bull (motif), 152, 188, 190
"Bull Site," 113, 114, 175
bullae, 206-9
burnishing (on pottery), 132, 133

Canaan, Canaanites, 110, 113-18, 122, 125, 143, 150, 267
capital, "palmette," 150-52, 241